T0325113

Privacy and Security Challenges in Location Aware Computing

P. Shanthi Saravanan
J.J. College of Engineering and Technology, Tiruchirappalli, India

S. R. Balasundaram
National Institute of Technology, Tiruchirappalli, India

A volume in the Advances in
Information Security, Privacy, and
Ethics (AISPE) Book Series

Published in the United States of America by
  IGI Global
  Information Science Reference (an imprint of IGI Global)
  701 E. Chocolate Avenue
  Hershey PA, USA 17033
  Tel: 717-533-8845
  Fax: 717-533-8661
  E-mail: cust@igi-global.com
  Web site: http://www.igi-global.com

Library of Congress Cataloging-in-Publication Data

Names: Shanthi Saravanan, P., 1971- editor. | Balasundaram, S. R., 1963- editor.
Title: Privacy and security challenges in location aware computing / P.
  Shanthi Saravanan and S. R. Balasundaram, editors.
Description: Hershey, PA : Information Science Reference, an imprint of IGI
  Global, [2021] | Includes bibliographical references and index. |
  Summary: "This book discusses how the availability of location data has
  given individuals enormous benefits but at the cost of exposing the
  location of the individual to the third parties, exposing location
  information that could be exploited for, among other things, theft,
  blackmail, or stalking of individuals"-- Provided by publisher.
Identifiers: LCCN 2020049647 (print) | LCCN 2020049648 (ebook) | ISBN
  9781799877561 (hardcover) | ISBN 9781799877578 (paperback) | ISBN
  9781799877585 (ebook)
Subjects: LCSH: Location-based services--Security measures. | Privacy,
  Right of.
Classification: LCC TK5105.65 .P75 2021 (print) | LCC TK5105.65 (ebook) |
  DDC 621.3841/92028558--dc23
LC record available at https://lccn.loc.gov/2020049647
LC ebook record available at https://lccn.loc.gov/2020049648

This book is published in the IGI Global book series Advances in Information Security, Privacy,
and Ethics (AISPE) (ISSN: 1948-9730; eISSN: 1948-9749)

British Cataloguing in Publication Data
A Cataloguing in Publication record for this book is available from the British Library.

For electronic access to this publication, please contact: eresources@igi-global.com.

Advances in Information Security, Privacy, and Ethics (AISPE) Book Series

ISSN:1948-9730
EISSN:1948-9749

Editor-in-Chief: Manish Gupta State University of New York, USA

MISSION

As digital technologies become more pervasive in everyday life and the Internet is utilized in ever increasing ways by both private and public entities, concern over digital threats becomes more prevalent.

The **Advances in Information Security, Privacy, & Ethics (AISPE) Book Series** provides cutting-edge research on the protection and misuse of information and technology across various industries and settings. Comprised of scholarly research on topics such as identity management, cryptography, system security, authentication, and data protection, this book series is ideal for reference by IT professionals, academicians, and upper-level students.

COVERAGE

- Cyberethics
- Privacy-Enhancing Technologies
- Data Storage of Minors
- CIA Triad of Information Security
- Network Security Services
- Global Privacy Concerns
- Computer ethics
- IT Risk
- Risk Management
- Cookies

IGI Global is currently accepting manuscripts for publication within this series. To submit a proposal for a volume in this series, please contact our Acquisition Editors at Acquisitions@igi-global.com or visit: http://www.igi-global.com/publish/.

Titles in this Series

For a list of additional titles in this series, please visit:
www.igi-global.com/book-series/advances-information-security-privacy-ethics/37157

Revolutionary Applications of Blockchain-Enabled Privacy and Access Control
Surjit Singh (Thapar Institute of Engineering and Technology, India) and Anca Delia Jurcut (University College Dublin, Ireland)
Information Science Reference • © 2021 • 297pp • H/C (ISBN: 9781799875895) • US $225.00

Multidisciplinary Approaches to Ethics in the Digital Era
Meliha Nurdan Taskiran (Istanbul Medipol University, Turkey) and Fatih Pinarbaşi (Istanbul Medipol University, Turkey)
Information Science Reference • © 2021 • 369pp • H/C (ISBN: 9781799841173) • US $195.00

Handbook of Research on Digital Transformation and Challenges to Data Security and Privacy
Pedro Fernandes Anunciação (Polytechnic Institute of Setúbal, Portugal) Cláudio Roberto Magalhães Pessoa (Escola de Engenharia de Minas Gerais, Brazil) and George Leal Jamil (Informações em Rede Consultoria e Treinamento, Brazil)
Information Science Reference • © 2021 • 529pp • H/C (ISBN: 9781799842019) • US $285.00

Limitations and Future Applications of Quantum Cryptography
Neeraj Kumar (Babasaheb Bhimrao Ambedkar University, Lucknow, India) Alka Agrawal (Babasaheb Bhimrao Ambedkar University, Lucknow, India) Brijesh K. Chaurasia (Indian Institute of Information Technology, India) and Raees Ahmad Khan (Indian Institute of Information Technology, India)
Information Science Reference • © 2021 • 305pp • H/C (ISBN: 9781799866770) • US $225.00

For an entire list of titles in this series, please visit:
www.igi-global.com/book-series/advances-information-security-privacy-ethics/37157

701 East Chocolate Avenue, Hershey, PA 17033, USA
Tel: 717-533-8845 x100 • Fax: 717-533-8661
E-Mail: cust@igi-global.com • www.igi-global.com

Table of Contents

Preface.. xiv

Chapter 1
Exploring Mobile Users' Daily Experiences in the United States and Taiwan:
An Experience Sampling Method to Study Privacy Concerns in Location-
Based Marketing Applications...1
    Yowei Kang, National Taiwan Ocean University, Taiwan
    Kenneth C. C. Yang, The University of Texas at El Paso, USA

Chapter 2
Mobility-Aware Prefetching and Replacement Scheme for Location-Based
Services: MOPAR..26
    Ajay Kumar Gupta, M. M. M. University of Technology, India
    Udai Shanker, M. M. M. University of Technology, India

Chapter 3
Location-Based Social Networking for Spatio-Temporal Analysis of Human
Mobility..52
    P. Shanthi Saravanan, J. J. College of Engineering and Technology,
        Tiruchirappalli, India
    Sabin Deori, Researcher, Sivasagar, India
    Balasundaram S. R., National Institute of Technology, Tiruchirappalli,
        India

Chapter 4
Human Detection/Tracking System for Video Surveillance With Noise
Removal 72
    Amany Sarhan, Department of Computers and Control Engineering,
        Tanta University, Egypt
    Nada M. Elshennawy, Tanta University, Egypt
    Ghadeer M. Diab, Tanta University, Egypt

Chapter 5
An Efficient Markov Chain Model Development based Prefetching in
Location-Based Services...109
 Ajay Kumar Gupta, M. M. M. University of Technology, India
 Udai Shanker, M. M. M. University of Technology, India

Chapter 6
Design of a Smart ATM Using a Bio-Inspired Watch Dog Mechanism............126
 S. Geetha, Sri Manakula Vinayagar Engineering College, India
 V. Prasanna Venkatesan, Pondicherry University, India
 Madhusudanan J., Sri Manakula Vinayagar Engineering College, India

Chapter 7
Security Attacks on Internet of Things 148
 Sujaritha M., Sri Krishna College of Engineering and Technology, India
 Shunmuga Priya S., Sri Krishna College of Engineering and
  Technology, India

Chapter 8
Towards the Design of a Geographical Information System for Tracking
Terrorist Attacks Online in Nigeria 177
 Jeremiah Ademola Balogun, Mountain Top University, Nigeria
 Funmilayo Kasali, Mountain Top University, Nigeria
 Ibidapo Olawole Akinyemi, Mountain Top University, Nigeria
 Bodunde Odunola Akinyemi, Obafemi Awolowo University, Nigeria
 Peter Adebayo Idowu, Obafemi Awolowo University, Nigeria

Chapter 9
An IoT-Based Soil Properties Monitoring System for Crop Growth and
Production 200
 Harshit Bhatt, Shoolini University of Biotechnology and Management
  Sciences, India
 Brij Bhushan Sharma, Shoolini University of Biotechnology and
  Management Sciences, India
 Aaditya Sharma, Shoolini University of Biotechnology and Management
  Sciences, India
 Ruchika Sharma, Shoolini University of Biotechnology and Management
  Sciences, India
 Meenakshi Sharma, Shoolini University of Biotechnology and
  Management Sciences, India

Chapter 10
An Improved Authentication Scheme for Wireless Sensor Network Using
User Biometrics 220
> *Ambika N., Dept of Computer Applications, Sivananda Sarma Memorial*
> *RV College, Bangalore, India*

Compilation of References 235

Related References 260

About the Contributors 290

Index 297

Detailed Table of Contents

Preface..xiv

Chapter 1
Exploring Mobile Users' Daily Experiences in the United States and Taiwan:
An Experience Sampling Method to Study Privacy Concerns in Location-
Based Marketing Applications...1

    Yowei Kang, National Taiwan Ocean University, Taiwan
    Kenneth C. C. Yang, The University of Texas at El Paso, USA

The advent of mobile communication devices has become an essential part of contemporary human experiences. However, what are consumers' experiences with their mobile devices on a daily basis? This exploratory chapter used an experience sampling method to extract quantitative and qualitative experiential data to understand how concerns over location-sensitive privacy issues affect how consumers feel about mobile phone in their daily lives. Participants from both Taiwan and U.S. took part in this study and recorded their daily experiences with the presence of smartphones at different parts of one single day. The findings suggest that cross-national consumers generally agree with the functional benefits of mobile devices, but at the same time, express their disruptive effects on their daily lives. Taiwanese consumer mood states are overall consistent with those of American participants who similarly feel more disrupted with their mobile phones. Discussions and implications are provided.

Chapter 2
Mobility-Aware Prefetching and Replacement Scheme for Location-Based
Services: MOPAR...26

    Ajay Kumar Gupta, M. M. M. University of Technology, India
    Udai Shanker, M. M. M. University of Technology, India

Location-based services (LBS) are gaining prominence in today's environment. When a mobile user submits a location-based query in LBS, an adversary may infer the locations or other related sensitive information. Thus, an efficient location privacy preservation model (LPPM) with minimal overhead needs to be built by considering contextual understanding and analytical ability. With consideration of service efficiency and privacy, a location privacy preservation policy, namely mobility-aware prefetching and replacement (MOPAR) policy, has been proposed by the cloaking area formulation through user location, cache contribution rate, and data freshness in LBS. An incorporation of prefetching and replacement to anonymizer and consumer cache with formulation of cloak area is being deployed to protect customer sensitive information. The Markov mobility model-based next-position prediction procedure is used in this chapter for caching and formulation of cloaking area. The results of the simulation show significant enhancement in the efficiency of the location-privacy preservation model.

Chapter 3
Location-Based Social Networking for Spatio-Temporal Analysis of Human
Mobility..52

    P. Shanthi Saravanan, J. J. College of Engineering and Technology,
        Tiruchirappalli, India
    Sabin Deori, Researcher, Sivasagar, India
    Balasundaram S. R., National Institute of Technology, Tiruchirappalli,
        India

Human location tracking and analysis have always been important domains with a wide range of implementations in areas such as traffic prediction, security, disaster response, health monitoring, etc. With the availability and use of GPS-enabled devices, it has become easier to obtain location traces of an individual. There may be situations when the current location may be difficult to trace due to device failures or any unforeseen situation. This is one reason why geo tagged social networking or LBSN (location-based social networking) data research is gaining popularity. This kind of geo-tagged data when collected over time from a crowd can be analyzed for various mobility patterns of the population. This chapter focuses on how to predict the location of the people during mobility. A sample study to predict the geographical location and points of interest of a user is explained with the help of random forest classifier. Also, the chapter highlights the security and privacy concerns when LBSN is used for human mobility analysis.

Chapter 4
Human Detection/Tracking System for Video Surveillance With Noise
Removal 72

    Amany Sarhan, Department of Computers and Control Engineering,
        Tanta University, Egypt
    Nada M. Elshennawy, Tanta University, Egypt
    Ghadeer M. Diab, Tanta University, Egypt

Object detection and tracking have been extensively used in many applications including security and surveillance. This chapter addresses the problem of human detection and tracking in surveillance videos with noise. The system proposed deals with video processing utilizing Kalman filtering to enhance the process in the presence of challenging weather conditions. To support the target idea, some experiments are introduced to measure the deviation between both the noiseless and the noisy videos and to study the effect of each filter within each noise type of video disturbance. The most efficient masking system is used to enhance the outcome in the presence of video degradations. The proposed tracking and detection technique achieves achieve an average correct assigned tracks accuracy of about 95% for noiseless video. This is due to the challenging video degradation depending on the type and level of noise. In case of noisy videos by applying the correct filter mask, the accuracy of tracking in the presence of a median filter comes to around 90%.

Chapter 5
An Efficient Markov Chain Model Development based Prefetching in
Location-Based Services...109
    Ajay Kumar Gupta, M. M. M. University of Technology, India
    Udai Shanker, M. M. M. University of Technology, India

A quite significant issue with the current location-based services application is to securely store information for users on the network in order to quickly access the data items. One way to do this is to store data items that have a high likelihood of subsequent request. This strategy is known as proactive caching or prefetching. It is a technique in which selected information is cached before it is actually needed. In comparison, past constructive caching strategies showed high data overhead in terms of computing costs. Therefore, with the use of Markov chain model, the aim of this work is to address the above problems by an efficient user future position movement prediction strategy. For modeling of the proposed system to evaluate the feasibility of accessing information on the network for location-based applications, the client-server queuing model is used in this chapter. The observational findings indicate substantial improvements in caching efficiency to previous caching policies that did not use prefetch module.

Chapter 6
Design of a Smart ATM Using a Bio-Inspired Watch Dog Mechanism............126
    S. Geetha, Sri Manakula Vinayagar Engineering College, India
    V. Prasanna Venkatesan, Pondicherry University, India
    Madhusudanan J., Sri Manakula Vinayagar Engineering College, India

The innovation of smart technologies has made the world into a connected network with "any where, any time, any thing" type of services. The current world has moved to a new environment where more smart gadgets and facilities are used by people. ATM is one such facility where context-aware features may be seen and also exposed to security threats. An intelligent and strong mechanism is needed to protect the ATM from attacks. Apart from the existing alert-based monitoring facility, there is a need to defend against the attackers. Currently, ATMs are said to be Smart ATMs, but really, whether they are smart enough to handle the critical situations is questionable. In this regard, this chapter focuses on designing phases considering the features such as context-awareness, monitoring, decision-making ability, and intelligence.

Chapter 7
Security Attacks on Internet of Things 148
    Sujaritha M., Sri Krishna College of Engineering and Technology, India
    Shunmuga Priya S., Sri Krishna College of Engineering and
        Technology, India

Today's digital world has been turned into a classy one due to the emerging technology, Internet of Things (IoT). IoT is about connecting any device to any other device or object or person or any entity of interest. Through internet, the connectivity span is increased making it a fully linked environment. An attack is a threat that can harm any component of a system. In case of IoT, such attacks may take place at any level, software, hardware, network, etc. Stakeholders of IoT, designers, developers, or users must know the range of attacks associated with every segment of IoT. In this regard, this chapter gives an eye opener for getting familiarity with various types of attacks at all levels. Also, to take care of attacks prone systems, the concepts of threat modeling with supporting details are discussed in this chapter.

Chapter 8
Towards the Design of a Geographical Information System for Tracking
Terrorist Attacks Online in Nigeria 177
    Jeremiah Ademola Balogun, Mountain Top University, Nigeria
    Funmilayo Kasali, Mountain Top University, Nigeria
    Ibidapo Olawole Akinyemi, Mountain Top University, Nigeria
    Bodunde Odunola Akinyemi, Obafemi Awolowo University, Nigeria
    Peter Adebayo Idowu, Obafemi Awolowo University, Nigeria

Currently in Nigeria, different crimes ranging from ethnic clashes, domestic violence, burglary, financial fraud, kidnapping, pipe-line vandalism, and random killings by terrorist organizations, to mention a few, continue to plague the country. The conventional system of intelligence and crime record have failed to live up to the expectations as a result of limited security personnel, deficiency in effective information technology strategies, and infrastructures for gathering, storing, and analyzing data for accurate prediction, decision support, and prevention of crimes. There is presently no information system in Nigeria that provides a central database that is capable of storing the spatial distribution of various acts of terrorism based on the location where the crime is committed. This chapter presents the design of an information system that can be used by security agents for the storage and retrieval of criminal acts of terrorism in order to provide improved decision support regarding solving and preventing criminal acts of terrorism in Nigeria using modern technologies.

Chapter 9
An IoT-Based Soil Properties Monitoring System for Crop Growth and
Production 200

Harshit Bhatt, Shoolini University of Biotechnology and Management
    Sciences, India
Brij Bhushan Sharma, Shoolini University of Biotechnology and
    Management Sciences, India
Aaditya Sharma, Shoolini University of Biotechnology and Management
    Sciences, India
Ruchika Sharma, Shoolini University of Biotechnology and Management
    Sciences, India
Meenakshi Sharma, Shoolini University of Biotechnology and
    Management Sciences, India

Agriculture is very important for the economic growth of a country. Soil properties such as soil type, nutrients, pH level, temperature, and soil moisture play active role in the field of agriculture for the proper growth of any crop. The common primitive methods for soil testing involve collection of soil samples and testing these samples in the lab to provide real-time information of the soil. For continuous monitoring of these factors and to get accurate results, there is a need to modernize the traditional methods by using smart technologies such as IoT and WSN. With sensors, all the mentioned soil properties can be detected continuously, making it easier for any farmer to know the status of the soil and to further act upon accordingly. The highlighting feature of this chapter is the detection of pH level to monitor the system for better crop and yield as well as to minimize the use of water and fertilizers in IoT environment. Protecting the pH level is the biggest concern. In view of this, a note on securing the system with various suggestions is given in this chapter.

Chapter 10
An Improved Authentication Scheme for Wireless Sensor Network Using
User Biometrics 220

Ambika N., Dept of Computer Applications, Sivananda Sarma Memorial
    RV College, Bangalore, India

Sensors are tiny devices deployed in an unsupervised environment. These devices monitor the readings, process them, and transmit them to the predefined destination. The internet has also availed the users to query the sensors and get the values directly.

Users are to register themselves with the gateway node. After registration, they increase flexibility to query the sensors. The sensors are to authenticate the users for their legitimacy before dispatching the requested information. The proposal increases security by minimizing the replay attacks and enhance reliability in sensor-user communication. The proposed work hikes reliability as well as conserves energy substantially. Also, it minimizes replay attacks that are vulnerable in WSN.

Compilation of References 235

Related References 260

About the Contributors 290

Index 297

Preface

Dynamic requirements of the globe and the move towards transformation have made, Location context as an essential entity for driving current day technologies and for defining consumer facilities. Smartphones with location enabled applications have revolutionized the ways in which people perform their activities and get benefits from the automated services. The needs for smartphones and location enabled applications have been growing exponentially. According to Mordor Intelligence Report, the LBS Market is expected to reach USD 155.13 billion by 2026 with CAGR growth of 23.2% (2021-2026 period). This is due to the changing scenario of one-person-one-device to one-with- many-gadgets.

In the products development or research in the field of location based applications, two broader terminologies exist namely, Location Aware Computing (LAC) and Location Based Services (LBS). LAC is about computing using the location (provides whereabouts or the granular geographical information) of people and objects to derive contextual information and it relies on LBS. LAC is the outcome of the convergence of location sensing, wireless and mobile computing domains. LAC has potential applications with broad spectrum covering navigation, tourism, government applications, disaster management, entertainment and gaming, object tracking, military, sports, healthcare etc.

On one hand, the research in LAC focuses on the design and deployment of effective applications or services; on the other hand, emphasizes the need for ethical, data protection, specifically towards the security and privacy aspects of such applications. Data security is protecting the data from third parties. Data privacy is a branch of data security concerned with proper handling of data. In case of LAC, location as well as related data needs to be protected from threats or attacks.

With low cost or even no cost services being offered by the service providers, it has become a common phenomenon among smart phone users to try launching such applications or increase the usage of such facilities. This paves ways for the hackers to utilize the space for bringing harm to the applications, devices, databases, software, hardware, network etc. Mainly through the location data. Geo-fencing, Geo-tagging, Geo-marketing etc. are all booming aspects of location enabled activities to promote the business cycle at various levels. No doubt, the LBS App Economy is growing substantially, but there is an increase in attacks and threats through the mobile world.

Also, some of the facts given below (Cyber Security Report by Check Point Research,2020) stress that the LAC and LBS need more attention in terms of securing the components at several levels.

1. Location data, photos, contacts, passwords, social media content are all accessible
2. Around 27% of cyber attacks are targeted towards the mobile devices only
3. Certain Trojans and RATs aim at financial mobile apps and the communication protocols
4. Geo-tagging pose threats to linking data at various levels

Towards these issues, the concern for emphasizing the need for protecting the security as well as privacy of mobile users has been continuously seen from the government and industrial levels. In this context, stakeholders are working towards devising policies, regulations and product/process level features.. For example, privacy controls have become part of Google services (Gadgets 360). Policies and regulations on consumer privacy, industry codes of self regulations, governance regarding the usage etc., are all being laid for data protection. But still the hacking entry exists. Though the research in the field of security enabled or privacy enabled location based services has a good track of contributions, there exist a gap in this area as the vulnerabilities posed are huge and diverse in nature.

In this regard, this book on *Privacy and Security Challenges in Location Aware Computing* has been aimed towards two major outcomes.

- Firstly, to discuss how the availability of location data has made revolution for the individuals to realize enormous benefits. Though this seems to be a boon, the services are provided at the cost of exposing the location of the individuals or objects to the third parties. This exposed location information could be exploited for security threats and vulnerabilities.
- To address these issues and for preserving privacy, solutions based on efficient techniques and innovative methodologies are covered in the other fold of this book.

OBJECTIVES

- To explore the necessity of location security/privacy preservation, issues and challenges related to the protection of location data.

- To be aware of potential threats seen in the location aware as well as location based systems.
- To acquire knowledge about the existing research available in handling security and privacy related issues in LAC.
- To realize the need for extending location security/privacy research over WSN, IoT and context aware applications.
- To understand the appropriate techniques used to mitigate the issues against security or privacy in location aware computing.

BOOK ORGANIZATION

Chapter 1 examines how mobile users describe their experiences with mobile Smartphone devices. This exploratory chapter uses an Experience Sampling Method to extract quantitative and qualitative experiential data applied over cross-cultural views (Taiwan and U.S.). This helps to understand the concerns over location-sensitive privacy issues and to analyze how consumers feel about mobile phones in their daily lives.

Chapter 2 proposes an efficient location privacy preservation model (LPPM) with minimal overhead called MObility aware Prefetching And Replacement (MOPAR). An incorporation of prefetching and replacement to anonymizer and consumer cache with formulation of cloak area is being deployed to protect customer sensitive information. Also, the markov mobility model based next position prediction procedure to preserve the user's location and other information from the untrusted entity is discussed.

Chapter 3 focuses on how to predict the location of the people using geo- tagged social networking data. This kind of geo-tagged data when collected overtime from a crowd can be analyzed for understanding various mobility patterns of the population. A sample study to predict the geographical location and points of interests of a user is explained with the help of Random forest classifier. Also, the chapter highlights the security and privacy concerns when geo-tagged data is used for human mobility analysis.

Chapter 4 deals with human tracking system. Object detection and tracking have been extensively used in many applications such as security and surveillance, human-computer interaction, traffic control, etc. Measuring and enhancing a pedestrian's tracking efficiency in a video is a challenging one. In this chapter, the proposed human tracking system involves video processing and Kalman filtering in order to enhance the detection and tracking in the presence of challenging weather conditions.

Chapter 5 explains how to securely store information for users of Location Based Services applications in order to quickly access the data items. One way to do this is to store data items that have a high likelihood of subsequent request. This strategy known as proactive caching or prefetching is discussed where selected information can be cached before it is actually needed. To evaluate the feasibility of accessing information on the network for location-based applications, the client-server queuing model is being implemented in this chapter.

Chapter 6 describes the design of a smart Automated Teller Machine (ATM) using a bio-inspired watch dog mechanism. ATMs that are helpful for customers to avail transactions such as cash withdrawal, deposit and fund transfers are certainly exposed to security threats. Apart from the existing alert-based monitoring facility, there is a need to defend against the attackers and to build intelligent and strong mechanisms. In this regard, this chapter focuses on designing phases of ATM considering the features such as Context-awareness, Monitoring, Decision Making etc.

Chapter 7 covers a wide spectrum of attacks possible in Internet of Things (IoT). IoT is about connecting any device to any other device or object or person or location or any entity of interest. While expanding the connectivity to all locations for better and smart applications, the rise of attacks is certain. In this regard, the developers of IoT applications and location based applications must be aware of attacks coming from various points. In this view, this chapter gives an eye opener for getting familiarity with such types of attacks happening at all levels in IoT and also the concepts of threat modeling.

Chapter 8 presents the design of an information system for solving and preventing criminal acts of terrorism. The proposed system can be used by security agents for the storage and retrieval of criminal acts of terrorism in order to provide improved decision support in Nigeria. System Design, Methodologies and Reports Generation are detailed with respect to the proposed information system.

Chapter 9 highlights the need to modernize the traditional methods of Agriculture by using smart agricultural techniques such as IoT and WSN. Soil properties such as soil type, nutrients, pH level, temperature and soil moisture play active role in the field of agriculture for the proper growth of any crop. In view of this, the proposed chapter addresses the detection of pH level of the soil. A note on various types of security threats expected in such an IoT environment is outlined.

Chapter 10 deals with the study of prominent works done in handling replay attacks expected in Wireless Sensor Networks. In this direction, a model has been proposed to handle replay attacks over sensors. Registration is done using hashed value of biometric extract with unique identity. By way of generating more hash keys in the registration process, the work done aims at proposing better approach for facing replay attacks.

This book is aimed at Professionals, Academicians and Researchers who are working in the field of Location Aware Computing. It is suitable for both beginners and expertise in this field.

We hope the discussions done in this book will be certainly useful for carrying out further academic as well as research activities in the fields of location aware computing and location-based services.

P. Shanthi Saravanan
J.J. College of Engineering and Technology, Tiruchirappalli, India

S. R. Balasundaram
National Institute of Technology, Tiruchirappalli, India

Chapter 1
Exploring Mobile Users' Daily Experiences in the United States and Taiwan:
An Experience Sampling Method to Study Privacy Concerns in Location-Based Marketing Applications

Yowei Kang
https://orcid.org/0000-0002-7060-194X
National Taiwan Ocean University, Taiwan

Kenneth C. C. Yang
https://orcid.org/0000-0002-4176-6219
The University of Texas at El Paso, USA

ABSTRACT

The advent of mobile communication devices has become an essential part of contemporary human experiences. However, what are consumers' experiences with their mobile devices on a daily basis? This exploratory chapter used an experience sampling method to extract quantitative and qualitative experiential data to understand how concerns over location-sensitive privacy issues affect how consumers feel about mobile phone in their daily lives. Participants from both Taiwan and U.S. took part in this study and recorded their daily experiences with the presence of smartphones at different parts of one single day. The findings suggest that cross-national consumers generally agree with the functional benefits of mobile devices, but at the same time, express their disruptive effects on their daily lives. Taiwanese consumer mood states are overall consistent with those of American participants who similarly feel more disrupted with their mobile phones. Discussions and implications are provided.

DOI: 10.4018/978-1-7998-7756-1.ch001

BACKGROUND

The advent of mobile communications in the late 20th century have played a vital part in modern human experiences and make the world become a global village (Silver et al., 2019). A global survey of 11 countries published by Pew Research Center in 2019 on cross-cultural consumers' attitudes toward mobile communication has also confirmed that the majorities of these participants feel that mobile phones are good for individuals and their daily lives, instead for the society overall (Silver et al., 2019). However, attitudes toward whether mobile devices are indispensable to their daily lives vary among countries in this survey (Silver et al., 2019). For example, over 50% of participants from these countries agree with the statement that mobile phone is something to free them, ranging from 40% in Lebanon to 86% in Kenya (Silver et al., 2019). On the other hand, positive assessment of what mobile phone can do for them seems consistent across countries. For example, among Kenyan consumers, 84% of them agree that mobile phone is something that helps them and 72% of them agree that technology is something that they cannot live without (Silver et al., 2019) (Refer to Figure 1).

Current rapid diffusion of smartphones and the deployment of 5G technology (Yang & Kang, 2020a) have promised a seamless integration of multi-media and personalized services, which has led to the emergence of many location-based applications and services in various business settings. The global 5G smartphone subscription is expected to triple and reach 600 million by the end of 2021 (Richter, 2021). This chapter is particularly interested in one aspect of mobile phone's impacts on human lives; that is how they would respond to this privacy-invasive technology into their daily lives. What will be the implications for direct marketers when considering this new location-sensitive technology for their practices?

According to a 2012 PEW Report, 74% of smartphone users get real-time location-based information through their smartphones. For example, the report also finds that 18% of them use a geosocial service to share their location information with friends. For example, in Figure 1, while 72% of participants from Kenya agree that mobile phone is something they cannot do without, 26% of them believe the technology is something they do not always need in their lives (Silver et al., 2019). Cross-country variations are noticeable in this 2019 Pew survey and these demonstrate how consumers from each country surveyed feel about mobile phone as a technology. For example, majorities of the participants from India (51%), Venezuela (62%), The Philippines (68%), Columbia (76%), Mexico (77%), and Vietnam (69%) expressed that mobile phone is a technology they do not always need (as shown in the figures within the parentheses) (Silver et al., 2019). However, in more economically advanced countries like the U.S., consumer attitudes have shown a different trend in the Pew's 2019 survey.

Figure 1.

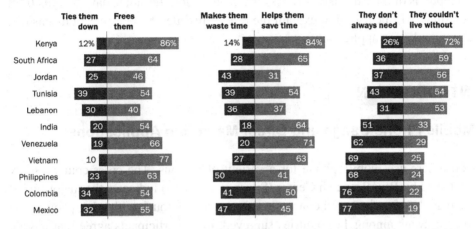

Mobile phone users divided over whether their phone is something they 'don't always need' or 'couldn't live without'

% of adult mobile phone users who say their phone is something that …

	Ties them down	Frees them		Makes them waste time	Helps them save time		They don't always need	They couldn't live without
Kenya	12%	86%		14%	84%		26%	72%
South Africa	27	64		28	65		36	59
Jordan	25	46		43	31		37	56
Tunisia	39	54		39	54		43	54
Lebanon	30	40		36	37		31	53
India	20	54		18	64		51	33
Venezuela	19	66		20	71		62	29
Vietnam	10	77		27	63		69	25
Philippines	23	63		50	41		68	24
Colombia	34	54		41	50		76	22
Mexico	32	55		47	45		77	19

Note: Respondents who gave other responses are not shown. Mobile phone users include those who say they own or share a mobile phone.
Source: Mobile Technology and Its Social Impact Survey 2018. Q16, Q17 & Q18.
"Mobile Connectivity in Emerging Economies"

PEW RESEARCH CENTER

Although quantitative research on what motivates people to use mobile communications and contents (such as mobile apps, mobile advertising, and direct marketing applications) is abundant, research is lacking to document and describe people's daily experiences with mobile smartphone devices in one single day. To better understand the effects of smart mobile devices on people's daily lives, we studied through an experiential sampling method to collect experiential data and narratives that will help examine the impacts of smart mobile device on people's daily life by creating a situation that people will be prompted to share their own experiences with mobile smartphone devices in one single day. There is a lack of systematic and programmatic mixed method research including both quantitative and qualitative approaches to examine mobile users' daily experience and, particularly, their privacy concerns when their mobile devices become an indispensable part of their lives. Due to the global diffusion of the intelligent mobile communications systems (such as smartphone), the examination of how people describe their experiences with mobile smartphone devices will be even more interesting if we compare cross-cultural data. The history of mobile communication diffusion in different countries helps account for the extent of mobile devices as integrated into people's daily lives. Therefore, the objectives of this study are to provide consumer experiential narratives and mood states using an Experience Sampling Method to collect data from cross-country consumers from Taiwan and the United States. Using a combination of qualitative and quantitative data, the authors aim to discover and record what consumers really feel about their smartphone or mobile devices and perceptions of their intrusive effects on their lives for one single day. Insights from this study will be useful to explain the role of mobile phone in location-sensitive direct marketing applications.

INTRODUCTION

Mobile Phone Usage and Direct Marketing Applications

Consumers use mobile phone for a variety of reasons. The cross-country study published by Pew Research Center (Silver et al., 2019) indicates the majorities of them are looking for social connections by staying in touch with other people who live far away; among 11 countries surveyed, most participants agree that mobile phone is helpful to connect users socially (Silver et al., 2019). Other motives to use mobile phone include seeking for information and news about important issues; over 70% of those surveyed have agreed that the news-seeking motive is consistently among countries (Silver et al., 2019). Other function-related motives include earning a living and get things done (Silver et al., 2019) (Refer to Figure 2).

As early as 2004, *The Economist* (2004) magazine once envisions the "disoriented" changes waiting for the traditional advertising and marketing practices. Factors leading to these many dramatic changes include the introduction of smartphone that allows consumers to be connected to the Internet all the time (Johnston, 2020). Particularly, among younger adults, 20% of them have accessed the Internet via their smartphone (Johnston, 2020). With the popularity of social media, smartphone has become a viable platform for not only mobile commerce, but also for social commerce (Papadopoulou, 2018). However, in spite of the claimed "tremendous opportunity" (Papadopoulou, 2018), highly privacy-invasive direct marketing applications, whether they are done via mobile or mobile-enabled social media platforms, have generated many privacy concerns.

To study the potential impacts of privacy in the age of social media, Koohang et al. (2018) introduced the term, *social media privacy concerns* (SMPC), to refer to "[t]he degree to which a user is concerned about a social media site's practices and procedures relating to his or her personal information (p. 1210) (Yang & Kang, 2020b). Heyman et al. (2014) once propose two types of privacy to explain the concept of social media privacy: "privacy as subject" and "privacy as object." According to their definitions, "privacy as subject" refers to "the management of information about one's identity *vis-a`-vis* the other users" (Heyman et el., 2014, p. 18; Yang & Kang, 2020b). On the other hand, "privacy as object" refers to a type of "lateral or social privacy" when "users are not seen by other users" but their behavior insights are analyzed through algorithms to generate monetary profits (Heyman et el., 2014, p. 18; Yang & Kang, 2020b).

Figure 2.

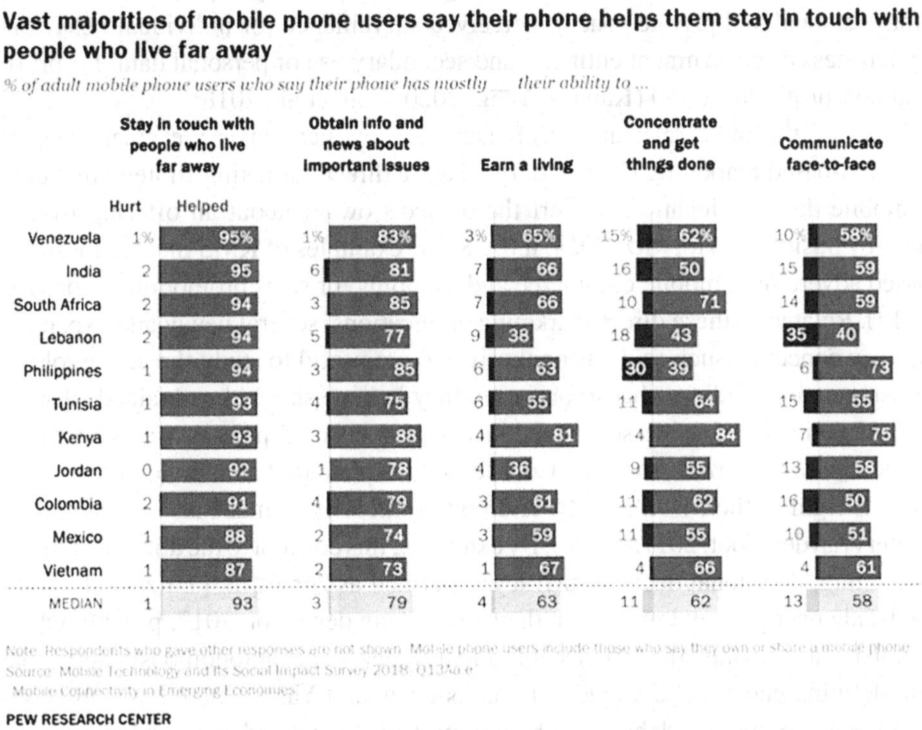

Vast majorities of mobile phone users say their phone helps them stay in touch with people who live far away

% of adult mobile phone users who say their phone has mostly ___ their ability to ...

	Stay in touch with people who live far away		Obtain info and news about important issues		Earn a living		Concentrate and get things done		Communicate face-to-face	
	Hurt	Helped								
Venezuela	1%	95%	1%	83%	3%	65%	15%	62%	10%	58%
India	2	95	6	81	7	66	16	50	15	59
South Africa	2	94	3	85	7	66	10	71	14	59
Lebanon	2	94	5	77	9	38	18	43	35	40
Philippines	1	94	3	85	6	63	30	39	6	73
Tunisia	1	93	4	75	6	55	11	64	15	55
Kenya	1	93	3	88	4	81	4	84	7	75
Jordan	0	92	1	78	4	36	9	55	13	58
Colombia	2	91	4	79	3	61	11	62	16	50
Mexico	1	88	2	74	3	59	11	55	10	51
Vietnam	1	87	2	73	1	67	4	66	4	61
MEDIAN	1	93	3	79	4	63	11	62	13	58

Note: Respondents who gave other responses are not shown. Mobile phone users include those who say they own or share a mobile phone
Source: Mobile Technology and Its Social Impact Survey 2018. Q13Aa-e
"Mobile Connectivity in Emerging Economies"

PEW RESEARCH CENTER

MAIN FOCUS OF THE CHAPTER

Theoretical Framework and Literature Review

ICTs and other connected mobile devices often incur privacy concerns among consumers (Irion & Helberger, 2017), resulting in strong demand of the protection of personal and individual data (Walden & Woods, 2011) from unwarranted and un-acknowledged use by business entities. Researchers have explained the management of an individual privacy often relies on their own decision-making process by which they will evaluate uncertainty about what their privacy-related behaviors could lead to and how they prefer different consequences (Kang & Yang, 2020). Ample academic research has been done to investigate consumers' concerns over an individual's privacy (Lom et al., 2018; Xu et al., 2011). In general, the term, privacy, often broadly is defined as "consumers' expected concerns about possible loss of their own online privacy in general or in a specific circumstance" (Kang & Yang, 2020; Xu et al., 2011). In academic literature, privacy concerns have often been studied as multi-dimensional that ranges from the study of perceived intrusion (into personal and private space), perceived surveillance (of individual behaviors by business or government entities), and secondary use of personal data (for profit and non-profit purposes) (Kang & Yang, 2020; Lom et al., 2018).

One of the most relevant direct marketing application is the emergence of location-based marketing (LMS), defined as "a direct marketing strategy that uses a mobile device's location to alert the device's owner about an offering from a near-by business" (Horwitz, 2014, n.p.). Some examples of KMS include location-based advertising, mobile commerce and shopping, or sales promotions (Horwitz, 2014). Related to these direct marketing applications, several newly and expanded privacy concepts (such as decisional privacy) are useful to study the active role of consumers in deciding what information they believe should be obtained, shared, and monetized by businesses. The concept of decisional privacy rights was first coined in *Roe vs. Wade* Supreme Court case to explain that an individual/a woman has the right to their own privacy and bodily integrity to make any decision they prefer (van der Sloot, 2017, p. 190). By extending this concept to the domain of direct marketing, decisional/decision privacy is defined as "grant[ing] citizens the right to decide over personal matters in their lives" (van der Sloot, 2017, p. 190). Other scholars have defined the term as individual rights "to act autonomously and make life-defining choice) (Levesque, 2017). As Kang and Yang (2020) have observed that the contemporary debates on how to protect consumers' privacy have moved from "privacy by design" to "privacy as control", in line with what many legal scholars have contended that "[c]onsumers are coming to treat privacy as a matter of control rather than an absolute prohibition on disclosure" (Fairfield, 2012, n.p.).

Using a mobile phone or smartphone device to receive location-based shopping services and mobile advertising often lead to concerns over consumer location data and their decision to share their privacy/private information. These are most relevant to this study. Concerns over their own privacy and conscious decision not to share have offered explanations about the feasibility of direct marketing application. According to a 2016 KMPG survey, 55% of consumers around the globe report that they sometimes decide against buying online because of their severe privacy concerns. Among many insights from this global survey of consumers, their most frequently raised concerns are the misuse of personal data for unwanted marketing, the monetization of personal data to a 3rd party user, and the lack of cyber-security system (KMPG, 2016b) (Kang & Yang, 2020). KMPG's data (2016a) also report several country-specific variations related to protecting and deciding their own online privacy. According to KMPG's data, consumers from three Asian countries, that is, China (39%), India (35%), and Singapore (32%), are the most worried about their own online privacy (Kang & Yang, 2020).

The study of privacy is important to many marketing researchers and practitioners because of its relationship to social media usage (Fox & Royne, 2018, cited in Hunter & Taylor, 2019). Hunter and Taylor (2019) also point out the biggest hurdle in studying privacy related to social media lies in variations in how people define and perceive privacy. Because the global diffusion of social media around the world, this issue can be particularly important because the socio-cultural variations among countries. This methodological problem will become worse after considering how marketers have been using personal information to develop personalized services and contents (Gal-Or et al., 2018). These categorizations and definitions of social media have allowed scholars to examine further many important issues related to users' privacy concerns. For this study, we reason that concerns over an individual's online privacy have been well documented not only in the academic literature (Lom et al., 2018; Xu et al., 2011), but also by the popular press (Friesland, 2018). Due to the rapid diffusion of social media technologies, it seems reasonable to assume that global consumers affected by these privacy-invasive technologies will think, feel, and act the same toward online privacy concerns. Empirical data have lent support to this claim of homogenization effects upon cross-cultural consumers.

As a direct marketing platform where mobile commerce activities can be delivered, global mobile commerce was about USD$119 billion by 2015 (EraInnovator, 2020). In the U.S. alone, mobile commerce activities was about USD$7.5 billion (EraInnovator, 2020). The popularity of mobile commerce is global in scale when 14 million Japanese consumers purchased through their mobile wallet in 2013 (EraInnovator, 2020). The cultural context provides what is considered to be private and how individuals should respond to any infringement upon their own privacy.

To account for the variations in perceiving privacy concerns related to mobile phone among American and Taiwanese consumers, Geert Geert Hofstede's 6-D cultural dimension framework was used to interpret cross-cultural data collected from ESM (Hofstede, https://geerthofstede.com/, 2021). Hofstede's (2010) cultural dimension framework has been widely applied in cross-cultural consumer research in international advertising and marketing areas (de Mooij, 2003; Hofstede, 1991). The national cultural characteristics in the current study have been chosen on the basis of Hofstede's (1991) well-known model in international research that examines the relationship between cultural values and their behaviors in an organization.

Hofstede (1991) developed his cultural value dimensions on the basis of extensive cross-national data from IBM employees during the 1960s. Each dimension ranges from 0 to 100, except for the LTO index. Hofstede's cultural value system includes the following cultural dimensions: collectivism/individualism (COL/IDV), uncertainty avoidance (UAI), power distance (PDI), masculinity-femininity (MAS-FEM), long term orientation (LTO), indulgence/restraint indices. Taiwan is different from the US with strikingly different cultural dimensions in IDV (Taiwan: 17; US: 91) and LTO (Taiwan: 93; US: 26). Taiwan has also a high PDI (58) (US: 40) and UAI (69) (US: 46), but lower MAS (45) (US: 62) and indulgence (49) (US: 68) (Hofstede, n.d., https://geert-hofstede.com/taiwan.html) (Refer to Figure 3).

Figure 3.

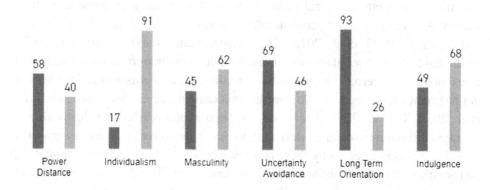

Deriving from this framework, the research expects to examine if mobile smartphone users' cultural differences help account for the influence of mobile smartphone usage on cross-country consumers' daily experiences with their own smart mobile devices in their daily lives.

On the basis of the preceding literature review and theoretical foundation, this book chapter answers the following research questions:

Research Question 1: What are mobile phone users' experiences when using mobile smartphone devices during different parts of their daily lives?

Research Question 2: What are mobile phone users' mood states when using mobile smartphone devices during different parts of their daily lives?

Research Question 3: Will there be cross-national differences in mobile users' experiences with their mobile smartphone devices?

RESEARCH METHOD

The Selection of Experience Sampling Method (ESM)

This chapter employed a modified experience sampling method (henceforth, ESM) to collect and analyze experiential narratives and mood states from both mobile phone users from U.S. (80.9% penetration rate) (Statista, 2016) and Taiwan (95% penetration rate) (Statista, 2020). These countries represent different, yet comparable, household penetration rates of mobile phones and are likely to view privacy differently as a result of their cultural dimensions (Hofstedes, 2021). Both countries are similar in terms of their political and economic systems, without a widespread fear of government surveillance such as in China. For example, mobile users in Taiwan are less likely to be concerned about their own personal privacy due to their highly collectivistic culture, while the US users are more likely to place more emphasis on individual privacy because of their individualistic tendency. On the other hand, the invasion of privacy into users' daily lives may be considered as creating uncertainty (and even risks) in people's lives and may be perceived equally unfavorable due to their similar UAI scores.

The ESM refers to a data collection method to gather "systematic self-reports of behaviors, emotions, or experiences as they occur in the individual's natural environment...... through event sampling, real-time data capture, ambulatory assessment, diary method, or ecological momentary assessment" (Sather, 2014, n.p.). The rationale behind the selection of the ESM method is mainly because the daily experiences that mobile user have is difficult to observe and analyze without a proper data collection method. In particular, if researchers are interested in collecting experiential narratives and mood state fluctuation among users, a traditional survey method is less likely to generate useful data. Because mobile device is a global technology that attracts users around the world, it is critical to understand how users feel about their experiences with mobile devices and applications in their daily lives. ESM also helps the researchers to understand how privacy concerns play any role in explaining mobile users' experiences. According to Khan et al. (2007), ESM is a quasi-naturalistic method that involves prompting participants to respond to questions designed by researchers. The techniques allow powerful tool to collect data to demonstrate participants' experiences (Khan et al., 2007).

Additionally, the benefits of ESM are its methodological advantages to "examine fluctuations in the stream of consciousness and the links between the external contents and the contents of the mind" (Hektner et al., 2007, p.6). Because of the pervasiveness of mobile devices in the modern world, ESM is able to capture not only what mobile phone users think of mobile devices to their life. Several ESM data collection strategies were used by scholars, including "interval-contingent sampling" (defined as when participants respond at pre-arranged times), "signal-contingent sampling" (defined as when participants are alerted and notified by beeper, text message, or mobile devices at pre-determined or randomly-selected intervals to provide their responses), or "event-contingent sampling" (defined as when participants offer responses at a pre-arranged event).

To follow the standard ESM protocols and strategies, this research used a signal contingent protocol to record participants' experiences upon prompted (Christensen et al., 2003). The signal-contingent protocols refer to "reporting on experience in responses to a signal at various times throughout the day" (Christensen et al., 2002, p. 60). The method is appropriate for observing on-going behaviors that are likely to be occurring when prompted (Christensen et al., 2003).

This study examined how people respond to new situations with their mobile devices by recording their daily experiences in one single day. The rationale behind the selection of ESM is mainly because the daily experiences mobile phones users have is difficult to observe and analyze. Furthermore, real-time interactions with other mobile phone users around the world have further introduced spatial, temporal, and cultural elements into their daily experiences. ESM is a quasi-naturalistic method that involves prompting participants to respond to questions designed by researchers (Khan et al., 2008). The techniques also provide a powerful tool to collect data to demonstrate participants' experiences (Khan et al., 2008).

In this study, the authors also used a multi-method approach by integrating a naturalistic experimental method to test how people respond to selected pre-determined tasks. For example, participants were prompted in the instruction card, asking them about their emotional and cognitive responses when they are asked to contact their friends, check their bank account, read news, find out what is going on in their offices, etc. Collected data were analyzed by examining country-specific differences in emotional and cognitive responses, as well as commonalities among cross-cultural mobile smartphone users. Analyses of these data help mobile researchers the relative importance of mobile devices to consumers from different countries.

Instrumentation

The 10-page IRB-approved questionnaire includes demographic questions (such as age, gender, nationality, or ethnic background), usage behaviors of mobile devices and applications (such as types of mobile devices used), attitudes toward and opinions about mobile devices and applications, and 18-item mood directory adapted from Hentner et al. (2007) and Williams' (2009) mood inventory. Both were revised to fit the purposes of this study. Some example of these 7-point semantic differential scales include two bipolar adjective. Among these bi-polar statements, the authors only reported nine items related to the privacy-invasive effects of mobile phone.

These items include angry-friendly, worried-relaxed, anxious-calm, nervous-relaxed, troubled-untroubled, satisfied-dissatisfied, disappointed-pleased, disturbed-stable, and annoyed-pleased.

Following the signal contingent protocol the study collected experiential narrative at 10 am (1st prompt), at 3 pm (2nd prompt), and at 8 pm (3rd prompt) at local times through mobile phone reminders to alert participants to complete each questionnaire section. The authors have used a non-app based approach by sending out signals to participants of the study (Conner, 2015). Once prompted, participants answered the following five questions to share their experiential narratives with a mobile phone or smartphone device in their daily lives. These questions include 1) What were you doing? 2) What was the main thing you were thinking? 3) What is your experience using the mobile devices when you were prompted? 4) What do you think about mobile devices and applications?; 5) If you felt a strong emotion since the last prompt, what did you feel and why did you feel that way?

Sampling and Sample Characteristics

A total of 10 participants (8 conveniently recruited from US and two from Taiwan) were included in the sample. However, some participants dropped out from the study; as a result, we had 5 participants. Their data were analyzed by examining country-specific differences in mobile users' experiential narratives and mood states.

The participant from Taiwan (labelled as Taiwan-1) is a male, 32 years old, and owns a traditional mobile phone. There are two female participants from the U.S. (labelled as US-2 and US-4); their ages are 24 and 26 years old. Both female participants are of Mexican/Hispanic origin. Two male participants from the U.S. age between 26 to 60 years old; the first one is a Mexican/Hispanic (labelled as US-1), while another one is a White (labelled as US-3) (Refer to Table 1). The average age of all four U.S. participants is 32.5 years old.

Table 1. Sample Characteristics

ID	Gender	Age	Nationality	Ethnicity	Type of Mobile Phone Owned
Taiwan-1	Male	32	Taiwan	Taiwanese	Traditional mobile phone
US-1	Male	26	USA	Hispanic	Samsung mobile phone
US-2	Female	24	USA	Mexican	Blackberry, Nokia, and Motorola
US-3	Male	60	USA	White	Droid2 Smartphone and iPad
US-4	Female	20	USA	Mexican	Traditional mobile phone

FINDINGS

Attitudes Toward Mobile Phone Devices and Applications

Most of the participants in this study have agreed the functional benefits of mobile phone devices and applications. The positive assessment of mobile phone seems to be consistent cross-nationally. For example, the Taiwanese participant (Taiwan-1) agrees with the convenience of mobile phone:

They are convenient if you have them by hands. Using the applications is a good way to keep in touch with friends and family. I know some of my friends take pictures and upload them to their Facebook account to share with people.

For participants from the U.S., US-1 also marvels at the communicative abilities of mobile phone to stay in touch with friends and family, as seen below:

I personally believe that mobile devices are necessary for communication with friends and family, and for work related communication. Many applications are not indispensable in our lives. Some may be really useful and some are just for leisure. Either way, cell phone and technology companies are making good profits marketing these applications.

I continue to marvel at their proliferation but have found them to be very useful and convenient for both business and personal use. They are certainly changing our culture by affecting our consumption of news and entertainment and facilitating a means of constant connection to other people and access to information. I like and appreciate the devices and most applications but dislike the distractions they provide and behavior changes that they produce in some people.

This is also echoed by US-2, a female consumer of 24 years old, as seen in the statements below:

They're great. They help me contact people right away, especially at work when things come up and we need a higher-up to tell us what to do.

It's a great way to be contacted whenever necessary. The applications are great and make finding things a lot easier. I personally use it for Facebook and it's only a click away for me to read updates. I also read news and again, it's very easy to access this things.

However, increasingly, consumers have become aware of the disruptive and "destructive" effects of mobile phone that invades consumers' daily lives. For example, the Taiwanese participant (Taiwan-1) points out the invasive nature of mobile phone that causes people to spend too much time on these devices and applications. Taiwan-1 also acknowledges the problem of text-and-driving as a mis-use of this ubiquitous communication technology.

I think people rely on their mobile devices too much and spend too much time on those applications. I also think people should not use their phones while driving. (from Taiwan-1)

Still I don't use my mobile phone other than making & receiving calls. Maybe that's because I am not using a smart phone for other purposes. But if I have one I think I will be willing to try out any kinds of applications available and useful. Hopefully they won't cost too much money. (from Taiwan-1)

It is likely that, due to similar diffusion and penetration rate between Taiwan and the U.S., consumers' responses to the mobile phone seem consistent cross-culturally. For example, US-4 believes the mobile phone has created a clutter for people's lives. Similarly, US-3, a White male consumer of 60 years old points out the negative effects of the mobile phone on the English language, as seen below:

I also personally dislike the destruction of the English language that I see in the use of texting and spilling over into e-mails and other forms of written communication.

On the other hand, the development of a new, "digital" language is a curious phenomenon to see and I will be interested in following its ongoing deployment.

I think that mobile devices have the power to affect our lives in more ways than we think. One way is that they may affect our mood after a phone call.

Consumers' Experiences With Mobile Devices

When asked about their experiences with mobile devices upon prompted during different parts of a day, the Taiwanese participant (Taiwan-1) has expressed "I use my mobile phone to make and receive calls" (1st Prompt), "I use my mobile phone only to make and receive calls. and those mobile ads I have been receiving are not relevant to my life" (2nd Prompt), and "I would really like to know what functions smart phones have if I have a chance" (3rd Prompt). The experiential narratives from Taiwan-1 demonstrate the functional benefits that mobile phone (1st and 2nd Prompt) and at the time, the technology also demands consumers' dedication to spend time in learning about the technology (3rd Prompt).

For the US participants, the age of consumers seems to be an important factor to understand their experiences with mobile phone devices. For example, the participant, US-1, is 26 years old Hispanic male and his experience with the mobile device is overall positive at three different prompts. For example, upon the first prompt to ask about his experience using the mobile device, he expresses that "[I]t was very natural. No different from any other phone call using my mobile device" (Prompt 1), "It was normal" (Prompt 2), "Same as before. Regular experience using a phone" (Prompt 3).

Old consumers seem to be more attentive to the mobile phone. For example, a US participant (US-3) is a 60-years-old White consumer and his experience with mobile phone is different from those expressed by younger consumers. Upon the first prompt, he shares the following narratives below:

As the mobile smartphone rang, I immediately looked at the number associated with the incoming call. It was an unfamiliar number and, therefore, did not have a name associated with it. I touched the answer button and answered with my name, as I always do when I receive an unrecognized call.

His attention paid to the mobile phone has affected his mood state in some way. Upon prompted the 3rd time, he said that "I felt very pleased that my choices on "American Idol" had been selected for the finals. I enjoyed a nice dinner with my wife and was very relaxed and happy."

Will the gender of consumers influences their experiences with the mobile phone? Their narratives do not seem to suggest a gender variation. For example a Hispanic female of 24 years old (US-2) similarly focuses on the functional benefits of mobile phone. Upon the 1st prompt, she expresses that

Like anything else. It was a device that helped the researcher contact me so I could start on the survey. It worked well, the reception was flawless and my phone is something I depend on for a lot of things...calling being the last thing I use my cell phone for.

She continues to have a positive experience with mobile phone, upon the 2nd and 3rd prompt as seen below:

Again, it was great, helped me be in contact with the researcher for the second call. Everything

was great.

I have had great experiences with mobile devices. So far every single one that I have owned have been reliable when I most need them and again, I am able to contact people right away and they are able to contact me just the same.

Similar to other media usage, consumers are also motivated to use mobile phone for escapism. For example, Participant US-4 is a Hispanic consumer of 20 years old, points out that mobile phone can give her "something to do meanwhile" while she is bored. It is noteworthy that the disruptive effects of mobile phone are experienced by consumers, young and old. For example, upon Prompt 2 and 3, Participant US-4 expresses the disruption caused by her mobile phone to her daily life:

I snapped out of my thoughts and had trouble re-focusing and getting into the book again.

(Prompt 2)

It is a disruption and it is hard for me to regain my focus after I am done with the device.

(Prompt 3)

Consumer Mood States With the Mobile Phone

Positive moods that consumers have is likely to suppress consumers' elaboration, promote heuristic processing, and to enhance persuasion of an advertising campaign (Myers & Sar, 2015; Wen et al., 2017). Therefore, the fluctuations of consumers' mood states with the mobile phone are likely to influence how they will be receptive to digital marketing messages delivered via their mobile phone and smartphone devices. The researchers used 9-item seven point semantic differential scales with a list of bipolar adjectives to measure how participants respond to their mobile phone at different parts of the day. The researchers particularly focus on the mood states related to the disruptive effects of mobile phone, such as worried vs. relaxed, angry vs. friendly, anxious vs. calm, nervous vs. relaxed, troubled vs. untroubled, satisfied vs. dissatisfied, disappointed vs. pleased, disruptive vs. stable, and annoyed vs. pleased.

In terms of the disruptive effects of mobile phone on consumers' mood states, both Taiwanese and US participants feel disrupted. As expected, their perceptions of disruption increase particularly at night. The mean score for American participants shows increased perceptions of being disruptive from Prompt 1 to Prompt 3. While Taiwanese consumers feel more calm with their mobile phone, American participants are noticeably feel more angry with the intrusion of their mobile phone in different parts of the day. American participants seem to have more negative mood states about their mobile phone. For example, they increasingly feel disappointed with mobile phone, particular at night (Mean $^{prompt\ three}$=.50, SD=1.92) (Refer to Table 2).

CONCLUSION

Given the global diffusion of mobile communications around the world, it is important to examine how mobile users in different countries have experienced this innovative technology and related applications. Specifically, it is also critical to examine how these location-sensitive mobile devices and applications could infringe upon users' privacy and if these users perceive these issues to be detrimental to their daily experiences with these technologies. As noted in this SEM study, the perceptions of privacy-invasion and –disruption have been shared in participants' experiential narratives and their narratives are cross-culturally consistent, regardless of their different cultural dimensions, suggesting a converging effect of mobile phone as a technology (Kang & Yang, 2021). In spite of the cultural variations between Taiwan and the U.S. as seen in Figure 3, participants from both countries have mostly agreed with the functional benefits of the mobile phone and its relevance to their daily lives. In general, their mood states in response to the mobile phone are noticeably

Table 2. Consumers' Mood State with the Privacy-Invasive Mobile Phone

	very	quite	some	neither	some	quite	very	
Worried	3	2	1	0	1	2	3	Relaxed
		Taiwan		Mean[1st Prompt] = 1.00		N/A		
				Mean[2nd Prompt] = 1.00		N/A		
				Mean[3rd Prompt] = 1.00		N/A		
		U.S.		Mean[1st Prompt] = .50		S.D.=2.38		
				Mean[2nd Prompt] = 2.25		S.D.=.96		
				Mean[3rd Prompt] = 1.50		S.D.=1.92		
Angry	3	2	1	0	1	2	3	Friendly
		Taiwan		Mean[1st Prompt] = 2.00		N/A		
				Mean[2nd Prompt] = 1.00		N/A		
				Mean[3rd Prompt] = 1.00		N/A		
		U.S.		Mean[1st Prompt] = 1.75		S.D.=1.89		
				Mean[2nd Prompt] = 1.75		S.D.=1.50		
				Mean[3rd Prompt] = 2.33		S.D.=1.16		
Anxious	3	2	1	0	1	2	3	Calm
		Taiwan		Mean[1st Prompt] = 2.00		N/A		
				Mean[2nd Prompt] = 1.00		N/A		
				Mean[3rd Prompt] = 2.00		N/A		
		U.S.		Mean[1st Prompt] = .50		S.D.=1.73		
				Mean[2nd Prompt] = 1.25		S.D.=2.62		
				Mean[3rd Prompt] = .50		S.D.=1.92		
Nervous	3	2	1	0	1	2	3	Relaxed
		Taiwan		Mean[1st Prompt] = 1.00		N/A		
				Mean[2nd Prompt] = 1.00		N/A		
				Mean[3rd Prompt] = 2.00		N/A		
		U.S.		Mean[1st Prompt] = 0		S.D.=2.45		
				Mean[2nd Prompt] = 1.50		S.D.=1.73		
				Mean[3rd Prompt] = 1.50		S.D.=1.92		
Troubled	3	2	1	0	1	2	3	Untroubled
		Taiwan		Mean[1st Prompt] = 1.00		N/A		
				Mean[2nd Prompt] = 1.00		N/A		
				Mean[3rd Prompt] = 2.00		N/A		
		U.S.		Mean[1st Prompt] = .50		S.D.=2.38		
				Mean[2nd Prompt] = 1.25		S.D.=2.06		
				Mean[3rd Prompt] = 2.00		S.D.=1.41		
Satisfied	3	2	1	0	1	2	3	Dissatisfied
		Taiwan		Mean[1st Prompt] = 0		N/A		
				Mean[2nd Prompt] = 0		N/A		
				Mean[3rd Prompt] = -1.00		N/A		
		U.S.		Mean[1st Prompt] = -1.50		S.D.= 1.92		
				Mean[2nd Prompt] = -1.50		S.D.= 1.73		
				Mean[3rd Prompt] = -1.00		S.D.= 2.45		
Disappointed	3	2	1	0	1	2	3	Pleased
		Taiwan		Mean[1st Prompt] = 1.00		N/A		
				Mean[2nd Prompt] = 0		N/A		
				Mean[3rd Prompt] = 2.00		N/A		
		U.S.		Mean[1st Prompt] = 1.00		S.D.= 1.16		
				Mean[2nd Prompt] = 1.00		S.D.=2.45		
				Mean[3rd Prompt] = .75		S.D.= 2.87		
Disturbed	3	2	1	0	1	2	3	Stable
		Taiwan		Mean[1st Prompt] = 0		N/A		
				Mean[2nd Prompt] = 1.00		N/A		
				Mean[3rd Prompt] = 0		N/A		
		U.S.		Mean[1st Prompt] = 1.25		S.D.=2.06		
				Mean[2nd Prompt] = .75		S.D.=2.87		
				Mean[3rd Prompt] = .50		S.D.=1.92		

continued on following page

Table 2. Continued

	very	quite	some	neither	some	quite	very	
Annoyed	3	2	1	0	1	2	3	Pleased
		Taiwan		Mean$^{1st\ Prompt}$= 1.00		N/A		
				Mean$^{2nd\ Prompt}$ = 1.00		N/A		
				Mean$^{3rd\ Prompt}$ = 2.00		N/A		
		U.S.		Mean$^{1st\ Prompt}$= 1.00		S.D.=1.16		
				Mean$^{2nd\ Prompt}$ = 2.00		S.D.= 1.41		
				Mean$^{3rd\ Prompt}$ = 1.00		S.D.= 2.45		

Notes:

1st Prompt at 10 am

2nd Prompt at 3 pm

3rd Prompt at 8 pm

similar, except when American consumers seem to be more likely to feel angry with the invasion of the mobile phone. In addition, these negative impacts of the mobile phone have generated less favorable mood states on consumers. In particular, cross-cultural consumers may feel anxious and disruptive as a result of the mobile phone.

The widespread use of direct marketing activities has severe implications on how consumers view and protect their own information privacy (Jordaan, 2007). Procedures to protect consumers' identity and name are essential for businesses to ensure the ethics and success of their direct marketing campaigns (Jordaan, 2007). With the increased awareness of consumers about how businesses use their own personal data, governments around the world have implemented new privacy regulations and directives (Flannery, n.d.). Some pertinent examples include General Data Protection Regulation ('GDPR') proposed by European Union (Flannery, n.d.). As a privacy-invasive technology, mobile phone and its associated direct marketing applications could pose the greatest challenges to personal privacy that needs to be studied particularly from the consumers' perspectives.

To better understand what consumers feel about these mobile devices and applications, this chapter used ESM as a methodological innovation to document how mobile users feel in their daily lives when encountering these mobile devices and applications. The study findings provides rich descriptive data to document the impacts of this technology by prompting participants to share their experiential narratives at three different parts of the day. Unexpectedly, the study did not find country-specific differences to account for mobile users' daily experiences and examine the intricate relationships that human beings have with these pervasive technologies. As a mixed method study, this chapter reports users' experiential data to help direct marketing practitioners and researchers to better investigate what people were thinking about when exposed to direct advertising messages.

In terms of methodological limitations, data collected from an ESM approach will be constrained by the number of sampling (prompts) to ask participants to provide their data (Sather, 2014). Therefore, the results from this exploratory study should be interpreted with caution and should not be extended to a larger mobile phone population. Future research may include more participants, as well as more sampling intervals to collect more consumer experiential data.

REFERENCES

Christensen, T. C., Barrett, L. F., Bliss-Moreau, E., Lebo, K., & Kaschub, C. (2003). A practical guide to experience-sampling procedures. *Journal of Happiness Studies*, *4*(1), 53–78. doi:10.1023/A:1023609306024

Conner, T. (2015, May). *Experience sampling and ecological momentary assessment with mobile phones*. Retrieved on February 28, 2021 from https://www.otago.ac.nz/psychology/otago047475.pdf

De Mooij, M. (2003). Convergence and divergence in consumer behaviour: Implications for global advertising. *International Journal of Advertising*, *22*(2), 183–202. doi:10.1080/02650487.2003.11072848

EraInnovator. (2020, September 1). EraInnovator. *Mobile Commerce*. Retrieved on February 27, 2021 from https://erainnovator.com/mobile-commerce/

Fairfield, J. A. T. (2012, Spring). Mixed reality: How the laws of virtual worlds govern everyday life. *Berkeley Technology Law Journal*, *27*(1), 55–116.

Flannery, N. (n.d.). *Direct marketing and privacy: Striking that balance*. Retrieved on March 3, 2021 from http://uir.unisa.ac.za/bitstream/handle/10500/13073/10542-10553.pdf?sequence=10501

Friesland, K. (2018, June 2). 10 Worst internet privacy scandals to Date. *TechNadu*. Retrieved on June 23, 2019 from https://www.technadu.com/worst-internet-privacy-scandals/30236/

Gal-Or, E., Gal-Or, R., & Penmetsa, N. (2018, September). The role of user privacy concerns in shaping competition among platforms. *Information Systems Research*, *29*(3), 698–722. doi:10.1287/isre.2017.0730

Hektner, J. M., Schmidt, A., & Csikszentmihalyi, M. (2007). Experience sampling method: Measuring the quality of everyday life. Thousand Oaks, CA: Sage Publications.

Heyman, R., Wolf, R. D., & Pierson, J. (2014). Evaluating social media privacy settings for personal and advertising purposes. *Info, 16*(4), 18-32.

Hofstede, G. H. (1991). *Cultures and organizations: Software of the mind*. McGraw-Hill.

Hofstede, G. H. (2021, February 27). Country comparison. *Hofstede Insights*. Retrieved on February 27, 2021 from https://www.hofstede-insights.com/country-comparison/taiwan,the-usa/

Horwitz, L. (2014). Location-based marketing (LBM). *TechTarget*. Retrieved on February 28, 2021 from https://searchcustomerexperience.techtarget.com/definition/location-based-marketing-LBM

Hunter, G. L., & Taylor, S. A. (2019). The relationship between preference for privacy and social media usage. *Journal of Consumer Marketing, 37*(1), 43–54. doi:10.1108/JCM-11-2018-2927

Irion, K., & Helberger, N. (2017). Smart TV and the online media sector: User privacy in view of changing market realities. *Telecommunications Policy, 41*(3), 170–184. doi:10.1016/j.telpol.2016.12.013

Johnston, M. (2020, March 26). Smartphones are changing advertising & marketing. *Investopedia*. Retrieved on February 27, 2021 from https://www.investopedia.com/articles/personal-finance/062315/how-smartphones-are-changing-advertising-marketing.asp

Jordaan, Y. (2007). Information privacy issues: Implications for direct marketing. *International Journal of Retail and Marketing*, 42-53.

Kang, Y. W., & Yang, K. C. C. (2020). Privacy concerns in the VR and AR applications in creative cultural industries: A text mining study. In Managerial Challenges and Social Impacts of Virtual and Augmented Reality (pp. 142-164). Hershey, PA: IGI-Global Publisher. doi:10.4018/978-1-7998-2874-7.ch009

Kang, Y. W., & Yang, K. C. C. (2021). Will social media and its consumption converge or diverge global consumer culture? In Analyzing global social media consumption (pp. 68-87). Hershey, PA: IGI-Global Publisher.

Khan, V. J., Markopoulos, I., & Jsselsteijn, W. A. (2007). Combining the Experience Sampling Method with the Day Reconstruction Method. *Proceedings 11th CHI Nederland Conference*.

KMPG. (2016a). *Creepy or cool? Staying on the right side of the consumer privacy line*. Retrieved on March 22, 2020 from https://home.kpmg.com/sg/en/home/insights/2016/2011/crossing-the-line.html

KMPG. (2016b, November 7). *Companies that fail to see privacy as a business priority risk crossing the 'creepy line'*. KMPG, Retrieved on June 23, 2019 from https://home.kpmg/sg/en/home/media/press-releases/2016/2011/companies-that-fail-to-see-privacy-as-a-business-priority-risk-crossing-the-creepy-line.html

Koohang, A., Paliszkiewicz, J., & Goluchowski, J. (2018). Social media privacy concerns: Trusting beliefs and risk beliefs. *Industrial Management & Data Systems*, *118*(6), 1209–1228. doi:10.1108/IMDS-12-2017-0558

Levesque, R. J. R. (2017). *Adolescence, Privacy, and the Law: A Developmental Science Perspective*. Oxford University Press.

Lom, H. S., Thoo, A. C., Sulaiman, Z., & Adam, S. (2018, June). Moderating role of mobile users' information privacy concerns towards behavioural intention and use behaviour in mobile advertising. *Advanced Science Letters*, *24*(6), 4259–4264. doi:10.1166/asl.2018.11584

Myers, J., & Sar, S. (2015). The influence of consumer mood state as a contextual factor on imagery-inducing advertisements and brand attitude. *Journal of Marketing Communications*, *21*(4), 284–299. doi:10.1080/13527266.2012.762421

Papadopoulou, P. (2018). Exploring M-Commerce and social media: A comparative analysis of mobile phones and tablets. In Mobile Commerce: Concepts, Methodologies, Tools, and Applications (pp. 849-869). IGI Publishers.

Pew Research Center. (2019, June 12). *Social Media Fact Sheet*. Washington, DC: Pew Research Center. Retrieved on July 31, 2019 from https://www.pewinternet.org/fact-sheet/social-media/

Richter, F. (2021, March 1). Global 5G Adoption to Triple in 2021. *Statista*. Retrieved on March 2, 2021 from https://www.statista.com/chart/9604/2025g-subscription-forecast/?utm_source=Statista+Global&utm_campaign=2670c2873f2029e-All_InfographTicker_daily_COM_AM_KW2005_2021_Fr_COPY&utm_medium=email&utm_term=2020_afecd2219f2025-2670c2873f2029e-301917341

Sather, T. (2014, November). Experience Sampling Method: An overview for researchers and clinicians. *CREd Library*. Retrieved on February 28, 2021 from https://academy.pubs.asha.org/2014/2011/experience-sampling-method/

Silver, L., Smith, A., John, C., Jiang, J., Anderson, M., & Rainie, L. (2019, March 7). Majorities say mobile phones are good for society, even amid concerns about their impact on children. *Pew Research Center*. Retrieved on February 27, 2021 from https://www.pewresearch.org/internet/2019/2003/2007/majorities-say-mobile-phones-are-good-for-society-even-amid-concerns-about-their-impact-on-children/

Statista. (2016, February 28). United States mobile phone penetration 2014-2020. *Statista*. Retrieved on February 27, 2021 from https://www.statista.com/statistics/222307/forecast-of-mobile-phone-penetration-in-the-us/

Statista. (2020, December 4). Household penetration of mobile phones in Taiwan 2007-2018. *Statista*. Retrieved on February 27, 2021 from https://www.statista.com/statistics/324757/taiwan-mobile-phone-household-penetration/

The Economist. (2004, June 24). The harder hard sell. *The Economist*. Retrieved on February 27, 2021 from https://www.economist.com/special-report/2004/2006/2024/the-harder-hard-sell

van der Sloot, B. (2017, August). Decisional privacy 2.0: the procedural requirements implicit in Article 8 ECHR and its potential impact on profiling. *International Data Privacy Law, 7*(3), 190-201, doi:https://doi.org/110.1093/idpl/ipx1011

Walden, I., & Woods, L. (2011). Broadcasting privacy. *Journal of Medicine and Law*, *3*(1), 117–141. https://dx.doi.org/110.5235/175776311796471323

Wen, J. T., Sar, S., & Anghelcev, G. (2017). The interaction effects of mood and ad appeals on type of elaboration and advertising effectiveness. *Journal of Current Issues and Research in Advertising*, *38*(1), 31–43.

Williams, M. (2009, July 10). Advertisers test alimented reality's durability. *Campaign*, 9.

Xu, H., Dinev, T., Smith, J., & Hart, P. (2011, December). Information privacy concerns: Linking individual perceptions with institutional privacy assurances. *Journal of the Association for Information Systems*, *12*(12), 798–824. doi:10.17705/1jais.00281

Yang, K. C. C., & Kang, Y. W. (2020a). Framing national security concerns in mobile telecommunication infrastructure debates: A text mining study of Huawei. In Huawei goes global (volume II): Regional, geopolitical perspectives and crisis management (pp. 313-339). Palgrave-Macmillan.

Yang, K. C. C., & Kang, Y. W. (2020b). What Facebook users' responses to advertising: A computational and ESM analysis. In IoT, digital transformation, and the future of global marketing. Hershey, PA: IGI-Global Publisher. doi:10.4018/978-1-7998-1618-8.ch001

ADDITIONAL READING

Baruh, L., Secinti, E., & Cemalcilar, Z. (2017). Online privacy concerns and privacy management: A meta-analytical review. *Journal of Communication, 67*, 26–53.

Bellman, S., Johnson, E. J., Kobrin, S. J., & Lohse, G. L. (2004). International differences in information privacy concerns: A global survey of consumers. *The Information Society, 20*(5), 313-324. *DOI, 3*. Advance online publication. doi:10.1080/01972240490507956

Bridwell, S. A. (2007). The dimensions of locational privacy. In H. J. Miller (Ed.), *Societies and Cities in the Age of Instant Access* (pp. 209–225). Springer.

Callanan, C., Jerman-Blažic, B., & Blažic, A. J. (2016). User awareness and tolerance of privacy abuse on mobile Internet: An exploratory study. *Telematics and Informatics, 33*, 109–128.

Dinev, T., & Hart, P. (2004). Internet privacy concerns and their antecedents: Measurement validity and a regression model. *Behaviour & Information Technology, 23*(6), 413-422. *DOI, 4*. Advance online publication. doi:10.1080/014492904100 01715723

Electronic Frontier Foundation (EFF). (2019). *Privacy*. San Francisco, CA: Electronic Frontier Foundation. Retrieved on March 16, 2020 from https://www.eff.org/issues/privacy

Krumm, J. (2008). *A Survey of Computational Location Privacy*. Redmond, Washington: Microsoft. Retrieved on March h16, 2020 from https://www.microsoft.com/en-us/research/wp-content/uploads/2016/12/computational-location-privacy-preprint.pdf

Merkovity, N., Imre, R., & Owen, S. (2015). Homogenizing social media - affect/effect and globalization of media and the public sphere. In Media and Globalization: Different Cultures, Societies, Political Systems (pp. 59-71). New York: Maria Curie-Sklodowska University Press (under Columbia University Press).

Mitry, D. J., & Smith, D. E. (2009). Convergence in global markets and consumer behaviour. *International Journal of Consumer Studies, 33*, 316–321.

Pasternak, O., Veloutsou, C., & Morgan-Thomas, A. (2017). Self-presentation, privacy and electronic word-of-mouth in social media. *Journal of Product and Brand Management, 26*(4), 415–428.

Thornthwaite, L. (2018). Social media and dismissal: Towards a reasonable expectation of privacy? *The Journal of Industrial Relations, 60*(1), 119–136.

Tucker, C. E. (2013). Social networks, personalized advertising, and privacy controls. *JMR, Journal of Marketing Research, 51*(5), 546–562.

Worley, B. (2010, Oct. 19). Facebook: Another privacy scandal. *ABC News.* Retrieved on March 31, 2018 from https://abcnews.go.com/GMA/Consumer/facebook-privacy-scandal-facebooks-watergate/story?id=11912201

KEY TERMS AND DEFINITIONS

Consumer Behavior: The study of consumers' decision-making processes to select, secure, use, and dispose of products or services. This term often refers to how consumers respond to advertising and marketing messages. The study of consumer behavior also examines social, cultural, regulatory, and other ecological factors in affecting their decision-making processes.

Direct Marketing: The term refers to a type of marketing activities that depends on direct communication with target consumers, instead of mediated through a third party or a mass media platform. Some example of direct marketing platforms include email, postal mail, social media, and texting.

Experience Sampling Method: A data collection method to gather systematic self-reports of behaviors, emotions, or experiences from research participants to record their experiences in the individual's natural context. The benefits of ESM are to offer researchers with real-time interactions through a quasi-

Information Privacy: This term refers to a type of privacy concerns about how personal information and data are stored and used. Types of information privacy include business-related data, criminal records, financial data, political records, and medical records.

Location-Awareness: A term commonly found in describing one of the functions in mobile, navigation, and GPS devices through which individual users' location privacy will be shared and monitored. In general, the term describes navigation, real-time location, and GPS positioning support at a local, regional, and global level.

Mixed Research Method: This term describes a combination of quantitative and qualitative research methods to collect data for a single study.

Mobile Advertising: An emerging platform of new digital media advertising formats that are delivered via mobile devices such as mobile phones, smartphones, tablets, or wearables, etc.

Mobile Commerce: Also known as m-commerce or mcommerce, the term relies on mobile devices to facilitate and conduct business transactions. Often thought to be an extension or an advancement of traditional e-commerce, this new type of

commercial activities will enable people to sell and buy goods and services from any locations users would prefer.

Mobile Communications: A term that emerges around 2000 refers to the use of a variety of technological systems to enable communication activities away from a fixed location without the use of any physical connectivity via cables or wired.

Mobile Social Media: A term to refer to social networking applications, media, or platforms such as Facebook, Foursquare, Instagram, Pinterest, Twitter, etc., that are often delivered via mobile devices such as smartphone, tablet, or laptop computer.

Privacy: Privacy is a term that describe people's right to be let alone, or their freedom from outside interference or intrusion without their prior consent from any noon-profit, profit-making, or government entities.

Smartphone: A mobile-based technology that integrates computing functions into a mobile device. Characteristics of a smartphone include strong hardware capabilities, comprehensive mobile operating systems, and computing capabilities similar to a minicomputer. A smartphone enables consumers to access the Internet and to use multimedia contents such as music, videos, and digital games.

Social Media: The term refers to a group of Internet-based applications to allow people to connect socially and includes collaborative projects (such as Wikipedia), microblogs and blogs, contents (such as YouTube), social networking services (such as Facebook) and virtual games.

Chapter 2
Mobility–Aware Prefetching and Replacement Scheme for Location–Based Services:
MOPAR

Ajay Kumar Gupta
iD https://orcid.org/0000-0001-9666-5047
M. M. M. University of Technology, India

Udai Shanker
iD https://orcid.org/0000-0002-4083-7046
M. M. M. University of Technology, India

ABSTRACT

Location-based services (LBS) are gaining prominence in today's environment. When a mobile user submits a location-based query in LBS, an adversary may infer the locations or other related sensitive information. Thus, an efficient location privacy preservation model (LPPM) with minimal overhead needs to be built by considering contextual understanding and analytical ability. With consideration of service efficiency and privacy, a location privacy preservation policy, namely mobility-aware prefetching and replacement (MOPAR) policy, has been proposed by the cloaking area formulation through user location, cache contribution rate, and data freshness in LBS. An incorporation of prefetching and replacement to anonymizer and consumer cache with formulation of cloak area is being deployed to protect customer sensitive information. The Markov mobility model-based next-position prediction procedure is used in this chapter for caching and formulation of cloaking area. The results of the simulation show significant enhancement in the efficiency of the location-privacy preservation model.

DOI: 10.4018/978-1-7998-7756-1.ch002

INTRODUCTION

LBS (Gupta & Shanker, 2020e) is a ubiquitous computer-based services that essentially provides all consumers with enormous valued resources by directly incorporating the location of the devices through global positioning system (GPS) or indirectly using other relevant details in the query. Centred on the upgraded approach, queries can be divided into two forms in any context-aware method, i.e., traditional queries as well as continuous queries (Gupta & Shanker, 2020a). Conventional query data items do not update by themself over period if mobile clients change their locations. Thus, mobile clients only send requests once in continuous queries, and then if any location update happens as clients travel to various areas, the server would be automatically alert about the position or new mobile client query results.

Even though GPS allows efficient outdoor positioning, there are certain portable devices not having the built-in GPS receiver. Therefore, they may not be suitable for location detection of wireless devices. Sukaphat (Sukaphat, 2011) has developed a location based application with an android based identifier API to solve this problem. The location tracking process is conducted as a background procedure in this system and the transfer of this information regularly takes place within a cycle. Geographic Information System (GIS) services on mobile gadgets are beginning to expand. GeoFairy (Sun et al., 2017) is an application of LBS that offers geospatial information in real-time for the users (Gupta & Shanker, 2018a). OpenLayers is another open-source JavaScript library similar to the Google Maps API that provides APIs for viewing map data and creating web-based geospatial applications. Raster and vector data can also be made by OpenLayers from a range of file types including the web servers. The implementation of GeoPackage (C. Zhang et al., 2016) is a smartphone application that allows users to view, monitor, interpret and simulate details on both OpenLayers and Google Maps.

If the inquired data is not found in the cache of mobile devices in primitive LBS implementations, then a Database Analyzer must accept system requests with its location and evaluate them to return the queried response. The drawback of previously suggested solutions is that they are likely to leak confidential user information such as the location of the user and associated business benefit data to untrusted third parties. There are various methods to fix privacy concerns for LBS. The reliable third party like Cloaking are commonly known as traditionally used LBS privacy policy for device location anonymization. This lowers the efficiency of resources (QoS) for points of interest (POI). In order to enhance user privacy with better caching efficiency, it should therefore be resolved while implementing the LBS. To be wise and positive, the existing context is not only understood by devices; instead, they should be capable of predicting context too. The device's ability to assess the potential location of the user is used in cache prefetching. (Ilayaraja et al., 2016). This tends to reduce the need for specific interaction with the Query Analyzer, which in essence improves customer protection. In several of the previous initiatives, there has been a trade-off between privacy and service quality. To meet the full POI for the query issued by the traveling client, the LBS compromises with user privacy. In comparison, preceding measures include high system overhead (processing and coordination costs). Further research goal is required to design multilevel caching to avoid unauthorised access to sensitive client information by cloaking area formulation to cope up with the above challenges. For improved user protection, the goal is to incorporate spatial k-anonymity and pre-fetching. Simply defining the algorithm one by one would influence the output of the method. Since, all the problems cannot be solved in one attempt, only few methods have been selected in our analysis to increase the efficiency of LBS. Caching Efficiency with Markov Predictor (CEMP) invalidation-replacement (Gupta & Shanker, 2020b) for cache invalidation- replacement and pre-fetching & spatial k-anonymity for client data security is used to suggest the solution to the above LBS problems. The above policies have used the nth order mobility model of Markov (Gupta & Shanker, 2020f) to predict the next travelling consumer position. This estimation of the next position of travelling client is used in procedures for replacement-invalidation and k-anonymity. The complete spatial k-anonymity, pre-fetching and caching framework lead to the protection of user data privacy; however, throughout all modules of the MOPAR model framework, the same next location prediction feature is used. In Anonymizer cache replacement, our analysis includes multi-users cache object cost calculation for improved cache hit ratio and reduces overhead. Therefore, incorporating suggested modules into one platform leads to enhancing device efficiency with limited incurred overhead.

The chapter is organised as follows. Section 2 describes the survey of the previous works carried out and the issue statement. In Section 3, the LBS design, conclusions, and the suggested strategy definition are discussed. Section 4 presents the specifics of the main results of our simulation. The future scope and conclusions are detailed in Section 5 and Section 6 of this chapter, respectively.

RELATED WORK

More recently, caching on terminal devices continues to draw attention from studies. Researchers are working to resolve important caching problems, such as cache strategies (Drakatos et al., 2009)(Akon et al., 2011), caching location (Wang et al., 2017) etc. Certain policies for spatiotemporal caching are Manhattan (Michael, 1996), PAID (Zheng et al., 2002) and MARS (Lai et al., 2004). There is another cache replacement technique called Furthest Away Replacement (FAR) (Ren &

Dunham, 2000) policy which involves eviction of those data items from cache whose valid scope area and client movement direction are opposite. This method facilitates eviction sequence based on the valid scope reference point distance of the client to the data item. The downside to this technique is that it does not consider the temporary access locality of the moving customer.

To pre-load the contents before being used, pre-fetching is used. Improving the pre-fetching accuracy is a vital consideration for improving the system's adaptability and thus performance as well. Adaptivity is a key problem with pre-fetching strategies particularly in the contexts of mobile technology where resources power, i.e., electricity, cache, and space are limited. Several researchers have proposed strategies for establishing policies for pre-fetching (Yin et al., 2002)(Drakatos et al., 2009) (Pallis et al., 2008); however, due to an unplanned policy to deal with the various device overhead, these pre-fetching policies incur excessive resource costs. The mobile client's Point of Interest (POI) (Al-Molegi, Jabreel, et al., 2018)(Al-Molegi, Alsmadi, et al., 2018) used in next place prediction module could easily be saved well in advance in the user's cache. The system will calculate prefetching costs and dynamically adjust the prefetching decision based on the assigned interest, current residual power level, access time, and update speed & data size.

Obfuscation, regulatory scheme, privacy policies, and anonymity policies are the four classes for latest security solutions for LBS user locations. Caching through a single grid for greater data protection has been proposed by Zhang et al. (S. Zhang et al., 2018). But, because of overlapping query limitations, the system's query overhead became daunting. A pair of dummy positions in caching have been suggested by Niu et al. (Niu et al., 2014) for stronger anonymity of user position. This method has its limitations in that it does not work with continuing requests. Due to essence of its service, personal location monitoring will intrude on privacy. The two prominent alternatives are k-anonymity and l-diversity. These methods, however, can still undermine the individual's privacy because they rely mainly on how to protect a fixed location, and information of this region may also be revealed by the surrounding areas. In comparison, instead of the low user audience, the scale may be considerably larger in cloaking region-based privacy-protection strategy schemes. The QoS show decreasing trends on increase of scale of cloaking area. In the case of low user density, the broad cloaking area formulated can minimise the QoS or sometimes result in denial of service. To overcome the constraint of prior laws, spatial cloaking technique can be paired with k-anonymity. In (Tian et al., 2018), the authors adopted a cloud-of-things system location privacy pre-protection strategy to preserve the credibility of user trajectories. Moving device patterns are measured and the proposed policy expands the restricted area to satisfy requirements for data protection. The exact location data are covered from attackers by this framework. However, in these policies, high device overhead (processing & communication cost) has been seen.

Mobility Aware Prefetching and Replacement (MOPAR) Scheme

In consideration of all the above problems, the policy implemented for the caching cost function is identical to SPMC-CRP (Gupta & Shanker, 2019) and invalidation identical to CELPB (Gupta & Shanker, 2018). The mobility Markov model of nth order is being used in module for prediction of next position. Apart from the Anonymizer cache replacement for improved cache hit ratio as well as lowering the overhead, our work has considered multiple clients cache data item cost estimation. The system performance and system availability have been enhanced by the use of mobile client caching additionally.

System Architecture

The mechanism that resides between the Query Analyzer and the recipient is introduced by a mediator called Anonymizer. The anonymizer hides the exact location of the device owner. When all user queries pass through the Anonymizer, it is the ultimate system performance bottleneck. By using the cloaking field obtained from Anonymizer, the pre-fetching and spatial k-anonymity strategy used in the proposed approach preserves the estimate of client location from an intruder. Query analyzer, mobile clients and anonymizer are used in the architecture of the system. The main function of Anonymizer is to cache the obtained query results of Query Analyzer by predicting moving users' next position. The anonymizer selects the cell that satisfies the k-anonymity criteria. Query probability is for the selection of cell between k cells as cloaking region. If few clients are found in each of the k cells, the probability that a single user sends the messages will be 1/K at most. In a related cell, Anonymizer does have the record of a query sent from the same user. The location-based programme connected to the corresponding cloaking region that Anonymizer gets, represents the Query Analyzer. In a shared collaboration basis, the mobile network software works with other neighbouring handset users. This has processing power, global positioning, storing of data, and the potential to communicate to other group smartphone devices.

The pre-fetching scheme is applied to LBS in conjunction to content caching to increase user interface and cache access optimization. Many variables like user behaviour, location, and log data are considered by the pre-fetch engine to forecast what there is to be pre-fetched. Plenty of the pre-fetching algorithm studied involve analysing the log data to obtain the client's access actions, calculate and rate element to be pre-fetched depending on the degree of interest. The Proxies PF is preferable over Server PF and User PF since pre-fetching content between clients is exchanged through the interpretation of mutual desires of various clients and servers; although, it is not feasible to evaluate a mutual query for a specific data item for all users. A portion of the database, proxies (Anonymizer), and Query Analyzer cache storage is allocated for pre-fetching in this chapter. In addition to the one allocated for pre-fetching, LBS implements the substitution and invalidation protocol in cache space. Here, in the allocated pre-fetching storage, we then use Markov model-based methodology to pre-fetch the hot data objects.

Assumptions

This was presumed that travelling users are trusted and show their true locations. Inside the network communication area, none of the peer nodes can relay damaging information to the neighbouring clients. To protect privacy and the authenticity of the transmitted data, LBS has encryption mechanisms such as cryptographic and hashing systems. From the standpoint of travelling users, the new law deals with the issue of location confidentiality. Moving consumers do have choice of choosing protection from high, medium, or low privacy requirements. Based on the degree of service and the sharing of privacy, a suitable standard is being used here. If the thresholds value is high, then LBS will breach the privacy of users and satisfy the need for full query POI of the smartphone user. The proposed MOPAR uses a PSKA framework to improve anonymity by establishing a cloaking area in a LBS system. To guarantee the status of the user's data to an unreliable entity, a multi-level caching is recommended.

The framework ensures that the full trajectory data is supposed to be processed on the server instead of on the device for the next position estimation. Sever passes the data with the greatest amount of route arbitration of mobile units from the complete pathway stored on the server at frequent time frames for the purpose of caching. We also built a strategy combined with the cache replacement, invalidation & prefetching protocol in the light of LBS challenges. With various method for data mining (Gupta, 2020), the next position prediction module has been developed. SPMC-next CRP's location prediction feature for caching and CELPB invalidation policy (Zheng et al., 2002) was replaced by the Markov's mobility model of nth order. In this case, validity testing is ideal if the travelling user assumes a new location after the query is given due to data access latency in the cellular region before the response is returned. The validity for a given data item of the geometry type or area is expressed by valid scope. The suggested MOPAR reference architecture and internal architecture of the Query Analyzer are outlined in Figure 1 and Figure 2 respectively.

Figure 1. Architecture of Proposed Location Based Service Framework

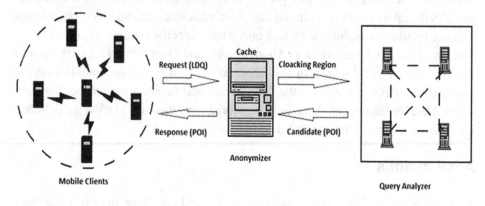

Figure 2. Detailed Architectural Description of Query Analyzer

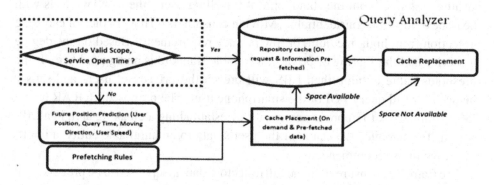

Markov Model Based Next Location Estimation

Mobility Markov Chain is a single stochastic process used to model the human mobility behaviour, where transitions likelihood distribution and former state are determinant parameters of transition. It uses node state as Markov processes and labelled edges as transition probability to show the directed acyclic diagram. The collection of the state is used depending on the order of importance to reflect a frequently set of Point of Interests (POIs). Mobility Markov model is used here to directly deduce and attach a semantic label such as "home," "job," "path," with such states. A transition probability matrix P (n×n) is used to define a set of transitions between states, where n is the count of Mobility Markov Chain participating states. In the first step of this mobility model, the mobile user dense GPS trajectory is processed for the extraction of stay points. The two GPS points $X(g_i, h_i, t_i)$ & $Y(g_{i+1}, h_{i+1}, t_{i+1})$ are assumed to be presented in the common region, if both met the given criteria.

$$\sqrt{\left(g_{i+1} - g_i\right)^2 + \left(h_{i+1} - h_i\right)^2} \leq D_r \text{ and, } \sqrt{\left(t_{i+1} - t_i\right)^2} \leq T_r$$

The mean of longitude and latitude with all trajectory points located in the common region shall be the location of the stay points. POIs are extracted from those stay points in the next stage. The region having density of distribution greater than that of other zones is termed as POI. Algorithm 1 demonstrates the steps of extracting POI from trajectories. It is derived by those trajectory clusters where stay points in given trajectory cluster exceeds system defined parameter minimum cluster stay count ($minC_s$). In Algorithm 4, the DBSCAN technique is used to determine the POI for users. The DBSCAN method uses the Haversine function to estimate points of stay distance. Input variables comprise of mobility traces (T) of stay point in the format of (g, h, t), $minC_s$, i.e., minimum cluster stay count. The points of interest final sequence for the users is achieved as output of Algorithm 1, which is further used as input in the iterative construction of the Markov mobility chain of nth order in algorithm 2. Algorithm 3 is used by LBS to determine the next user position directly according to the formed Transition Probability Matrix of nth order.

Algorithm 1: Trajectory T Preprocessing

```
Input: stay_points (g, h, t) mobility traces (T)
minC_s: Least stay count for cluster
Eps: expanding clusters local radius
Begin
Mark "unvisited" to each stay point's pt ∈ T;
For All moving user from all_user do
For All pt ∈ T do
If cluster or pt ∈ noise
Continue;
Else If minC_s ≥ num(Neighbour_Eps(pt))
Mark p as noise;
Else
Create a new POI cluster C with center pt and add each pt of
Neighbour_Eps(pt) into it;
For All Not_visited u∈ Neighbour_Eps(pt) do
Find Neighbour_Eps(u) if minC_s ≥ count(Neighbour_Eps(u));
```

```
Not_visited points fetching into cluster C from Neighbour_
Eps(u);
End For_All
End if
End For_All
End For_All
For All user
If continuous POI AND same day
Take any POI and Assign time = Initial POI time;
End if
End For_All
Return Cluster C
End
```

Algorithm 2: Creation of Markov Transition Probability Matrix

```
Input: stay points (g, h, t) mobility traces (T)
Cw: merging width of POI Cluster
n: Number of past location visited
minCs: Minimum Cluster stay count
Eps: expanding clusters local radius
Begin
Extract most significant clusters using Algorithm 1;
Merge shared clusters having common point;
Find Clist by the merge of all POI clusters falls within
semantic distance Cw;
For All cluster Ci∈Clist do
Calculate C time interval, radius, and, density;
End For_All
Based on densities descending sort of clusters listed in Clist;
For All cluster Ci ∈ Clist
For point pti, use Markov Transition Probability for assignment
of a state in matrix;
End For_All
For All POI do
If the radiusi is greater than cluster Ci centre and POI
distance width
Update Ci current location and FIFO n - 1 past locations;
```

```
Past n - 1 locations and C_i current location labeling on trace
m;
Else
Trace m "Unidentified" marking;
End if
End For_All
Deletion of all Traces having marks of "Unidentified";
Substitution of subsequent similar traces into single pattern;
With all Markov Chain states pair, estimate transition
probability and put into nth order Transition Probability
Matrix;
Return Matrix of Transition Probability;
End Algorithm 3: Predict_Next_POI
```

Algorithm 3: Predict_Next_POI

```
Input: Transition Probability Matrix (nth order)
User FMP set L: point_1→point_2→···→point_m, m ≤ n
Begin
Search for row Y in Transition Probability Matrix which have m
past visited points point_1→point_2→···→point_m ;
Return POI corresponding to the column in row Y;
End
```

In algorithm 3, Transition Probability Matrix of nth order is used to find a row Y (or POI) that has a maximum probability of transition. The topological distance between two locations is inversely proportional to the relationship. Here, the measure of semantic similarity is called the semantic distance between the p_i and p_j of any two position points. This set of semantic distances is stored in n×n matrix. It is a topological distance obtained by calculating the number of edges that one needs to deduce from the state representing point pt_i to the point pt_j state. Semantic distances are directly inserted into the probability transformation matrix of the low order Markov model. A post pruning process is executed in the nth order of the Markov model to prune the outliers in the Markov model state.

Forming Cloaking Region

The Anonymizer selects k cells which meet the k-anonymity criteria by using the cache contribution rate and predicted next location with data freshness. The cloaking region is then picked from the k cells that have the highest request probability. The unit has a rectangular M*M grid service area in which each cell has a particular identifier (c_i, r_j) and the same dimensions. A shared software cache method is designed by the computer.

In our approach here, cooperative caching relies on the tree structure of the signature supplement close to that suggested in (Lubbe et al., 2011) being used. It is assumed that both the Anonymizer and the consumers are potentially reliable in this system and reveal their actual roles. A false location may be introduced together with a fake request if the network has any fake users inside it. The possibilities for location disclosure are also significantly greater than 1/k. The LBS specification assumes that the point density within the cell implies the possibility that the client will ask a query within the cell. We assumed that the individual, who sends a query, travels somewhere in the cells. We choose the other cell in the cloaking region with equivalent question probability to that of the mobile user cell. As in this case, the intruder does not infer the associated background data in the cloaking field from the population of participant cells. In LBS implementation, I_q is represented by cell identifiers set with query POI. I_c is described by cell identifiers matched to the cache of the user.

The matching cell identifier from the device's neighbouring cache is expressed by I_n. D_u represents the user location initiating the query. The optimum degree threshold (θ) ranges in between 0 and 1. The threshold value shows trade-off between privacy and service quality. User anonymity is reduced by the high value of this threshold and meets the required POI of more mobile apps. The minimum number of cell identifiers (λ) equals $\theta *\text{Num}(I_q) - \text{Num}(I_n) - \text{Num}(I_c)$ where, Num() function is used to count the cell identifiers.

In PSKA, if the inquired answer is not found in the Anonymizer cache, then next location estimate of user trajectories is applied to the nth order mobility Markov model. Then, as per the cloaking area selection protocol, it executes spatial k-anonymity feature using mobile device inputs in LBS. In this particular case, the number of cell identities to be matched in the Anonymizer cache is supplied by $k - \text{Num}(I_u^3)$ where $I_u^3 = I_q - I_c - I_n - I_a$.

The creation of a cloaking area comprises the following procedures.

i). The LBS selects Z cells around L_p (Z > 2k and is a framework parameter) according to the next expected location of the client L_p. In addition, it selects 2k cells from Z cells with the greatest likelihood of query.

ii). As a candidate set, $W = k - \text{Num}\left(i_u^3\right)$ cells are chosen randomly of 2k cells. For every one of the W cells, cache contribution rate and data freshness are determined.

iii). The computer would assign the cell (C_d) with the least data freshness and highest cache contribution rate to be a cloaking region in the final step.

The formulation approach for the cloaking area chooses the cell with cache's maximum contribution rate. Assume $\sum_{i=1}^{M \times M} P_i = 1$ and Pi be customer's probability of query in i^{th} cell & M be the cell size, then rate of Anonymizer cache contribution can be mathematically represented by the equation 1.

$$\textbf{Rate of cache contribution} = \sum_{i=1}^{k-\text{Num}\left(i_u^3\right)} P_i \tag{1}$$

Any cache data assumes to be expired after its lifetime. To enhance the usefulness of the system cache hit ratio, the application has to refresh the allocated cache information after the data has expired. Assume $T \geq t$, where t is a caching time for data in any cell and T represents the lifetime of the cached data, then the cell's freshness (F) can be expressed by the equation 2.

$$F = 1 - \sqrt{\frac{t^2}{T^2}} \tag{2}$$

The overall average freshness with the use of selected cell counts, i.e., $k - \text{Num}(I_u^3)$ can be defined by equation 3.

$$\textbf{Data Freshness}_{Avg} = \frac{\sum_{i=1}^{k-\text{Num}\left(i_u^3\right)} F}{k - \textbf{Num}\left(i_u^3\right)} \tag{3}$$

As defined by equation 4, for cloaking area formulation, Anonymizer selects the cell (Cd) with the minimum data freshness and highest contribution rate to caching.

$$C_d = Maximum \sum_{i=1}^{k-Num(i_u^3)} \frac{\sum_{i=1}^{k-Num(i_u^3)} \sqrt{\frac{t^2}{T^2}}}{k - Num(i_u^3)} \times P_i \qquad (4)$$

The replacement strategy is meant to recognise minimally expensive data items that can be eliminated from the client and Anonymizer cache. One may formally describe the replacement function as finding S with the conditions defined in equation 5.

$$d_{new} < \sum_{d_i \in S} objSize \text{ and } Min(\sum_{d_i \in S} cost(i)) \qquad (5)$$

The cost method of proposed model being introduced in equation 6, which is fairly similar to the PPRRP (Kumar et al., 2006). When the area of data item valid scope be broad, then the likelihood of access to the defined data item would be greater. The data item cost is dependent on the size, access likelihood, valid scope area, and the distance from the valid scope reference point to the present position of the consumer. The user current location is being used for cost calculation of client cache data item, while the positioning of each travelling user moving in the cell with the highest contribution rate is used for Anonymizer cache. In the second case, the cost of replacement is the amount of the cost measured in the cloaking area for each travelling person.

$$Cost_i = \begin{cases} \dfrac{\gg_i}{\mu_i.min(L_r, D(vs(d_i)))} \cdot \dfrac{Prob_i.A(vs(d_i))}{S_i} .if\ vs(d_i) \in predicted\_Region \\[2em] \dfrac{\gg_i}{\mu_i.D'(vs(d_i))} \cdot \dfrac{P_i.A(vs(d_i))}{S_i} .if\ vs(d_i) \notin predicted\_Region \end{cases} \qquad (6)$$

$Prob_i$ refers for the probability of accessing the ith data object in the cache of Anonymizer. The default value of $Prob_i$ be the zero. The area of valid scope attached to v is specified by $A(vs(d_i))$. Markov model based models are used for the replacement, invalidation, and pre-fetching strategies to predict user next positions as specified in the preceding sub-sections. By providing information of the next forecast position, the distance from the next position of the anticipated client to the reference point of data item valid scope can be identified. In this framework, mobility rules are being framed based on the similarities among user movement logs. The strategy provides detailed next position estimation used for cost computing of data items, which essentially increases the cache hit ratio relative to previous strategies.

In the replacement method, $D(vs(d_i))$ is the point of reference to the actual position distance of the user with valid scopes. The function for $D(vs(d_i))$ is given in equation 7. For the future queried data item (d_i), the possibly next position of the user is described by $L_{am} = (Lx_{am}, Ly_{am})$ and the point of reference of relevant scopes is described by $L_i = (Lx_i, Ly_i)$.

$$D(vs(d_i)) = |(L_{am} - L_i| = \sqrt{\left(Ly_{am} - Ly_i\right)^2 + \left(Lx_{am} - Lx_i\right)^2} \qquad (7)$$

$D'(vs(d_i))$ as given by equation 8, represents the length between the ith data item valid scope reference point and the centre of predicted region.

$$D'(vs(d_i)) = |L_p - L_i| \sqrt{\left(Ly_p - Ly_i\right)^2 + \left(Lx_p - Lx_i\right)^2} \qquad (8)$$

The variable μ_i reflects the average update rate of the ith data objects. The average query rate for the ith data item is λ_i. The current position of the m client is specified by $L_m = (L_{xm}, L_{ym})$ at the moment of the query arrival. At the time of the query arrival [19], the ith data item reference point valid scopes is given by $L_i = (L_{xi}, L_{yi})$. The proposed scheme involves the revised cost function in terms of temporal as well as spatial features. The ratio λ_i/μ_i is described as the relative query rate to the update rate.

EXPERIMENTATION CONFIGURATION AND REVIEW OF RESULTS

In the suggested system, the defined server and client configuration is the same as that defined in (Gupta & Shanker, 2019)(Gupta & Shanker, 2020c). Using OpenSSL 1.0.1, the MOPAR architecture was implemented in Java. The production testing was carried out on a 3.2 GHz quad-core and Intel i7 processor computer with a 64 GB RAM Microsoft windows operating system. The device has a 100 km covering area approximately and is divided into M * M cells. .We have used the public Geolife dataset available in Microsoft Research Asia throughout the nth order Markov (with Baum-welch steps) mobility model. This set of data involves 182 persons for 18,670 trajectories with a total distance of nearly 1200,000 km over a cumulative duration of 48,000+ hours. The $pt_i \in Pt_{in}$ point includes $pt_i.lng, pt_i.lat, pt_i.t,$ as longitude, latitude and timestamp, respectively in the trajectory. We chose randomly 3465 distinct sets for the scenario of the simulations. We also preserved traces of mobility with the span of points from 10 and 15 positions in the trace. In our model, it took minimum 16 minutes, while at most 154 minutes for the PC with defined configuration to train the next position prediction function using the Markov n^{th} order mobility system with a varying states count.

For experimenting with user's request data item log, different location-specific datasets may be taken such as Blood Bank, Hospital, Fire Station, Police, Film, ATM, Hotel, etc. In the log or request file, each record is considered to be a query. One transaction can ask more than one cached object. A good proportion of user data item queries were considered for this experimental study in order to eliminate the warm-up effect of client cache. The transactions files must be preprocessed before they could be applied in the testing phase. The preprocessing approach involves adding related variables, and labelling of the attributes of the cached file found invalid or in duplicate order.

The database generator produces location-dependent queries with different pieces of data continuously. The data information is maintained such that 0th data item be the most commonly accessed data item and $(DB_{Size} - 1)^{th}$ data item be the most frequently accessed data item. The probability of access of the ith data item is calculated using Zipf probability function given in the equation 9.

$$\mathbf{Zipf_{Prob}}\left(\mathbf{i}\right) = \frac{\dfrac{1}{i^{Zipf_{access}}}}{\displaystyle\sum_{j=1}^{U}\left(\dfrac{1}{j^{Zipf_{access}}}\right)} \tag{9}$$

Where $Zipf_{access}$ is described as the measure of Zipf and the cumulative number of data objects is U. When $Zipf_{access} = 0$, for all data objects, $Zipf_{prob}(i) = 1/U$, so in this case, the same probability and uniform access pattern is being used. With the high value of $Zipf_{access}$, higher skewness in the access pattern has been shown. We began experimenting by adjusting the cache size and inter-arrival time of queries. The query interval is the time between consecutive client queries. With inter-arrival time (d) of the demand, the exponentially distributed pattern is considered in this chapter. The data object sizes range from S_{min} to S_{max}. Increasing size distribution (INCRT) together with skewed access patterns is implemented favouring the client's often querying smaller data object. To approximate the size of the data object, the equation 10 is being used.

$$\frac{1+\left(1-i\right)\times\left(S_{min}-S_{max}\right)}{DB_{size}} + S_{min} \quad 1 \leq i \leq DB_{Size} \tag{10}$$

One may numerically describe the cache-size as given by equation 11.

$$Cache_{Size} = Cache\ Ratio \times DB_{size} \times \frac{S_{max} - S_{min}}{2} \qquad (11)$$

The Cache$_{Size}$ contains space necessary for data item parameters such as space and that of the data item itself to ensure fairness in various caching approaches. The Para$_{Size}$ bytes are required by each cache parameter. In a rectangular area, ten thousand objects are spread. The section of Voronoi Diagrams for default scope distributions of POIs (Gupta & Shanker, 2018) is shown in Figure 3.

Figure 3. The Distribution of Valid Scope in Rectangular Area Cache Data Object

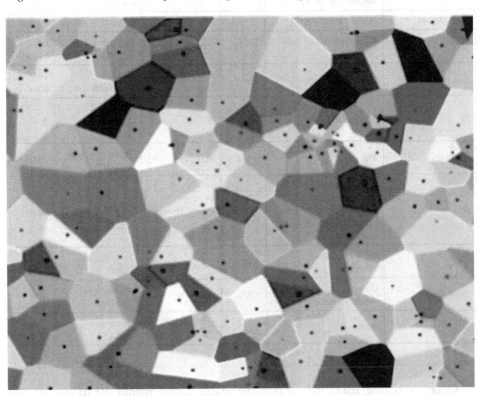

Table 1. Experimentation Variable Default Value

Parameter	Description	Initial Value	Parameter	Description	Initial Value
Zipf$_{access}$	Zipf Parameter	0.5	Size_Rect	Size of Service Area	10km* 10km
T$_r$	Trajectory pre-processing time threshold	2 minute	D$_r$	Distance Threshold of Trajectory pre-processing	2 mtr
N	Count of states	10	C$_w$	Width of POI Merge Cluster	5 mtr
Eps	Expanding clusters local radius	20 mtr	minC$_s$	Count of Lowest Cluster stay	4
Interval_Prediction	Interval of Predicted Region Calculation	240.0s	C_Size_Rate	Size of cache to database	10%
Max_Speed	Highest user speed	20 mps	Min_Speed	Lowest client user	10 mps
S$_{max}$	Maximum size of data object	1024 bytes	S$_{min}$	Minimum size of data object	64 bytes
Bandwidth_Up	Uplink Bandwidth	4 bytes	Bandwidth_Down	Downlink bandwidth	144 kbps
M	Number of Cells	1000-10,000	N	Number of trajectories dataset	3465
Theta (è)	Threshold	0.1–1.0	POI_Num.	Number of point of interest	10,000
Á	Constant concern for assessing the significance of the most current likelihood access estimate	0.70	Query_Interval	Subsequent Query Interval	60.0 s
conf$_{min}$	Least confidence Threshold	50%	R	Query range Radius	0.5 km
Num_Scope	Count unique data object values at multiple places	220	sup$_{min}$	Least Support Threshold	30%
O	Outlier	Vary	K	Anonymity degree	10 to 50

Query initiating users can search the entire cache within 50 metres of the neighbouring customer. Table 1 provides the default values of the various parameters in the experiment. The First Come First Serve approach is used in the infinite list buffer for the user's request. A marginal overhead is taken out by the server software for order control and process planning. A uniformly distributed quadratic time function is used for velocity parameter and falls within v_{min} to v_{max}. The θ is an acceptable degree threshold based on the operating standard and privacy trade-off. On higher value of threshold, LBS violates user privacy and satisfies full POI queries for the mobile user.

In the caching technique, the location information held helps to distinguish the lowest cost data objects that can be displaced from the cache. As given in the previous segment, the relevance of the suggested MOPAR replacement cost function was contrasted to those of prior anonymization techniques e.g. MobiCrowd (Shokri et al., 2014), CaDSA(Niu et al., 2015) and CSKA (S. Zhang et al., 2019) as depicted in Figure 4, .

Figure 4. Cache Hit Rate for User and Anonymizer

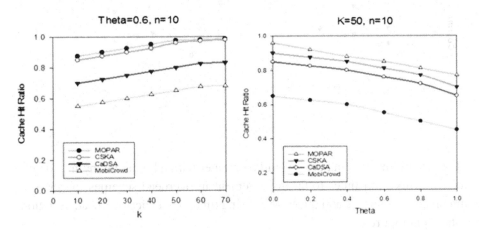

In addition, the total transmission and communication cost estimate (Swaroop & Shanker, 2011)(Swaroop et al., 2011)(Gupta & Shanker, 2020d) are also assessed. As the cell count (M) and the level of anonymity (k) increase, the system overhead method also rises in proportion. Higher the value of k, better is the cloaking region that will be formed by Anonymizer. For higher the value of k, it produces higher data entity outcomes for client and Anonymizer caches; therefore, the cache hit-ratio improves. If the required data item is present in the cache, then it is not required to send this query request to the web server resulting in privacy security and overhead minimization. In addition, if a certain smartphone app request is sent to the Database Analyzer, the privacy of the mobile user will be decreased and also incurs a high overhead to the system. The threshold size increment reduces the cache hit rate of the CSKA, CaDSA, MobiCrowd, and MOPAR policies. In contrast, with respect to operating overhead and cost of communication of LBS applications, the proposed

MOPAR method outperformed those of CSKA, CaDSA, and MobiCrowd with an expansion in the order of n. This assessment is shown in Figure 5.

Figure 5. Overhead of System Implementation

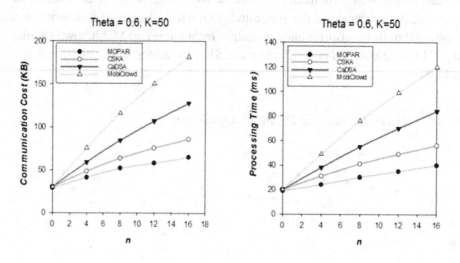

The size of the cloaking area would be greater with a higher anonymity degree value (k). This contributes to an improvement in overhead schemes. In terms of communication expense and query processing time, the device overhead variations are shown in Figure 6.

Figure 6. Results of Degree for Anonymity with Differing Cell Count (M)

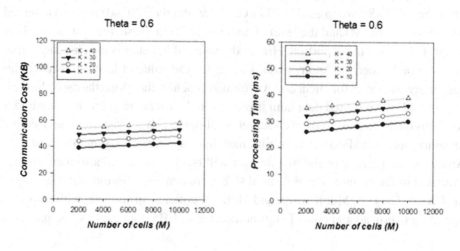

Figure 7. POI and Cloaking Region Size Variation

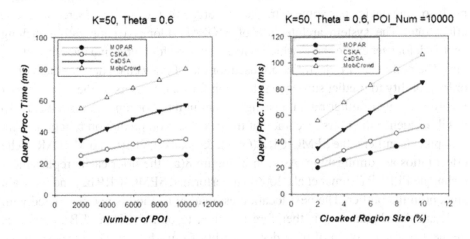

Upon adjusting the cloaking region size of the experimental zone as a whole, we evaluated the processing time. Figure 7(a) shows the time of processing in cloaking region formulation for different region sizes. In addition, the query processing time is calculated with different POI number to see the effect of POIs count variation in the simulated environment. Figure 7(b) shows the processing complexity for various policies.

Figure 8. Outlier Ratio and Cache Size Variations

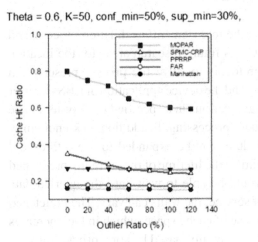
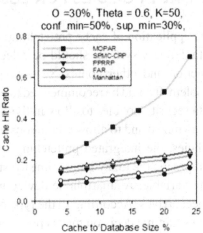

Due to the incorporation of cache into an Anonymizer-identified trustworthy mediator, the device has some extra cache storage that leads to an increased cache effect rate. The system architecture of MOPAR adopts a cooperative caching approach for user cache share, which is itself a reason for increasing the cache effect rate. The mobile user trajectories are used for the Markov chain development of nth order mobility to predict subsequent location for mobile users. If the route dataset involves a higher outlier rate, i.e., a significant number of random movements, so it will influence the users' accuracy of the next location prediction function. With the spike in outliers, the SPMC-CRP (Gupta & Shanker, 2019) and MOPAR cache effect ratios are diminishing. As seen in Figure 8(a), the prior cache replacement technique PPRRP (Kumar et al., 2006) outperformed SPMC-CRP beyond a certain amount in the outlier. The next location estimation method is not associated with FAR and Manhattan and is therefore invariant to outliers. Here, LBS combines the next-position notion of nth order versatility from Markov. The purpose of the Markov mobility model based next position prediction method is to formulate the chain of Markov mobility for a current travelling consumer position. Trust level threshold $conf_{min}$ is used by the previous SPMC-CRP method to filter the rules on mobility. With the drop in confidence level $conf_{min}$ threshold, the sum of formulated mobility rules increases. Figure 8(b) depicts an increase in the cache hit ratio of MOPAR and that of previous LBS policies such as SPMC-CRP, PPRRP, FAR, and Manhattan by increasing the cache size. In comparison, cache hit rate, as seen in the graphical analysis for different LBS policies, MOPAR efficiency is higher than the past caching and location privacy preservation schemes.

FUTURE RESEARCH SCOPE IN LOCATION PRIVACY POLICIES FOR LBS QUERY

The application of cache prefetching, cache replacement/invalidation process, and data delivery systems should be selected as future research areas for the location function and other context security protocols to solve the privacy preservation problem. It could be recommended to expand the device application of LBSs for user data security policies to allow individual locations in a specified road system to be anonymized and to allow continuous query processing. In addition, in k-anonymity policies, the integrated prefetching module may be expanded to use a threshold comprising the fuzzy-length time to estimate the lifetime of the currently prefetched data variable. A smartphone device would be able to wait until the queried data object arrives. According to the type of service, the waits can vary. The prefetched data's lifetime decision makes practical use of cache space, which in fact increases the cache hit ratio. In LBS, the former k-anonymity-based location privacy policies did not consider multiple users' location prediction cases for the development of the cloaking region by selecting the cells. If several mobile users have LBS requests, choosing the correct cell to form a clocking area is a tough task. None of the previous procedures, though, have offered some solution for this issue. Thus, modelling for many users to create a cloaking area for the next likely position predictor may be a possible study domain. In comparison, all existing LBS proposals use Euclidean distance in user motions, but mobile users in fact ride via a fixed road system where the offender can infer potential user locations using the road system details in query. Therefore, in order to promote the anonymization of unique locations in a predefined road structure, it is also necessary and important to establish a query processing scheme with consumer privacy preservation in mind.

CONCLUSION

The proposed policy MOPAR preserves the user's location and other information to the untrusted entity. The spatial cloaking technique paired with k-anonymity has been used to overcome the cloaking area size constraint. The use of precise n^{th} order Markov model-based mobility next position prediction algorithm in caching, prefetching and PSKA results in higher cache hit rate. Therefore, MOPAR offers a greater tradeoff between QoS and user query privacy than that of past approaches. It promotes quality-enhancing adaptability and full request of POI as demanded by a smartphone customer without sacrificing the extent of user privacy. The device overhead has also been greatly reduced.

REFERENCES

Akon, M., Islam, M., Shen, X., & Singh, A. (2011). OUR: Optimal Update-based Replacement policy for cache in wireless data access networks with optimal effective hits and bandwidth requirements. *Wireless Communications and Mobile Computing, 13*. doi:10.1002/wcm.1182

Al-Molegi, A., Alsmadi, I., & Martínez-Ballesté, A. (2018). Regions-of-interest discovering and predicting in smartphone environments. *Pervasive and Mobile Computing, 47*, 31–53. doi:10.1016/j.pmcj.2018.05.001

Al-Molegi, A., Jabreel, M., & Martínez-Ballesté, A. (2018). Move, Attend and Predict: An attention-based neural model for people's movement prediction. *Pattern Recognition Letters, 112*, 34–40. doi:10.1016/j.patrec.2018.05.015

Drakatos, S., Pissinou, N., Makki, K., & Douligeris, C. (2009). A future location-aware replacement policy for the cache management at the mobile terminal. *Wireless Communications and Mobile Computing, 9*(5), 607–629. doi:10.1002/wcm.606

Gupta, A. K. (2020). Spam Mail Filtering Using Data Mining Approach: A comparative performance analysis. In Handling Priority Inversion in Time-Constrained Distributed Databases (pp. 253–282). Hershey, PA: IGI Global. doi:10.4018/978-1-7998-2491-6.ch015

Gupta, A. K., & Shanker, U. (2018). CELPB: A cache invalidation policy for location dependent data in mobile environment. *ACM International Conference Proceeding Series*. 10.1145/3216122.3216147

Gupta, A. K., & Shanker, U. (2018a). Location dependent information system's queries for mobile environment. Lecture Notes in Computer Science (Including Subseries Lecture Notes in Artificial Intelligence and Lecture Notes in Bioinformatics), 10829 LNCS. doi:10.1007/978-3-319-91455-8_19

Gupta, A. K., & Shanker, U. (2019). SPMC-PRRP: A Predicted Region Based Cache Replacement Policy. In Lecture Notes in Networks and Systems (Vol. 39). doi:10.1007/978-981-13-0277-0_26

Gupta, A. K., & Shanker, U. (2020a). A Literature Review of Location-Aware Computing Policies: Taxonomy and Empirical Analysis in Mobile Environment. *International Journal of Mobile Human Computer Interaction, 12*(3), 21–45. doi:10.4018/IJMHCI.2020070102

Gupta, A. K., & Shanker, U. (2020b). CEMP-IR: A Novel Location Aware Cache Invalidation & Replacement Policy. *International Journal on Computer Science and Engineering, 2020*(1).

Gupta, A. K., & Shanker, U. (2020c). OMCPR: Optimal Mobility Aware Cache Data Pre-fetching and Replacement Policy Using Spatial K-Anonymity for LBS. *Wireless Personal Communications, 114*(2), 949–973. doi:10.100711277-020-07402-2

Gupta, A. K., & Shanker, U. (2020d). *Study of fuzzy logic and particle swarm methods in map matching algorithm.* doi:10.100742452-020-2431-y

Gupta, A. K., & Shanker, U. (2020e). Some Issues for Location Dependent Information System Query in Mobile Environment. *29th ACM International Conference on Information and Knowledge Management (CIKM '20)*, 4. doi:10.1145/3340531.3418504

Gupta, A. K., & Shanker, U. (2020f). MAD-RAPPEL: Mobility Aware Data Replacement &Prefetching Policy Enrooted LBS. *Journal of King Saud University - Computer and Information Sciences*.

Ilayaraja, N., Mary Magdalene Jane, F., Safar, M., & Nadarajan, R. (2016). WARM Based Data Pre-fetching and Cache Replacement Strategies for Location Dependent Information System in Wireless Environment. *Wireless Personal Communications*, *90*(4), 1811–1842. doi:10.100711277-016-3425-3

Kumar, A., Misra, M., & Sarje, A. K. (2006). A Predicted Region Based Cache Replacement Policy for Location Dependent Data in Mobile Environment. *2006 International Conference on Wireless Communications, Networking and Mobile Computing*, 1–4. 10.1109/WiCOM.2006.405

Lai, K. Y., Tari, Z., & Bertok, P. (2004). Location-aware cache replacement for mobile environments. *Global Telecommunications Conference, GLOBECOM '04*, 3441-3447. 10.1109/GLOCOM.2004.1379006

Lubbe, C., Brodt, A., Cipriani, N., Großmann, M., & Mitschang, B. (2011). DiSCO: A Distributed Semantic Cache Overlay for Location-Based Services. *2011 IEEE 12th International Conference on Mobile Data Management, 1*, 17–26. 10.1109/MDM.2011.56

Michael, S. D. (1996). Semantic Data Caching and Replacement. *Proceedings of the 22th International Conference on Very Large Data Bases*, *22*(4), 333–341. 10.1.1.45.683

Niu, B., Li, Q., Zhu, X., Cao, G., & Li, H. (2014). Achieving k-anonymity in privacy-aware location-based services. *IEEE INFOCOM 2014 - IEEE Conference on Computer Communications*, 754–762. 10.1109/INFOCOM.2014.6848002

Niu, B., Li, Q., Zhu, X., Cao, G., & Li, H. (2015). Enhancing privacy through caching in location-based services. *2015 IEEE Conference on Computer Communications (INFOCOM)*, 1017–1025. 10.1109/INFOCOM.2015.7218474

Pallis, G., Vakali, A., & Pokorny, J. (2008). A clustering-based prefetching scheme on a Web cache environment. *Computers & Electrical Engineering*, *34*(4), 309–323. doi:10.1016/j.compeleceng.2007.04.002

Ren, Q., & Dunham, M. H. (2000). Using Semantic Caching to Manage Location Dependent Data in Mobile Computing. *6th ACM/IEEE Mobile Computing and Networking (MobiCom)*, 3, 210–221.

Shokri, R., Theodorakopoulos, G., Papadimitratos, P., Kazemi, E., & Hubaux, J. (2014). Hiding in the Mobile Crowd: LocationPrivacy through Collaboration. *IEEE Transactions on Dependable and Secure Computing*, *11*(3), 266–279. doi:10.1109/TDSC.2013.57

Sukaphat, S. (2011). An implementation of location-based service system with cell identifier for detecting lost mobile. *Procedia Computer Science*, *3*, 949–953. doi:10.1016/j.procs.2010.12.155

Sun, Z., Di, L., Heo, G., Zhang, C., Fang, H., Yue, P., Jiang, L., Tan, X., Guo, L., & Lin, L. (2017). GeoFairy: Towards a one-stop and location based Service for Geospatial Information Retrieval. *Computers, Environment and Urban Systems*, *62*, 156–167. doi:10.1016/j.compenvurbsys.2016.11.007

Swaroop, V., Gupta, G., & Shanker, U. (2011). Issues in mobile distributed real time databases: Performance and review. *International Journal of Engineering Science and Technology*, 3.

Swaroop, V., & Shanker, U. (2011). *Concept and Management Issues in Mobile Distributed Real Time Database*. Academic Press.

Tian, Y., Kaleemullah, M., Rodhaan, M., Song, B., Al-Dhelaan, A., & Ma, T. (2018). A privacy preserving location service for cloud-of-things system. *Journal of Parallel and Distributed Computing*, *123*, 215–222. Advance online publication. doi:10.1016/j.jpdc.2018.09.005

Wang, S., Zhang, X., Zhang, Y., Wang, L., Yang, J., & Wang, W. (2017). A Survey on Mobile Edge Networks: Convergence of Computing, Caching and Communications. *IEEE Access: Practical Innovations, Open Solutions*, *5*, 6757–6779. doi:10.1109/ACCESS.2017.2685434

Yin, L., Cao, G., Das, C., & Ashraf, A. (2002). Power-aware prefetch in mobile environments. *Proceedings 22nd International Conference on Distributed Computing Systems*, 571–578. 10.1109/ICDCS.2002.1022307

Zhang, C., Sun, Z., Heo, G., Di, L., & Lin, L. (2016). A GeoPackage implementation of common map API on Google Maps and OpenLayers to manipulate agricultural data on mobile devices. *2016 Fifth International Conference on Agro-Geoinformatics (Agro-Geoinformatics)*, 1–4. 10.1109/Agro-Geoinformatics.2016.7577654

Zhang, S., Choo, K.-K. R., Liu, Q., & Wang, G. (2018). Enhancing privacy through uniform grid and caching in location-based services. *Future Generation Computer Systems*, *86*, 881–892. doi:10.1016/j.future.2017.06.022

Zhang, S., Li, X., Tan, Z., Peng, T., & Wang, G. (2019). A caching and spatial K-anonymity driven privacy enhancement scheme in continuous location-based services. *Future Generation Computer Systems*, *94*, 40–50. doi:10.1016/j. future.2018.10.053

Zheng, B., Xu, J., Member, S., & Lee, D. L. (2002). *Cache Invalidation and Replacement Strategies for Location-Dependent Data in Mobile Environments*. Academic Press.

Chapter 3
Location–Based Social Networking for Spatio– Temporal Analysis of Human Mobility

P. Shanthi Saravanan
https://orcid.org/0000-0003-0189-7369
J. J. College of Engineering and Technology, Tiruchirappalli, India

Sabin Deori
Researcher, Sivasagar, India

Balasundaram S. R.
National Institute of Technology, Tiruchirappalli, India

ABSTRACT

Human location tracking and analysis have always been important domains with a wide range of implementations in areas such as traffic prediction, security, disaster response, health monitoring, etc. With the availability and use of GPS-enabled devices, it has become easier to obtain location traces of an individual. There may be situations when the current location may be difficult to trace due to device failures or any unforeseen situation. This is one reason why geo tagged social networking or LBSN (location-based social networking) data research is gaining popularity. This kind of geo-tagged data when collected over time from a crowd can be analyzed for various mobility patterns of the population. This chapter focuses on how to predict the location of the people during mobility. A sample study to predict the geographical location and points of interest of a user is explained with the help of random forest classifier. Also, the chapter highlights the security and privacy concerns when LBSN is used for human mobility analysis.

DOI: 10.4018/978-1-7998-7756-1.ch003

INTRODUCTION

Mobility is an essential aspect of humans for the sake of fulfilling their needs for survival. Depending on the individuals the mobility factor may be viewed for any kind of study. People go to different places for jobs, for food, for purchase, for visiting places etc. Mobility relates to geography and human needs. With the tremendous growth of information and communication technologies, it becomes possible to link the physical world with the digital space thereby providing ample opportunities to understand and provide services to the moving people (Roth et al. 2011; Lenormand et al., 2014; Song et al., 2006; Abou-zeid et al., 2013). It becomes possible to extract knowledge on human location details with the help of GPS, wearable devices, etc. This knowledge helps to monitor health aspects, seamless computing, disaster management, traffic prediction, etc. Much research can be seen in modeling and understanding human mobility patterns based on individual levels to groups pertaining to varieties of applications. Broadly speaking, understanding the patterns of mobility and applying them in transportation planning, resource allocation, spreading of diseases(Ravenstein1885; Siminiet al., 2012; Merler&Ajelli, 2010; Marguta&Parisi, 2015).

Many questions are possible with respect to human mobility. How far an individual or group of people will travel? Whether the mobility follows patterns? Whether time and space parameters contribute to the study of human mobility? Is it possible to know the future locations of humans based on past history? Other than location based details, by any other means, whether the location prediction of human mobility be tracked.

Hess et al. (2015) focused on classifying human mobility models into two groups namely trace based and synthetic(Hess et al., 2015).Trace based models are based on GPS, Cell Detail Records etc. Whereas synthetic models are outcomes of simulations based on mathematical computations. When technologies help to extract the location data of individuals to analyze the movements, data coming through social interactions also help to model the human mobility.

These models are predominantly observed in varieties of domains at general level such as people walking in a constrained space, walking to markets or any other business locations, etc. to more specific as well as broader domains such as urban planning, epidemic studies, traffic predictions etc. Lazer et al. (2009) specify digital traces as records of human activities collected through and stored by means of digital devices. Lima, Antonio (2016) et al. focus on models related to digital traces that include large number of forms of data gathered from devices and related societies.

In case of Calling Description Records (CDRs), generated from telephone exchange, the time, location, duration, and position of base stations, source and destination number etc. that are associated with each phone call could be used to predict the mobility(Horak, 2012).Whenever a call is done by a user, the nearest cellular network tower routing that call is recorded. This in turn yields the user's geographical location.

LBSN

Even though mobility analysis is important and GPS devices are widely used, it is difficult to obtain the actual GPS traces of the people due to issues related to privacy and security (Sushama et al. 2021; Mohapatra et al., 2021). This is why another kind of location trace data called "geotagged check-in" data from LBSN is gaining popularity among the researchers. Today most social network data has the geo-tagging facility i.e. when a user posts something (text, image, video, etc.) publicly, he/she has the option to tag the GPS location from where the post was made from. As shown in Figure 1, the components of LBSN are the Contents, Social Networks and location details based on geography linked with the above.This kind of geo-tagged data (check-in data) when collected overtime from a crowd can be analyzed for predicting various mobility patterns; in the extreme case an individual mobility can also be predicted.

Figure 1. LBSN – Components

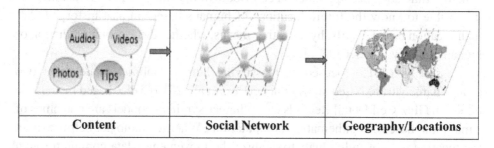

Location-Based Social Networks (LBSN) is a type of social networking where geographic services and features including Geotagging are used in the context of social dynamics(Quercia et al., 2010). According to Zheng &Zhou(2011), LBSN focuses on:

- Adding location value in social networks.
- People share location related data
- Geotagged i.e. location tagged information such as text, photos and videos are shared among people in the network.

- Apart from locations, interests, behaviors, activities etc. can be inferred from humans' location history and location related data.

Research in the field of human mobility pattern analysis as well as prediction modeling has gained the interests of many.On one hand, with the help of personal devices or gadgets and positioning systems such as GPS or WPS (WiFi positioning systems), the mobility can be tracked for analysis. In this line of ubiquitous connectivity, social network adds another dimension to do further analysis on mobility.

General Properties of LBSN

Properties pertaining to LBSN integrate the properties of both geography and social networks. In this direction, Gao et al. (2013) have summarized the following properties of LBSN (Figure 2).

Figure 2. Properties of LBSN

Various researchers have tried to approach the problem in different ways. The authors Andrea Cuttoneet al.(2018) predicted the next locations of an individual through two formulations: next-cell and next-place. In next cell approach, space is discretized into grid cells and prediction of the cell is done in the next time slot. In the next place method, visits to places are detected and predictions of the next place visited are detected. The Markov model was used for both formulations and it was observed that the accuracy of the model in the next cell formulation(0.7) was higher than next place formulation (0.4).

The LBSN check-in data was analyzed by Zhang et al. (2013). LBSN are large scale geosocial mobility traces with a large userbase who creates an event by checking into various locations as they move around the geographic areas. In this work the authors tries to classify the check-in location values by comparing the check in trace with the GPS trace. The check-in trace contained 14927 check-ins while the GPS trace included 30835 visits. After passing through a matching algorithm three categories of check-ins are created:

- Honest check-ins: only 3525 check-in events matched up with the GPS visits.
- Extraneous check-ins: 10772 checking events (75% of total check-ins) do not match up with GPS trace.
- Missing Check-ins: 27310 visits in the GPS trace do not match any Foursquare check in events.

The spatial and temporal activity preference of the users can help to design a wide spectrum of ubiquitous applications. This includes personalized context-aware location recommendation systems and group oriented advertisements. Yang et al.(2014) proposed a model called STAP considering the spatial and temporal activity preference separately. The model uses a principle way to combine them for getting preference inferences. Also, Cuenca-Jaraet al.(2017) introduced a novel approach to extract personal mobility patterns by using the fuzzy c-means (FCM) algorithm.

The proposed work in this chapter shows how the overall population of a city moves with respect to the temporal and spatial domain with the help of the Foursquare dataset. The results show that the proposed method effectively predicts the type of venue and the geographical location area where the user might be in at a given time period. For the purpose of predicting the type of venue and the geographical location area, Random Forest classifier is used. A random forest is a meta estimator that fits a number of decision tree classifiers on varioussub-samples of the dataset. It uses averaging to improve the predictive accuracy and controlover-fitting. It can be used for both classification and regression tasks.

Now location data is susceptible to random locations being visited by the volunteers or some venues having really low check-in counts which can be considered as outliers. Random Forest is usually robust to outliers and can handle them automatically. It is also comparatively lessimpacted by noise.

EXAMPLE

This section describes how to predict the type of venue and the geographical locationarea where the user might be in at a given time. The simulation of the entire work is relying on the top of temporal and spatial domain analysis (Figure 3).

Using the temporal domain analysis, what type of venues the population visit the most during each of the time frames and also how the population in these venues change with respect to thetemporal blocks are found out. The distributions of the population, venues and users check-ins over the geographical area are carried out under the analysis in the spatial domain phase.With the help of these two analysis one can predicts the type of venue a user might be in and would like to visit at a given time period are doneusing the Random Forest classifier. The implementation details are described in the following subsections.

Figure 3. Phases of the Proposed Work

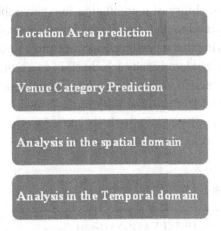

TEMPORAL DOMAIN ANALYSIS

Temporal domain analysis analyses the check-in data of the Foursquare dataset with respect to time. The dataset containing check-in data spans from Tuesday April 3rd 2012 to Saturday February 16th 2013. The data is confined to the city of New York in the USA. The dataset consists of 2,27,428 rows and 8 columns. These check-ins are done by 1083 unique users from 38,333 unique locations. The following table (Table 1) shows the information contained in the dataset. For the implementation of the proposed work the libraries such as Numpy, Pandas, Matplotlib, Seaborn, gmaps are used.

Table 1. Attributes of the Foursquare Dataset

User id	The unique identification record of the user
Venue id	The unique identification record of the venue from which the user checkedin.
Venue category:	The type of venue the user logged in from. e.g. home, office, subway,etc.
Venue Category Id:	This holds a unique id value for the category.
Latitude	Latitude value of the checked in location.
Longitude	Longitude value of the checked-in location.
UTC Timestamp	Holds the time at which the check-in was made.
Time-zone Offset	Holds the offset values.

To understand the mobility of a population in a geographic area across the 24 hours of a day it is required to understand which venues people populate more and at what time. Considering that a person checks in from a location and that check-in value is true it can be considered each such check-in as a representation of mobility. A collection of such check-in values from a huge population over a long period of time will provide some patterns of mobility of the crowd.

For the experimentation purpose, in the proposed work the 24 hours of a day is divided into six time-blocks and is shown in the following table (Table 2).

Table 2. Time Blocks of a Day

NO.	TIME BLOCKS	OBSERVATIONS (Generalised)	CHECKIN COUNTS
1	7 am to 10 am	Early morning hours	7,274
2	10 am to 2 pm	Morning to Afternoon hours	41,246
3	2 pm to 6 pm	Afternoon to Evening hours	45,908
4	6 pm to 10 pm	Evening to Night hours	48,417
5	10 pm to 2 pm	Night to late night hours	54,782
6	2 pm to 7 am	Late night to early morning hours	29,815

Figure 4. Check-in Data and Heat Map of 7AM to 10AM

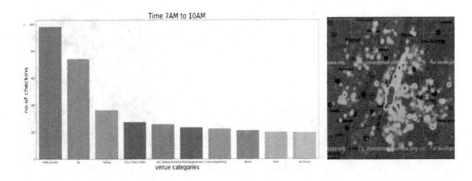

For the time period between 7 am to 10 am (Early Morning hours) there are 7274 check-in values are observed. This is the lowest number of check-ins recorded of all the temporal blocks. One possible reason might be that people use social media less during early morning period. Analysis reveals that out of 248 categories of locations users checked in only from 190 categories. While most of the check-ins came from locations like home, subway, bars, etc. the lowest check-ins came from locations like nail salons, jewellery stores, etc. The Figure4(left side) represents the bar plot for the top ten categories of locations people visited during this time block. The right side of the Figure 4 shows the corresponding heat map (points were plotted on Google maps).

In the Morning to Afternoon Hours (10am to 2pm)41,246 check-ins are recorded and it is increased approximately by almost 600% from the early morning hours' time block. Now out of 248 categories of locations, analysis reveals that users checked in

Figure 5. Check-in Data and Heat Map of 10AM to 2 PM

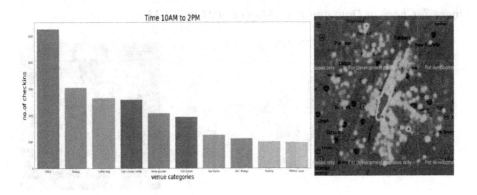

Figure 6. Check-in Data and Heat Map of 2PM to 6PM

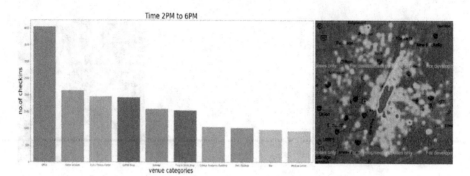

from 222 categories. While most of the check-ins are locations like office, subway, coffee shop, home, etc., the lowest check-ins are from locations like music store, pet service, etc. Like previous figure the results are show as below (Figure 5).

The check-ins (Figure 6) generated during Afternoon to Evening Hours(2pm to 6pm) is nearly similar to the previous time block (45,908 check-ins are recorded). However there is a slight increase in the number of check-in values. Out of 248 categories people checked in from 241 categories. The highest number of check-ins are from office, home, subways, etc., while the lowest are from Distillery, Internet cafe, etc.

Figure7 represents the top ten categories of locations that are visited by the people during the time block Evening to Night Hours (6 pm to 10 pm). The number of check-ins recorded during this period was 48,417. Out of 248 categories people checked in from 246 types of locations. Home, Food and drink shops, Office, Bars are topped the category list while the lowest no. of check-ins are recorded from pet service, bike rental etc.

Figure 7. Check-in Data and Heat Map of 6PM to 10PM

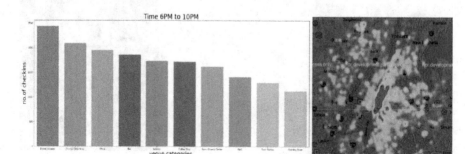

The highest no of check-ins (54,782) are recorded during the Night to Late Night Hours (10 pm to 2 am) time block (Figure 8). It is observed that all of the 248 location categories are checked-in during this time block. Also the most of the check-ins are the locations like Bars, home, gyms, subways, etc., while the lowest number of check-ins are from locations like Photography lab, Recycling facility, etc.

Figure 8. Check-in Data and Heat Map of 10PM to 2AM

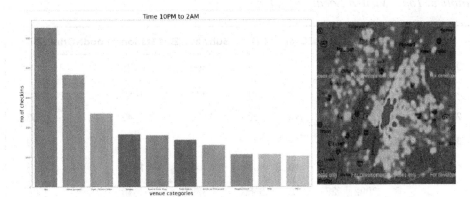

It is observed that during the Night to Late Night Hours(2 am to 7 am) time block the number of check-ins (29,815) are dropped to almost half of the number of check-ins (Figure 9) during the previous temporal block. One of the reasons for it might be a majority of the people are asleep by this time.Also the analysis reveals the check-ins are recorded from 231 locations and the highest number of check-ins are from bars, home, etc., while the lowest number of check-ins are from locations like planetarium, camera store etc.

Figure 9. Check-in Data and Heat Map of 2AM to 7AM

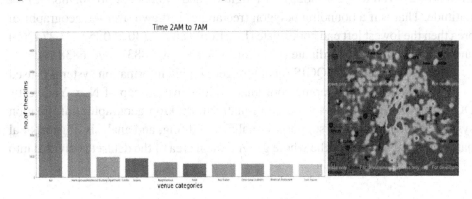

61

From the experimental results of the temporal analysis it can be inferred that people are more at home during the early morning hours before 10 am while during 10 am to 6 pm people are at work places while after 6 pm people are back home. After 10 pm the highest number of check-ins are recorded from Bars. This shows that people are more inclined towards leisure during the late night to early morning hours in the city. Table 3 summarizes the top 7 visited location categories.

Table 3. Top 7 Visited Location Categories

	timeblock	Home	Gym	Office	Bar	Subway	BusStation	FoodNDrinkShop
0	1	981	272	133	741	360	195	85
1	2	2079	2583	5250	511	3042	1246	740
2	3	2135	1958	4035	966	1569	542	1535
3	4	2439	1618	1953	1862	1732	860	2093
4	5	3757	2458	1029	5339	1767	1022	1731
5	6	3992	283	343	6560	879	610	413

SPATIAL DOMAIN ANALYSIS

How the population and venues are distributed across the geographical area is analyzed in this sub section. This analysis helps in observing patterns like which geographical areas are moreor less visited by people. So that contributes for infrastructures planning, disaster management, business ventures, etc. in a fixed area.

As mentioned in the previous subsection the Foursquare dataset is used for the experimental purpose. The locations in this dataset are spread across the geographical location whose latitude and longitude are bounded by the values rages from (-74.274766 to -73.683825) for longitude and (40.550852 to 40.988332) for Latitude. That is if a bounding polygon (rectangle) is drawn over the geographical area then the lowest left end coordinate (Lat, Lon) value is (40.550852,-74.274766) and highest right end coordinate (Lat, Lon) value is (40.988332,-73.683825).

In the experiments the QGIS (quantum geographic information system) is used to plot the check-in geographic coordinate values over a map of New York City. QGIS is a free and open-source cross-platform desktop geographic information system application. QGIS supports visualizing, editing, and analysis of geospatial data. For our experiments the whole geographical area of the dataset is divided into a grid containing small square cells of side 5km. So that the area covered by each grid cell is 25 sq. km.

Figure 10. Map Grid of New York City

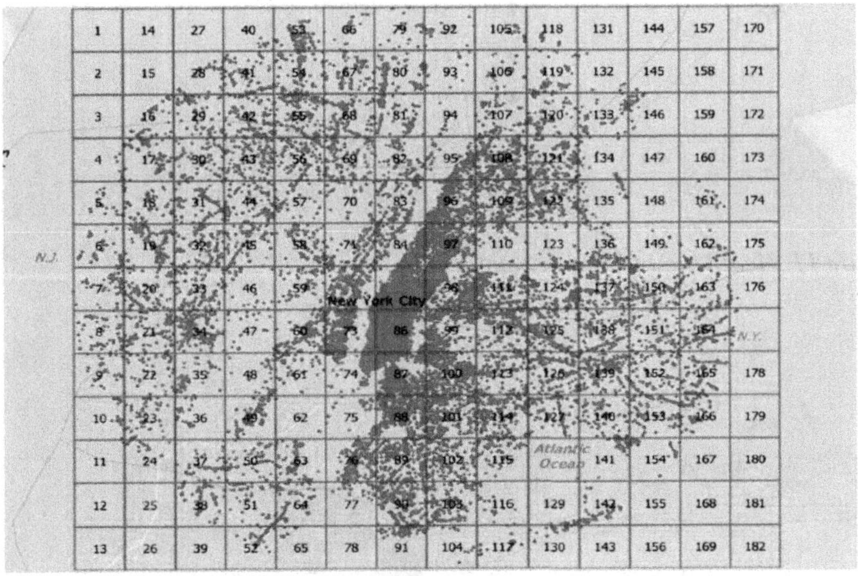

In the Figure10 the green points are the coordinates of the check-ins, the red lines represent the grid cells and the number inside the cell represents the unique identity of the cell. From the results it is observed that totally there are 182 cells are generated over the study area. Also it is inferred that only 148 of the grid cells are having the check in values the remaining 34 cells don't have any check-in values. After the generation of the grid cells over the study area the cell identity is added to the dataset.

The inclusion of the cell id in the existing dataset helps in determining how many unique venues that the users are checked in from which cell.The Table 4lists out top six cells with more number of unique venues in the study area.

The heat map (Figure 11) shows the number of uniquevenues in each cell. The higher the venue counts the darker the cells. It can be observed from the heat map that the central part of the city has higher unique venuesthat the crowd visited. This inference is used to predict the cells with higher check-in values have greater crowd mobility.

Table 4. Venue Counts

	cellId	counts
0	86	6641
1	85	5426
2	87	1472
3	98	1457
4	73	1357
5	74	926

Figure 11. Heat Map of Unique Venues

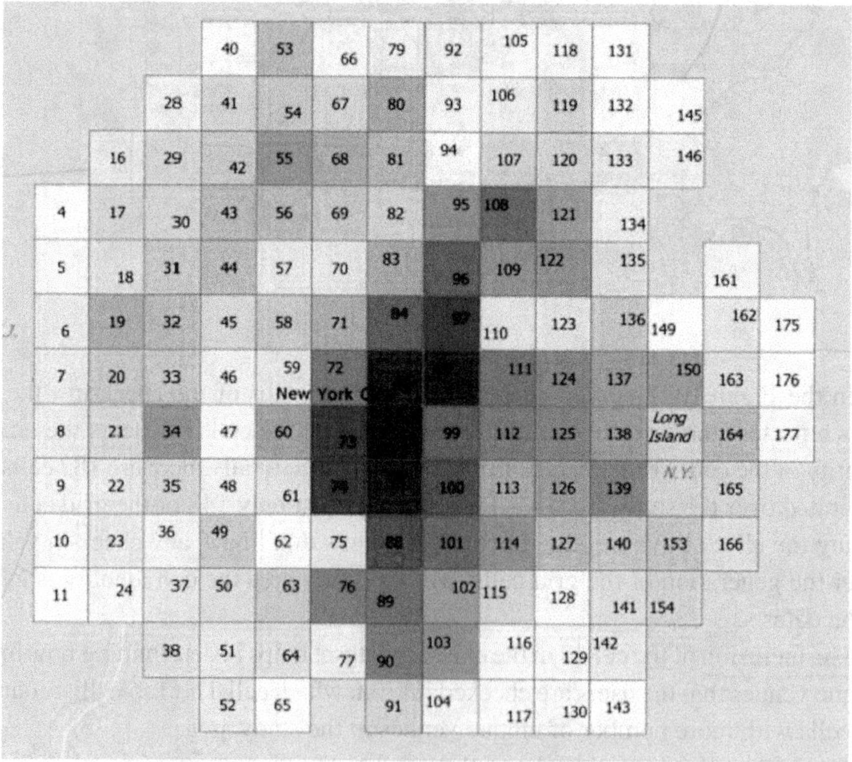

Also the number of unique users' visited each of the above top six grid cells can be extracted from the dataset (Table 5 and Figure 12). This information is used to predict the cell with higher user mobility. That is more the number of unique users visiting a cell indicates higher the mobility.

Table 5. Unique User Counts

	cellId	counts
0	85	1012
1	86	985
2	87	697
3	73	671
4	98	561
5	74	543

Figure 12. Heat Map of Unique User Counts

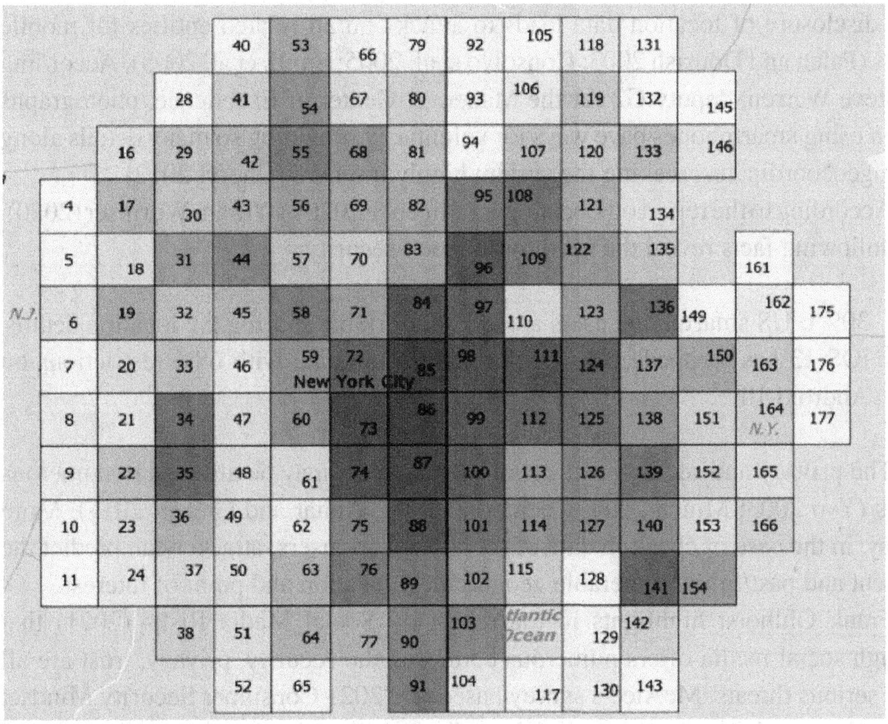

The geographic location (i.e. cell id) and the type of venue(venue category) a user might visit at a given time of day can be predicted with good accuracy. This has been done using the Random forest classifier with the backbone of both temporal and spatial domain analysis. From the experiments it is observed that the proposed work returns an accuracy of 97.18% for predicting the type of venue category theuser might visit at a given time; and an accuracy of 97.67% for the geographical locationarea(cellid) in which the user might be at a given time. From the results it could be concluded that the location and the venue category of an individual can be predicted with higher evidence.

CHALLENGES

Privacy and Security are the prime challenges of geotagged applications. It is certain that location based services must ensure trustful server (Giaglis et al., 2003). But there are possibilities for contradictory outcomes happening when both security and privacy are aimed at LBSN.

Based on studies done over social data towards privacy breaches, it became evident that disclosure of location data leads to attacks on all related entities for mobile users (Palen and Dourish 2003; Consolvo et al. 2005; Smith et al. 2005). According to Steve Warren, deputy G2 for the Maneuver Center of Excellence, photographs taken using smartphones pave ways for voluntarily providing so many details along with geocoordinates, making the system highly insecure (Cheryl 2012).

According to the report on Location Intelligence 2020 by Yoram Wurmser (2020), the following facts reveal the need for location security:

1. 30% o US smartphone users are not comfortable sharing the location details
2. iOS 13 has stopped certain types of location data with 68% restrictions on Android 10

The privacy and security aspects of mobile users may be affected in numerous ways (Yvo 2003; Minch 2004; Chen et al. 2008; Anuar and Gretzel 2011). More to say, in the case of check-in data of social network users, attacker can predict the current and past/future preferable geographical location and point of interest.

Frank Ohlhorst highlights in the report on Social Media Risks (2021) that though social media offers numerous comforts, the security, privacy, trust are all face serious threats. McAfee's survey based on "2021 Consumer Security Mindset Report", reveals the fact that social media is still a risky endeavor in terms of security, privacy and trust.

Abbas et al. (2015) link various factors such as privacy, security, control and trust association with location based applications Figure 13.

1. Privacy requires Security
2. Security improves the control over the information.
3. Control reduces the level of trust
4. Trust improves Privacy
5. Control and Privacy are mutually exclusive

Figure 13. Human Mobility Using Locations and Social Networks

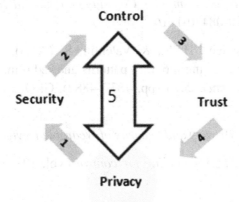

Need for balanced pipeline and processing mechanisms need to be deployed in Location Based Social Networks when dealing with human mobility.

CONCLUSION

Advancements in Information and Communication technologies have sparked growth in social networks, which continue to have a large impact in users' day today activities. An attacker or an individual may use the check-in data of the users to predict present, past and future geographical location and preferable venue (i.e. points of interest). Towards this end, this paper discusses one of the ways to predict users' location and venue category using the Random Forest classifier. Using evaluation based on the Foursquare, we find that the proposed model can effectively predicts the venue category and the location with the accuracy of 97.18% and 97.67% respectively.

A sample scenario of geo tagged social networkbased way of understanding human mobility is discussed. It is mandatory that while services are possible to be given through social network based mobile applications, while involving data related to human mobility proper balance is to be enforced for adopting technologies and research findings towards location as well as human security and privacy.

REFERENCES

Abbas, R., Michael, K., & Michael, M. G. (2015). Location-Based Privacy, Protection, Safety, and Security. In S. Zeadally & M. Badra (Eds.), *Privacy in a Digital, Networked World. Computer Communications and Networks. Springer.* doi:10.1007/978-3-319-08470-1_16

Abou-zeid, H., Hassanein, H. S., & Valentin, S. (2013). Optimal predictive resource allocation: exploiting mobility patterns and radio maps. In *IEEE global communications conference 2013* (pp. 4877–4882). GLOBECOM. doi:10.1109/GLOCOMW.2013.6855723

Alrababah, Z. (2020). *Privacy and Security of Wearable Devices*. Academic Press.

Babuška, R. (2012). *Fuzzy modeling for control* (Vol. 12). Springer Science & Business Media.

Beiró, M. G., Panisson, A., Tizzoni, M., & Cattuto, C. (2016). Predicting human mobility through the assimilation of social media traces into mobility models. *EPJ Data Science, 5*(1), 1–15. doi:10.1140/epjds13688-016-0092-2

CherylR. (2012). https://www.army.mil/article/75165/Geotagging_poses_security_risks

Cuenca-Jara, J., Terroso-Saenz, F., Valdes-Vela, M., Gonzalez-Vidal, A., &Skarmeta, A. F. (2017, June). Human mobility analysis based on social media and fuzzy clustering. In *2017 Global Internet of Things Summit (GIoTS)* (pp. 1-6). IEEE.

Cuttone, A., Lehmann, S., & González, M. C. (2018). Understanding predictability and exploration in human mobility. *EPJ Data Science, 7*(1), 1–17. doi:10.1140/epjds13688-017-0129-1

Dobson, J. E., & Fisher, P. F. (2003). Geoslavery. *IEEE Technology and Society Magazine, 22*(1), 47–52. doi:10.1109/MTAS.2003.1188276

Gabrielli, L., Rinzivillo, S., Ronzano, F., & Villatoro, D. (2013, September). From tweets to semantic trajectories: mining anomalous urban mobility patterns. In *International Workshop on Citizen in Sensor Networks* (pp. 26-35). Springer.

Gao, H., & Liu, H. (2013). Data Analysis on Location-Based Social Networks. *Mobile Social Networking*, 165–194. . doi:10.1007/978-1-4614-8579-7_8

Giaglis, G. M., Kourouthanassis, P., & Tsamakos, A. (2003). Towards a classification framework for mobile location-based services. In B. E. Mennecke & T. J. Strader (Eds.), *Mobile commerce: technology, theory and applications* (pp. 67–85). Idea Group Publishing. doi:10.4018/978-1-59140-044-8.ch004

Hess, A., Hummel, K.A., Gansterer, W.N., & Haring, G. (2015). Data-driven human mobility modeling: a survey and engineering guidance for mobile networking. *ACM Comput. Surv., 48*(3), 38:1–38:39.

Horak, R. (2012). *Telecommunications and Data Communications Handbook.* Wiley-Interscience.

Ikram, A. A. (2020). Privacy and Security Issues in Online Social Networks (OSN). *LGURJCSIT, 4*(4), 43–54.

Lazer, D., Pentland, A. S., Adamic, L., Aral, S., Barabasi, A. L., Brewer, D., & Van Alstyne, M. (2009). Life in the network: The coming age of computational social science. *Science, 323*(5915), 721. doi:10.1126cience.1167742 PMID:19197046

Lenormand, M., Tugores, A., Colet, P., & Ramasco, J. J. (2014). Tweets on the road. *PLoS One, 9*(8), e105407. doi:10.1371/journal.pone.0105407 PMID:25141161

Lima, A. (2016). *Digital traces of human mobility and interaction: models and applications.* University of Birmingham. Retrieved from https://etheses.bham.ac.uk/id/eprint/6833

Marguta, R., & Parisi, A. (2015). Impact of human mobility on the periodicities and mechanisms underlying measles dynamics. *Journal of the Royal Society, Interface, 12*(104), 20141317. doi:10.1098/rsif.2014.1317 PMID:25673302

Merler, S., & Ajelli, M. (2010). The role of population heterogeneity and human mobility in the spread of pandemic influenza. *Proc R Soc Lond B, 277*(1681), 557-565.

Mohapatra, M. R., & Mohanty, J. R. (2021). Overview of IoT Privacy and Security Challenges for Smart Carpooling System. In *Proceedings of Second International Conference on Smart Energy and Communication* (pp. 727-733). Springer. 10.1007/978-981-15-6707-0_71

Ohlhorst, F. (2021). Social Media Risks Increasing in 2021. *Security Boulevard.* Retrieved from https://securityboulevard.com/2021/03/social-media-risks-increasing-in-2021

Palen, L., & Dourish, P. (2003, April). Unpacking" privacy" for a networked world. In *Proceedings of the SIGCHI conference on Human factors in computing systems* (pp. 129-136). 10.1145/642611.642635

Quercia, D., Lathia, N., Calabrese, F., Di Lorenzo, G., & Crowcroft, J. (2010). Recommending social events from mobile phone location data. *International conference on data mining,* 971–976. 10.1109/ICDM.2010.152

Ravenstein, E. G. (1885). The laws of migration. *Journal of the Statistical Society of London, 52*(2), 167–235. doi:10.2307/2979181

Ritter, A., Etzioni, O., & Clark, S. (2012, August). Open domain event extraction from twitter. In *Proceedings of the 18th ACM SIGKDD international conference on Knowledge discovery and data mining* (pp. 1104-1112). 10.1145/2339530.2339704

Roth, C., Kang, S. M., Batty, M., & Barthèlemy, M. (2011). Structure of urban movements: Polycentric activity and entangled hierarchical flows. *PLoS One, 6*(1), e15923. doi:10.1371/journal.pone.0015923 PMID:21249210

Simini, F., González, M. C., Maritan, A., & Barabási, A.-L. (2012). A universal model for mobility and migration patterns. *Nature, 484*(7392), 96–100. doi:10.1038/nature10856 PMID:22367540

Song, L., Kotz, D., Jain, R., & He, X. (2006). Evaluating next-cell predictors with extensive wi-fi mobility data. *IEEE Transactions on Mobile Computing, 5*(12), 1633–1649. doi:10.1109/TMC.2006.185

Sushama, C., Kumar, M. S., & Neelima, P. (2021). Privacy and security issues in the future: A social media. *Materials Today: Proceedings.* Advance online publication. doi:10.1016/j.matpr.2020.11.105

Thilakarathna, K., Seneviratne, S., Gupta, K., Kaafar, M. A., & Seneviratne, A. (2017). A deep dive into location-based communities in social discovery networks. *Computer Communications, 100,* 78–90. doi:10.1016/j.comcom.2016.11.008

Wurmser. (2020). *Location Intelligence 2020 - Privacy Concerns Start to Squeeze the Supply of Mobile Location Data.* Report. Retrieved from https://www.emarketer.com/content/location-intelligence-2020

Yang, D., Zhang, D., Zheng, V. W., & Yu, Z. (2014). Modeling user activity preference by leveraging user spatial temporal characteristics in LBSNs. *IEEE Transactions on Systems, Man, and Cybernetics. Systems, 45*(1), 129–142. doi:10.1109/TSMC.2014.2327053

Zhang, Z., Zhou, L., Zhao, X., Wang, G., Su, Y., Metzger, M., & Zhao, B. Y. (2013, November). On the validity of geosocial mobility traces. In *Proceedings of the Twelfth ACM Workshop on Hot Topics in Networks* (pp. 1-7). 10.1145/2535771.2535786

Zheng, Y., & Zhou, X. (Eds.). (2011). *Computing with spatial trajectories*. Springer Science & Business Media. doi:10.1007/978-1-4614-1629-6

Chapter 4
Human Detection/Tracking System for Video Surveillance With Noise Removal

Amany Sarhan
Department of Computers and Control Engineering, Tanta University, Egypt

Nada M. Elshennawy
Tanta University, Egypt

Ghadeer M. Diab
Tanta University, Egypt

ABSTRACT

Object detection and tracking have been extensively used in many applications including security and surveillance. This chapter addresses the problem of human detection and tracking in surveillance videos with noise. The system proposed deals with video processing utilizing Kalman filtering to enhance the process in the presence of challenging weather conditions. To support the target idea, some experiments are introduced to measure the deviation between both the noiseless and the noisy videos and to study the effect of each filter within each noise type of video disturbance. The most efficient masking system is used to enhance the outcome in the presence of video degradations. The proposed tracking and detection technique achieves achieve an average correct assigned tracks accuracy of about 95% for noiseless video. This is due to the challenging video degradation depending on the type and level of noise. In case of noisy videos by applying the correct filter mask, the accuracy of tracking in the presence of a median filter comes to around 90%.

DOI: 10.4018/978-1-7998-7756-1.ch004

INTRODUCTION

For many applications such as security and surveillance, human-computer interaction, video communication, and traffic control, object detection and tracking have been extensively used. Video analysis needs three crucial steps: identification of interesting moving objects, monitoring of these objects from frame to frame, and analyzing object tracks to identify their activities. Object detection in images and videos is the method of identifying instances of a particular class of objects. Tracking objects is the method of locating movable objects in different frames of a video while preserving the correct identities. In the context of video surveillance, detection and tracking of pedestrians objects are usually combined to locate the objects of interest through the video. First, we need to detect pedestrians in each video frame, and then track them through multiple frames.

In this study, we concentrate on human objects, as humans are most likely to be the object of concern in applications such as visual surveillance video communication, and road traffic control. The literature contains various techniques for solving tracking tasks in vision and can generally be divided into two groups: i) classical applications, where targets do not interact much with each other, behave independently and ii) application in which targets do not act independently (people), their identification is not always quite distinguishable. There is usually a close link between the representations of object and the tracking algorithms. Object representations are usually selected by application domain. On the other hand, tracking several similar targets poses its own problems as the targets move near each as can be seen in Figure 1 (Sidenbladh & Black, 2003).

Early object detection efforts presented by Elgammal, et al. (2000) were focused on a subtraction of the background. Although this technique is very effective in detecting individual moving objects, when they are close to each other, it is not able to detect static objects or distinguishing individual humans. Current methods of tracking also suffer from issues of variations in visibility. Noise and cluttered backgrounds are most common problems in our surveillance information. These issues cause the tracker to quickly drift into the background.

To solve this problem, we propose a technique of local frame differencing, which can detect foreground and background in the search region. This technique is very effective in keeping the tracker from drifting into the background and greatly increases the overall accuracy of tracking.

Video analysis involves three critical steps: detection of interesting moving objects, tracking of such objects from frame to frame, and analyzing object tracks to recognize their behavior. Recently, a large number of algorithms have been proposed due to the importance of human tracking methods from video, and many of them have been used to deal with human tracking issues. Nearly all algorithms, however,

Figure 1. Examples of appearance change of pedestrian (Sidenbladh & Black, 2003)

face the same problems while tracking the human, complexity and computational time (Konard, 2000). Human detection functions by defining the actual object from the background. So, the tracking process can be done where this object's trajectory is the desired result of the consecutive frame from the video sequence (Puri & Devale, 2012). However, a major challenge is to estimate correctly the area of interest in the corresponding video frames.

In predicting and keeping track of the pedestrian course, the algorithm must know the pedestrian to be identified, in terms of their representation. Consequently, due to the extremely complex behavior of the pedestrians, accurate assessment of the pedestrian's actual and future locations is important. Responsive prediction visions are therefore usually small, for instance in several seconds. In addition, the monitoring system will depict the video as a series of still images in human detection and tracking. For this sequence, we need to model and subtract the background to extract the foreground. Reducing noise artifacts is also important to enhance performance. We have presented a preliminary work in (Diab et al., 2019) for discovering the proper filter for noise in this problem. We build upon the results reached in this work.

This chapter is aimed at analyzing and evaluating the performance of the algorithms selected based on the dataset, which will act as ground truth. In this study, it was suggested that video analysis consider human tracking under various weather conditions (e.g., foggy, rainy, snowy day). To analyze multiple moving pedestrians, we used two different types of video degradation (salt & pepper and speckle noises) with different variances (i.e., the presence of noise in the test video). In addition, a filter system has been applied to the degraded version of the tested videos in order to make a reasonable decision for efficient tracking (Diab et al., 2019).

This chapter is concerned with the development and implementation of the human tracking system under different video degradations. The contributions of this chapter are summarized as follows:

Reviewing different traditional techniques of human detection and tracking and conclude the main drawbacks of each system.

- Proposing a new human tracking system using Kalman filter to enhance the human detection and tracking in the presence of challenging noise conditions in videos.
- Developing a decision making criteria for best tuning that increases the efficiency of human tracking.
- Designing a combined hybrid filters system to satisfy the least deviation between the noiseless and noisy video of human tracking to evaluate the effect of each filter mask within each noise type of video disturbances.
- Testing the performance and accuracy of the proposed technique using different performance metrics. Moreover, for surveillance applications, we have tracked all moving humans in a test video, where each human has been assigned a predefined randomly chosen IDs. After detecting and tracking all the moving humans according to Kalman filter, we have proposed an algorithm for extracting all needed positions of each human according to its assigned IDs of interest. Moreover, we have proposed an algorithm for detecting the trajectory path of different humans.

BACKGROUND AND RELATED WORK

Feature Selection for Tracking

Object tracking, in general, is a challenging problem due to sudden object movement, shift in object and scene presence patterns, and camera movement. Generally, the most desirable property of a visual feature is its individuality, so that objects can be easily differentiated within the feature's space. Selection of the feature is closely related to representation of the object. In general, a combination of those features is used by many tracking algorithms. The boundaries of the objects produce large variations in the source image intensities. Edge detection is used to identify those changes. Algorithms that monitor the boundary of the objects typically use edges as the representative feature. Bowyer et al. (2001) provide an overview of the edge detection algorithms. The bulk of the features are selected by the user manually depending on the application domain. Automated methods for selecting features can be split into both filter methods and wrapper methods (Blum & Langley, 1997).

The filter methods attempt to select the features based on a general criterion, while the wrapper method selects the features based on the effectiveness of the features in a specific problem area. Jepson et al. (2003) used steerable filter responses to improve tracking performance.

Object Detection

Every tracking system involves a mechanism to detect objects either in each frame or when the object once arises in the video. A common technique to object detection is the processing and storage of information in one frame. Even so, some methods of object detection makes use of the temporal information derived from a frame sequence to minimize the number of false detections. This temporal information is generally in the form of frame variance, highlighting the changing regions inside consecutive frames. Given the position of the object in the image allows object correspondence to be performed from one frame to the next to generate tracks. In Table 1, we summarize several traditional methods for object detection.

Table 1. Some recent methods for object detection

Categories	Representative Work
Point detectors	Lowe (2004), Mikolajczyk & Schmid (2002)
Segmentation	Comaniciu & Meer (1999), Shi & Malik (2000)
Background Modeling	Stauffer & Grimson (2000), Oliver et al. (200), Monnet et al. (2003)
Supervised Classifiers	Viola et al. (2003)

Object Tracking

An object tracker is designed to produce an object's trajectory over time by finding its location within each frame of the video. Additionally, object tracker can include the whole region in the picture that the object occupies at any given time. The tasks of detecting the object and establishing the relationship between object instances across frames may either be performed separately or jointly. In the first case, potential object regions in each frame are obtained using an object detection algorithm, and then the tracker corresponds to objects across frames (Diab et al., 2019). In the latter case, the object region and its correspondence are jointly determined by the iterative updating of the object position and the area details collected from previous frames. The objects are represented in any of the tracking approaches using the shape and/

or appearance models. The chosen model for representing objects restricts the type of motion or deformation it may exists.

Integration of Human Detection and Tracking

Figure 2 displays a simplified structure for human detection and tracking system. It contains three major parts: background subtraction (to get foreground detection), human detection, and human tracking (Diab et al., 2019). Firstly, to detect foreground blobs, we apply background subtraction. In order to improve the detection rate, we combine background subtraction with a short term frame difference. The subtraction module on the background is designed to cope with global changes in lighting.

The resulting foreground boxes are connected together to form preliminary tracks. Then, faulty tracks are removed. A cascade of filters is used to delete irrelevant moveable objects and preserve only tracks which correspond to humans. In most scenarios, frame-by-frame object detection is difficult to track directly, because the detection process always takes time and can only be carried out at very low frame rates. In addition, the image quality in surveillance videos is generally poor, making proper detection more challenging (Puri & Devale, 2012). Several other research extracted additional features from a camera based on video analysis.

Figure 2. Main components of human tracking system

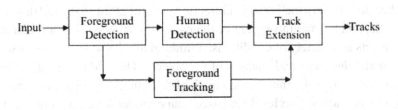

Figure 3. Human detection process (Benezeth et al, 2011)

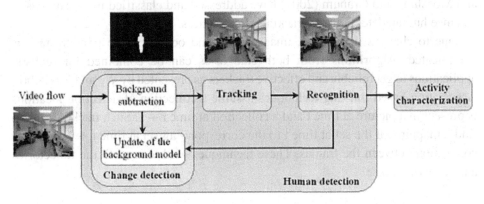

Figure 3 summarizes the human detection process, in which various intermediate results are obtained in the human detection chain. Operating with a fixed camera, the search area may be declined by detecting regions of interest in the image where a person is highly likely to be found. This method is accomplished by means of a background subtraction: from an environment model and observation to defining what has changed, based on the results obtained in the background subtraction algorithms comparative study presented by Fan et al, (2016). The first step of tracking after recognition of the foreground pixels is to collect and combine these pixels into linked components, called blobs. Every blob refers to an object inside the scene, whether human or not. There is comprehensive literature on tracking (Viola & Jones, (2001) and Fan et al, (2016)).

Review of Human Tracking Methods From Video

Video analysis requires three crucial steps: detecting interesting moveable objects, tracking these objects from frame to frame, and analyzing tracks of objects to identify their behavior. Multiple methods have been proposed for tracking objects. These vary mainly according to object representation, used picture attributes, and motion, size and shape of the object modelling.

A large number of monitoring approaches have been proposed for a variety of scenarios which aim to address such questions. Haritaoglu et al. (2000) detected regions of interest by using methods of background subtraction for fixed cameras. This is because modern methods of subtraction have the ability to model the changing light, noise, and normal movement of the background areas, and thus can reliably detect objects in a variety of conditions. Yilmaz et al. (2004) used a set-based level model, model the shape and changes of the objects. The grid points of the level set in this model reflect the means and standard deviations of point's distances from the object's boundary. The level set-based shape model removes target occlusions during monitoring. There has been extensive research on tracking individuals using articulated object models that Aggarwal and Cai (1999), Gavrilla (1999), and Moeslund and Granum (2001) have addressed and classified in the surveys to enhance human detection and tracking effectiveness.

Due to changes in lighting, image noise, and occlusion the tracking task is complicated. Algorithms from both categories can be combined for realistic applications to get reliable and effective trackers as presented by Wu and Yu (2006). Association-based tracking techniques assume a collection of detection locations is present in a picture at time t and a collection at time t + 1. Such trackers seek to find a mapping of the set at time t to the corresponding set at time t + 1, to detect correlation between the frames. These techniques tend to smooth the trajectories and removing noise.

The KF is one of those filtering approaches which is simplest and most common (Yilmaz et al, (2006) and Mehta et al., (2010)). The KF is a state-space model that predicts the object's location and velocity at time t + 1 as a linear function of the object's position at time t plus some additive Gaussian noise. Such assumptions allow the model to determine the optimal positions from the data locations (assuming that the object's motion obeys the model's assumptions). In addition, the KF has become more useful technique for very complicated real-time applications, with the recent growth of high-speed computers (Jyotsna & Sunita, (2013) and Mahmoud et al, (2008)).

Consequently, a growing number of algorithms have been developed to deal with human tracking problems. Nearly all algorithms, however, face the same problems with complexity, and expense computational time. The most selected approach for tracking is through a combination of the detection process as in Bodor et al, (2003). The tracking technique can be conducted where the desired outcome is the trajectory of the objects from the consecutive frame of the video by Di Lascio et al, (2013). Nevertheless, a major challenge is to measure the region of interest in the specific video frames precisely. In tracking an object of interest, the algorithm must recognize the object which is to be detected in terms of its representation (shape and appearance).

Review of Human Tracking Algorithms

This section is structured to evaluate and asses the efficiency of the algorithms chosen. The analysis would be based on significant factors, such as computational time, as well as the impact of human activity relative to the frame rate. While the selected algorithms perform the tracking, the effect of these parameters will be analyzed. Three tracking algorithms- KF, Mean-Shift Filter (MSF), and Partial Least Square (PLS)-are considered for further study. Their choice is due to their extensive use and ability in tracking moving objects (Di Lascio et al, (2013), Balan et al, (2005) and Lee et al, (2012).

The Mean-Shift Filter (MSF)

The Mean-Shift Filter (MSF) is a non-parametric technique as in Salhi & Jammoussi (2012), in which the search window size for that technique is set in the video sequence. However, it is an iterative method that calculates the Mean-Shift value for the viewable point position in the initial frame, before attempting to shift the point as the location in the consecutive frame to a new Mean-Shift value until it fulfills a particular condition for creating match. The algorithm is then initialized with a large number of hypothesized cluster centers, distributed randomly from the data. Then each cluster center is moved to the mean of the data lying within the multidimensional ellipsoid centered cluster. The vector defined by the old and new cluster centers is called the Mean-Shift vector where it is calculated iteratively until the cluster centers do not change their positions.

Partial Least Square (PLS)

Partial Least Square (PLS) is one of the useful tracking algorithms, where the object representation is determined by a partial least square analysis. This approach will respond to the shift in appearance of the active area (foreground) and background while minimizing drift when the object is involved with the best tracking dynamic distribution. A collection of adaptive discriminative appearance models will be acquired to adapt to any representation of objects (Abdul Shukor et al, 2012). Since the presence of an object in consecutive frames is briefly correlated and is likely to repeat over time. PLS can calculate, learn, and adapt to multiple appearance models to achieve reliable tracking. The higher the dimensionality of the features, the more complexity to compute the tracking process.

Kalman Filter (KF)

KF has been commonly used for tracking in several domains (Yilmaz et al, 2006). The KF significant preference and efficiency is due to its low computation requirement, efficient recursive properties, and its status as the optimal estimator for a one-dimensional linear system with Gaussian error statistics. It estimates the location of the object in each frame of the sequence by evaluating the state vector of a linear system in which a Gaussian distribution assumes distribution of the state vector (Balan et al, 2005 and Abdul Shukor et al, 2012). The KF important process in tracking humans is to predict and estimate the location of people or human state and covariance in the upcoming frame, which enhances human body tracking (Abdul Shukor et al, 2012).

   KF requires two basic steps, prediction and correction. The step / time update equation prediction uses the state model to predict the new status of the variables, which calculates the area of interest location in the next frame (Bodor et al, 2005, Salhi & Jammoussi 2012, and Li et al, 2010). It uses the current observation to update the object's state for the correction step or measurement update equations, which updates the object's location afterwards. On the other side, the histogram of oriented gradients is considered one of the shape-based classification methods that can be used for human detection and tracking. Finally, human activity analysis can happen. For that, human body parts must be classified and labeled. Based on human body part motion, the human activity analysis can occur. If abnormal behavior is detected, an alarm can be triggered.

Due to human motion's randomness in complex environments, the multiple pedestrians tracking becomes challenging as in Li et al, (2014). In addition, complex backgrounds, posture changes, pedestrian-scale changes affect the tracking process, and accuracy. Generally, the methods which can be used for object tracking in videos can be categorized into pattern matching- based methods, classification- based methods, and object-state estimation- based methods. In the pattern matching- based methods, the visual tracking is transformed to object matching of consecutive video frames (Hu et al, 2015). Such methods include the mean shift, which can realize the rapid detection and tracking of pedestrians (Kim, 2006). Nevertheless, it has degraded performance for detecting and tracking in moving background. In the classification- based methods (Nuevo, et al, 2010), classification methods are used to classify the objects into background and foreground using the machine learning method.

In the object state estimation-based methods by Idler et al. (2006), the Bayesian theory is used. The object tracking is performed iteratively to find the maximum posterior probability of the object's state. Accordingly, video object tracking can use multiple hypothesis properties and nonlinear assumptions as presented in Li et al, (2015). Numerous detection methods were settled based on classical techniques such as background subtraction, optical flow, and Gaussian mixture model that suffer from several limitations, including processing a long time, and detection costs. To overcome such limitations, different techniques were carried out for automated data collection and analysis with short required time length and a large amount of acquired information.

In conclusion, the discussed techniques and previously selected parameters have impacts towards the performance of these algorithms in tracking human, can act as a guide in developing a more robust algorithm. Accordingly, the main goal of the present chapter is to develop an efficient technique for human detection and tracking based on foreground detection and Kalman filter algorithm methodology. Moreover, different video degradation due to different noise conditions will be studied to determine the best tuning that increases the efficiency of human tracking.

Proposed Human Detection and Tracking System

Foreground human detection aims to detect changes in successive video frames sequence, presenting the amount of the appropriate changes in each frame. The foreground detector typically analyzes the video patterns in real-time, which is being recorded using a stationary camera. Different foreground detection techniques are based on modeling the background of the image and detecting which changes have been occurred (Li et al, (2015) and Sivaraman & Trivedi (2013)). Representing the background can be challenging when it involves shapes, shadows, and moving objects. In the determination of the background, it is assumed that stationary objects vary in color and intensity over time. They tend to be very diverse in different scenarios (Krishna et al, (2005) and Jing & Wen-xing (2009)).

Highly fluctuating sequences may occur, such as frames with very unusual lighting, interiors, outdoors, temperature and noise. Also, systems need to be able to adapt to these in real time applications. Figure 4 shows the main block diagram of the proposed system. Initially noisy video is the input for the system, where filter mask is used to clean the video. Then, human detection based on background subtraction model is used. KF is used to estimate the location of the object in each frame of the sequence by evaluating the state vector of a linear system in which a Gaussian distribution assumes distribution of the state vector.

The tracking process is then initiated with the connected components that are detected with the background subtraction. Finally check tuning progress is used to conclude the level of confidence of the tracking process. A decision making component is used to differentiate between correct and incorrect tracking and finalize the process. A detailed flowchart for detection and tracking process of the proposed system is shown in Figure 5. Highly fluctuating sequences can arise, such as frames

Figure 4. Main block diagram of the proposed system

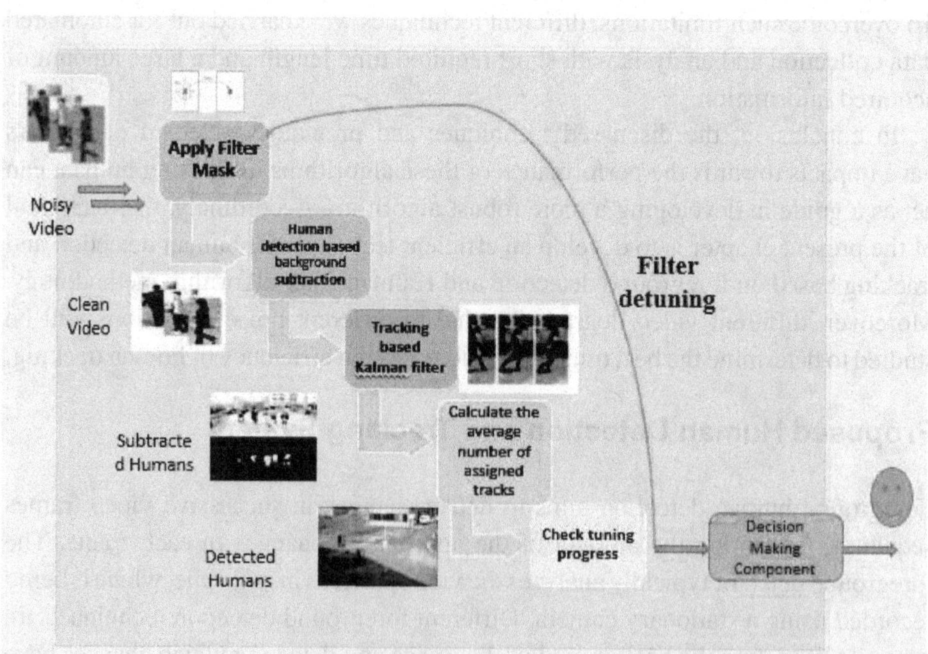

Figure 5. Flowchart for detection and tracking process of the proposed technique

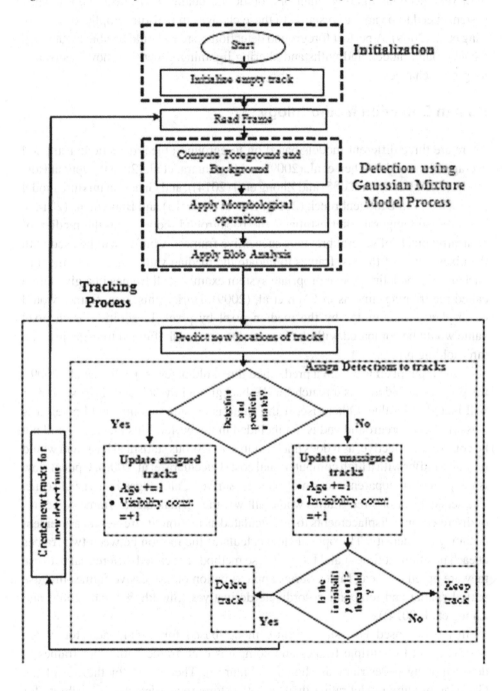

with very peculiar lighting, interiors, outdoors, quality and noise. Additionally, systems need to be able to respond to these changes in real-time applications as in Ling et al, (2009). A perfect foreground detection system should be able to: develop a background model, and withstand altering lightning, repetitive movements, and long-term changes.

Human Detection Methodology

There are three different models based on foreground object detection: Temporal average filter model (Chen et al, (2009) and Cucchiara, et al, (2003)), Optical flow model (Sheikh & Shah (2005) and Zhong et al (2014)), and Gaussian mixture model (Barnich & Van Droogenbroeck (2011), Guo et al, (2013) and Bouwmans (2014)). The average temporal filter estimates the background model from the median of all nearby pixels of several previous successive frames. A buffer will be used with the pixel values of the last frames to update the median value for each frame. For background modeling, the appropriate system examines all frames in a given time called the training time as in Chen et al, (2009). During this time, frames would be displayed and funded by the median pixel by pixel. In addition, each pixel value would be compared with the input value previously funded to make use of a thresholding process.

If the input pixel is within a predefined threshold pixel as in Chen et al, (2009), the pixel is considered as a match for the background model, and the pixel buffer will include its value. Otherwise, if the value is outside this threshold pixel, it is classified as a foreground and is not included in the buffer. This method would not be considered effective, as it does not introduce a rigorous statistical basis and would require a buffer with a high computational cost (Cucchiara, et al, 2003). Optical flow is the pattern of apparent motion of objects, surfaces, and edges in a visual scene. The sequence of ordered frames would allow either instantaneous frame velocities or discrete frame displacements to be calculated as motion. It stresses measurement accuracy and density. The optical flow calculates the motion between two frames at each position, at times t and $t + \delta t$. These methods are called differential because they are based on local Taylor Series approximation of successive frames that use partial spatial and temporal co-ordinate derivatives (Sheikh & Shah (2005) and Zhong et al (2014)).

In the proposed Gaussian mixture model-based foreground detector, video is subsequent to multiple frames and compares each frame with other frames to detect moving pedestrians as shown in Figure 6. The reason for the use of the Gaussian mixture model rather than any other foreground detector is its ability for fast detection. As this algorithm would maximize only the detection probability (Barnich & Van Droogenbroeck (2011), Guo et al, (2013) and Bouwmans (2014)).

Figure 6. Gaussian mixture model-based foreground detector pedestrians

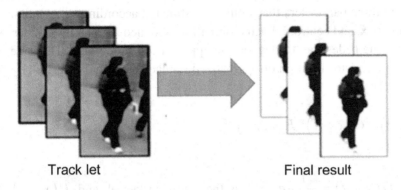

Track let   Final result

Gaussian mixture model relies on two main steps; initialize foreground detector, and detecting pedestrians in initial video frames. In the first step, moving pedestrians are segmented from the background. There are 3 Gaussian parameters; (μi, σi, ωi), which express mean, variance, and weights, respectively (Krishna et al, 2005). For accepted results, the chosen values of the appropriate parameters must be estimated relative to the total number of consecutive video frames.

In the second step, pedestrian detection would be applied according to the state of the art of the traditional background subtraction model as follows (Xue et al, 2012):

$$x_t(s) = \begin{cases} 1 \, d\left(K_{s,t}, R_s\right) > \tau \\ 0 \, elsewhere \end{cases} \tag{1}$$

where: K: observed video sequence, R: static background, A: threshold which obtained by using means of try and error, x_t: motion mask, d: distance between $K_{s,t}$ the color at time t and pixel s, and Bs: the background model at pixel s (Ling et al, 2009).

The probability of occurrence of color K at pixel s is given by (Xue et al, 2012):

$$p\left(K_{s,t}\right) = \sum_{i=1}^{k} w_{i,s,t} \cdot N\left(\mu_{i,s,t}, \pounds_{i,s,t}\right) \tag{2}$$

where $N\left(\mu_{i,s,t}, \pounds_{i,s,t}\right)$: is the ith Gaussian model and $w_{i,s,t}$ is the appropriate weights.

Next, a blob analysis algorithm is applied to remove any undesired moving objects in the video as presented by Xue et al, (2012). The blob detector's main objective is to distinguish the moving person (blobs) in a binary frame (Guo et al, 2014). The blob detector consists of a group of connected pixels in successive video frames. There are three parameters that would be estimated according to each blob; area, bounding box, and centroid. Each blob will be assigned with an ID number, which identifies the pedestrian throughout its appearance in the video. The state of the art of blob detector is based on normalized Laplacian of Gaussian (LOG)$_{\text{norm}}$(Xue et al, 2012):

$$L(x,y,t) = G(x,y,t) * F(x,y,t) \tag{3}$$

where: $G(x,y,t) = \dfrac{1}{2\pi t^2} e^{-\frac{x^2+y^2}{2t^2}}$ is the Gaussian kernel, and $F(x,y,t)$ is the video frame of interest. The (LOG)$_{\text{norm}}$ can be estimated as follows (Xue et al, 2012):

$$\nabla^2_{norm}L = t\left(L_{xx} + L_{yy}\right) \tag{4}$$

The final phase in the detection procedure is to fill undetectable pixels in the pedestrian window. By completing the detection process, a tracking algorithm based on Kalman filter would be applied to guarantee keep tracking of the moving pedestrian (Chen et al, 2009). The morphological operations are used to preprocess the appropriate test video and remove undesirable objects. We have concerned with the calculation and the assignment of the following properties of each detected pedestrian: (i) Area of the object, (ii) Bounding box of the object, (iii) Coordinates box of the blob's centroid, as indicated in Eq. (3)

Human Tracking Based on KF

Figure 7 shows the flowchart of the proposed human tracking based on KF techniques that suggests a fine tuning in two case studies for moving human detection and tracking; human video without any means of video degradation (noiseless video) and with video degradation (after adding noise), which could be considered as a simulated analysis for challenging weather conditions. In the proposed analysis the main performance indices were targeted by calculating the average number of tracks allocated in the video. The designated tracks are the correct pedestrian to keep each pedestrian's tracking process from the first frame until the end of the video. After finalizing the detection process, a tracking procedure would be initialized to keeping track of the detected pedestrian by using means of KF. After finalizing the detection process, a tracking procedure would be initialized to keeping track of the detected pedestrian by using means of KF.

Figure 7. Flowchart of the proposed human tracking based on KF algorithm

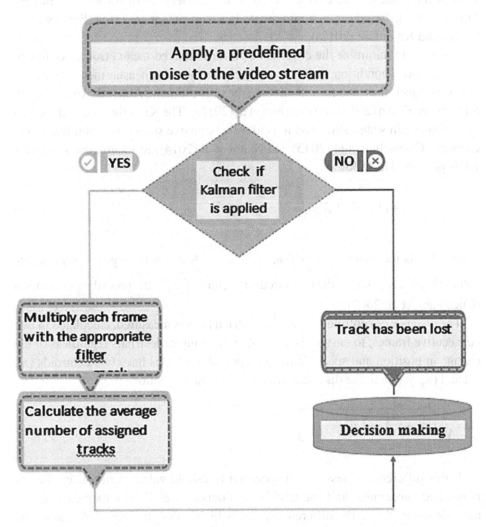

KF introduces three main facilities-based on multiple object tracking; its ability to predict moving pedestrians in future locations, its ability to minimize incorrect detections. Finally, it provides some kind of facilitating the process of combining multiple pedestrians with their tracks (Cucchiara, et al, 2003). To ensure proper pedestrian monitoring despite changing locations, we calculate the distance of each blob's centroids which were measured using the Euclidean equation in two consecutive frames (Bewley et al, 2016). If this difference is found to be less than a specified threshold value, (KF gain), then this prediction is considered "accurate," and the level of trust in the track is increased. If the difference value is greater than the threshold value, the forecast will be deemed 'inaccurate' and the confidence level of the track will be decreased. KF is an efficient estimator and its filtering functionality is based on an approximate linear mean square error (Bewley et al, (2016) and Ko & Lee (2012)).

It is used to minimize the covariance of the estimated mean error according to some presumed condition. A KF not only cleans the data measurements, however, but also projects these measurements onto the state estimate (Abada & Aouat (2016), Suganthi & Korah (2016) and Lakshmi et al (2016)). The KF is the standard method of preference in state-estimation to achieve a recursive state maximum likelihood estimate (Christaline et al (2015) and Nanni et al (2014)).Mathematical model for KF is presented as follows:

$$\widehat{X_k} = K_K.Z_K + \left(1 - K_K\right).\widehat{X_{K-1}} \tag{5}$$

where $\widehat{X_k}$ is the current estimation, K_K is the Kalman filter gain with discrete values ($K_1, K_2, K_3,..$), Z_k is the measured value, and $\widehat{X_{K-1}}$ is the preceding estimation (Cucchiara, et al, 2003).

The distance of centroids of each pedestrian blob is measured, calculated in two consecutive frames, to ensure the process of tracking pedestrians regardless of the change in position and speed. When two pedestrian blobs have two centroids (x_1, y_1) and (x_2, y_2), then the distance will be determined as follows:

$$d = \sqrt{\left[\left(x_2 - x_1\right)^2 + \left(y_2 - y_1\right)^2\right]} \tag{6}$$

If this difference is less than a specified threshold value, then this prediction is deemed "accurate," and the track's confidence level is incremented (express an assigned track). If the difference value is higher than the threshold value, the prediction is deemed 'inaccurate,' and the track's confidence level is decremented (express a lost track).

The steps for detection and tracking are:

Step 1: Object Setup

1. Generate a reader for the video files.
2. Develop a player for video display of the original video.
3. Produce a video player that shows the distance.
4. Construct a Foreground Detector piece.
5. Create Blob Analyzer object.

Step 2: Initialize Tracks

Build an empty array of tracks using the following parameters: Electronic ID, Bounding Box, Instance from the KF, Age, Total visible count, and Consecutive invisibility count.

Step 3: Observe the appropriate frame

Step 4: Detect objects

1. Use the Foreground detector object to get the mask for the frame.
2. Apply morphological operations on the frame.
3. Using the Blob analyser components, identify the blobs and their characteristics (Centroids and Bounding Boxes).

Step 5: Assign every detected blob to a track structure.

Step 6: Predict New Tracks Locations

Predict the blob's the location in the next frame by using the (KF).

Step 7: Detection to track assignment

1. Build a cost matrix
2. Assign a Cost of Non Assignment value
3. Call the Assign Detections to track function which, based on the cost matrix, will decide which predictions are acceptable and which aren't. (As in which predictions match the detections and which ones don't match any detections).

Step 8: Update Assigned Tracks

1. Increase age by 1 for every matched track.
2. Set the invisibility count of that track to zero.
3. Set the centroid and bounding box of the track to the currently detected values instead of the previously predicted ones to be used for the next prediction.

Step 9: Update Unassigned Tracks

Increase by 1 the invisibility count for unassigned tracks by 1.

Step 10: Delete Lost Tracks

Delete a track if the invisibility count exceeds the threshold of acceptable invisibility count.

Step 11: Create New Tracks

1. Generate new tracks for detections not assigned to it.
2. Add them to the track array

Figure 8. Pedestrian detection process

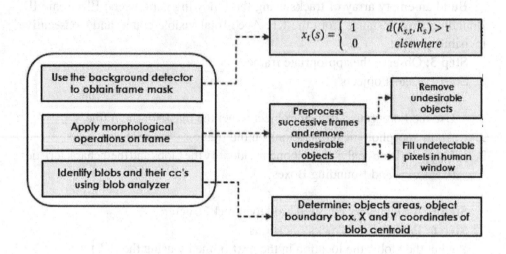

Figure 9. The proposed tracking algorithm (Diab et al., 2019)

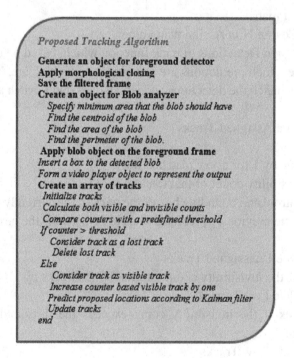

Figure 8 shows the process of pedestrian detection. We evaluate the distance of centroids of each pedestrian blob which is measured in two consecutive frames using equation (6) to ensure the process of tracking pedestrians regardless of the change of location. If this difference is found to be less than a specified threshold value, then this prediction is considered "accurate," and the level of confidence of the track is increased (express an assigned track).

As we intended to refrain from using the complex model of tracking objects in order to respect the computational time constraints, and to save memory space, the process of tracking process is initiated with the connected components which are detected with the background subtraction. Figure 9 shows the proposed tracking algorithm.

EXPERIMENTAL RESULTS & DISCUSSION

A big challenge is to estimate correctly the area of interest in the corresponding video frames. When tracking an object of interest, the algorithm must recognize the object that will be identified. We have run our proposed algorithm using Matlab 9.4 release 2018 (a) with PC (core i5 processor and 4GB RAM).

Results of Original Images With Background Subtraction

On the other hand, and based on the results obtained in the comparative analysis of background subtraction algorithms, we planned to apply each background pixel by means of a Gaussian probability density function (Kaur & Singh, 2015). This reasonably easy model represents a fair compromise between detection efficiency, computation time and memory requirement. Because the scene never gets completely static. The model must be tailored to suit the various environmental changes. Figure 10 presents sample results of our model of a snapshot of original images obtained from various videos, along with obtained results after subtraction of the background.

The tracking mechanism is being easily initialized with the detected connected components with the subtraction of the background. Through time, t, we have to pair the list of detected blobs and the list of tracked pedestrian in previous frames. The relationship between tracked pedestrian and blobs is defined if the pedestrian is associated with a minimum fixed percentage of the interest points present on a blob. Once regions of interest are detected and managed, we have to determine the morphological operations, as stated in section 3.2., to preprocess the appropriate test video and remove undesirable objects such as smaller (i.e. animals). This approach would be concerned in the state of art of adaptive thresholding (Ajitha et

Figure 10. Snapshot of ID22, ID23, and ID25 after background subtraction

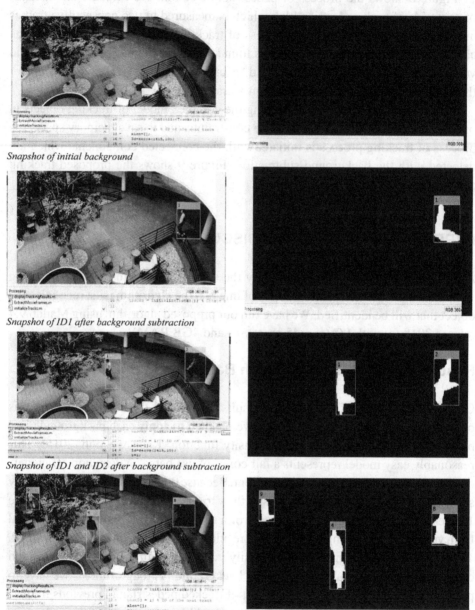

Snapshot of initial background

Snapshot of ID1 after background subtraction

Snapshot of ID1 and ID2 after background subtraction

Snapshot of ID4, ID8, and ID9 after background subtraction

Figure 11. Some snapshots of our results according to both detection and tracking algorithm

al, 2017). Figure 11 shows some snapshots obtained from the proposed detection and tracking algorithm.

After detecting and tracking all moving humans according to Kalman filter, and to investigate the range of number of successive video frames for different ID, we designed the algorithm shown in Figure 12 for extracting all needed positions of each human according to its assigned IDs of interest.

Figure 12. Estimation of ID position from successive video frames

```
Algorithm: Estimation of ID position
Input: Video frames
Output: ID position
Begin
  Initialize tracking parameters;
  Create Track_array[];
  Set id=1;
  Use KF to detect moving objects
  For i=1:n_frames
      Xleni=length(id)
      Id_Pad=double(Id,zeros(1,(100-length(id)))
      Id(i,:) = Id_Pad;
      i=i+1;
  End for
End
```

We have tracked all moving humans in a test video, as shown in Figure 13. Each human has been assigned to a predefined randomly chosen IDs. Video properties are defined as follows:

Duration: 47 sec, Width: 640, Height: 360, Frame Rate: 30, Bits Per Pixel: 24 and Video Format: RGB24.

Figure 13. Some selected frames of the test video

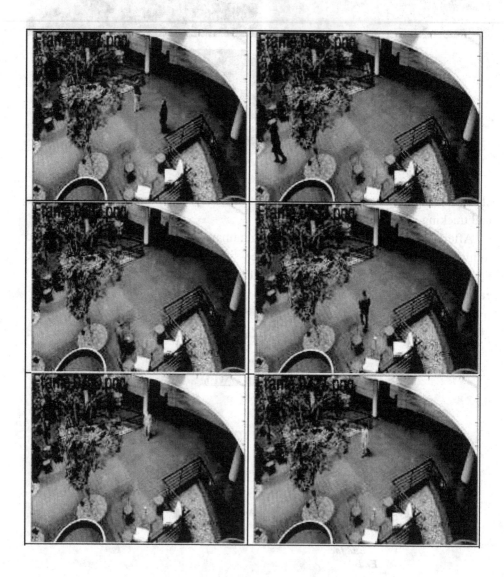

Figure 14. Spectrum of successive video frames for human ID =1 and 2

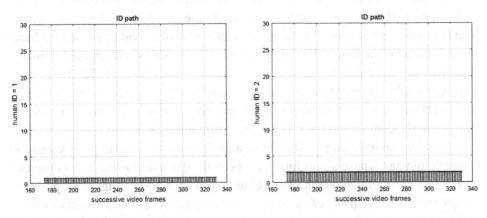

Figure 15. Step by step draing the trajectory of ID #1

Snapshot of initial position and starting point of trajectory of ID#1, Centroid trajectory: starting point coordinate (508.1294, 183.0644)

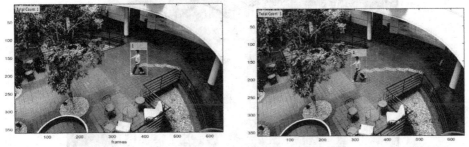

Snapshot of trajectory of ID#1 at end point coordinate (369.4483 , 173.5502) and (293.8730 , 178.7896)

Examples for the data extracted of the relation between the positions of each ID with respect to the number of successive video frames are shown in figure 14, where X-axis represents the range of the number of consecutive video frames, and the y-axis represents the human ID number. According to Kalman filter, the following IDs have been detected randomly: 1, 2, 3, 4, 8, 9, 11, 14, 15, 16, 18, 22, 23, 25, and 27, respectively. For example, ID =1, shown in Figure 4. 28, has been detected in frames 166 through 331. Each vertical bar represents the discrete position of interest. We can easily identify and track each human through its assigned ID.

Moreover, we have proposed an algorithm for detecting the trajectory path of different humans. These algorithms have been designed according to background subtraction algorithm and centroids estimation in each frame. Figure 15 presents sample results of a snapshot of the trajectory of original images at different locations obtained from the same test videos at different coordinates as explained using algorithm shown in Figure 12.

Figure 16 shows two trajectories of ID 1 and 2 persons. As can be shown trajectory of ID#2 starts to be observed in this frame at start point coordinate (521.8861, 140.6345) and end point coordinate (501.6239, 141.4146). Figure 17 summarizes the trajectory path of human ID#1 according to its centroid in each frame, where x coordinates represent the number of frames.

Figure 16. Trajectory of ID#1 at end point coordinate (172.6824, 227.9464) while trajectory of ID#2 at end point coordinate (461.6313, 138.5531)

Figure 17. The trajectory path of human ID#1 according to its centroid in each frame

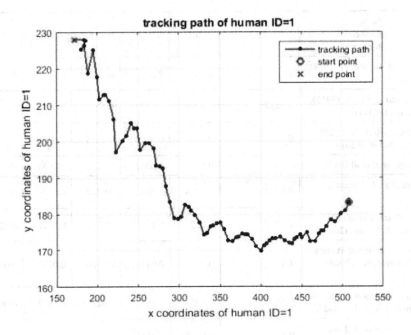

Effect of Noise on Test Videos

The following results have been proved in (Diab et al., 2019), however, we add them again here to make this work coherent. Tables 2 and 3 represent the effect of all filtering masks on salt & pepper noise according to both test videos 1 and 2, respectively with respect to the percentage of noise presence in videos (variance). Nine filters were used to remove the noise namely; Average, Disk, Laplacian, LoG, Motion, Sobel, Prewit, Median, and Gaussian. From the tables, it is noticed that the **Median filter** has achieved the best mask among all filters with the least deviation on the value of the average number of assigned tracks according to the no noise case study (9.5356).

Tables 4 and 5 represent the effect of all filtering masks on speckle noise according to both test videos 1 and 2, respectively. It is noticed that the disk filter has targeted the best mask among all filters with the least deviation on the value of the average number of assigned tracks according to the no noise case study (5.197183).

Table 2. Effect of all filtering masks on salt & pepper noise according to test video 1

Noise variance Filter type	0.03	0.1	0.3	0.5	0.8	1
Average (Joshua et al (2019), Ajitha et al (2017))	10.4133	9.9911	7.32	0.4289	0	0
Disk (Kaur & Singh, (2015), Ajitha et al (2017))	9.9467	9.9489	9.9333	9.4111	0.9578	0
Laplacian (Kong et al, 2013 and Hambal et al 2017)	0	0	0	0.0178	0.0289	0.0089
LoG (Hambal et al 2017)	0	0	0.0022	0.0133	0.0044	0
Motion (Fan & Namazi, 2000)	9.7244	9.7578	5.0044	0.0244	0	0
Sobel (Sharma et al (2013), Gonzalez & Woods (2002))	1.22	0.0022	0.1	0.0356	0.0311	0.0689
Prewit (Gonzalez & Woods (2002), Dhankhar & Sahu (2013))	1.4	0	0.0844	0.0756	0.0222	0.0311
Median (Joshua et al (2019), Gonzalez & Woods (2002))	9.5956	9.5356	9.5533	8.642	0.1822	0.0044
Gaussian (Boyat & Joshi (2015), Hambal et al (2017))	9.3178	6.8178	0.0111	0	0	0

Table 3. Effect of all filtering masks on salt & pepper noise according to test video2

Noise variance Filter type	0.03	0.1	0.3	0.5	0.8	1
Average (Joshua et al (2019), Ajitha et al (2017))	5.7606	5.8028	4.1268	0.3944	0	0
Disk (Kaur & Singh, (2015), Ajitha et al (2017))	5.3803	5.507	5.1972	4.338	0.1268	0
Laplacian (Kong et al, 2013 and Hambal et al 2017)	0	0	0.0563	0.1972	0.1972	0.0845
LoG (Hambal et al 2017)	0	0	0.1408	0.1976	0	0
Motion (Fan & Namazi, 2000)	5.6901	5.4789	3.0986	0	0	0
Sobel (Sharma et al (2013), Gonzalez & Woods (2002))	1.9155	0.0141	0.3944	0.2817	0.1831	0.2676
Prewit (Gonzalez & Woods (2002), Dhankhar & Sahu (2013))	1.2535	0	0.169	0.3521	0.2817	0.169
Median (Joshua et al (2019), Gonzalez & Woods (2002))	5.3099	5.2676	5.06761	5.8169	0.2113	0.022
Gaussian (Boyat & Joshi (2015), Hambal et al (2017))	5.7465	4.7042	0	0	0	0

Table 4. Effect of all filtering masks on speckle noise according to test video 1

Noise variance Filter type	0.02	0.04	0.05	0.07	0.08	0.1
Average (Joshua et al (2019), Ajitha et al (2017))	9.9244	10.0867	10.1133	10.12	10.12	9.9844
Disk (Kaur & Singh, (2015), Ajitha et al (2017))	9.9556	9.9622	9.98	9.9222	9.94	9.8889
Laplacian (Kong et al, 2013 and Hambal et al 2017)	0	0	0	0	0	0
LoG (Hambal et al 2017)	0	0	0	0	0	0
Motion (Fan & Namazi, 2000)	9.8756	9.8867	9.8644	9.8356	9.8333	9.7511
Sobel (Sharma et al (2013), Gonzalez & Woods (2002))	0.0044	0	0	0.0022	0	0.0111
Prewit (Gonzalez & Woods (2002), Dhankhar & Sahu (2013))	0.0111	0	0	0	0	0
Median (Joshua et al (2019), Gonzalez & Woods (2002))	9.9933	10.1333	10.0511	9.8667	9.7356	9.3978
Gaussian (Boyat & Joshi (2015), Hambal et al (2017))	9.9244	9.5978	9.0933	7.7822	6.9867	5.0489

Table 5. Effect of all filtering masks on speckle noise according to test video2

Noise variance Filter type	0.02	0.04	0.05	0.07	0.08	0.1
Average (Joshua et al (2019), Ajitha et al (2017))	5.5352	5.8451	5.9014	5.8732	5.8451	5.8028
Disk (Kaur & Singh, (2015), Ajitha et al (2017))	5.4366	5.493	5.5493	5.4507	5.4225	5.5634
Laplacian (Kong et al, 2013 and Hambal et al 2017)	0	0	0	0	0	0
LoG (Hambal et al 2017)	0	0	0	0	0	0
Motion (Fan & Namazi, 2000)	5.6479	5.6761	5.6901	5.7465	5.662	5.6056
Sobel (Sharma et al (2013), Gonzalez & Woods (2002))	1.662	0.3662	0.2113	0.0141	0.0141	0.0423
Prewit (Gonzalez & Woods (2002), Dhankhar & Sahu (2013))	1.4085	0.3944	0.1972	0	0	0
Median (Joshua et al (2019), Gonzalez & Woods (2002))	5.662	5.8873	5.6761	5.7324	5.6479	5.7887
Gaussian (Boyat & Joshi (2015), Hambal et al (2017))	5.7887	5.7606	5.831	5.2254	4.9296	4.3521

Comparison of The Proposed Method With Recently Published State-of-the-art Techniques

In this section, we perform a comparison of state-of-the-art techniques used for human detection and tracking with our proposed system. Our main focus is to detect and track human in more difficult environment. Recently, several studies have been done in the literature for human detection and tracking having different classification and accuracy rate. Hambal et al. (2017) proposed improved Convolutional neural network CNN method for fast human detection in real time which obtained an accuracy of 88%. While Wang et al. (2005) proposed a significant method based on two streams unified deep network for human detection as it consumes less computational time and enhanced human detection accuracy which obtained an accuracy of 91.4%. Whereas Adlakha et al. (2016) reported accuracy of 92% using video analytics technique.

As can be noted, the experiments demonstrate that our proposed techniques achieved high accuracy (95%) for noiseless and 90% for noisy videos respectively. Moreover, it achieves a running time with about 25 ms per frame and still effective in complex situations such as noisy videos as a result of different weather conditions. Thus, the proposed approach outperforms other existing techniques with highest accuracy and fast running time.

CONCLUSIONS & FUTURE WORK

Enhancement of the human algorithm's real-time surveillance (RTS) for identifying and monitoring pedestrians under video disturbance is being studied. In the state of the art of video processing, we've introduced human detection and tracking techniques. Two steps were used to develop such technique under both ideal and challenging weather conditions. We propose using a median filter in case of video degradation due to salt & pepper noise as a simulation of real rainy weather conditions. While we recommend using a disk filter to minimize video degradation due to speckle noise as a simulation of fog weather condition. The proposed techniques achieve an average correct assigned tracks accuracy of about 95% for noiseless video. This value is degraded due to challenging video degradation depending on the type and level of noise. In this case and after applying the correct filter mask, the accuracy of recognition in the presence of a median filter is around 90%.

Moreover, for surveillance applications, we have tracked all moving humans in a test video, where each human has been assigned to a predefined randomly chosen IDs. After detecting and tracking all moving humans according to Kalman filter, we have proposed an algorithm for extracting all needed positions of each human according to its assigned IDs of interest. Moreover, we have proposed an algorithm for detecting the trajectory path of different humans. These algorithms have been designed according to background subtraction algorithm and centroids estimation in each frame.

Future work of interest will be targeted by further use of assessments of other datasets, tracking of human in groups, and taking both indoor and outdoor considerations.

REFERENCES

Abada, L., & Aouat, S. (2016). Facial shape-from-shading using features detection method. *International Journal of Advanced Intelligence Paradigms*, *8*(1), 3–19. doi:10.1504/IJAIP.2016.074774

Abdul Shukor, S. A., Amiruddin, S., & Ilias, B. (2016). Analysis and Evaluation of Human Tracking Methods from Video. *The 6th IEEE International Conference on Control System, Computing and Engineering*, 310-315.

Adlakha, D., Adlakha, D., & Tanwar, R. (2016). Analytical Comparison between Sobel and Prewitt Edge Detection Techniques. *International Journal of Scientific and Engineering Research*, *7*(1), 1482–1488.

Aggarwal, J. K., & Cai, Q. (1999). Human motion analysis: A review. *Computer Vision and Image Understanding*, *73*(3), 428–440. doi:10.1006/cviu.1998.0744

Ajitha, J. M, & Jaba, K., & M.phil, M. (. (2017). Video Image Filtering Technique - A Review. *International Journal of Engineering Trends and Technology*, *46*(3), 159–161. doi:10.14445/22315381/IJETT-V46P227

Balan, A., Sigal, L., & Black, M. (2005). A Quantitative Evaluation of Video-based 3D Person Tracking. *The IEEE International Workshop on Visual Surveillance and Performance Evaluation of Tracking and Surveillance*, *5*, 349–356. 10.1109/VSPETS.2005.1570935

Barnich, O., & Van Droogenbroeck, M. (2011). The vibe: A universal Background subtraction algorithm for video sequences. *IEEE Transactions on Image Processing*, *20*(6), 1709–1724. doi:10.1109/TIP.2010.2101613 PMID:21189241

Benezeth, Y., Laurent, H., Emile, B., & Rosenberger, C. (2011). Towards a sensor for detecting human presence and activity. *Energy and Buildings, Elsevier*, *43*(2-3), 305–314. doi:10.1016/j.enbuild.2010.09.014

Bewley, A., Ge, Z., Ott, L., Ramos, F., & Upcroft, B. (2016). Simple online and real-time tracking. *The IEEE International Conference on Image Processing (ICIP)*, 3464-3468.

Blum, A. L., & Langley, P. (1997). Selection of relevant features and examples in machine learning. *Artificial Intelligence, 1-2*(1-2), 245–271. doi:10.1016/S0004-3702(97)00063-5

Bodor, R., Jackson, B., & Papanikolopoulos, N. (2003). Vision Based Human Tracking and Activity Recognition. *The 11th Mediterranean Conference on Control Automation*, 18–20.

Bouwmans, T. (2014). Traditional and recent approaches in background modeling for foreground detection: An overview. *Computer Science Review, 11-12*, 31–66. doi:10.1016/j.cosrev.2014.04.001

Bowyer, K., Kranenburg, C., & Dougherty, S. (2001). Edge detector evaluation using empirical ROC curve. *Computer Vision and Image Understanding, 10*(1), 77–103. doi:10.1006/cviu.2001.0931

Boyat, A. K., & Joshi, B. K. (2015). A review paper: Noise modes in digital image processing. [SIPIJ]. *Signal and Image Processing: an International Journal, 6*(2), 63–75. doi:10.5121ipij.2015.6206

Chen, X., Huang, Q., Hu, P., Li, M., Tian, Y., & Li, C. (2009). Rapid and Precise Object Detection based on Color Histograms and Adaptive Bandwidth Mean Shift. *International IEEE/RSJ Conference on Intelligent Robots and Systems*, 4281-4286. 10.1109/IROS.2009.5354739

Christaline, J. A., Ramesh, R., & Vaishali, D. (2015). Critical review of image analysis techniques. *International Journal of Advanced Intelligence Paradigms, 7*(3/4), 368–381. doi:10.1504/IJAIP.2015.073715

Comaniciu, D., & Meer, P. (1999). Mean shift analysis and applications. *The IEEE International Conference on Computer Vision (ICCV), 2*, 1197–1203.

Cucchiara, R., Piccardi, M., & Prati, A. (2003). Detecting Moving Objects, Ghosts, and Shadows in Video Streams. *IEEE Transactions on Pattern Analysis and Machine Intelligence, 25*(10), 1337–1342. doi:10.1109/TPAMI.2003.1233909

Dhankhar, P., & Sahu, N. (2013). A Review and Research of Edge Detection Techniques for Image Segmentation. *International Journal of Computer Science and Mobile Computing, IJCSMC, 2*(7), 86–92.

Di Lascio, R., Foggia, P., Percannella, G., Saggese, A., & Vento, M. (2013). A real-time algorithm for people tracking using contextual reasoning. *Computer Vision and Image Understanding*, *117*(8), 892–908. doi:10.1016/j.cviu.2013.04.004

Diab, G. M., El-Shennawy, N., & Sarhan, A. (2019). Implementation of Human Tracking System under Different Video Degradations. *The International Japan-Africa Conference on Electronics, and Communications (JAC-ECC 2019).*

Elgammal, A., Harwood, D., & Davis, L. (2000). Non-parametric model for background subtraction. *The International Conference on Computer Vision (ECCV 2000)*, 751-767. 10.1007/3-540-45053-X_48

Fan, C. M., & Namazi, N. M. (2000). Simultaneous Motion Estimation and Filtering of Image Sequences. *IEEE Transactions on Image Processing*, *8*(12), 1788–1795. PMID:18267454

Fan, L., Wang, Z., Cail, B., Tao, C., Zhang, Z., Wang, Y., Li, S., Huang, F., Fu, S., & Zhang, F. (2016). A survey on multiple objects tracking algorithm. *The IEEE International Conference on Information and Automation (ICIA)*, 1855-1862. 10.1109/ICInfA.2016.7832121

Gavrila, D. M. (1999). The visual analysis of human movement: A survey. *Computer Vision and Image Understanding*, *73*(1), 82–98. doi:10.1006/cviu.1998.0716

Gonzalez, R. C., & Woods, R. E. (2002). *Digital Image Processing* (2nd ed.). Prentice Hall.

Guizi, F., & Kurashima, C. S. (2016). Real-time people detection and tracking using 3d depth estimation. *The IEEE International Symposium on Consumer Electronics (ISCE)*, 39–40. 10.1109/ISCE.2016.7797359

Guo, J., Williams, B. M., & Huang, W. (2014). Adaptive Kalman filter approach for stochastic short-term traffic flow rate prediction and uncertainty quantification. *Transportation Research Part C, Emerging Technologies*, *43*(1), 50–51. doi:10.1016/j.trc.2014.02.006

Guo, J. M., Hsia, C. H., Liu, Y. F., Shih, M. H., Chang, C. H., & Wu, J. Y. (2013). Fast background subtraction based on a multilayer codebook model for moving object detection. *IEEE Transactions on Circuits System Video Technology*, *23*(10), 1809–1821. doi:10.1109/TCSVT.2013.2269011

Hambal, A. M., Pei, Z., & Ishabailu, F. L. (2017). Image Noise reduction and Filtering Techniques. *International Journal of Scientific Research*, *6*(3), 2033–2038.

Haritaoglu, I., Harwood, D., & Davis, L. (2000). Real-time surveillance of people and their activities. *IEEE Transactions on Pattern Analysis and Machine Intelligence, 22*(8), 809–830. doi:10.1109/34.868683

Hu, W., Li, W., Zhang, X., & Maybank, S. (2015). Single and Multiple Object Tracking Using a Multi-Feature Joint Sparse Representation. *IEEE Transactions on Pattern Analysis and Machine Intelligence, 37*(4), 816–833. doi:10.1109/TPAMI.2014.2353628 PMID:26353296

Idler, C., Schweiger, R., Paulus, D., Mahlisch, M., & Ritter, W. (2006). Real-time vision based multi-target-tracking with particle filters in automotive applications. *The 13th IEEE Intelligent Vehicle Symposium*, 188–193.

Jepson, A., Fleet, D., & Elmaraghi, T. (2003). Robust online appearance models for visual tracking. *IEEE Transactions on Pattern Analysis and Machine Intelligence, 25*(10), 1296–1311. doi:10.1109/TPAMI.2003.1233903

Jing, W., & Wen-xing, B. (2009). A video supported moving object detection technique based on a different algorithm. *Computer Applications and Software, 26*(12), 68–70.

Joshua, O., Ibiyemi, T. S., & Adu, B. A. (2019). A Comprehensive Review on Various Types of Noise in Image Processing. *International Journal of Scientific and Engineering Research, 10*(11), 388–393.

Jyotsna, P., & Sunita, J. (2013). A Comparative Study of Image Denoising Techniques. *International Journal of Innovative Research in Science, Engineering and Technology, 2*(3), 787–794.

Kaur, S., & Singh, R. (2015). Image De-Noising Technique: A Review. *International Journal for Technological Research in Engineering, 2*(8), 2347–2352.

Kim, Z. (2006). Real-time obstacle detection and tracking based on constrained Delaunay triangulation. *The IEEE Intelligent Transportation Systems Conference (ITSC)*, 548–553.

Ko, C. N., & Lee, C. M. (2012). Short-term load forecasting using SVR (support vector regression)-based radial basis function neural network with dual extended Kalman filter. *Energy, Elsevier, 49*, 413–416.

Konard, J. (2000). Handbook of Images and Video Processing. Academic Press.

Kong, H., Cinar, H., Sanjay, A., & Sanjay, S. (2013). A Generalized Laplacian of Gaussian Filter for Blob Detection and its Applications. *IEEE Transactions on Cybernetics, 43*(6), 1719–1733. doi:10.1109/TSMCB.2012.2228639 PMID:23757570

Krishna, M. K., Hexmoor, H., & Sogani, S., (2005). At-step ahead constrained optimal target detection algorithm for a multi-sensor surveillance system. *IEEE Intelligent Robots and Systems*, 357–362.

Lakshmi, R. S., Ravichandran, K. S., Nathan, P. S., & Alagapan, A. N. (2016). Information retrieval by mining text and image. *International Journal of Advanced Intelligence Paradigms*, 8(4), 451–459. doi:10.1504/IJAIP.2016.080199

Lee, B. Y., Liew, L. H., Cheah, W. S., & Wang, Y. C., (2012). Measuring the Effects of Occlusion on Kernel-Based Object Tracking Using Simulated Videos. *Procedia Engineering*, *41*, 764–770.

Li, C., Guo, L., & Hu, Y. (2010). A new method is combining HOG and Kalman filter for video-based human detection and tracking. *The 3rd International Conference on Image Signal Processing*, *1*, 290–293.

Li, H., Liu, Y., Xiong, S., & Wang, L. (2014). Pedestrian detection algorithm based on video sequences and laser point cloud. *Frontiers of Computer Science*, *9*(3), 402–414. doi:10.100711704-014-3413-2

Li, M., Cai, Z., Wei, C., & Yuan, Y. (2015). A Survey of Video Object Tracking. *International Journal of Control and Automation*, 8(9), 303–312. doi:10.14257/ijca.2015.8.9.29

Ling, S., Shuo, W., & Qing-Xia, L. (2009). A target detection method based on an adaptive threshold mixed difference. *Computer Applications and Software*, 26(10), 94–97.

Lowe, D. (2004). Distinctive image features from scale-invariant key points. *International Journal of Computer Vision*, *60*(2), 91–110. doi:10.1023/B:VISI.0000029664.99615.94

Mahmoud, R. O., Faheem, M. T., & Sarhan, A. (2008). Intelligent Denoising Technique for Spatial Video Denoising for real-time applications. *International Conference on Computers Engineering and Systems (ICCES08)*, 407-412. 10.1109/ICCES.2008.4773037

Mehta, M., Goyal, C., Srivastava, M., & Jain, R. (2010). Real-time object Detection and Tracking: Histogram Matching and Kalman Filter Approach. *The 2nd International Conference on Computer and Automation Engineering*, 796-801.

Mikolajczyk, K., & Schmid, C. (2002). An affine invariant interest point detector. *The European Conference on Computer Vision (ECCV)*, 1, 128–142.

Moeslund, T., & Granum, E. (2001). A survey of computer vision-based human motion capture. *Computer Vision and Image Understanding, 81*(3), 231–268. doi:10.1006/cviu.2000.0897

Monnet, A., Mittal, A., Paragios, N., & Ramesh, V. (2003). Background modeling and subtraction of dynamic scenes. *The IEEE International Conference on Computer Vision (ICCV)*, 1305–1312. 10.1109/ICCV.2003.1238641

Nanni, L., Lumini, A., & Brahnam, S. (2014). Ensemble of shape descriptors for shape retrieval and classification. *International Journal of Advanced Intelligence Paradigms, 6*(2), 136–156. doi:10.1504/IJAIP.2014.062177

Nuevo, J., Parra, I., Sjoberg, J., & Bergasa, L. (2010). Estimating surrounding pedestrians' pose using computer vision. *The 13th IEEE Intelligent Transportation Systems Conference (ITSC)*, 1863–1868.

Oliver, N., Rosario, B., & Pentland, A. (2000). A Bayesian computer vision system for modeling human interactions. *IEEE Transactions on Pattern Analysis and Machine Intelligence, 22*(8), 831–843. doi:10.1109/34.868684

Puri, N. V., & Devale, P. R. (2012). Development of Human Tracking in Video Surveillance System for Activity Analysis. *Journal of Computational Engineering, 4*, 26–30.

Salhi, A., & Jammoussi, A. Y. (2012). Object tracking system using Camshaft, Meanshift and Kalman filter. *World Academy of Science, Engineering and Technology, 6*(4), 674–679.

Sharma, P., Singh, G., & Kaur, A. (2013). Different Techniques of Edge Detection in Digital Image Processing. *International Journal of Engineering Research and Applications, 3*(3), 458–461.

Sheikh, Y., & Shah, M. (2005). Bayesian Modeling of Dynamic Scenes for Object Detection. *IEEE Transactions on Pattern Analysis and Machine Intelligence, 27*(11), 1778–1792. doi:10.1109/TPAMI.2005.213 PMID:16285376

Shi, J., & Malik, J. (2000). Normalized cuts and image segmentation. *IEEE Transactions on Pattern Analysis and Machine Intelligence, 22*(8), 888–905. doi:10.1109/34.868688

Sidenbladh, H., & Black, M. J. (2003). Learning the statistics of people images and video. *International Journal of Computer Vision, 54*(1/2), 189–209. doi:10.1023/A:1023765619733

Sivaraman, S., & Trivedi, M. (2013). Integrated lane and vehicle detection, localization, and tracking: A synergistic approach. *IEEE Transactions on Intelligent Transportation Systems*, *14*(2), 907–917. doi:10.1109/TITS.2013.2246835

Stauffer, C., & Grimson, W. (2000). Learning patterns of activity using real-time tracking. *IEEE Transactions on Pattern Analysis and Machine Intelligence*, *22*(8), 747–767. doi:10.1109/34.868677

Suganthi, G., & Korah, R. (2016). Computer-aided detection and identification of mine-like objects in infrared imagery using digital image processing. *International Journal of Advanced Intelligence Paradigms*, *8*(4), 400–411. doi:10.1504/IJAIP.2016.080193

Viola, P., & Jones, M. (2001). Rapid object detection using a boosted cascade of simple features. *The IEEE Computer Society Conference on Computer Vision and Pattern Recognition (CVPR)*, 511–518. 10.1109/CVPR.2001.990517

Viola, P., Jones, M., & Snow, D. (2003). Detecting pedestrians using patterns of motion and appearance. *The IEEE International Conference on Computer Vision (ICCV)*, 734–741. 10.1109/ICCV.2003.1238422

Wu, Y., & Yu, T. (2006). A field model for human detection and tracking. *IEEE Transactions on Pattern Analysis and Machine Intelligence*, *28*(5), 753–765. doi:10.1109/TPAMI.2006.87 PMID:16640261

Xue, L., Jiang, C., Chang, H., Yang, Y., Qin, W., & Yuan, W. (2012). A novel Kalman filter for combining outputs of MEMS gyroscope array. *Measurement, Elsevier*, *45*(4), 745–746. doi:10.1016/j.measurement.2011.12.016

Yilmaz, A., Javed, O., & Shah, M. (2006). Object Tracking: A Survey. *ACM Computing Surveys*, *38*(4), 1–45. doi:10.1145/1177352.1177355

Yilmaz, A., Li, X., & Shah, M. (2004). Contour based object tracking with occlusion handling in video acquired using mobile cameras. *IEEE Transactions on Pattern Analysis and Machine Intelligence*, *26*(11), 1531–1536. doi:10.1109/TPAMI.2004.96 PMID:15521500

Zhong, Q., Chen, Z., Zhang, X., & Hu, G. (2014). Feature-Based Object Location of IC Pins by Using Fast Run Length Encoding BLOB Analysis. *IEEE Transactions on Components, Packaging, and Manufacturing Technology*, *4*(11), 1887–1898. doi:10.1109/TCPMT.2014.2350015

ADDITIONAL READING

Li, P., Wang, D., Wang, L., & Lu, H. (2018). Deep visual tracking review and experimental comparison. *Pattern Recognition*, *76*, 323–338. doi:10.1016/j.patcog.2017.11.007

Puri, N. V., & Devale, P. R. (2012). Development of Human Tracking in Video Surveillance System for Activity Analysis. *Journal of Computational Engineering*, *4*(2), 26–30.

Xu, C., Wang, G., Yan, S., Yu, J., Zhang, B., Dai, S., Li, Y., & Xu, L. (2020). *Fast Vehicle and Pedestrian Detection Using Improved Mask R-CNN. In Mathematical Problems in Engineering*. Hindawi.

Chapter 5
An Efficient Markov Chain Model Development based Prefetching in Location-Based Services

Ajay Kumar Gupta
ⓘD https://orcid.org/0000-0001-9666-5047
M. M. M. University of Technology, India

Udai Shanker
ⓘD https://orcid.org/0000-0002-4083-7046
M. M. M. University of Technology, India

ABSTRACT

A quite significant issue with the current location-based services application is to securely store information for users on the network in order to quickly access the data items. One way to do this is to store data items that have a high likelihood of subsequent request. This strategy is known as proactive caching or prefetching. It is a technique in which selected information is cached before it is actually needed. In comparison, past constructive caching strategies showed high data overhead in terms of computing costs. Therefore, with the use of Markov chain model, the aim of this work is to address the above problems by an efficient user future position movement prediction strategy. For modeling of the proposed system to evaluate the feasibility of accessing information on the network for location-based applications, the client-server queuing model is used in this chapter. The observational findings indicate substantial improvements in caching efficiency to previous caching policies that did not use prefetch module.

DOI: 10.4018/978-1-7998-7756-1.ch005

INTRODUCTION

In the modern age, access to the information is quite easy (Ben et al., 2017)(Gupta & Shanker, 2020d)(Gupta & Shanker, 2020a). Users can quickly access data stored in videos, images, and sounds enabling the internet service providers to serve users in a better way. Proactive caching is a well-known methodology for performance optimization that significantly improves data look-ups. The past research claimed that latency (Cao, 2003) could be greatly decreased by embedding proactive caching phenomenon by helping the consumer to have easy access to the data without requesting from server and reduction in unnecessary overhead. Proactive caching (Darwish et al., 2018) focuses on the user's ability to anticipate mobility trends by travelling from one place to another in an environment in order to assess which data objects should be placed on which cache node depending on the frequency of content demanded by the users. The traditional prefetching strategies overcome the latency state of the processor only; the encouraging aim of the prefetching approach to be used against mobile devices, however, is to minimize both the time of processing as well as time for communication (Gupta & Shanker, 2020b)(Gupta & Shanker, 2020c). The problem statement for prefetching is also to suggest a new approach to reinforce the prefetch processing of a low network communication mobile device system (Gupta & Prakash, 2018). With the support of machine learning techniques, this approach improves customer satisfaction and optimizes cache access. Prefetching has been reported in recent studies to be a hot subject for research on computer-based web services. Informed mobile prefetching (IMP) architecture had been designed in (Patterson et al., 1995) to prefetch data using least recently used (LRU) cache, which utilizes costs & benefits analysis to handle the allocation of the disk buffer to competitive users. Previous prefetching research was built specifically for desktop environments, and is agnostic to resource limitations imposed by CPU, memory and mobile device's battery power (Gupta & Shanker, 2018a). As the main aim of prefetching was to minimize access latency, all of the prefetching logic might historically operate on the end computer. However, for a smartphone and tablet, the prefetching approach is a necessity to minimize the number of system resources request. Therefore, this chapter presents the prefetching process that may be appropriate for content caching in the mobile world by looking at this promising solution. This chapter's key contribution is to make a model to decide the data objects to be prefetched using the Markov model. Using the user's movement trajectory, the process of next location prediction through the mobility Markov chain model has the better accuracy and least error than that of previous forecasting methods used in caching.

Preliminary

This subsection has the definition of the terms used in this chapter.

Definition 1: Road Network- The road network is defined by an undirected graph G= (V, E), comprising set of road segments represented as E and set of intersections represented as V.

Definition 2: Location- It is the recorded position of given moving object in terms of latitude and longitude coordinates in two dimensional area of interest.

Definition 3: Markov chain- Let S be the set of all states. The sequence $\{M_t, 0 \le t\}$ is said to be a Markov chain, if for any i, j $\in$ S and $0 \le t$, the condition defined by equation 1, and equation 2 are true.

$$P\left\{M_{n+1} = j | M_0, \ldots\ldots, M_n\right\} = P\left\{M_{n+1} = j | M_n\right\} \tag{1}$$

Table 1. Terminology Description

Symbol	Description	Symbol	Description
O	Outlier	Z_{access}	Zipf access distribution parameter
Size_Rect	Size of the service area	Num_Scope	At different locations, the number of data items single values
D	Periodicity	π_j	Restrictive distribution
Query_Interval	Subsequent query average time interval	A	Latest estimation access probability biasing constant
POI_Num.	Point of interest count	$conf_{min}$	Minimum confidence threshold
N	Trajectories dataset count (number of users)	Query_Interval	Subsequent query average time interval
Band_Range	Bandwidth range	Moving Interval	Predicted region computation time interval
S_{min}	Minimum size of the data item	G	Road network undirected graph
C_Size_Ratio	Cache vs. database size	S	Set of all states
$P(S_j)$	Probability of jth state transition	m_{ij}	mean return time to identify the average time for particular states to return to itself,

$$P\left\{M_{n+1} = j | M_n = i\right\} = p_{ij} \tag{2}$$

The P_{ij} is the probability of transition to j^{th} state from i^{th} state. The matrix $P = (p_{ij})$ is the transition matrix of the chain and the transition probabilities satisfy $\sum_{j \in S} p_{ij} = 1$, where $i \in S$. This means that the likelihood that it will make a transition to another j^{th} state depends only on the ith state regardless of its past prior to time n (Pitman & Yor, 2018). It should be remembered here that it does not matter if the particle was in that state for just a fleeting moment or a lengthy period of time. Table 1 describes the various terminologies used in the chapter.

Problem Statement, Motivation & Summary of Contributions

To find the solution of real-world problems, there are number of well-known prediction approaches available. Examples of such predictive models include the ANN-Support Vector Machine (SVM), Empirical Mode Decomposition (SVR-Hybrid, & IMFs-Hybrid) (EMD-SVR-Hybrid), Autoregressive Moving Average Model (ARIMA), Seasonal ARIMA (SARIMA), Artificial Neural Networks (ANN), Fuzzy Time Series (FTS) (Gupta & Shanker, 2020e). Each model of prediction has its own strengths and expertise in tackling different problems in the real world. The Markov chain (Miguel, 2012) is one of the influential techniques developed to solve complex real-world problems such as model interrelationships, peak energy consumption estimation etc.

A special case of the stochastic process is the Markov chain which was termed after the Russian mathematician Andrei Andreevich Markov (Ruiz Espejo, 2002). This Methodology has recently been used to approximate the transitive matrix from the system observation states. It is a random mechanism in which the current state records all the information about the future. Furthermore, state transformation matrix and probability are the key components in designing the Markov chain model (Lee et al., 2016); both of which would summaries all the critical dynamic transformation parameters.

Through incorporating a revised solution to the unique next position prediction system and the cost role of data items capable of addressing LBS issues, the research challenge is to improve the cache hit ratio of the successful caching strategy (Gupta & Shanker, 2018c). The problem description can be described as below.

Problem Definition- Let $T = \{T_1, T_2, ..., T_N\}$ be the N trajectories containing historical trajectories from database. Here, the goal is to find the set of maximum data items that can be stored in prefetch cache storage to maximize the cache hit rate. To predict the set of data items, system finds the probable future location L_i through Markov chain model. The major contributions of this work are outlined below.

1. Proposal of a revised approach to improve the precision of the next location prediction procedure for designing of efficient prefetching method and reduction in the processing overhead.
2. Proposal of a revised data item's cost function using the distance between the client's estimated next locations to the reference point of a valid scope contributing to the cache hit ratio improvement using prefetching.
3. Analysis of efficiency and overhead of proposed caching scheme as compared to the previous schemes.

The composition of the chapter is as follows. The proposed methods are defined in section 2. Section 3 consequently illustrates the design and study of the simulation. Finally, the chapter is concluded in section 4 with the list of scopes for potential LBS study.

Proposed Method

In this research, the Markov chain technique was adopted to improve the precision of the next location prediction procedure for the designing of efficient prefetching method and reducing the processing overhead. Incorporation of the simplest method of statistical dependency in prediction model of the proposed method is a stochastic operation. The future functioning in prediction model is not concerned with previous behavior. The hierarchical caching design in proposed policy has shown in Figure 1.

Figure 1. System Architecture

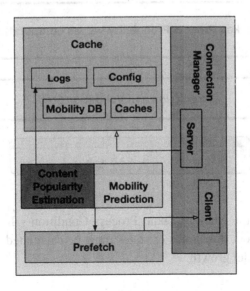

Markov Chain Based Mobility Prediction

Past mobility models, such as Apriori feature-based candidate generate-test techniques have the drawback that they form a large number of candidate sets and are repeatedly evaluated by matching patterns. To reduce this processing overhead, efficient Markov chain (EMC)- prefetching is being proposed in this chapter. As the movement of users satisfies the Markov property, EMC-prefetching is based on the Markov chain. The proposed Markov chain process algorithms consist of five steps that are being shown in Figure 2.

Figure 2. Steps in Markov chain model

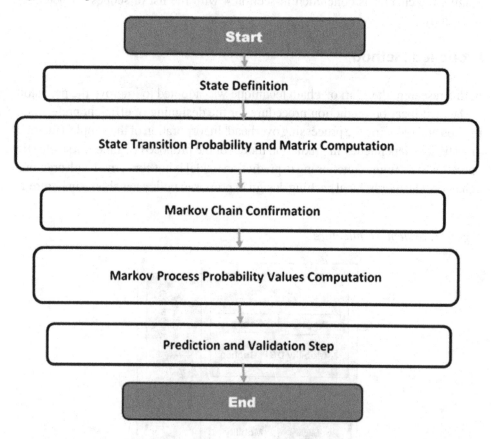

Step 1. Define the Markov Chain Process Condition - In this phase for the Markov chain method, thresholds or states must be calculated on the basis of the data used in the model growth.

Step 2. Build the matrix of state transition, N, and probability of state transition- As defined by the Markov chain, the transition matrix N of state indicates the observed frequency of state transition. Therefore,

$$N = \begin{vmatrix} n_{11} & \cdots & \cdots & n_{1s} \\ . & \cdots & \cdots & . \\ . & \cdots & \cdots & . \\ n_{s1} & \cdots & \cdots & n_{ss} \end{vmatrix}$$

Where transitions count of state i to state j is depicted by n_{ij}. For each state of the Markov chain model, we assumed P be the transition matrix which represents all the concerned transition probabilities. P is, therefore, denoted as per given below.

$$P = \begin{vmatrix} p_{11} & \cdots & \cdots & p_{1s} \\ . & \cdots & \cdots & . \\ . & \cdots & \cdots & . \\ p_{s1} & \cdots & \cdots & p_{ss} \end{vmatrix}, i, j \in I,$$

Then,

$$P\left\{ M_{n+1} = j | M_n = i \right\} = p_{ij} \tag{3}$$

The terms given in equation 3 are used for one-step probability of homogenous or stationary Markov chain. The transition probabilities in this Markov chain are independent of time t. The property given by equation 4 is prevalent in the transition matrix P.

$$P(n) = P \times P^{n-1} = P^n \tag{4}$$

Step 3. The ergodic properties confirmation in Markov chain- In order to define the presence of restrictive distribution in this chain by classifying the condition of P, proof of an ergodic Markov chain must be made. The existence of aperiodic states and positive recurrent are concluded as ergodic. The ergodic properties can be classified into three pieces as given below.

1. Irreducible-. The Markov chain could be deduced as irreducible when there is just one class and the two states communicate in this same class.

2. Periodicity- Let d is the largest integer and n is not divisible by d, then d is said to be period of State i. In this case, $P_{ii}^{(n)} = 0$. The Markov Chain is known as aperiodic because of each state of this model has a period of one.

3. 3. Transient and Recurrent States- Assume f_i be the probability of re-entering the given state from its starting state i, then state i is said to be transient if f_i < 1 and recurrent if $f_i = 1$. The recurrent condition for finite Markov chain is met only in case given by equation 5.

$$\sum_{n=1}^{\infty} P_{ii}^{(n)} = \infty \tag{5}$$

Step 4. Probability values computation for Markov process- The mean return time and stationary probability distribution for Markov process can be obtained for this step. In long-term forecasting, stationary probability distribution can be characterized by the behavior of air emissions, where the chain is appropriate for a long period of time with stable-state probability which do not depends on the starting conditions (Trivedi, 2016). The restrictive distribution π_j exists for the stationary distribution of probability for an ergodic Markov chain and can be defined by equation 6.

$$\pi_j = \lim_{n \to \infty} P\{M_n = j | M_0 = i\} \tag{6}$$

Then, $P_j(n) = \sum_k P_k(n-1) P_{kj}$ becomes $\sum_k \pi_k P_{kj}$ as n $\to \infty$ for j = 0, 1, 2, . etc.

Therefore, the likelihood of having the process in state j is independent of the starting condition over a long period of time in the process. If the likelihood of the incidence of state j is high, the value of π_j will be more (Grinstead & Snell, 2021). In addition to it, it is important to measure the mean return time to identify the average time for the particular states to return to itself, m_j. It can be given by $m_{ij} = 1 / \pi_j$.

Step 5. Forecasting and model validation- The forecast measure can be derived from the equation using the initial likelihood and probability of state transition. It is given by equation 7.

$$P\left(S_j\right) = \sum_{i=1}^{n} P\left(S_i\right) P_{ij} \tag{7}$$

where, P_{ij} is a probability of state transition and $P(Si)$ is an initial probability. The Chi-square test is used for model validation to verify the validity of the Markov chain based on the independence assumption (Zhou et al., 2018). The alternate hypothesis is that the consecutive time data selected is dependent, while the null hypothesis is that the consecutive time data selected is independent.

$$\chi^2_{calculated} = \sum \frac{\left(Expected - Observed\right)^2}{Expected} \tag{8}$$

The null hypothesis is rejected when $\chi^2_{calculated}$ given by equation 8 is greater than $\chi^2_{tabulated}$ on the 0.05 critical regions (Zhou et al., 2018).

Efficient Markov Chain (EMC) Enrooted Next Location Prediction Based Prefetching

A proactive caching framework focused on the mobility paradigm known as EMC-prefetching is being suggested in this chapter. EMC-prefetching method has been proposed to estimate future movement routes, which is included in the revised cost feature to increase the cache impact ratio. Prefetching is performed to keep the hot data items in cache for subsequent request. The proposed policy is intended to identify the cache data items having the maximum cost for data item. The formal definition of the prefetching function can be given by equation 9.

$$\max(\sum_{di \in S} \cos t\left(i\right)) \, And \, \sum_{d_i \in S} objSize\left(d_i\right) > \text{Total Prefetch Occupied Cache Size} \tag{9}$$

If the valid scope of data items has a larger area, then the probability of revisiting it in the region is greater. The different input parameters in the estimation of data item cost as defined in equation 10 for cache replacement are the distance from the relevant scope to the actual client location, data item size, valid scope, and probability of the access.

$$\text{Cos}\,t_i = \begin{cases} \dfrac{1}{D'(vs(d_i))} \cdot \dfrac{P_i \cdot A(vs(d_i))}{S_i} \cdot \dfrac{\lambda_i}{\mu_i} & \text{if } vs(d_i) \notin \text{pred\_Reg} \\[4mm] \dfrac{1}{\min(L_r, D(vs(d_i)))} \cdot \dfrac{P_i \cdot A(vs(d_i))}{S_i} \cdot \dfrac{\lambda_i}{\mu_i} & \text{if } vs(d_i) \int \text{pred\_Reg} \end{cases} \quad (10)$$

The access possibility is represented by P_i and has zero as its initial value. The area of any data items' valid scope is represented by function $A()$. Let, the last access time to the ith data element is t_i^1, then the update function of access likelihood can be described by the equation 11 as given below.

$$P_i = \frac{1-\alpha}{P_i} + \frac{\alpha}{t_c - t_i^l} \quad (11)$$

The next position anticipation algorithm is used for selecting the data items for prefetching in the cache. The user next position estimation integrated with Markov chain matrix-based procedure is described in the earlier section. Using the next predicted location, the distance from the client's next predicted location to the reference point of the data object's valid scope may be defined. The mobility regulations were interpreted through the Markov mobility matrix depending upon the similarity between the users' movement logs. The approach effectively increases the cache hit ratio relative to earlier policies due to the specific integration of the next location prediction feature in data item cost computation. The distance between reference point $L_i = (Lx_i, Ly_i)$ for the valid scope of ith data item and client's estimated next locations $L_{am} = (Lx_{am}, Ly_{am})$ for the next query data item (d_i) is given by $D(vs(d_i))$ as defined by equation 12.

$$D(vs(d_i)) = |(L_{am} - L_i)| = \sqrt{(Ly_{am} - Ly_i)^2 + (Lx_{am} - Lx_i)^2} \quad (12)$$

The distance between the predicted region center to the reference point of valid scope is expressed by $D'(vs(d_i))$ as given in equation 13.

$$D'(vs(d_i)) = |L_p - L_i| \sqrt{(Ly_p - Ly_i)^2 + (Lx_p - Lx_i)^2} \quad (13)$$

At the query issue time for client m, the velocity, current position, and reference point of valid scope are rpresented by V_m, $L_m = (L_{xm}, L_{ym})$ and $L_i = (L_{xi}, L_{yi})$ respectively.

The average update rate and average query rate are defined by μ_i and λ_i respectively for the ith data set. In this strategy, the revised cost function is proposed that enhances the temporal locality functionality by query rate to update the rate ratio.

EVALUATION OF PROPOSED MODEL

The evaluation was conducted on Octa-core 3.2 GHz, RAM of 64 GB, Windows 8 operating system, and Intel i7 processor. The processing time overhead (Sadri et al., 2021) of the query and service schedule are assumed to be negligible in the proposed model. LBSs have drawn millions of users and their digital footprints are massively contained. The query process and interval process are the two modules executed for the simulation of the proposed model.

Data Collection and API States

The 10 month's duration data of foursquare check-in in New York is used to evaluate the feasibility of our proposed approach and the data availability. The cumulative points count is about 227,428 check-ins with each check-in is associated with 8 attributes. A location-dependent k-nearest neighbor query (e.g. nearest hospital profile info) is continuously generated by the query process with the exponential distributed query interval. We used Fortune's algorithm to create a Voronoi diagram (O'Rourke, 1994) from a series of points in a plane. The Fortune algorithm uses the logical surface of the sweep to solve various challenges of Euclidean space. The fortune algorithm follows empty circle condition as depicted in Figure 3.

Figure 3. Voronoi Diagram Properties

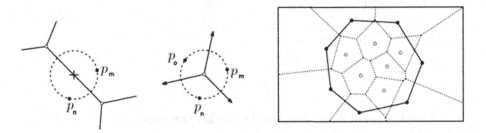

Empty Circle Condition- In a given edge of Voronoi diagram, every point is equidistant from its two nearest neighbors p_m and p_n. Thus, there is a circle centered at any such point, where p_m and p_n lie on this circle and no other site is interior to the circle. In Figure 4, the Voronoi diagrams for 110 and 220 data objects are represented.

Figure 4. Scope Distribution

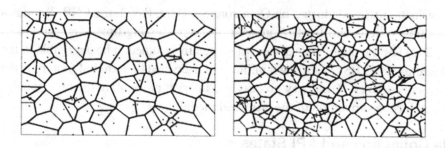

In the Foursquare data set, an extra attribute namely queried data item is also added. This attribute defines the details of the data item associated with a given check-in location using the corresponding valid scope of the Voronoi diagram.

For performance analysis of the model, the effects of variation in query inter-arrival time and cache size are plotted with the cache hit ratio. The interval process is also exponentially distributed for the computation of predicted regions. The access pattern for data items follows a Zipf distribution (Kumar et al., 2008) to simulate non-uniform distribution for access to a data item. The data items are arranged in such a way that 0th data item be the most frequently accessed and $(DB_{Size} - 1)^{th}$ data item be the least frequently accessed. The Zipf probability equation given below is used for i^{th} data item access probability.

$$\text{Zipf}_{\text{Prob}}(i) = \frac{\dfrac{1}{i^{Z_{access}}}}{\sum_{j=1}^{U}\left(\dfrac{1}{j^{Z_{access}}}\right)}$$

where, the total count of data items and Zipf ratio are represented by U and Z_{access} respectively. In the case of $Z_{access} = 0$, the uniform access pattern with common likelihood is used for every data item. Skewness in access pattern has been shown with the increasing value of Z_{access}.

Discussion

In this subsection, we discuss the simulation results from the application of the Proactive caching strategy. For simulation of proposed strategies, we use Matlab software. Here, we have compared the various existing caching policies such as LRU (Xu et al., 2004), FAR (Ren & Dunham, 2000), MPRRP (Gupta & Shanker, 2018b) and SPMC-CRP (Gupta & Shanker, 2019) content caching without prefetch and then we use with integration of proposed EMC-prefetch based model. The various cache

Figure 5. Cache Replacement Schemes without Prefetching Procedure

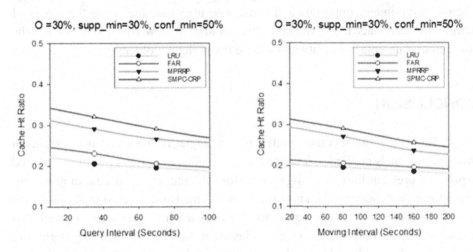

Figure 6. Cache Replacement Schemes with EMC-Prefetching Procedure

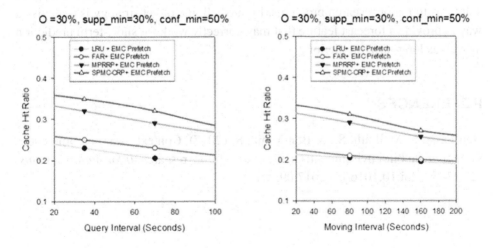

replacement policies compared for caching efficiency with and without proposed prefetching policy as depicted in Figure 5 and Figure 6 respectively. The proposed policy uses a cost/benefit analysis to decide when and if to prefetch the given data object in available prefetch size of cache. The prefetching is done such a way that the hot data items of user current location are prefetched with a threshold time interval or on displacement of user from its previous location. The EMC-prefetching method is used to fill the data items in cache with its full capacity in proactive manner prior to user request.

One may see how prefetching policy logic separates the different ordinary page and loads to analyze vulnerability existing in the prefetching. There is a vulnerability existing in prefetching if a malicious page is pre-fetched rather than visited directly. Therefore, it is indeed important to do further security research giving the benefit of marginally faster page loads. In future, we would try to develop the model for cache continuous data object security and reduce the prefetch vulnerability.

CONCLUSION

We analyzed the issue of current prefetching strategies from various perspectives in this article, namely prediction functions, access methods, and uncertainty. Compared to previous prefetch-based caching policies for LBS, the projected area computation-based location-dependent data prefetching performed as described in the proposed policy achieves substantial cache hit ratio performance improvement. We concluded that it is essential for the database researchers to think to offer scalable, generic, and complete caching solutions over Spatio-temporal data for mobile objects feasible to be combined with traditional DBMSs. We have also addressed key research challenges that researchers should take into consideration while planning to construct solutions to major research problems. In nutshell, the target strategy is to devise a way to provide a forecast feature that may correctly work for short-term prediction as well as long-term prediction.

REFERENCES

Ben Sassi, I., Mellouli, S., & Ben Yahia, S. (2017). Context-aware recommender systems in mobile environment: On the road of future research. *Information Systems*, *72*, 27–61. doi:10.1016/j.is.2017.09.001

Cao, G. (2003). A scalable low-latency cache invalidation strategy for mobile environments. *IEEE Transactions on Knowledge and Data Engineering*, *15*(5), 1251–1265. doi:10.1109/TKDE.2003.1232276

Darwish, S. M., El-Zoghabi, A., & El-Shnawy, A. G. (2018). Proactive cache replacement technique for mobile networks based on genetic programming. *IET Networks*, *7*(6), 376–383. doi:10.1049/iet-net.2017.0261

Grinstead, C., & Snell, J. L. (2021). Introduction to probability (2nd rev. ed). Academic Press.

Gupta, A. K., & Prakash, S. (2018). Secure Communication in Cluster-Based Ad Hoc Networks: A Review. In D. K. Lobiyal, V. Mansotra, & U. Singh (Eds.), *Advances in Intelligent Systems and Computing* (pp. 537–545). Springer Singapore.

Gupta, A. K., & Shanker, U. (2018a). Location dependent information system's queries for mobile environment. Lecture Notes in Computer Science (Including Subseries Lecture Notes in Artificial Intelligence and Lecture Notes in Bioinformatics), 10829 LNCS. doi:10.1007/978-3-319-91455-8_19

Gupta, A. K., & Shanker, U. (2018b). Modified predicted region based cache replacement policy for location-dependent data in mobile environment. *Procedia Computer Science*, *125*, 917–924. Advance online publication. doi:10.1016/j.procs.2017.12.117

Gupta, A. K., & Shanker, U. (2018c). CELPB: A cache invalidation policy for location dependent data in mobile environment. *ACM International Conference Proceeding Series*. 10.1145/3216122.3216147

Gupta, A. K., & Shanker, U. (2019). SPMC-PRRP: A Predicted Region Based Cache Replacement Policy. In Lecture Notes in Networks and Systems (Vol. 39). doi:10.1007/978-981-13-0277-0_26

Gupta, A. K., & Shanker, U. (2020a). A Literature Review of Location-Aware Computing Policies: Taxonomy and Empirical Analysis in Mobile Environment. *International Journal of Mobile Human Computer Interaction*, *12*(3), 21–45. doi:10.4018/IJMHCI.2020070102

Gupta, A. K., & Shanker, U. (2020b). MAD-RAPPEL: Mobility Aware Data Replacement &Prefetching Policy Enrooted LBS. *Journal of King Saud University - Computer and Information Sciences*.

Gupta, A. K., & Shanker, U. (2020c). OMCPR: Optimal Mobility Aware Cache Data Pre-fetching and Replacement Policy Using Spatial K-Anonymity for LBS. *Wireless Personal Communications, 114*(2), 949–973. doi:10.100711277-020-07402-2

Gupta, A. K., & Shanker, U. (2020d). Some Issues for Location Dependent Information System Query in Mobile Environment. *29th ACM International Conference on Information and Knowledge Management (CIKM '20)*, 4. doi:10.1145/3340531.3418504

Gupta, A. K., & Shanker, U. (2020d). Study of fuzzy logic and particle swarm methods in map matching algorithm. doi:10.100742452-020-2431-y

Kumar, A., Misra, M., & Sarje, A. K. (2008). A Predicted Region based Cache Replacement Policy for Location Dependent Data in Mobile Environment. *10th Inter-Research-Institute Student Seminar in Computer Science, IIIT Hyderabad, 7*(February), 1–8.

Lee, S., Lim, J., Park, J., & Kim, K. (2016). *Next Place Prediction Based on Spatiotemporal Pattern Mining of Mobile Device Logs*. 1–19. doi:10.339016020145

Miguel, N. (2012). *Next Place Prediction using Mobility Markov Chains*. Academic Press.

O'Rourke, J. (1994). *Computational geometry in C* (2nd ed.). Cambridge University Press.

Patterson, R. H., Gibson, G. A., Ginting, E., Stodolsky, D., & Zelenka, J. (1995). Informed Prefetching and Caching. *Proceedings of the Fifteenth ACM Symposium on Operating Systems Principles*, 79–95. 10.1145/224056.224064

Pitman, J., & Yor, M. (2018). *A guide to Brownian motion and related stochastic processes*. Academic Press.

Ren, Q., & Dunham, M. H. (2000). Using Semantic Caching to Manage Location Dependent Data in Mobile Computing. 6th ACM/IEEE Mobile Computing and Networking (MobiCom), 3, 210–221.

Ruiz Espejo, M. (2002). Review of Statisticians of the Centuries. Computational Statistics & Data Analysis, 40, 209–210.

Sadri, A. A., Rahmani, A. M., Saberikamarposhti, M., & Hosseinzadeh, M. (2021). Fog data management: A vision, challenges, and future directions. *Journal of Network and Computer Applications, 174*, 102882. Advance online publication. doi:10.1016/j.jnca.2020.102882

Trivedi, K. (2016). *Discrete-Time Markov Chains*. doi:10.1002/9781119285441.ch7

Xu, J., Hu, Q., Lee, W.-C., & Lee, D. L. (2004). Performance evaluation of an optimal cache replacement policy for wireless data dissemination. *IEEE Transactions on Knowledge and Data Engineering*, *16*(1), 125–139. doi:10.1109/TKDE.2004.1264827

Zhou, Y., Wang, L., Zhong, R., & Tan, Y. (2018). A Markov Chain Based Demand Prediction Model for Stations in Bike Sharing Systems. *Mathematical Problems in Engineering*, *2018*, 1–8. doi:10.1155/2018/8028714

Chapter 6
Design of a Smart ATM Using a Bio–Inspired Watch Dog Mechanism

S. Geetha
Sri Manakula Vinayagar Engineering College, India

V. Prasanna Venkatesan
Pondicherry University, India

Madhusudanan J.
Sri Manakula Vinayagar Engineering College, India

ABSTRACT

The innovation of smart technologies has made the world into a connected network with "any where, any time, any thing" type of services. The current world has moved to a new environment where more smart gadgets and facilities are used by people. ATM is one such facility where context-aware features may be seen and also exposed to security threats. An intelligent and strong mechanism is needed to protect the ATM from attacks. Apart from the existing alert-based monitoring facility, there is a need to defend against the attackers. Currently, ATMs are said to be Smart ATMs, but really, whether they are smart enough to handle the critical situations is questionable. In this regard, this chapter focuses on designing phases considering the features such as context-awareness, monitoring, decision-making ability, and intelligence.

DOI: 10.4018/978-1-7998-7756-1.ch006

1. INTRODUCTION

Now-a-days portable devices have become a part of everyday life. The pervasive computing environment includes a wide variety of devices and services from different manufacturers and developers. As these systems have become smart and act according to the context of the situation they are also termed as Smart Systems. Therefore achieving platform and Vendor independence as well as architecture openness have become more efficient before pervasive computing spaces become common places for communication. Privacy, Trust on the devices in the environment and security of the connected network devices are the major security issues in the pervasive world. Whether the smart devices are connected through a secured network connection? Are the security provided to these smart systems are not adequate to handle the attacks done on them.

Context is one of the major keyword in the pervasive smart environments where the security requirements have to be provided based on the context of the devices working environment. The Smart devices and environments are connected with unknown networks for continuous communication of data to the users. The knowledge about the security of these networks is not provided to the users.

Due to the lack of proper security, Smart systems attackers have evolved more and more threats into this field. Handling of these threats has become a big challenge for the researchers in the smart world.

Since the smart environment is connected and open, the network monitoring of the devices and environment continuously is a necessary task. Monitoring the activities of the devices and users in the environment will help to find whether any abnormal behavior is carried out in the smart world. Thus if any abnormal behavior is identified security measures can be provided according to the context of the environment.

Therefore a decision making mechanism with intelligence provided to decide on the needed solutions for security is necessary for the Pervasive smart environment. This work is an attempt to develop a security model with context-awareness, intelligence, monitoring and decision making process for the Pervasive Smart Systems.

Sensing plays a major role in the smart world. Sensing the activities of the devices will help in improving the security of the environment. The model includes sensing as one of the process to monitor the activities of the various devices that are present in the smart environment. Location context plays an important role in the pervasive environment. The location of the devices has to be monitored for their abnormal activities to identify where the critical activity is carried out. The rest of the content is organized as section 2 with literature review, section 3 briefs about the proposed system; section 4 explains a case study on smart ATM, section 5 is the discussion about the performance of model compared with other existing security models and section 6 is the conclusion.

2. LITERATURE REVIEW

The challenges and requirements to develop a security model for the Pervasive Smart Environment are very difficult as the heterogeneity and complexity of these systems are very high. The security policies developed should operate across the multiple domains of the Pervasive Smart Environment automatically according to the context which should be easier to use and self-adaptive. An intelligent system should support the quality of analyzing the security issues according to the context and should adapt accordingly. Therefore an efficient security model which suitably adapts according to the changes in the environment is needed in the current state of pervasive smart environment security (Tapalina Bhattasali et al, 2017).

According to Yuxin Chen, et.al,(2012), smart appliances are not yet equipped with smart security protection mechanisms to defend against cyber attacks. Petteri Alahuhta, et.al (2010) has stated that, remote surveillance of the smart home is not enough to secure it. Security requires on-the-spot checks and back-up systems if something goes wrong. False 'automatic' alarms could be an issue in the future to the extent that they become counterproductive and ignored. GMV Soluciones Globales Internet, S.AU, (2011) has discussed about various ATM risks as "Many security incidents in ATM networks are currently not detected and thus the rate of occurrence of breaches is usually underestimated". Based on the report of Security Digest on skimming a global ATM threat, December 2013, it is clear that, a strong ATM room is necessary and is the first level of defense against ATM attacks. This also indicates the location of ATM room is to be monitored. According to the January 2016 report of Bank info Security, malwares are designed to trick the users to get diverted into their websites by the links and pop-ups that are being displayed on the screen to make all kinds of phishing attacks in the device. Md. Shoriful Islam (2014), have suggested improving the user's knowledge level about the threats and their smartness needed to overcome these issues. According to Jason Cornwell, et al., (2006), the demand for increasing flexibility grows in a pervasive environment and it is essential to develop a security policy that is understandable for the users to be used at various contexts accordingly. According to Max Landman (2010), the unusual mix of personal and business use for smart phones as well as their unique combination of capabilities creates a number of challenges to manage their risk. According to Petros Belimpasakis and Vlad Stirbu (2012), home network when attached to the public Internet, is exposed to the threats of hackers and viruses.

Sensing the activities of the devices will help in improving the security of the environment. When comparing the sensing capability of dog and humans, the dog's sensing power is found to be ten thousand times more than humans (Bruce Dwyer, Dog Walkers, Melbourne). The sensing process of dogs has been taken as an inspiration for the design of bio-inspired smart security model for pervasive smart environment.

3. PROPOSED SYSTEM

The idea of pervasive computing has changed the world in such a way that almost every device we see today is capable of communicating and exchanging the data in collaboration with one another. The objective of the proposed work is to develop a generic security model to provide better security to the pervasive systems. The architecture consists of Context layer, Device layer, Security manager, Autonomy Manager and Intelligent manager. People are connected to many computational devices simultaneously without even knowing their existence in the smart environment. This sudden change from a normal environment to a smart one has raised more and more security issues to the smart world. Thus to handle the security of the smart environment a better and an intelligent model is required to continue with its successes in the future.

The Proposed architecture model is developed with various layers like Threat Analyzer Layer, Threat Knowledge Manager Layer and Threat Handler Layer. To develop a better and intelligent security model, the proposed model is divided into various phases considering the features such as Context-awareness, Monitoring, Decision Making ability and Intelligence. The various phases of the security model are

1. Sensing Process
2. Inferencing Process
3. Decision Making
4. Action Performing

Sensing

Various activities carried out in the Smart Environment are sensed. The activities are compared with the stored activities in the database. If any change in the activity is identified, it has to be monitored and security measures have to be provided.

Inferencing

The sensed activity is analyzed for its levels of criticality that will be created by its action in the smart environment, if allowed to proceed. The Inferencing Engine will evaluate the criticality of the activity with the data stored in the database and will infer the level of criticality as dangerous or non-dangerous. The Inferencing engine will send these details to the Threat handler for deciding on the security measures that are to be taken for that particular activity in the environment and also according to the various contexts of the environment.

Decision Making

For the identified dangerous and critical situations, smarter security action has to be provided. The Threat handler will act as a decision maker in the proposed model. It will make decision on what security steps are to be carried out for the identified critical activity/situation. It will suggest the security measure that is to be taken based on the dangerous level of the activity/situation. If additional verification and validation are needed, then it also will be specified for the security of the smart environment.

Action Performing

The suggested security measure has to be implemented in the system. These security actions are performed by various devices that are available in the environment. The Policy implementor will inform who has to carry out the security action. Based on the context, the policy implementor will select the implementor (Access Control, Authenticator and Cryptography) to perform the action that is to be carried out. Warning and Alert signals are raised by the Access Control Implementor.

Informing Transactions with Location Details

All the observed activities in the ATM room, either done by the customer or by the hacker are sent to both the bank as well the customer. This involves the location details of the ATM for future analysis.

Figure 1. Proposed Architecture Layers with various Phases

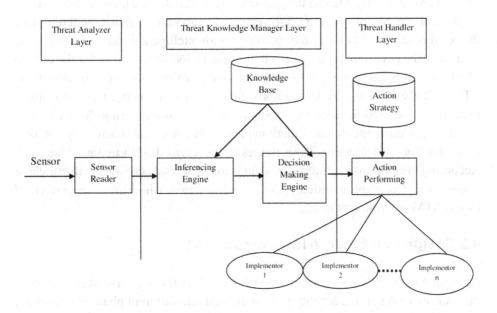

4. CASE STUDY ON SMART ATM

4.1 Introduction

In recent years, more criminal activities are carried out in ATM centers. Fraud of attacking the ATM machine for cash has increased more. Hacking the pin number of the card or placing skimming devices in ATM to steal the customer's account information has also been increased. The fradulers have become so smart that they make cloning of the ATM cards and directly transfer the cash from the machine or customer's account to their accounts. Though more security measures are being followed to avoid these types of attacks to ATMs, they are not yet completely stopped. The report of CDAC's Information Security Awareness about ATM threats, **(CDAC Report, May 2016)** states that fraudsters place a folded piece of plastic film into the ATM card slot which holds the card and will not allow to be expelled by the machine.

Diebold **(Axis Solutions Report, 2016)**, a worldwide ATM machine supplier has analyzed about various risks related to ATM and has concluded that the risks for ATM come in three categories, namely physical threat (Breaking the ATM machine), Logical threat (Malwares) and frauds (Skimming).

The literature review clearly describes that an intelligent and strong mechanism is needed to protect the ATM's attack. The existing alert based monitoring is not sufficient enough to defend against the attackers. Currently ATMs are said to be Smart ATMs but really whether they are smart enough to handle the critical situations is questionable. Simply adding smart security features and activities will not make the ATM Smarter. They have to be provided with intelligence and according to the context of the environment they have to make decision on their own for the critical situations. Monitoring the various activities and emotions of the person coming to ATM will also help the banks to improve its security in a better way. IR Camera Sensors can be used to sense the emotions of the person entering the ATM. The emotions are differentiated as Emotional and Non emotional where they can be a Critical or Non-critical action. The activities are categorized as Normal and Abnormal. According to emotions captured, the normal and abnormal activities with critical or non-critical effects are provided with a remedial action, which are to be performed by the ATM environment itself.

4.2 Design of a Smart ATM Environment

According to the proposed security model, to achieve the objective of smartness in the security of ATM, the activity flow is divided into different phase like Sensing, Inference, Decision Making and Action Performer phase.

Sensing Phase

In this phase the IR (Infrared) Camera inside the ATM will capture the emotions of the person. The **camera** converts that **infrared** data into an electronic image that shows the apparent surface temperature of the object being measured. Based on the temperature measured, the emotions are compared with the emotion level stored in the database. If it matches the user is said to be emotional and is monitored to identify whether any activity is done wrongly due to his emotional state. The CCTV camera parallelly monitors the activities of the person. The activities captured are compared with the various abnormal activities stored in the database. If the activity matches with the wrong activity in the database then the user is performing an abnormal activity. The normal activity is again compared with the routine activity to find whether any irregular activity is carried out by the person.

Figure 2. Design of a Smart ATM environment

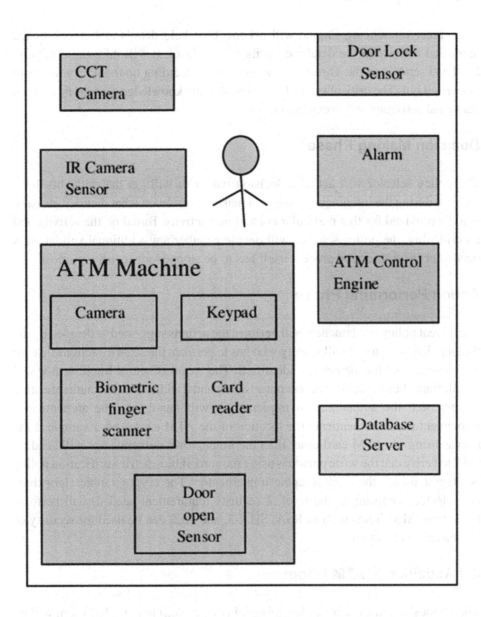

If the activity is irregular then validation has to be done. Based on the user's emotional state and operations done in the ATM machine, the trust analyzer will analyze the trust value of the user every time. The context of the user, Activity and trust levels are taken for generating the threshold value of the threat identified.

Inferencing Phase

The Threat Inferencing Engine will get the Threshold details and compares the identified activity in the database for its critical level. It will infer the criticality level and sends it to the Threat policy selector for deciding on the policy that is to be carried out. The criticality levels are stored in the knowledge repository for both abnormal activities and irregular activities.

Decision Making Phase

The policy selector will act as a decision maker. It will get the criticality level inferred during the inferencing phase and makes decision on what security measure is to be provided for that particular context and activity. Based on the activity and its criticality, the policy selector will decide whether any additional validation is needed or the transaction process itself has to be stopped for security purpose.

Action Performing Phase

The Threat policy implementor will perform the actions suggested or decided by the threat policy selector. It will specify who has to perform the security actions that are to be carried out for the activity identified. The Access Control Implementor will handle the policies related to access permissions and if additional OTP authentication is suggested the authentication implementor will handle it. The authenticator implementor will authenticate the location of the ATM card used. Example if the user is using his ATM card other than the home, town authenticator will send an OTP to verify that the write person is using the card. If bio-metric verification policy is suggested then the cryptographic implementor (The cryptographic algorithms are selected according to the level of security requirement needed) will perform the action. Algorithms such as RSA, SHA-3, and AES can be used for security of bio-metric verification.

4.3 Activities in ATM Room

The various activities (like card swiping, pin entry, etc.,) in the ATM room will be stored in the database for monitoring purpose. The abnormal activities and irregular activities that are identified to be performed in the ATM are tabulated in the Table 1 and Table 2. The criticality level and the corresponding activity are specified. If any new activities are identified then they will be updated in the database. The threshold ranges for the various actions in the ATM environment are given in the Table 3.

Table 1. Abnormal Activities for ATM Room

Criticality Level	Activity Identified
Critical 1	Placing any Skimming device or camera on the ATM machine.
Critical 2	Doing any changes to the card reader point, keyboard and Monitor of the ATM.
Critical 3	Trying to open the ATM machine or breaking the Machine using any tool.
Critical 4	Switching off the cameras, sensors, Routers, light, AC, Alarms placed, Switches in the ATM Room.
Critical 5	Placing any object over the camera, ATM machine and sensors to divert the camera footage capturing.
Non-Critical	Spoiling the ATM room by splitting on the floor or wall. Laying or sitting inside the ATM room.

Table 2. Irregular Activities for ATM Room

Criticality Level	Activity Identified
Critical 1	Withdrawal of huge amount from the account than usual by the person.
Critical 2	Making any changes to the account details, i.e., trying to change the PIN frequently or changing the personal details emotionally other than usual manner.
Critical 3	Taking cash on unusual time than his/her regular cash withdrawal time. Entering the PIN wrongly for more times.
Non-Critical	Performs a normal transaction process.

Table 3. Threshold Ranges for Action Performing in ATM Environment

	NORMAL	LOW	HIGH
IR SENSING	22^0 C-34.9^{0}C	<21^{0}C	35^{0}C-45^{0}C
ACTIVITY SENSING	-20>0<20	<-20	>20
OPERATION SENSING	= = 20%	<20%	>20%

4.4 Experimentation Results of Smart ATM Environment

The experimentation was conducted to evaluate the performance of all the layers with different cases. A sample size of 30 test cases with users with emotional state and non-emotional state were taken. The images of the person were captured using a IR camera and the thermal images captured was tested for their emotions using the Lunapic tool which is an open tool available for calculating the emotions of a given image using the thermal color ranges available.

Table 4. Actual Test Case for Smart ATM

Test Cases	Input Sensed	Input Context	Input Behavior	Threshold Value	Test Cases	Input Sensed	Input Context	Input Behavior	Threshold Value
Test Case 1	U,N	E	R	0,1,0	Test Case 16	U,N	NE	R	0,0,0
Test Case 2	U,N	NE	R	0 ,0,0					
Test Case 3	U, N	E	I	0,1,1	Test Case 17	U,N	NE	I	0,0,2
Test Case 4	U,N	NE	I	0,0,2					
Test Case 5	U,A	E	R	1,1,0	Test Case 18	U,A	E	R	3,1,0
Test Case 6	U,A	NE	R	2 ,0,0					
Test Case 7	U, A	E	I	3,1,1	Test Case 19	U,A	E	I	2,1,0
Test Case 8	U,A	NE	I	3,0,2					
Test Case 9	U,N	NE	R	0,0,0	Test Case 20	U,N	E	I	0,1,1
Test Case 10	U,N	NE	I	0,0,2					
Test Case 11	U,A	E	R	3,1,0	Test Case 21	U,N	E	R	0,1,0
Test Case 12	U,A	E	I	3,1,0					
Test Case 13	U,A	NE	R	2,0,0	Test Case 22	U,N	NE	R	0 ,0,0
Test Case 14	U,N	NE	R	0,0,0					
Test Case 15	U,A	E	I	1,1,2	Test Case 23	U. N	E	I	0,0,1
					Test Case 24	U,N	NE	I	0,0,2
					Test Case 25	U,A	E	R	4,1,0
					Test Case 26	U,A	NE	R	5,0,0
					Test Case 27	U,N	NE	I	0,0,3
					Test Case 28	U,A	E	R	3,1,0
					Test Case 29	U,A	E	I	4,1,0
					Test Case 30	U,N	E	I	0,1,1

U-User; N-Normal; A- Abnormal; E-Emotional; NE-Non-Emotional; O-Other; H-Home; R-Regular; I-Irregular

The Threat Analyzer layer considers the various context of the environment, the activity of the input sensed and the trusted behavior of the input sensed for performance evaluation. A description about the various data sensed for analysis and the method of generating the threshold value for each test case in Smart ATM is shown in Table 4. Here, if the input activity is normal, it is set as 0, the value 1 is set for critical activity 1, 2 for critical 2, 3 for critical 3, 4 for critical 4 and 5 for critical 5. For emotional state, the value is 1 and for non-emotional, it is 0. If it is a regular behavior, it is represented as 0 and for irregular behavior - 1 is set for irregular behavior 1, 2 for irregular 2 and 3 for irregular behavior 3.

Table 5. Predicted Output for Test Cases

Test Cases	Input Sensed	Input Context	Input Behavior	Threshold Value	Test Cases	Input Sensed	Input Context	Input Behavior	Threshold Value
Test Case 1	U,N	E	R	0,1,0	Test Case 16	U,N	NE	R	0,0,0
Test Case 2	U,N	NE	R	0,0,0	Test Case 17	U,N	E	R	0,1,0
Test Case 3	U, N	E	I	0,1,1	Test Case 18	U,A	E	R	3,1,0
Test Case 4	U,N	NE	I	0,0,2	Test Case 19	U,N	E	I	0,1,2
Test Case 5	U,A	E	R	1,1,0	Test Case 20	U,N	E	I	0,1,1
Test Case 6	U,A	NE	R	2,0,0	Test Case 21	U,N	E	R	0,1,0
Test Case 7	U, A	E	I	3,1,1	Test Case 22	U,N	NE	R	0,0,0
Test Case 8	U,A	NE	I	3,0,2	Test Case 23	U, N	E	I	0,0,1
Test Case 9	U,N	NE	R	0,0,0	Test Case 24	U,N	NE	I	0,0,2
Test Case 10	U,N	NE	I	0,0,2	Test Case 25	U,A	E	R	4,1,0
Test Case 11	U,A	E	R	3,1,0	Test Case 26	U,A	NE	R	5,0,0
Test Case 12	U,A	E	R	3,1,0	Test Case 27	U,N	NE	I	0,0,3
Test Case 13	U,A	E	I	2,1,1	Test Case 28	U,A	E	R	3,1,0
Test Case 14	U,N	NE	R	0,0,0	Test Case 29	U,A	E	I	4,1,0
Test Case 15	U,A	E	I	1,1,2	Test Case 30	U,N	E	I	0,1,1

U-User; N-Normal; A- Abnormal; E-Emotional; NE-Non-Emotional; O-Other; H-Home; R-Regular; I-Irregular

The formula to generate the threshold value to identify the threat is as follows

Threshold Value Composer (TC) = {Activity (Input), Context (Input), Behavior (Input)}

= { (0,1,2,3,4,5),(0,1),(0,1,2,3)}

Table 6. Threat Criticality level identified

Threshold Value Received	Threat Criticality Level Inferred
{(0,0,0), (0,1,0)}	T0
{(0,0,1), (0,1,1)}	T1
{ (0,0,2) (0,1,2)}	T2
{ (0,0,3), (0,1,3)}	T3
{(1,0,0)(1,1,0)(1,0,1)(1,1,1) (1,0,2)(1,1,2)(1,0,3)(1,1,3)}	T4
{(2,0,0)(2,1,0)(2,0,1)(2,1,1)(2,0,2)(2,1,2)(2,0,3)(2,1,3)}	T5
{(3,0,0)(3,1,0)(3,0,1)(3,1,1)(3,0,2)(3,1,2)(3,0,3)(3,1,3)}	T6
{(4,0,0)(4,1,0)(4,0,1)(4,1,1)(4,0,2)(4,1,2)(4,0,3)(4,1,3)}	T7
{(4,0,0)(4,1,0)(4,0,1)(4,1,1)(5,0,2)(5,1,2)(5,0,3)(5,1,3)}	T8

For example, if the critical activity identified is 3, context state is emotional and the behavior critical is identified as 3, then the threshold value composed would be

TC = {3, 1, 2}

The output values predicted by the model for the test cases given are shown in the Table 5

Therefore, the performance of the Security Threat Analyzer layer can be evaluated using the formula for the three inputs sensed as.

$$Activity\ Identification\ Ratio = \frac{No.of\ Activities\ Identified\ Correctly}{Total\ number\ of\ actual\ activities\ sensed} = \frac{29}{30} = 0.96 = 96\%$$

$$Context\ Identification\ Ratio = \frac{Number\ of\ context\ Identified\ Correctly}{Total\ number\ of\ actual\ context\ saved} = \frac{28}{30} = 0.93 = 93\%$$

$$Behaviour\ Identification\ Ration = \frac{Number\ of\ Activities\ Identified\ Correctly}{Total\ number\ of\ actual\ activities\ sensed} = \frac{29}{30} = 96\%$$

The above evaluation parameters show that the model is predicting the criticality of the Smart Environment in a better manner.

The overall performance of the Security Threat Analyzer (STA) Layer is

Table 7. Policy Selected for the Threat inferred

Threat Criticality Level Inferred	Policy Selected	Threat Criticality Level Inferred	Policy Selected
T0	**P0:** Routine Process	T5	**P5:** a) Machine Should be Locked. b) Alarm to Bank and Police. c) Close ATM door.
T1	**P1:** a) OTP and Bio-metric Verification. b) Warning should be given.		
T2	**P2:** OTP and Bio-metric verification.	T6	**P6:** a) Alarm to Bank and Police. b) Close ATM door.
T3	**P3:** Warning should be given.		
T4	**P4:** a) Machine Should be Locked. b) Alarm to Bank and Police. c) Close ATM door.	T7	**P7:** a) Warning should be given. b) Send photo to Police and Bank
		T8	**P8:** Warning should be given.

Table 8. Threat Inferring and Policy Selection

Test Cases	Threshold Value	Criticality Inferred	Policy Selected	Test Cases	Threshold Value	Criticality Inferred	Policy Selected
Test Case 1	0,1,0	T0	P0	Test Case 16	0,0,0	T0	P0
Test Case 2	0,0,0	T0	P0	Test Case 17	0,1,0	T0	P0
Test Case 3	0,1,1	T1	P1	Test Case 18	3,1,0	T6	P6
Test Case 4	0,0,2	T2	P2	Test Case 19	0,1,2	T2	P2
Test Case 5	1,1,0	T4	P4	Test Case 20	0,1,1	T1	P1
Test Case 6	2,0,0	T5	P5	Test Case 21	0,1,0	T1	P1
Test Case 7	3,1,1	T6	P6	Test Case 22	0,0,0	T0	P0
Test Case 8	3,0,2	T6	P6	Test Case 23	0,0,1	T1	P1
Test Case 9	0,0,0	T0	P0	Test Case 24	0,0,2	T2	P2
Test Case 10	0,0,2	T2	P2	Test Case 25	4,1,0	T7	P7
Test Case 11	3,1,0	T6	P6	Test Case 26	5,0,0	T8	P8
Test Case 12	3,1,0	T6	P6	Test Case 27	0,0,3	T3	P3
Test Case 13	2,1,1	T5	P5	Test Case 28	3,1,0	T6	P6
Test Case 14	0,0,0	T0	P0	Test Case 29	4,1,0	T7	P7
Test Case 15	1,1,2	T4	P4	Test Case 30	0,1,1	T1	P1

$$STA\,Performance\,Ratio = \frac{Activity\,Ratio + Context\,Ratio + Behaviour\,Ratio}{3}$$

$$= \frac{(0.96+0.93+0.96)}{3} = \frac{2.85}{3} = 0.92 = 92\%$$

The Knowledge Manager Layer is responsible for inferring the criticality levels of the identified threats and to decide on the policies according to the criticality. The threshold value composed in the analyzing phase is given as input to the knowledge manager phase. The inferencing engine will infer the criticality level of the threat identified. The Criticality levels of the threat are represented in Table 6. The Policy selector will select the appropriate policies based on the criticality inferred. Table 7 shows the selection of policy decided by the policy selector according to the threat inferred. The threat level identification and the policy selection actions are carried out based on the data stored in the Knowledge Manager. The process of inferring the threats criticality and the selection of policy done accordingly for the test cases chosen is shown in Table 8.

Here, the non-critical threats identified are shown in green color; so there are total of 6 non-critical threats for the test cases chosen. The critical levels of the test case 17 and test case 19 are not inferred correctly, as the actual threat criticality level is T2 for both the cases. Though test case 13 is analyzed with incorrect prediction, the threat criticality level is same as the actual test case threat level. Thus, from the above table, it is clear that the inferencing engine has inferred two incorrect threat levels by which the policy selected is also incorrect for these cases. Therefore the performance of the Threat Inferencing Engine and the Threat Policy Selector module can be calculated as

$$Threat\,Inferencing\,Ratio = \frac{Number\,of\,critical\,threats\,inferred\,correctly}{Total\,number\,of\,actual\,threats} = \frac{22}{24} = 0.916 = 92\% \cdot$$

$$Threat\,Policy\,Selection\,Ratio = \frac{Number\,of\,policy\,selected\,correctly}{Total\,number\,of\,policies\,selected} = \frac{28}{30} = 0.93 = 93\%$$

The overall performance of the Security Threat Knowledge Manager is calculated as
The Threat Handler layer is responsible for handling the various threats identified by performing the necessary action strategy. The Handler will receive the policy

decided for the threat from the policy selector and sends it to the policy implementor. The policy implementor will compare the policy with the action strategy database and will select the implementor based on the action that is to be performed. For example, if a bio-metric verification is to be done for the user, the cryptographic implementor will be selected for action performing. Table 9 shows the action mapping strategy carried out by the policy implementor according to the policy received from the policy selector. The action that is to be performed for each policy is defined and is stored in the action strategy database.

Table 9. Action Performed for the Policy Decided

Policy Selected for the Threat Identified	Action Performing implementor	Policy Selected for the Threat Identified	Action Performing implementor
P0: Routine Process	A0: Routine Process	P5: a) Machine Should be Locked.	A5: Access Control & Authenticator Implementor
P1: a)OTP and Bio-metric Verification b) Warning should be given.	A1:a)Cryptographic Implementor b) Access Control & Authenticator Implementor	b) Alarm to Bank and Police. c) Close ATM door.	
		P6: a) Alarm to Bank and Police. b) Close ATM door.	A6: Access Control & Authenticator Implementor
P2: OTP and Bio-metric verification.	A2: Cryptographic Implementor	P7: a) Warning should be given. b) Send photo to Police and Bank	A7: Access Control & Authenticator Implementor
P3: Warning should be given.	A3: Access Control & Authenticator Implementor		
P4: a) Machine Should be Locked. b) Alarm to Bank and Police. c) Close ATM door.	A4: Access Control & Authenticator Implementor	P8: Warning should be given.	A8: Access Control & Authenticator Implementor

Based on the above table, the number of actions that would be mapped with the policy selected for the test cases chosen will be 30. But the number of actions executed correctly would be varying if any conflict occurs in performing the action. For example, for policy P1, 2 actions have to be performed; if the implementor is same for both actions, then there will be no conflict. If the action has to be performed by different policy implementor, the priority will be given to the highest security measure that has to be applied. If that action is not possible to perform due to unavailability of resources for performing, the alternate action implementor will be chosen to perform the action.

Table 10. Action Performing carried out for Policy Selected

Test Cases	Criticality Inferred	Policy Selected	Action Performed	Test Cases	Criticality Inferred	Policy Selected	Action Performed
Test Case 1	T0	P0	A0	Test Case 16	T0	P0	A0
Test Case 2	T0	P0	A0	Test Case 17	T0	P0	A0
Test Case 3	T1	P1	A1	Test Case 18	T6	P6	A6
Test Case 4	T2	P2	A2	Test Case 19	T2	P2	A2
Test Case 5	T4	P4	A4	Test Case 20	T1	P1	A1
Test Case 6	T5	P5	A5	Test Case 21	T1	P1	A1
Test Case 7	T6	P6	A6	Test Case 22	T0	P0	A0
Test Case 8	T6	P6	A6	Test Case 23	T1	P1	A1
Test Case 9	T0	P0	A0	Test Case 24	T2	P2	A2
Test Case 10	T2	P2	A2	Test Case 25	T7	P7	A7
Test Case 11	T6	P6	A6	Test Case 26	T8	P8	A8
Test Case 12	T6	P6	A6	Test Case 27	T3	P3	A3
Test Case 13	T5	P5	A5	Test Case 28	T6	P6	A6
Test Case 14	T0	P0	A0	Test Case 29	T7	P7	A7
Test Case 15	T4	P4	A4	Test Case 30	T1	P1	A1

Here, according to the policy selected, 5 policies are to be implemented with action A1. For test case 3, 20, 23 and 30, the highest priority of cryptographic implementor will be selected as the person emotion context is higher in the threshold value composed. For test case 21, the behavior threshold value is 0 but his emotion value is high, so the inferencing engine has inferred as T1. The policy selected for this case is a warning; therefore, in this case, the action mapping has to be done with the access control and authenticator implementor. Thus, from the discussion on the actions performing carried out, the performance of the Threat Handler Layer can be calculated as

$$Action\ Mapping\ Criticality\ ratio = \frac{Number\ of\ Actions\ Mapped\ to\ the\ Critical\ Threats}{Total\ No.of\ Avg.Critical\ Actions\ Mapped}$$

$$= \frac{23}{24} = 0.958 = 96\%$$

$$Actual\ Action\ Executed\ Ratio = \frac{Number\ of\ Actions\ Executed}{Total\ No.of\ Actions\ Identified} = \frac{30}{30} = 1 = 100\%$$

Though the number of actual critical threats is 24, since the analyzer has analyzed the test case 17 as TN value, the inferred criticality has changed to non-critical. So, the Action mapping ratio for the critical threats is being done only for 23 threats, thereby the ratio of action mapping for critical threats is reduced.

The Overall Performance of the Security Threat Handler Layer is calculated as

$$STH\ Performance\ Ratio = \frac{Criticality\ Action\ Mapping + Action\ Executed\ Ratio}{2} = \frac{(0.96 + 1.0)}{2} = \frac{1.96}{2} = 0.98 = 98\%$$

The overall performance of the model for Smart ATM can be calculated as.

$$Overall\ Performance\ Ratio = \frac{Performance\ of\ (STA + STKM + STH)}{3}$$

$$\frac{(0.95 + 0.93 + 0.98)}{3} = \frac{2.86}{3} = 0.95 = 95\%$$

The performance of the Smart Security model Layers for Smart ATM is shown as a chart with x-axis showing the layers of the model and with y-axis showing their performance in percentage. STA is Security Threat Analyzer, STKM is Security Threat Knowledge Manager to identify the various threats and STH is Security Threat Handler to Handle the Threats. The overall performance shown in Figure 3 is based on the test case chosen for testing the performance of the model in the smart ATM environment. From the chart it is clear that if the performance of the Knowledge Manger Component is improved, the overall performance of the model would also increase. Though the number of wrong criticality level inferred is less, the performance ratio of the component is reduced due to the number of test cases chosen; if the number of test case is increased, the performance ratio also will increase accordingly.

Figure 3. Performance of Layers in Smart ATM Environment

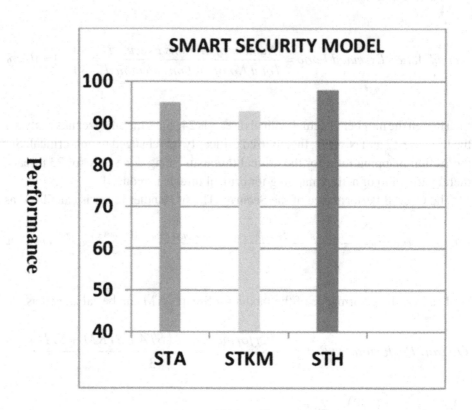

Table 11. Comparison with Existing Security Models for ATM Environment

MODEL	Success Ratio of Operations in ATM		Alternate Policies Decided		Context Awareness in applying the policy	
	No. of Test Cases	Success Ratio	No. of Test Cases	Success Ratio	No. of Test Cases	Success Ratio
An Enhanced ATM Security System Using Second Level Authentication	30	30%	30	23%	30	23%
Design of Highly Secured ATM by Using Aadhaar Card and Finger Print	30	43%	30	36%	30	36%
A Bio-inspired Smart Security model for Pervasive Smart Environment	30	96%	30	93%	30	93%

Figure 4. Comparison of Performance of Models for Success Ratio

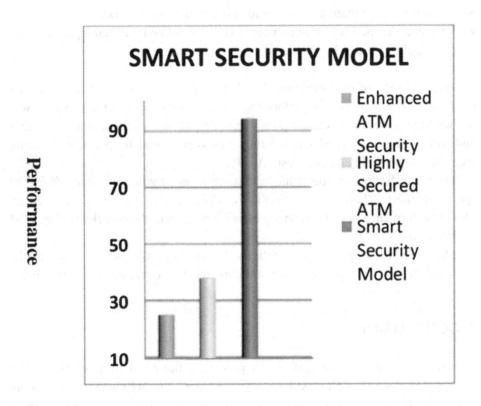

5. DISCUSSION

The threats and the attacks on ATMs has become a big issue for the financial institutions to safeguard their customer's hard earned money. The convenience that is provided by the technology also creates a more problematic situation for both the banks and the customers. Though video surveillance camera, security person and Alarm are placed for the ATMs the attackers perform their criminal activities overcoming all these measures taken by the banks. The proposed system is one such attempt to develop a better security to the ATM. This will help the banks to stop the criminal activities and there by the security of the ATM will also be improved to a better extent.

To compare the performance of the smart security model with existing security models, two models designed for the security of the ATM environment are taken and the results are tabulated below.

The approach for comparing the model with other models involves

- Finding the success ratio of the operation behavior ratio of the models.
- Number of alternate policies decided if conflict in policy occurs.
- Comparing the context awareness feature considered for security measure to be applied for the threats identified.

The limitation of the other model is that it achieves only 30% and for second model 43% of success ratio in performing the operations. For other test cases, it was not working correctly. In deciding the alternate policies for the threats, only 23% and 36%. could be achieved. Considering context awareness for providing security measures, it was 23% and 36% respectively.

The Smart Security model achieved a success rate of 96%, 93% and 93% for the specified criteria. Therefore, it is clear and evident that the proposed Smart Security Model performance is better than the existing models in the security of the ATM environment.

The overall performance ratios of the models are 25%, 38% and 94% respectively. The comparison of the performance of the models is shown as graph in figure 4.

6. CONCLUSION

This work describes a new method for protecting the ATM from attackers. The architecture consists of Context layer, Device layer, Security manager, Autonomy Manager and Intelligent manager. People are connected to many computational devices simultaneously. To develop a better and intelligent security model, the proposed model is divided into various phases considering the features such as Context-awareness, Monitoring, Decision Making ability and Intelligence. The modules are supported by Sensing Process, Inferencing Process, Decision Making and Action Performing.

The performances of the various layers of the model are described with their implications for the input sensed. When compared to the existing models the proposed model shows a better performance and it is evident that the model can be applied to any pervasive smart environments security.

REFERENCES

A report on awareness of ATM Threats to Parents by CDAC. (n.d.). Available at https://www.infosecawareness.in/parents/atm-threats

A Report on —Updated Mobile Malware Targets Android‖, Bank Info Security. (2016). https://bankinfosecurity.com/

Alahuhta. (2010). *SWAMI- Dark scenarios in ambient intelligence: Highlighting risks and vulnerabilities.* Information Society Technologies, Sixth Frame Work Programme.

Belimpasakis & Stirbu. (2012). A survey of techniques for remote access to home networks and resources. *Journal on Multimedia Tools and Applications.*

Bhattasali, T. (2017). Study of Security Issues in Pervasive Environment of Next Generation Internet of Things. In *12th International Conference on Information Systems and Information Management (CISIM).* Springer.

Checker ATM Security Report. (2011). *Protect your automatic teller machines against logical fraud.* GMV Soluciones Globales Internet.

Chen & Luo. (2012). *S2A: Secure Smart Household Appliances.* CODASPY'12, San Antonio, TX.

Cornwell, J., & ... User-Controllable Security and Privacy for Pervasive Computing. *Eighth IEEE Workshop on Mobile Computing Systems and Applications.* 10.1109/HotMobile.2007.9

Dwyer, B. (n.d.). *Report on Dog's Sense of Smell by Dogwalkers.* http://dogwalkersmelbourne.com.au

Islam. (2014). Systematic Literature Review: Security Challenges of Mobile Banking and Payments System. *International Journal of u- and e- Service, Science and Technology, 7*(6), 107-116. doi:10.14257/ijunesst.2014.7.6.10

Landman, M. (2010). Managing Smart Phone Security Risks. In *InfoSecCD'10, 2010* (p. 10). ACM.

Udupa. (2011). *ATM Security Digest India, Skimming- the global threat.* Secure Systems Pvt. Ltd.

Wazid, Katal, Goudar, Singh, Tyagi, Sharma, & Bhakuni. (2013). A Framework for Detection and Prevention of Novel Keylogger Spyware Attacks. *7th International Conference on Intelligent Systems and Control (ISCO 2013).*

Chapter 7
Security Attacks on Internet of Things

Sujaritha M.
Sri Krishna College of Engineering and Technology, India

Shunmuga Priya S.
Sri Krishna College of Engineering and Technology, India

ABSTRACT

Today's digital world has been turned into a classy one due to the emerging technology, Internet of Things (IoT). IoT is about connecting any device to any other device or object or person or any entity of interest. Through internet, the connectivity span is increased making it a fully linked environment. An attack is a threat that can harm any component of a system. In case of IoT, such attacks may take place at any level, software, hardware, network, etc. Stakeholders of IoT, designers, developers, or users must know the range of attacks associated with every segment of IoT. In this regard, this chapter gives an eye opener for getting familiarity with various types of attacks at all levels. Also, to take care of attacks prone systems, the concepts of threat modeling with supporting details are discussed in this chapter.

INTRODUCTION

Introduction to IoT

Technology is endeavouring to reach it's pinnacle. Technology is getting evolved at a very faster rate. Internet of Things is one such devastating technology. There is a huge growth in this great field due to the significant development and easily

DOI: 10.4018/978-1-7998-7756-1.ch007

affordable powerful devices such as sensors, Radio Frequency Identification (RFID) tags, Near Field Communication (NFC) cards, IoT, etc. But there are certain grey areas pulling it backward. One such is the security attacks triggered by intruders or hackers or malicious entities to shatter the privacy and security of any computing system (Atzori,2010). These attacks topple the privacy and security.

Many researchers are building security solutions like Honeypots, IDS, secure kernels, etc to overcome this problem (Biradar, 2018). It is essential to have a clear knowledge about the security attacks for developing a security model. Only a clear knowledge about the security attacks will pave way to achieve a perfect security model. So it is essential to have a deliberate idea about the security attacks. This chapter provides the security attacks targeting the internet of things.

IoT Applications and Challenges

IoT extends its beneficial hand to various disciplines viz., Smart Agriculture, Smart City, Supply Chain and Logistics, Smart Infrastructure, Healthcare systems and so forth. Many tasks like monitoring the system, tracking the inventory, enhancing customer service, data exchange etc has become very easy due to the advent of IoT (Suo, H, 2012). It is predicted that by 2022, the count of IoT devices connected to internet will cross 18 billion (Mosenia, 2010).

The system concentrates on device to device interaction, human to device interaction and performs data exchange. Though IoT renders many advantages, it is vulnerable to many security threats due to huge amount of system access and crippling IoT features (Sengupta,2020).

IoT Layers

IoT is the connection of interconnected objects with unique address and standard protocol for communication through internet infrastructure at any time (Kouicem, 2018). Based on the functionalities of IoT, it is broadly grouped into three layers namely Perception Layer, Network Layer and Application Layer. Figure 1 gives the illustration of the layers of IoT. Each layer is discussed in details so that it facilitates to know the security attacks on each of these layers.

Figure 1. Three tier layer architecture of IoT

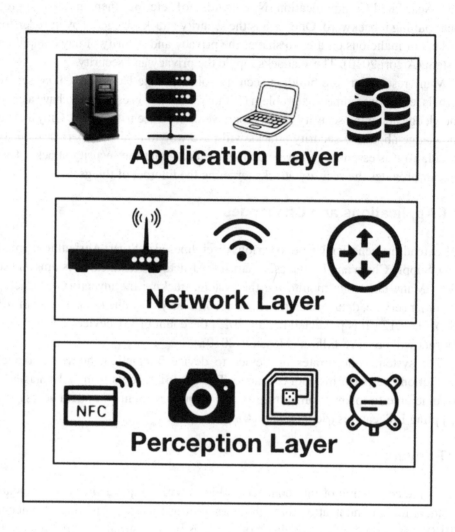

Perception Layer

Sensing the environment, identifying small objects and gathering required data is the major functionality of the Perception layer. It has sensing nodes or sensing devices with communication capability. Many types of devices are used to sense the environment like temperature sensor, humidity sensor, vibration sensor, proximity sensor, position sensor, radiation sensor, vision and imaging sensors, RFID tags,

NFC cards GPS system, web camera, etc. With the help of these devices the remote location is sensed and the data about it is made ready for exchange.

Network Layer

This layer is in charge for data exchange and communication among all the nodes and device. It uses standard protocols for establishing the communication. Gateway is one of the significant components in this layer. It goes through all the data exchanges. Gate way is the protocol converter that sophisticates smooth communication. Gateway is capable to convert the data packets as per the protocol requirement of destination and as per the needs of architecture. Gateway is installed either at the starting point or at the end point of the network.

Application Layer

The application layer is responsible for service providing and determines set of protocols required for message exchange. This layer manages the whole IoT system which includes applications, business and profit models. User sophistication is taken care by this layer.

BACKGROUND

Many researchers had worked on the security and privacy issues faced by IoT. Attacks are broadly classified into active attack and passive attack. Attack which compromises the devices or nodes and create harmless to the device or data or any other resources, is called Active attack. Attack which listens and analyses to the data or resources without disturbing the system, is called passive attack. Both active attack and passive attack can be triggered on any IoT system.

Attacks are also classified based on the attacks triggered on the resources of IoT systems. Such attacks are classified as Physical Attacks, Network Attacks, Software attacks and Data Attacks. This categorisation deals with how each attack affects the functionalities and layers of IoT. Physical Attack attempts to make attack physically on the hardware which are readily accessible by the intruders. Network attacks affects the communication link and data exchange and network connectivity of the legitimate nodes. Software attacks are purely performed by software and logically affect the IoT system. Data attacks deal with the encryption of data that is exchanged.

Categorisation can be done by grouping the attack targeted on the layers of IoT System. These attack targets the unique functionality of the IoT system which are deliberated in detail below.

Figure 2. Classification of IoT Attacks

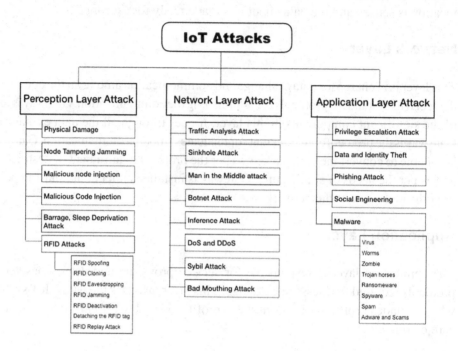

MAIN FOCUS OF THE CHAPTER

All the three layers of IoT (Perception layer, Network Layer, Application Layer) are prone to various attacks that affect the security and privacy of the system. To overcome these attacks many secure systems like honeypots, Intrusion Detection System, anti-malware softwares, Secure gateways and secure networking devices are being built (Tournier, 2020). To make a secure model it is essential to have a clear knowledge about the security attacks. Let us see the list of attacks that affect each layer of IoT system.

Taxonomy of Threats

Each layer in IoT is prone to many security attacks. Figure 2 provides the classification of the security attacks based on the Layers.

Perception Layer Attacks

Uke, S and et. al. (2013) has detailed about attacks on layer perspective. Always there is a tradeoff between availability and security. Availability of devices and nodes are prioritised in the perception layer. Sensing of environment is the crucial task to be done. For sensing of information, the nodes are implanted in many remote areas that are readily accessible to general public. This creates a rostrum to trigger attacks and to eavesdrop the exchanged message.

Network Layer Attacks

Tasks like real-time data collection and processing those collected data are carried out s on IoT platforms. Attacks of Network layer targets the IoT platform which results in serious consequences. The network layer on the IoT is the bull's eye of several cyber attacks and hence it faces many challenges. Network layer attacks are triggered by the attacker by manipulating the network traffic, network devices, information exchange, etc. Many attacks are launched to exhaust the network bandwidth so that the entire communication gets collapsed.

Application Layer Attacks

Application layer is the podium where many services are launched. End users and clients are closely connected with the functionality of this layer. Attackers target this layer to create inconvenience to the users and create greater impact. Attackers mostly try to generate software attacks on this layer.

Attacks in each layer is explained in detail as follows.

PERCEPTION LAYER ATTACKS

Physical Damage

The nodes or devices present in the perception layer are readily available in the remote area and they can be easily accessed by any third person. These devices include RFID tags, NFC cards, GPS systems, various sensors, camera, camcorder, etc. These devices can be accessed by any general public. The attacker can either hit the device and demolish it completely or he can damage it, so that the device starts to malfunction. For instance, the attacker can cause partial damage to the sensor so that the sensor starts to measure and send inaccurate reading. This is worse than damaging the device completely. Because if the device like sensor is damaged completely the server will not receive the sensing information from that device at all. So the system will recognise the absence of the device and try to take actions to overcome this type of physical damage. On the other hand, if the device is partially damaged, the server will be receiving the data from the devices but the server will be unaware of the fake or inaccurate value and believes it to be true. This affects the performance of the system. Most of the time the physical damage is made intentionally by the attackers. Occasionally, there is a chance of unintentional physical damage to the devices or components of IoT system.

Figure 3. Node Jamming Attack

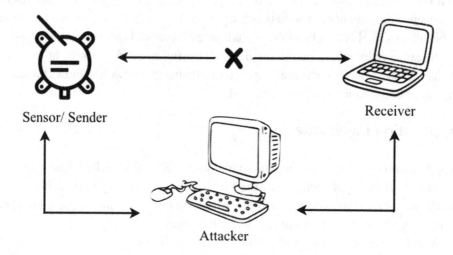

Node Tampering

In this attack, the main motive of the attacker is to collapse the system by his physical actions on the devices or the communication link. The attacker modifies the information of the compromised node physically or alters the communication link or tampers the entire device. The sensitive information like encryption key, log file, personal information can be conquered easily. With these the communication can be corrupted or even the entire system can be collapsed.

Node Jamming

The nodes in the IoT system gets connected with the help of wireless communication system. In Node Jamming attack, the attacker uses powerful devices like jammer to distort the communication. The attacker sends a signal called jamming signal that is of same frequency of the sensor nodes. This prevents the sensors to send or receive the signals. Thus the sensors are isolated from communication and thereby the attacker achieves denial of service by the legitimate sensors. This attack is illustrated in figure 3.

Malicious Node Injection

In the IoT architecture, unintended and unauthorised nodes may be physically injected by the attacker. It is a quiet simple task for the attacker to inject these malicious nodes into the perception layer. The malicious node interjects between two genuine nodes and modifies the information and passes the false content to the adjacent nodes. The attacker replicates the victim node and it uses more number of malicious nodes to perform this attack. Due to this the verifier node or the monitoring node gets collapsed completely. The verifier node or the monitoring node is the node which checks the genuine and trustworthy status of all the nodes present in the system. As a result of this attack, the verifier nodes may report a legitimate genuine node as a suspicious node.

Malicious Code Injection

The attacker processes invalid data and creates computer bugs. These bugs are often injected via database connecting languages like SQL, NOSQL queries, etc or OS commands, SMPT headers, XML parsers, program parameters etc. With the help of malicious code injection the attacker gains complete control of the IoT system and gets privilege escalations to root access as well as the critical part of the system. The result of this attack leads to loss of data, corruption of information, access denial and so on. Thus the attacker performs required malicious activities as he intends.

Barrage Attack and Sleep Deprivation Attack

All the nodes enter the sleep mode state when there is no interaction with them. This process saves power and helps for long life of the network. (Pirretti, 2006). If the node entering the sleep mode is disrupted the nodes will loose their power and node dead condition will occur. So it is essential for every node to enter sleep mode at periodic intervals. Barrage attack and Sleep Deprivation attacks try to break this process and aim to achieve node dead condition. Matthew et. al. (2006) have detailed the consequences of this attack in their work in detail.

Figure 4. Barrage and Sleep Deprivation Attack

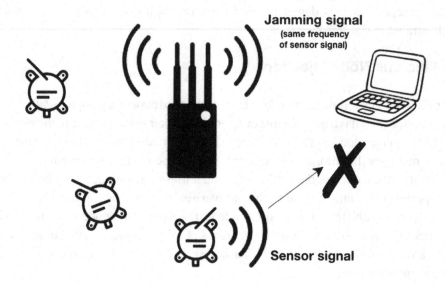

The attacker sends legitimate requests to the sensor nodes with the intention to avoid the nodes entering the low power sleep mode. This is called Barrage Attack.

Another type of attack is sleep deprivation attack. In this the attacker sends request to victim node at periodic intervals. The interval is chosen in such a way that the IoT nodes never enter the low power sleep mode at all. Due to these unnecessary requests, the IoT nodes will never enter the sleep mode at all. After certain while, node dead condition will occur due to power depletion. If many nodes die then the entire network will be depleted and the life of network vanishes. Thus the attacker gains advantage by demolishing the entire network. Both the attacks are explained in figure 4. The barrage attack will not have the timer with it.

RFID Attacks

The working of RFID technology is first deliberated here. RFID is Radio Frequency Identification. RFID technology has a rfid reader and rfid tags. It uses electromagnetic fields to automatically identify and track the rfid tags. The tags are attached to the objects or components of the IoT system. For instance, In supply chain using IoT system, the rfid tags will be attached to the product which is shipped. The rfid reader tracks the tags there by the objects can be tracked. RFID technology is widely used in many wireless communications, Internet of Things and many soft computing networks. The attacker performs various attacks by affecting rfid technology like capturing or malfunctioning the RFID tag and RFID reader. Attacks targeted on this RFID technology are discussed here. The working of RFID technology is illustrated in figure 5.

Figure 5. Working of Radio Frequency Identification (RFID)

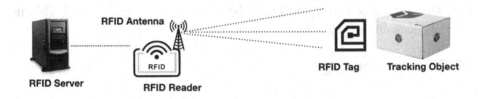

RFID Spoofing

The literal meaning of spoofing is "someone or something pretends to be something else". There are many Spoofing attacks like email spoofing, caller id spoofing, website spoofing, gps spoofing, ip spoofing and so forth. In RFID spoofing a malicious node imitates the RFID signals. The intend of the attacker is to capture the informations about the security related protocol used in the RFID system. Using this details, the attacker rewrites the obtained data with the similar format of his own RFID tags that is blank. This is called tag duplication. Due to this activity, the original reader things that the data is from the original genuine tag but actually it is from the spoofed malicious tag. The attacker manipulates the sensitive information like price, manufacture date, expiry date, product name etc.

RFID Cloning

The attacker replicates the information of the original tag into an empty black chip. This malicious tag will appear to be the original tag. The attacker owns this tag.

This malicious node uses the malicious RFID tag before the genuine node performs its intended action. Thus the duplication of tag paves way for access to private and critical information of the system. All the sensitive information access can be revealed to the attacker with the help of the duplicated tag. One more thing to be noted is the verifier node or the monitoring node in the IoT system will believe the fake tag to be the original tag. At times when the malicious tag approaches the verifier node before the original tag, the verifier will think the malicious tag to be genuine and when the original tag approaches the verifier node, the verifier suspects the original tag to be suspicious and the system collapses.

RF Interference

The attacker targets on RFID tags. Noise signals are produced by the attacker and sent over the Radio frequency signal or the sensor signals. Thereby the RFID communication gets interrupted due to the effect of heavy noise signal. Thus the entire devices suffer from communication collapse.

RFID Eavesdropping

The attacker creates a fake RFID reader. The attacker sets the frequency of the fake reader such that it resembles the same frequency of the original reader. With this fake RFID reader, the information is stolen by the attacker. All the information received by the original reader can be accessed by the fake reader too. Due to the constrained storage in RFID system, the nodes transfer non-encrypted text. This facilitates the attacker to eaves drop the entire communication with the help of the fake reader. This attack is considered to be a passive attack because this attack does not harm the victim node. It just eavesdrops the messages transferred to the victim. But still this attack paves way to many other attack like Replay attack.

RFID Jamming

In perception layer, always there will be communication establishment between the rfid tag and the rfid reader. Jamming affects the air interface between the reader and the tag which prevents their communication. Disrupting the air medium is an easy task. To collapse the communication between the tag and reader, the attacker produces radio noise signal at the same frequency of the RFID system. Thus the communication between the tag and reader is destroyed very easily.

RFID Deactivation

The target of this attack is to deactivate the rfid tag without the acquaintance of the RFID reader. The attacker impersonates the reader and sends deactivating commands like kill command, delete command to the rfid tag. On receiving the commands, the tag believes that this command is from genuine reader and performs self deactivation. The most deplorable thing here is the genuine reader will be unable to identify the presence of the tag even though it is available in the detection range. The reader will miss all the information from the deactivated rfid tag and also ignores the presence of the tag due to the deactivating command from the fake rfid reader.

Detaching the RFID tag

This attack is generally targeted on systems which has tracking as its main task. For instance in supply chains and logistics system, the core task is to track the product during shipping process to its destination. To perform this task, RFID tags are attached physically to the ordered items or objects. The client will be notified about his shipping details periodically and accurately with the help of this attached rfid tag. The attacker actually physically removes the tag from the original thing and either demolishes it or switches it to another object/thing. The reader does not have this information and assumes that the tag is attached to the original object. The tracking information produced by the tag will be the information of another unintended object. Thus the detaching of the rfid tag produces great confusion in the IoT system.

RFID Replay Attack

The intend of the reply attack is to make the victims believe that there is no happening of passive attack in the system. To perform this the attacker introduces a fake reader in the perception layer. The fake reader listens the communication in the system for long time so that it is perfectly capable to make believe the victims that passive attack is absent in the system. As a next step, the fake reader performs eavesdropping attack and gains all essential information. Then it replicates the message to the original reader or the rfid tag by personification as the original source. With the stolen information, the attacker affects the business of the system or tries to earn money with stolen data.

NETWORK LAYER ATTACKS

Traffic Analysis Attack

This is a passive attack which means the nodes in the system do not get affected explicitly. The attacker does not directly affect the system either physically or logically. The attacker eavesdrops the traffic occurring in the network without creating any harm to the victim nodes. With the number of packets transferred, file size transferred, number of logs, etc many information can be derived. This information acts as a stepping stone for many other attacks.

Sinkhole Attack

Sinkhole attack is one of the most destructive attacks when compared to other routing attacks. The attacker advertises that it has good route knowledge so that it knows the shortest path to reach the desired receiver. All the nodes prefer to choose shortest path for quick communication. Thus all the traffic is attracted towards the attacker. The attacker receives all the data being as an intermediated node. Then it discards the packets and demolishes the network communication. The sender and receiver will be unaware of this sinkhole attack.

Man in the Middle Attack

Let us see an analogy to understand this attack easily. Alice posts a letter to Bob. Eve is the postman, he opens the letter and modifies it before delivering it to Alice. Bob posts a reply letter to Alice. Again Eve, the postman modifies the letter before delivering it back to Alice. Here, Eve acts as a Man in the middle between

Alice and Bob. Same way the attacker sits in the mid between the sender and receiver. The attacker either eavesdrop the message exchange or modifies the message content between the sender and the receiver. This is depicted in figure 6. The most pathetic thing to be noted is that the sender and receiver will be unaware about the attacker playing in the middle. This attack paves way for many more attacks like session hijacking, evil twin, ARP cache poisoning, sniffing, SSL Hijacking, DNS Spoofing and so forth. Zoran et. al. have pinpointed the severity and outcome of this attack.

Figure 6. Man in the Middle Attack

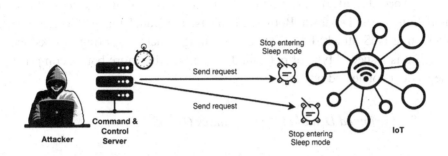

Botnet Attack

Figure 7. Botnet Attack

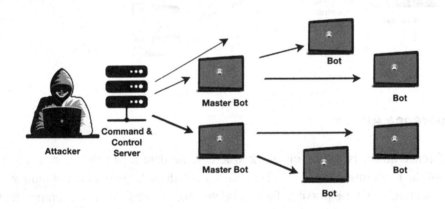

The attacker conquers more number of devices by compromising the nodes and forms an interconnected network called botnet. These compromised nodes are called zombies or bots. The bots are made so much powerful that they are capable to compromise more devices and strengthen the interconnected network by adding more number of compromised bots to it. The attacker can take remote control over this compromised network from anywhere. There are special servers called Command and Control Servers (also called C&C Servers) to control the bots and make them do malicious activities. Figure7 illustrates this attack. The bot network can be triggered to do many malicious and suspicious activities like sending large amount of spam messages to the targeted victim, exploit online data like banking data, steal private and crucial system and personal information, steal credentials, spy on other device and so forth. Botnets can be used to launch many other devastating attacks like DoS attack, DDoS attack, phishing attacks, spoofing attacks and so on. There is a special type of bot called Thing bot, the entire botnet comprises of independent connected objects.

Figure 8. Distributed Denial of Service Attack (DDoS)

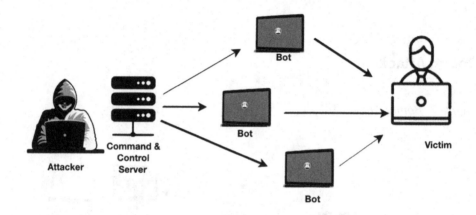

Inference Attack

Inference attack is a type of attack where some data about the user is inferred from the randomised data. This is because even though the data is randomized in the dataset, it will be possible for us to determine some facts. For example, let us assume that data is about cancer inference, it would be possible to determine that city would be from Hiroshima or Nagasaki assuming its a health data of people in Japan. With more details in the randomized set of data, the personal identity is revealed and much of the data is often available in public repositories assuming it as a randomized set of data.

But there are often simple methods available in public that reveal the data about the randomised data. That is referred to the highly documented techniques such as the frequency analysis and sorting.

Denial of Service Attack (DoS)

The intention of the attacker is to make the system resource unavailable for the genuine intended users. A successful attacker consumes all available system resource, network resource, denies server responses completely and slows down the entire system. Powerful DoS attacks create server crash or system crash. (Liang, L, 2017)

Distributed Denial of Service Attack (DDoS)

Multiple sources of DoS attack co-ordinate together to form Distributed Denial of Service Attack (DDoS).

In standard DDoS attack, the attacker directly targets the server or the network with heavy network traffic formed by malfunctions. Generally the attackers prefer to use botnet to trigger this attack. When many zombies or victim computer trigger DoS attack it is difficult for the server to identify it. The attacker can use bots from different locations. So the original server will think that the requests are from various countries and various sources and thinks them to be genuine. The server keeps responding for the bots. On the other hand, the original servers will be waiting for the reply or will be trying to access the system but gets denied due to heavy network traffic. Thus the attacker's intention is achieved that is denying the genuine users to access the system resources (Kumar, U, 2020). The sketch of this attack is presented in figure 8.

In a Reflection DDoS attack, the attackers mask themselves as the intended victim by spoofing their IP address. The system then sends legitimate requests to the public-facing servers. The server will accept these request and send responses to the intended victim nodes. Thus both legitimate servers and legitimate victims will be pooled with unintended request and respond. In course of time the network bandwidth and other resources will be exhausted. The worser part in the reflection DDoS attack is Amplification process. In amplification, the attacker impersonates a chosen victim by spoofing it's IP and sends request to the server for all known data which of larger size. So, the attacker requests with small amount of data to the server and the server in turn will respond with larger size of data to the victim and a huge network traffic is unnecessarily created by the attacker and this process is called Amplification (Gupta, 2009).

Another way to generate DDoS attack is with the available tools. Many online tools are available for free (free open source software tools/ FOSS tools) that includes LOIC (Low Orbit Ion Cannon), HOIC (High Orbit Icon Cannon), Metasploit, Pyloris, Slowloris and so forth. LOIC floods the network with TCP (Transmission control protocol) packets and UDP (User Datagram Protocol) Datagrams. HOIC floods the network with HTTP traffic. Thus each tool creates network traffic in each form and exhaust the network resource and denies the service to genuine users.

Few more DDoS attacks are discussed here. SYN Flood attack sends successive TCP Synchronize (SYN) requests to the targeted victim so that enough amount of resources are consumed by this and the server will be unavailable for the legitimate users. Once the SYN request of the attacker is accepted by the legitimate server, the server sends back an acknowledgement to the attacker, establishes an open connection and waits for the reply. But the attacker will never respond to it. The server's resource will be completely wasted until the connection gets time out. The attacker can easily exhaust the server resources by sending several TCP SYN requests and thus launch a successful DDoS attack using SYN Flooding.

UDP flooding is similar to TCP SYN but differs slightly. The server responds with an Internet Control Message Protocol (ICMP) Destination Unreachable packet instead of acknowledging the attacker. During an attack, a large number of UDP packets arrive, each with a different destination Port. In most instances, this aids the server's ability to process and respond to each one.This form of attack will easily lead to all available bandwidth being consumed.

The attacker uses the zombies in the botnet to send a large number of ICMP packets to the targeted victim server in an ICMP Flood attack. This consumes all available bandwidth and denies the access of legitimate users. For instance, ping command is used to test network connectivity.

In HTTP GET Flood attack, the attacker generates considerable number of HTTP Get requests and sends to the legitimate server in the attempt to consume all the network resources and make the server unavailable for genuine users.

Sybil Attack

The attacker creates fake identities. These identities are either stolen or fabricated. With this fake identities used, multiple distinct nodes acquire disproportionate level of control and reduce the effectiveness of the network. This attack is capable of affecting data integrity, resource utilisation and overall network performance (Zhang, K, 2014).

Bad Mouthing Attack

This attack is popularly seen in trust based system and recommendation system. The attacker sends false recommendations targeting the legitimate nodes to get lower trust values there by increasing the trust value of the intruder systems. This attack performs collusion. Malicious nodes work together in this phase to submit bad recommendations to a specific target node.

APPLICATION LAYER ATTACKS

Privilege Escalation Attack

The attacker looks for the bugs and weakness present in the device. Taking advantage of these bugs as entry point, the attacker intrudes into the system. This intrusion will be unknown to the genuine users of the system. The attacker performs many malicious tasks like deployment of malware, data stealing, etc.

Data and Identity Theft

Due to the advent of many handheld devices like mobile phone, iPad, kindle, smart watches, fitness trackers, smart meters, laptops, tablets, etc people get many sophistications but fail to take care about the security parameters. The attackers find opportunities over the careless use and unsafe usage of these internet connected handheld devices. With this advantage the attacker steal the personal identity of the user, the credentials like security pattern, passwords, etc are stolen. Since many people are exposed over the social network, they knowingly or unknowingly reveal their personal information and paves way to the attacker to steal them. With the stolen credentials, the attackers take control of the entire system when possible.

Phishing Attack

The attacker attempts to lure the credentials of user using counterfeit email id or websites or both. These attackers are called phishers. The phishers select the target victim (it may be an organisation, or targeted network or person) Phishers create a phishing website and sends huge number of spam emails. When the targeted victims unknowingly or accidentally clicks the link, the victim is redirected to the phishing site from which the targeted credentials are stolen by the phisher. Spoofed email is one technique by which the user or victim is convinced by emails and made to click the link of the phishing site. Phishers perform few tasks to perform this attack namely, To create a fake connection, certain strings are concatenated at the end of a legitimate domain, or certain characters of a legitimate URL are exchanged with similar characters that are difficult to detect. Phishers even hide the address bar using languages like javascript. Due to these actions the victims are deceived to click the phishing link. Figure 9 gives the step by step process of launching phishing attack (Gupta, 2018).

Phishing can be performed using techniques like Cross-site scripting, session-hijacking, malware phishing, DNS poisioning, Key/screen loggers (Arachchilage, 2016).

Figure 9. Phishing Attack

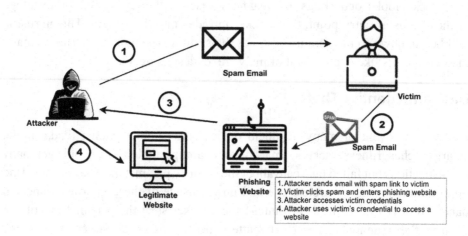

1. Attacker sends email with spam link to victim
2. Victim clicks spam and enters phishing website
3. Attacker accesses victim credentials
4. Attacker uses victim's crendential to access a website

Cross site scripting (abbreviated as XSS) targets the victim having insecure web application. Attacker installs malicious javascript and hijacks the login credentials and misuse them.

Session hijacking, also known as cookie hijacking, is when a DoS attack is used to steal the session key. The intruder takes the victim's identity and uses it to obtain unauthorized access to services. The attacker's primary goal is to manipulate the mobile station and disrupt the link to a standard access point.

Malware phishing is a form of phishing attack in which malicious software stores credentials on the victim's device and sends them to the phisher.

The phisher uses a fake DNS server to connect with the client in a DNS poisoning attack. If a link with the victim has been developed, he will be led to malicious websites. The phisher infects their computers with malware.

The screenshots and mouse movements of the victim are captured by a key/screen logger and sent to the attacker at a remote location. The knowledge of hidden credentials can be accessed by the phisher using this process.

Social Engineering

This is a type of phishing attack since the intention of the attack is to lure the credentials of the victims. This attack manipulates the people psychologically with the intend to steal secret and personal credentials and information from them. To gain access to the device, network, or physical location, the intruder relies on human interaction and manipulates people into breaching general security processes and procedures. The users are deceived to enter their personal information like bank information, password, identity numbers, etc in fake portfolios. The attacker creates fake shopping or banking websites that looks too legitimate and traps the people to enter their secret information.

Malware

Malware is an abbreviated acronym for Malicious software. Many malicious softwares are created by the attackers to destroy the IoT system. Each malicious software work in unique way and accomplishes a particular target. There are many malware like worms, virus, zombies, Trojan horses, Ransomware, Adware, Scams, Spyware, Spams, etc. These malware are discussed one by one.

Virus

Virus are self replicating programs. Virus are in the form of an executable file. Initially they are dormant. Once it gets activated it starts to self replicate and damage the entire system. Also it spreads itself via infected websites, email attachment, file sharing, downloads and so on. Viruses expose themselves to all the connected device in the IoT System. They are propagated as executable attachment coming from trustworthy source but it is actually not so. When the victims open this exe files, the virus gets activated and demolishes the system.

Worms

Once if worms are installed successfully in a machine, it infects the whole machine and also spreads itself to all the network connected devices and in turn infect them too. Worms are more powerful since it is capable to infect the whole network. They can alter or trash files, inject suspicious software onto the devices attached to the network; it can replicate itself again and again to deplete the entire system resources, steal confidential information, install sophisticated backdoor for hackers. Also worms can infect huge number of devices very fast and consumes bandwidth and overload the server.

Zombie

Zombie otherwise called as bot is a compromised device that can be accessed remotely by the attacker. Zombies are created by malicious codes that compromise and control the device and convert it into bot. Zombies are very essential to launch many attacks like DDoS attack, keylogging, spreading other malware, triggering phishing message.

Trojan Horse

It is a suspicious programming file that disguises itself as legitimate one. It creates a backdoor in the device for the attacker. Attackers use it to trash, alter and conquer data and compromise the captured device as a bot, snoop on the device, obtain access to the network and so on.

Ransomeware

Ransomware prevents or limits the access to your own files. Then it demands for ample amount of money (generally in the form of crypto-currencies) in order to let the victim back in. In May 2017, a ransomware attack escalated through 150 countries, infecting more than 200,000 machines in just a single day. The assault, dubbed WannaCry, is estimated to have cost hundreds of millions to billions of dollars.

Spyware

Spyware tracks the victim's web activity secretly. It gathers victim's data, sensitive information such as user name, password, pattern of surfing etc. Spyware is a common threat, typically distributed as freeware or shareware that has an enticing feature on the front end that you might never see with a hidden mission running in the background. It is widely used for identity theft and credit card fraud. Spyware relays your data to advertisers or cyber criminals while on your computer. Some spyware automatically installs other malware that modifies the system settings.

Spam

Spam is also referred to as junk email, is unsolicited message sent in bulk by email (spamming). Most spam messages from emails are commercial in nature. Many are not only irritating, but also harmful, whether commercial or not, since they can include links that lead to malware hosting phishing websites or sites - or have malware as file attachments.

Adware and Scams

Some users are willing to put up with adware in return for free software (games for example). However, not all software is created equal. It's at best annoying, and it slows down the machine. In the worst-case scenario, the advertisements lead to pages where unsuspecting users are awaiting malicious updates. Adware can also deliver spyware and is easily hacked, making it a soft target for hackers, phishers, and scammers on computers that have it installed.

Location Based Attacks

When Location Based Services help in numerous ways, there are potential threats aimed for it. By hacking the location of victims with information from Global Positioning System, these types of attacks are carried out.

THREAT/ATTACK MODELING FRAMEWORK

Threat modelling is a defensive measure to security attacks. It is a process to identify, enumerate and mitigate the security vulnerabilities. According to W.Xiong et al. (2019), threat modeling refers to as a solution for secure application development and system security evaluations. As a proactive aim, it makes more difficult for the attackers to perform their malicious tasks. According to Uzunov and Fernandez (2014), threat modeling is used to analyze potential attacks or threats. The process is supported by libraries or taxonomies. Modeling helps the analysts to identify, classify, and prioritize threats to ensure appropriate documentation and reporting are done. (Tedeschi,2019)

The process inputs the nature of the system, the probable attacker's profile, the most likely attack vectors, the assets most desired by an attacker and so forth. It then outputs the systematic analysis of what controls or defences need to be incorporated to the system. Many threat models are available. Let us see one by one in brief.

1. Attack Trees and its Significance

They are diagrams that illustrates the attacks or vulnerabilities on a system in a tree form. For complex system, attack trees are built for each component separately and thus there will be a set of attack trees produced by the system threat analysis such that each tree is built for each goal. The goal of the attack is placed in the root of the tree and the leaves pave way to achieve that goal.

Initially, the attack system was used as stand alone method and now it is incorporated with other methods like STRIDE, CVSS, and PASTA (discussed below) and used.

Example for Attack Tree:

An example for Attack tree is depicted in figure 10. The root of the tree has the goal of the threat that is "Break Password of the system". The leaves of the attack tree gives the way to reach the root of the tree.

Figure 10. Sample attack graph

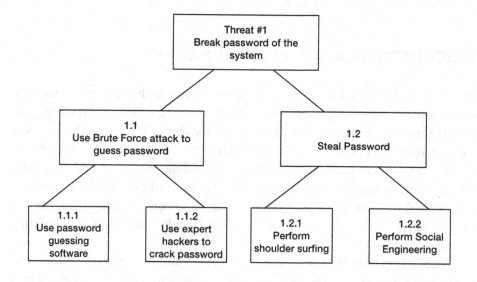

2. STRIDE

STRIDE (Spoofing Identity, Tampering with data, Repudiation, Information Disclosure, DoS, Elevation of Priviege), developed by Microsoft is the most matured model. Based on Data Flow Diagram, STRIDE is used to identify entities of the system, events and system boundaries.

3. DREAD

Another product of Microsoft is DREAD (damage potential, reproducibility, exploitability, affected users, discoverability) with a different approach for assessing threats. Currently with OpenStack, provides a mnemonic for risk rating the threats due to security issues.

4. PASTA

Developed in 2012, PASTA has 7 stages namely Define Objectives, Define Technical Scope, Application Decomposition, Threat Analysis, Vulnerability and Weakness Analysis, Attack Modeling, Risk and Impact Analysis. This involves dynamic threat identification and rating (Xiong,2019).

5. LINDDUN

LINDDUN stands for Link ability, Identifiability, Nonrepudiation, Detectability, Disclosure of information, Unawareness, Noncompliance. It has six steps, viz., Define DFD, Map privacy threats to DFD elements, Identify threat scenarios, Prioritise threats, Elicit mitigation strategies and Select corresponding PETS. The first three steps focus on problem space and the last three steps focus on solution space.

6. CVSS

CVSS stands for Common Vulnerability Scoring System. It inputs the principal characteristics of a vulnerability and outputs a numerical severity score. This score is a standardised score and can be calculated by a readily accessible online cvss calculator. CVSS method is widely incorporated with other threat modeling methods for efficient usage.

7. Quantitative Threat Modeling Method

This is a hybrid model incorporating the methods of attack trees, STRIDE and CVSS. Model is built over defining intrinsic factors of attack tree for five categories of STRIDE and the scores computation for three components based on CVSS.

Table 1. Comparison of Threat Modeling methods

Threat Modeling Method	Features	Disadvantage	Applications Used
Attack Tree	Best choice when it is used repeatedly because it gives consistent results. It helps to identify relevant mitigation techniques.	Simple to use only when you have a thorough knowledge of the system beforehand.	SCADA networks, Biometric, GSM Radio Access Networks
STRIDE	Most mature method and helps to identify relevant mitigating techniques	Though usability is easy it consumes more time	E-Banking to Software Defined Networking
DREAD	Helps to figure out relevant mitigation techniques and directly supports risk management	Labor intensive	From small businesses to enterprises and militaries.
PASTA	Direct contribution to risk management and encourages stakeholder's collaboration	Laborious due to rich documentation.	Consumer Electronics
LINDDUN	It has built-in prioritisation of threat mitigation. It helps to identify relevant mitigation techniques.	Involves extreme Labor effort and time	Smart Grids
CVSS	Comprises of built-in prioritisation techniques. Best choice when it is used repeatedly because it gives consistent results. It has automated components.	Score calculations are not transparent.	Useful for manufacturers in post-marketing phase.
Quantitative Threat Modeling	Comprises of built-in prioritisation techniques. Best choice when it is used repeatedly because it gives consistent results. It has automated components.	Time consuming	Extension of STRIDE
VAST Modeling	Explicitly designed to be scalable. It has automated components.	Few documentations are publicly available.	

Threat Model Construction

Threat modelling process has the following major steps to implement application security. This is supported by DFDs, UMLs, Graph Representations etc.

1.   Identify the use case, assets for protection, external entities

The item focused for threat modelling is to be identified.
Assets such as credentials, communication, logs, keys etc. to be known.

The external factors or persons linked to this must be identified.

2. Identify trust areas, possible adversaries and threats

From whom or from where the attacks are going to happen must be known.
What are the anticipated threats based on the entity under consideration must be analysed.

3. Deciding the high level security objectives

High Level security components such as confidentiality, availability, integrity, etc. must be clearly considered for the analysis purpose.

4. Defining security requirements based on the objectives

For every objective and its associated elements, appropriate action points related to them must be clearly focused i.e. failure thresholds setting, roles definition, authorization settings etc.

5. Documentation w.r.t. all details

Using tables, charts/graphs, diagrams, the system must be well documented. This will help in further analysis and mitigation.

Further Challenges

As the number of applications adopting IoT increase as well as the number of IoT devices deployed in these application grow exponentially, lot of challenges are ahead. Few of them are highlighted to focus more on research and products deployments.

1. Testing of IoT applications must be multidimensional
2. Cryptocurrencies may be favourable to attackers than the real users.
3. Ransomware and Malware attacks grow intelligently
4. Data Protection w.r.t. web, cloud and mobile must be seen as an integrated activity.

CONCLUSION

In this chapter, List of security attack on IoT system is discussed in detail. The emphasis and impact of each attack is stated clearly. Security of IoT is very much essential to have smooth real time projects. So the list of attacks affecting the security of IoT is identified and presented in this chapter. Thread Modelling Methods to mitigate these attacks are outlined. The future work is to identify countermeasures to overcome these security issues in IoT and utilise the available threat modelling tools effectively to overcome the security attacks.

FUTURE RESEARCH DIRECTIONS

Many Security model are built to prevent each types of attack. The solution to overcome the above attacks can be given process by process. Attack Detection, Pinpointing the attack location, Attack elimination and Attack prevention. Attack Detection is the process in which it is identified that few nodes or few components of the system is suffering from attack. On detecting the attack, alerts can be passed to all the components of the IoT system so that each device and user can make their own security measures. This is just level1 solution.

Pinpointing the attack location is the next level of solution. Here, the nodes or components which are affected is identified and broadcasted to all. This can give alert to other nodes to take security measures. Attack elimination is the level 3 solution. The attackers are identified or in least level the compromised nodes are identified and they are isolated from the IoT system or repaired and then reintroduced into the system. Attack Prevention is the level 4 solution which is a top notch approach in which the attack is totally avoided in the system. The system is built so secure that there is no possibility to trigger the prevented attack in the system.

ACKNOWLEDGMENT

This research received no specific grant from any funding agency in the public, commercial, or not-for-profit sectors.

REFERENCES

Arachchilage, N. A. G., Love, S., & Beznosov, K. (2016). Phishing threat avoidance behaviour: An empirical investigation. *Computers in Human Behavior, 60,* 185–197. doi:10.1016/j.chb.2016.02.065

Atzori & Iera. (2010). The internet of things: A survey. *Elsevier Journal on Computer Networks, 54,* 2787–2805.

Biradar, A., & Patil, S. S. (2018). Secure Communication Between Sensors in IoT. *International Journal of Computing, 7*(4).

Braganza, D., & Tulasi, B. (2017). RFID security issues in IoT: A comparative study. *Oriental Journal of Computer Science and Technology, 10*(1), 127–134. doi:10.13005/ojcst/10.01.17

Cekerevac, Z., Dvorak, Z., Prigoda, L., & Cekerevac, P. (2017). Internet of things and the man-in-the-middle attacks–security and economic risks. *MEST Journal, 5*(2), 15–25. doi:10.12709/mest.05.05.02.03

Gupta, B. B., Arachchilage, N. A., & Psannis, K. E. (2018). Defending against phishing attacks: Taxonomy of methods, current issues and future directions. *Telecommunication Systems, 67*(2), 247–267. doi:10.100711235-017-0334-z

Gupta, B. B., Joshi, R. C., & Misra, M. (2009). Defending against distributed denial of service attacks: issues and challenges. *Information Security Journal: A Global Perspective, 18*(5), 224-247.

Kouicem, D. E., Bouabdallah, A., & Lakhlef, H. (2018). Internet of things security: A top-down survey. *Computer Networks, 141,* 199–221. doi:10.1016/j.comnet.2018.03.012

Kumar, U., Navaneet, S., Kumar, N., & Pandey, S. C. (2020). Isolation of DDoS Attack in IoT: A New Perspective. *Wireless Personal Communications, 114*(3), 2493–2510. doi:10.100711277-020-07486-w

Liang, L., Zheng, K., Sheng, Q., & Huang, X. (2016, December). A denial of service attack method for an iot system. In *2016 8th international conference on Information Technology in Medicine and Education (ITME)* (pp. 360-364). IEEE. 10.1109/ITME.2016.0087

Liang, L., Zheng, K., Sheng, Q., Wang, W., Fu, R., & Huang, X. (2017, August). A denial of service attack method for iot system in photovoltaic energy system. In *International Conference on Network and System Security* (pp. 613-622). Springer. 10.1007/978-3-319-64701-2_48

Mosenia, A., & Jha, N. K. (2016). A comprehensive study of security of internet-of-things. *IEEE Transactions on Emerging Topics in Computing*, *5*(4), 586–602. doi:10.1109/TETC.2016.2606384

Pirretti, M., Zhu, S., Vijaykrishnan, N., McDaniel, P., Kandemir, M., & Brooks, R. (2006). The sleep deprivation attack in sensor networks: Analysis and methods of defense. *International Journal of Distributed Sensor Networks*, *2*(3), 267–287. doi:10.1080/15501320600642718

Sengupta, J., Ruj, S., & Bit, S. D. (2020). A comprehensive survey on attacks, security issues and blockchain solutions for IoT and IIoT. *Journal of Network and Computer Applications*, *149*, 102481. doi:10.1016/j.jnca.2019.102481

Suo, H., Wan, J., Zou, C., & Liu, J. (2012, March). Security in the internet of things: A review. In 2012 international conference on computer science and electronics engineering (Vol. 3, pp. 648-651). IEEE.

Tedeschi, S., Emmanouilidis, C., Mehnen, J., & Roy, R. (2019). A design approach to IoT endpoint security for production machinery monitoring. *Sensors (Basel)*, *19*(10), 2355. doi:10.339019102355 PMID:31121892

Tournier, J., Lesueur, F., Le Mouël, F., Guyon, L., & Ben-Hassine, H. (2020). A survey of IoT protocols and their security issues through the lens of a generic IoT stack. *Internet of Things*, 100264.

Uke, S. N., Mahajan, A. R., & Thool, R. C. (2013). UML modeling of physical and data link layer security attacks in WSN. *International Journal of Computers and Applications*, *70*(11).

Van Le, T., Burmester, M., & de Medeiros, B. (2007). Forward-secure RFID Authentication and Key Exchange. *IACR Cryptol. ePrint Arch.*, *2007*, 51.

Xiong, W., & Lagerström, R. (2019). Threat modeling–A systematic literature review. *Computers & Security*, *84*, 53–69. doi:10.1016/j.cose.2019.03.010

Zhang, K., Liang, X., Lu, R., & Shen, X. (2014). Sybil attacks and their defenses in the internet of things. *IEEE Internet of Things Journal*, *1*(5), 372–383. doi:10.1109/JIOT.2014.2344013

Chapter 8

Towards the Design of a Geographical Information System for Tracking Terrorist Attacks Online in Nigeria

Jeremiah Ademola Balogun
(iD) https://orcid.org/0000-0002-6510-6127
Mountain Top University, Nigeria

Mountain Top University, Nigeria

Bodunde Odunola Akinyemi
Obafemi Awolowo University, Nigeria

Funmilayo Kasali
Mountain Top University, Nigeria

Peter Adebayo Idowu
(iD) https://orcid.org/0000-0002-3883-3310
Obafemi Awolowo University, Nigeria

Ibidapo Olawole Akinyemi

ABSTRACT

Currently in Nigeria, different crimes ranging from ethnic clashes, domestic violence, burglary, financial fraud, kidnapping, pipe-line vandalism, and random killings by terrorist organizations, to mention a few, continue to plague the country. The conventional system of intelligence and crime record have failed to live up to the expectations as a result of limited security personnel, deficiency in effective information technology strategies, and infrastructures for gathering, storing, and analyzing data for accurate prediction, decision support, and prevention of crimes. There is presently no information system in Nigeria that provides a central database that is capable of storing the spatial distribution of various acts of terrorism based on the location where the crime is committed. This chapter presents the design of an information system that can be used by security agents for the storage and retrieval of criminal acts of terrorism in order to provide improved decision support regarding solving and preventing criminal acts of terrorism in Nigeria using modern technologies.

DOI: 10.4018/978-1-7998-7756-1.ch008

1. INTRODUCTION

Crime is as old as man himself and efforts have been directed for ways to combat and reduce it. Criminal activities such as robbery, assaults, theft, internet fraud, alteration of documents, impersonation, advance fee fraud, homicides, kidnapping amongst others are everyday occurrence in all parts of the world (Ejemeyovwi, 2015). According to World Population Review (2020), Venezuela has the highest crime rate worldwide with crime index of 84.86 percent while in the United States, it is 46.73 percent. Also, the prevalence of crime in South Africa and Nigeria is still relatively very high (Nwankwo & James, 2016). The alarming increase in rate of criminal activities in Nigeria is reported in local and international media (print and electronic) in reflection of the index for measured status. This is aggravated by the harsh economy coupled with the rush for quick wealth especially among the youths. Idhoko and Ojaiko (2013), described Geographic Information Systems (GIS) as a computer system capable of capturing, storing, analyzing, and displaying geographically referenced information which works by relating information from different sources.

A geographic information system (GIS) can be described as a location-based information system modeling the real world. Wang (2012), gave an in-depth review on the numerous benefits of using GIS applications by security personnel which include the fact that GIS can be used as tool for preventing, monitoring and investigating crimes. It can also be used for mapping how various geographical locations of different crimes relate to one another. The power of a GIS comes from the ability to relate different information in a spatial context and to reach a conclusion about this relationship. Since the emergence of the Internet in the 1990s, there has been a paradigm shift in all aspects of GIS. The way GIS applications are designed have metamorphosed from an isolated architecture to an interoperable framework; from a standalone solution to a distributed approach; from individual proprietary data formats to open specification exchange of data; and from a desktop platform to an Internet environment (Chow, 2008).

Current technological advancements have increased the awareness of GIS's potential among the general public and also encouraged researchers and other stakeholders to explore more powerful GIS techniques (Smiatek, 2005). The recent development of web services, 3-dimensioanl (3D) visualization tools (e.g., Google Earth, World Wind) and Maps Application Programming Interfaces (APIs) have certainly contributed to the ever-increasing attention to the development and implementation of distributed GIS through the Internet (Butler, 2006). In emergency situations and highly critical missions, information about the location of incident suspect or victim in crime is often crucial to determination of the manner and size of the response by law enforcement agencies.

Most of the information available about terrorism today is location-based and can be referenced to a spatial location. Spatial data play a very important role in the fight against insurgency and terrorism. Terrorists' uprising in Nigeria which started in 2009 as a small riot has now metamorphosed into a global threat and this has drastically increased the rate of insecurity in the country (Adelaja, Labo & Penar, 2018). Nigeria is currently being faced with different acts of terror which include ethnic clashes, kidnapping, pipe-line vandalism and random killings by some herdsmen to mention a few. For crime to occur, there are offenders, their target (victims) and properties which are usually located at a point in any given period of time. The conventional system of intelligence and crime record may fail to live up to expectations of the existing crime scenario as they have been found to be deficient in terms accuracy, reliability and comprehensive data availability required for prediction and decision support for enhanced productivity and effective utilization of materials and manpower (Adigun, Folorunso & Uzoh, 2018).

1.1 Problem Statement

The problem of crime in Nigeria is multifaceted and it ranges from cybercrimes, corruption, money laundering, kidnapping, terrorism, robbery, bribery, cultism, rape, and fraud amongst others (Oguntade, Ojo, Okagbue, & Oguntade, 2015). The commonest and most heinous amongst these crime types include kidnapping, terrorism and robbery as a result of high rate of poverty, social, economic and political instability in the country. The crime index of Nigeria currently stands at 64.64 according to World Population Review (2020). There is a need for reliable emergency communication at national level. There is presently no information system in Nigeria that provides a central database that is capable of storing the spatial distribution of various acts of terrors based on the location where the crime was committed. Hence the focus of this work is to develop a spatially enabled information system that can be used by security agencies for the storage and retrieval of criminal acts of terror in order to improve the ways some of these crimes are solved in Nigeria.

2. LITERATURE REVIEW

Crime is one of the major challenges that most governments around the world are currently plagued with (Bornman, 2012) and it affects quality of life negatively (Chaudhuri, Chowdhury & Kumbhakar, 2015). Crime could be in the form of cyber-crime, robberies, burglaries, vandalism, sexual harassment, murder, kidnapping, terrorism amongst others. In Malaysia, using a ten-year period of 2004 to 2013 archival analysis showed that a total number of 314,675 violent crime incidents were recorded and majority of the violent crimes occurred in a fluctuating pattern (Amin *et al.*, 2014). In the United States of America (USA), it was reported that in 2018 alone, there were more than a million reported violent crimes, 16,214 reported murders and non-negligent manslaughter cases (Statista, 2019).

In the Philippines, the total crime volume for the last four years has been fluctuating. It registered 80,108 in 2000, 76,991 in 2001, 85,776 in 2002 and 83,704 in 2003. For the period January to November 2004, the total crime volume registered is 8.5% lower compared with the same period last year (Mwiya, Phiri & Lyoko, 2015) and the current crime rate in Philippines is 41.09 (World Population Review, 2020). In 2018, there were about 2.79 million thefts alone committed in China (Statista Research Department, 2020) although there was a little decrease compared to the previous year. The crime rate is so high especially in some South American countries that they are considered dangerous to live in as a result of economic, political and social crisis (Asmann & O'Reilly, 2020).

For example, it was recently reported in the BBC news that the homicide rate in Mexico continues to increase annually since 2014 and ranks 19th globally in the list of countries with highest homicide rate in the world although still way below countries like Honduras, Venezuela, Jamaica and El Savador (BBC News, 2020). Currently, as at 2019, the crime index for South Africa (SA) is 77.02 just a little below that of Venezuela and Papua New Guinea making SA to be listed as one of the countries with the highest crime rate in the world according to World Population Review (2020). The crime rate in SA is actually much worse than what is reported according to BusinesTech (2019) as shown in Table 1. There has been an increment in the rate of murder, sexual offences and assault according to a research done by Africa Check (2019).

Falaye *et al.* (2013), worked on the development of a Crime Investigation System which uses Biometrics for the Nigerian Police Station. The study proposed a system that captures information about suspects reported for committing crimes including the fingerprints of the suspect. The user and system requirements of the system were identified following which the system design was done using flowcharts. The system was implemented a standalone desktop application using Visual Basic. The study was limited to the storage and retrieval of information about criminals reported in the past and does not consider the spatial distribution of the information stored.

Mwiya, Phiri and Lyoko (2015) developed a crime reporting and management tool using GSM and GIS technologies with the aim of reducing crime rates especially in developing countries using Zambia as the case study. The app was designed for Android mobile platforms using PHP, MySQL and Google API was used for location mapping. The study was limited due to the fact that the tool was designed to be used by crime victims to make crime reports to security agencies and consequently, the app cannot keep record of crimes and monitor the distribution of crimes across different locations.

Table 1. Incidence of Crime levels in SA

Type of Crime	Incidents (VOCS)	Reported (SAPS)	% Not Reported
Robbery at residential premises	264,054	22,431	92
House breaking	1,345,196	220,865	84
Common robbery	581,438	191,797	67
Hijacking	32,465	17,208	47
Theft of motor vehicles	82,867	48,324	42
Assault with intent to cause Grave Body Harm (GBH)	497,093	332,991	33
Sexual offences	26,460	52,240	-
Murder	12,079	32,622	-
Damage to Properties	69,896	117,172	-

VOCS – Victims of Crime Survey, SAPS – South Africa Police Service
Source: BusinessTech (2019)

Ahishakiye (2017), worked on the development of a web-based records management system for Ugandan Prisons. The study was embarked upon because of a lot of loopholes in the system because there is no tracking and/or monitoring of the information available in the different Departments and there are no security measures in place to safe guard the available information. If no tracking and/or monitoring of information is possible, it leads to unsafe situations. The study was limited to the development of a web-based system without spatial functions required for storing information about Ugandan Prisons.

Yasser *et al.* (2018), in their study reviewed the importance of using GIS for combating terrorism in Saudi Arabia. Different tools and methods related to GIS technology was discussed and their applications in ensuring effective security measures was focused on. GIS provides the technology that enables geographical data collection from LIDAR, aerial photography and satellite imagery, data that is captured, stored, analysed and displayed in maps. The maps can reflect hot-spot gas field and oil field where terrorist activities are carried out. This also makes geography a key subject in understanding such activities. The study did not consider the implementation of a spatially-enabled system based on the review made.

3. MATERIALS AND METHODS

This section presents the materials and methods that were required for the design and development of the geographical information system that is needed for tracking terrorists' attacks based on information provided by various security agencies.

3.1 Study Area

In order to determine the types and severity of crimes committed and the format in which those crimes are reported, interview was done with several security agents belonging to various security agencies. The study located for this study is Ogun State, located in the south western part of Nigeria which has twenty local government areas as depicted in Figure 1.

Figure 1. Map of Ogun State showing the 20 local governments
Source: Adedeji, Adebayo & Sotayo (2014)

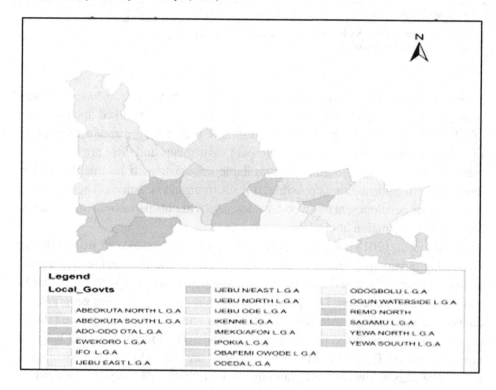

The outcome of the interview/interaction and audio recordings showed that in virtually all the police stations visited, the traditional approach is still being used.

This involved the use of paper-based case files for the collection and storage of crime information based on victims' reports. The limitations of this approach as indicated by the system users include: inaccurate crime reports, unreported crimes as a result of brutality and intimidation by security personnel, low response and high rate of unsolved crimes, scarcity of financial resources, lack of manpower and tools needed to fight crimes, lack of administrative resources, and time consuming and laborious ways of file organization. This system was designed with the aim of proffering solutions to all the identified challenges.

3.2 Software Development Model

The Rapid Application Development (RAD) model was used because the users wanted to test run and get a working prototype as fast as possible. The model also ensures that a quality product is produced on time and thus saving resources. It is also highly interactive in nature. RAD consists of four phases which are requirements planning phase, user design phase, construction phase and the cutover phase (Naz & Khan, 2015). RAD encourages incremental prototyping and giving out deliverables in phases (Beynon-Davies, Carne, Mackay & Tudhope, 1999). After a deliberate interview and interaction process with the proposed users of the system, highlighted are the functional requirements that are expected to be met by the system.

The system will only allow authorized users access to the system using usernames and passwords provided by system administrator. New users and existing users must be able to change their default passwords to their preferred password. The system must allow new security agencies and new users to be created when required. Existing users must be able to provide information of new criminal events upon reporting. Existing criminal events records can be viewed by users using tables and charts. System must provide a digital map showing the distribution of the location of criminal events recorded by security agents. For the non-functional requirements, the users wanted a system that is easy to use, has a simple graphical user interface, reliable, learnable, secured, operable, effective and efficient to use.

3.3 System Modelling

The user requirements of the system was modelled using use case diagrams as depicted in Figure 2 and class diagrams was used for data modelling as depicted in Figure 3. Figure 2 shows the relationship between all the users of the system with their respective responsibilities.

The System Administrator is the super-user of the system. He is responsible for creating access to the system by an authorized user. The primary responsibilities of the system administrator are as follows. Creation of user profiles for newly registered security agencies based on their respective wards in the selected local government areas. Creation of profiles for newly registered security agents and data collators within their respective security agencies. Management of user profiles of registered security agencies and respective users. View information stored about security agencies created, users created and crime events reported.

Figure 2. Use case Diagram showing User Activities

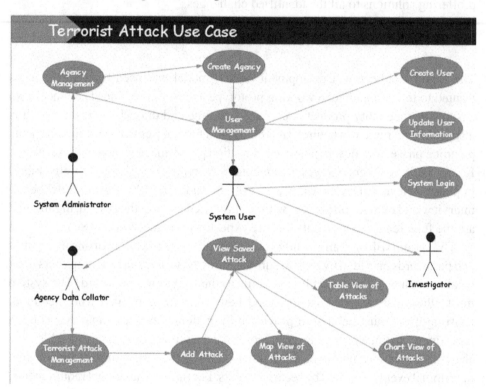

Agency Data Collator is one of the primary users of the system and is responsible for creating the crime events reported alongside their respective information required for properly identifying the crimes reported based on number of people affected, type of crime reported, location of crime and located affected to mention a few. Their primary responsibilities are as follows. They are responsible for the creation of new crime events reported; they can view information about reported crime events stored using tables; and ability to view crime events stored as charts and maps.

The investigator is another primary user of the system who is responsible for using the information of crime events reported by the data collator in order to make informed decisions. The primary responsibilities are as follows. They are required to query the system for reported crime events based on a number of criteria which includes the people affected, type of location affected, time of attack to mention a few using charts. They can view the results of the crime events reported using maps.

Figure 3 was used to identify the various types of classes, objects and their respective instances alongside their relationships within the context of the designed system. The system has a main class defined as the users of the system who were either a system administrator, a data collator from a security agency and an investigator. The user class is a generalization of the system administrator, data collator and the investigator classes while the users whom were created for each role were the instance of those class objects. Furthermore, each user was allocated to a particular type of security agency such that a user can only belong to only one security agency. Also, the different security agencies which were created for the system were located at a particular ward in their respective local government area.

Figure 3. Class Diagrams for Data Modeling

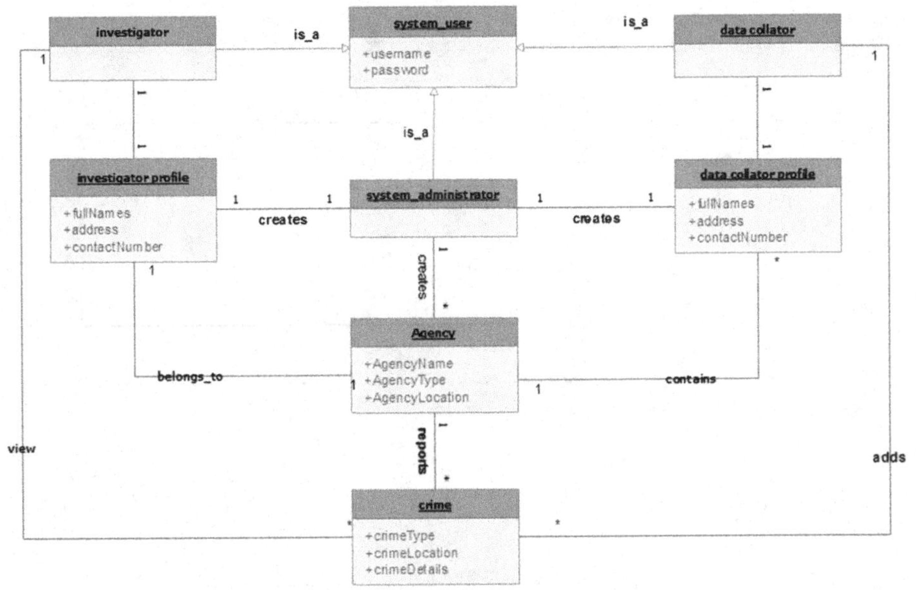

Therefore, there can be one or more security agencies that are registered within a particular ward. Also, the classes named investigator profile and data collator profile can be used to manage the systems users by creating new users, updating the information of existing users and for removing non-existing users from the system.

Also, the agency class can also be used by the data collator to manage the crime events reported to the security agency.

Figure 4 shows the sequence diagram of the timing operations of the GIS. As shown in the diagram, all authorized users are required to provide their username and password in order for the system to grant access to their respective profile. At the point of providing the username and password, the system checks the user database for the presence of the username and password as provided by the user and thus directs the user to their respective dashboard depending on the role of the user as provided in the database. However, if the username and password provided by the user are not consistent with information stored in the database then the user is not granted access to the system thus denied login to the system. Upon successful login to the system user's dashboard by the system to an authorized system user, the user can store information provided about reported fire outbreaks to the report database.

Figure 4. Sequence Diagram of Information System

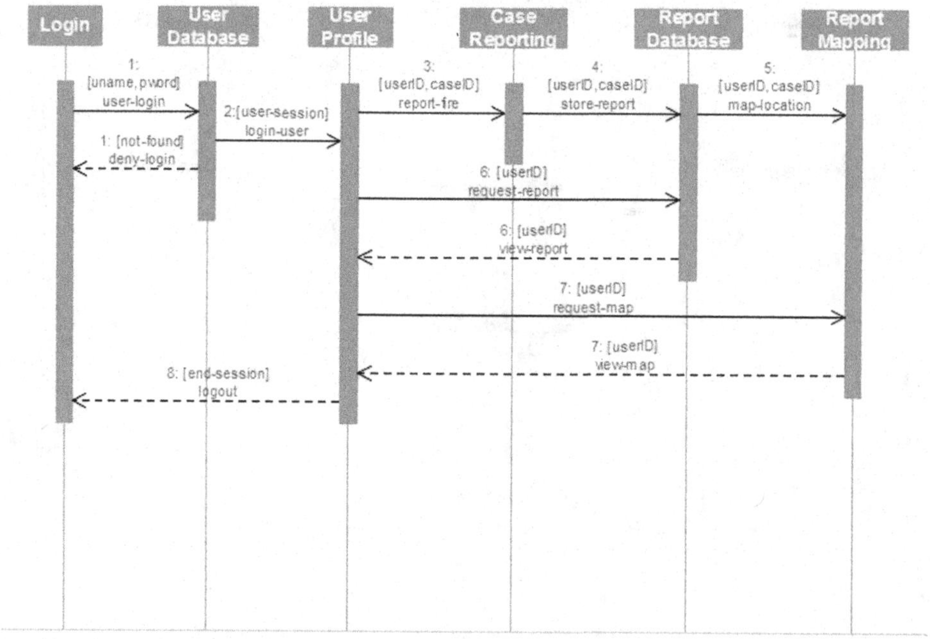

Following the process of providing information about reported fire outbreaks, the information is stored by the system to the report database in addition to information about the location of fire outbreak reporting by the system to the reporting map. Thus, there is a many-to-one correspondence between the numbers of fire outbreaks to the location of fire outbreak reporting. Therefore, information stored about fire outbreaks can also be viewed by the authorized user from their respective dashboard about the distribution of information stored about fire outbreaks in addition to the spatial distribution of the reported fire outbreaks via a digital map. Also, information about the user who reported the fire outbreak is stored by the system in order to keep track of the providers of information about fire outbreaks thus maintaining accountability of reports.

Figure 5. System Architecture of Terrorist Attack Monitoring System

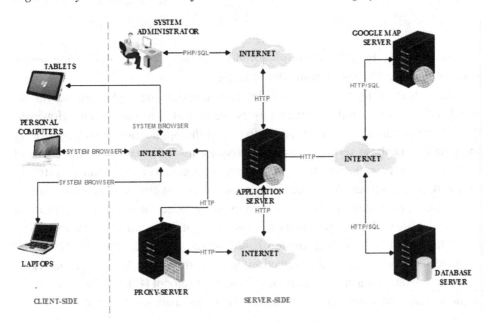

3.4 System Architecture

Figure 5 shows a conceptual diagram of the architecture of the spatial-based fire outbreak monitoring system. The system architecture of the system is an n-tier architecture that consists of a client-side and a server side. The client side provides an interface for the primary users of the system to interact with using their system browser over the Internet. The client-side provides access to system users using various hardware consisting of portable devices (e.g. smartphones, tablets, laptops etc.) alongside personal computers via either LAN or wireless LAN networks. On the server side, a proxy server was required for hiding information about the IP addresses of system users so as to protect user information from system intruders.

Figure 6. Wgis_terrorist.sql Database showing its 5 Relational Tables

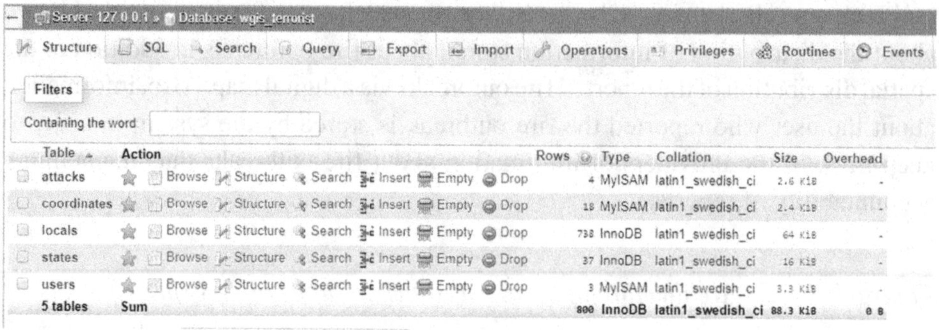

Table	Action	Rows	Type	Collation	Size	Overhead
attacks	Browse Structure Search Insert Empty Drop	4	MyISAM	latin1_swedish_ci	2.6 KiB	-
coordinates	Browse Structure Search Insert Empty Drop	18	MyISAM	latin1_swedish_ci	2.4 KiB	-
locals	Browse Structure Search Insert Empty Drop	738	InnoDB	latin1_swedish_ci	64 KiB	-
states	Browse Structure Search Insert Empty Drop	37	InnoDB	latin1_swedish_ci	16 KiB	-
users	Browse Structure Search Insert Empty Drop	3	MyISAM	latin1_swedish_ci	3.3 KiB	-
5 tables	Sum	800	InnoDB	latin1_swedish_ci	88.3 KiB	0 B

The information about the system is provided to users via the application server which is managed by the system administrator.

The system administrator uses the Internet to access the application server via which information about authorized users are provided to the system. However, data stored on the system were separated from the application server by storing them on the database server. Thus, every request for information provided to and retrieved from the system by users via the application server were managed strictly by the database server. Also, the Google map server which was accessed online was required for accessing the Google Map API needed for mapping the location of reported fire outbreaks based on the coordinates of the location. The information about the coordinates were provided based on the longitude and latitude of the required location. In general, interaction between the severs located at the server side was guaranteed using the hypertext Transfer Protocol (HTTP) for transferring requests made from one server to another during information processing.

3.5 System Development Tools

The software development tools used in development of the system include: Cascading Style Sheet (CSS) for design purpose, JavaScript which is usually used by most websites was used to create visually engaging webpages, user interfaces for web applications and mobile applications, Hypertext Pre-processor (PHP) was used as scripting language, Structured Query Language (SQL) for database along with Apache HTTP server and Google Map API.

4. RESULTS AND DISCUSSIONS

Figure 6 depicts the system's database which was used for information storage and retrieval. The database was named wgis_terrorist.sql and it consisted of five (5) database tables used for managing the various types of information stored and manipulated by the system.

The results of the implemented table called *attacks* as shown in Figure 7 was used to manage information about the crime events that were reported by a data collator from a security agency. The table contains attributes, such as: the unique Id of each record, the type of attack, state, LGA and ward where the crime was reported to have taken place for determining physical location, the type of location affected, time of attack and the longitude and latitude of the security agency for storing geographical location of the ward to which the security agency belongs to.

Figure 7. Table attacks showing its respective records and attributes

Show all | Number of rows: 25 | Filter rows: Search this table | Sort by key: None

Options	id	type_of_attack	loc_state	loc_lga	loc_name	latitude	longitude	loc_type	time_of_attack	no_injured	no_dead	suspect	attack_day
Edit Copy Delete	1	Car and Truck Bombings	Ogun State	Abeokuta South	Kuto	7.1635	3.3548	Market	15-06-2018 12:59	34	4	Boko Haram	Friday
Edit Copy Delete	7	Oil Pipeline Vandalism	Ogun State	Ewekoro	Ajaie	6.9356	3.2228	Hospital	15-06-2018 00:00	53	16	ISIS	Friday
Edit Copy Delete	5	Fulani Herdsman Attacks	Ogun State	Shagamu	Sabo	6.8322	3.6319	Market	18-06-2018 05:10	23	5	Hardsmen	Monday
Edit Copy Delete	6	Religious Attacks	Ogun State	Ijebu Ode	Molepa	6.83	3.9165	Religious Building	08-06-2018 05:32	12	5	Unknown	Friday

Check all   With selected: Edit Copy Delete Export

The results of the implemented Table called *users* as shown in Figure 8 was used to manage information about the users who are authorized to access the system. The table contains 11 attributes, namely: the unique ID of each user record, the type of user (data collator, admin or investigator), full names of users, gender, ethnicity, state of origin of user, the agency to which the user belonged, the rank of the user, the data information was reported alongside the username and password required by the user to log into the system. For each Table created in the database for storing and retrieving crime events reported, the primary keys of were defined by the unique ID provided at the first column for each respective table.

Figure 8. Table users showing its respective attributes and records

Options	id	user_type	full_name	gender	ethnicity	state_of_origin	agency	rank	date_added	username	password
Edit Copy Delete	1	Admin	Administrator	NULL	NULL	NULL	NULL	NULL	NULL	admin	admin
Edit Copy Delete	3	Record Officer	Kunle Oripenaiye	Male	Ibo	Benue State	Nigerian Navy	Rank II	13-06-2018	kunle	kunle
Edit Copy Delete	4	investigator	Drey Dreydoller	Male	Yoruba	Ogun State	National Intelligence Agency (NIA)	Rank V	13-06-2018	drey	drey

Check all   With selected: Edit Copy Delete Export

Figure 9. Login Page for Information System Users

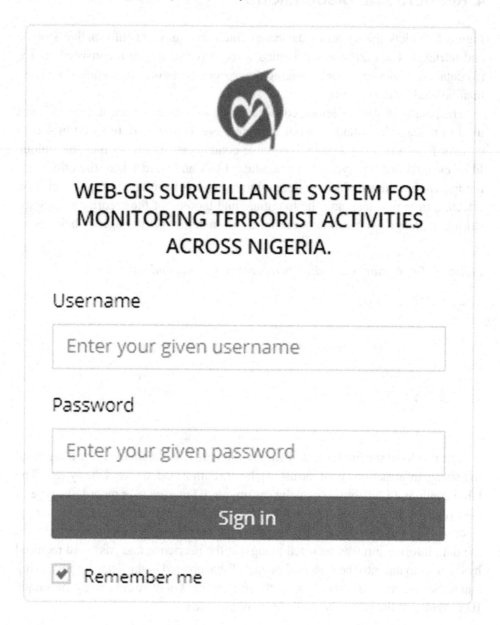

Figure 9 shows the system Login page also called the Home Page. Users are required to provide their username and passwords which is used by the system to determine the session which is to be created following user access authentication by the system.

Figure 10 shows the interface of the dashboard of the system administrator upon providing his username and password to the system. The results of this interface showed the different information stored on the system so far such as number of system users, number of injured and number of dead affected in the crime and record officers.

Figure 10. Screenshot of System Admin dashboard upon Login

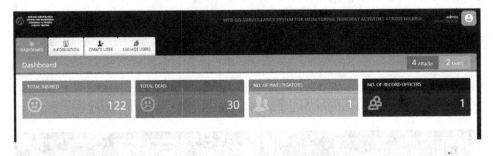

Figure 11 shows the results of the interface when an administrator is to create a new user to the system which requires the user to provide the names of the users, ranks, gender, state of origin, agency name alongside the default username and password provided by the administrator to the user. Figure 12 depicts the administrator's interface that is used to manage existing security personnel information.

Figure 13 shows the results of the interface required by the administrator for viewing information about existing crimes events reported. Thus, the interface shows the requirement of details such as the date of the reported crime, the agent that reported the crime, the data of occurrence of crime event, the agency reporting the crime and the type of crime event that was reported.

Figure 11. Screenshot of Admin Interface for Creating New Users

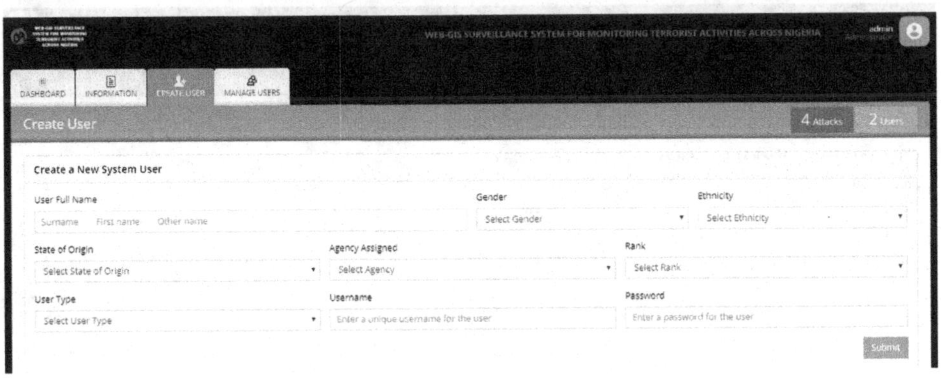

Figure 12. Screenshot of Admin Interface for managing Existing Users

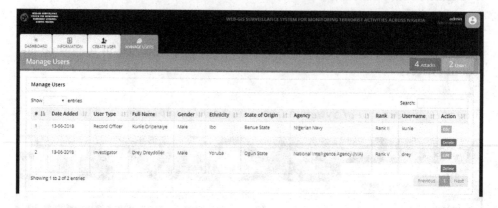

Figure 13. Screenshot Admin Interface for Viewing Reported Crimes

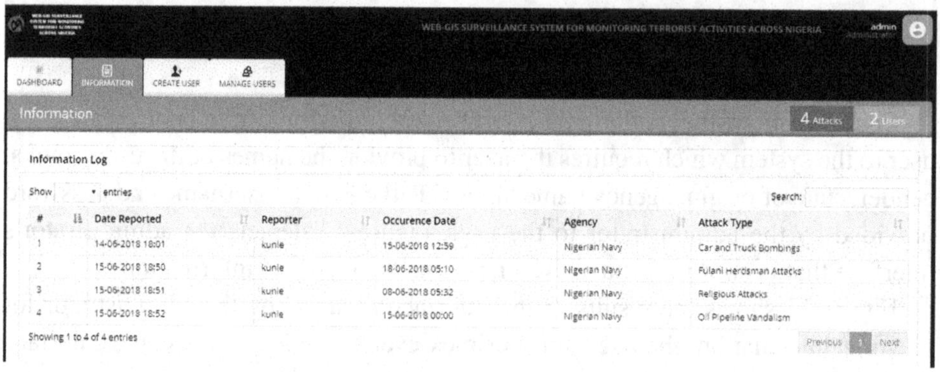

Figure 14. Data Collator Interface for adding new Crime Events

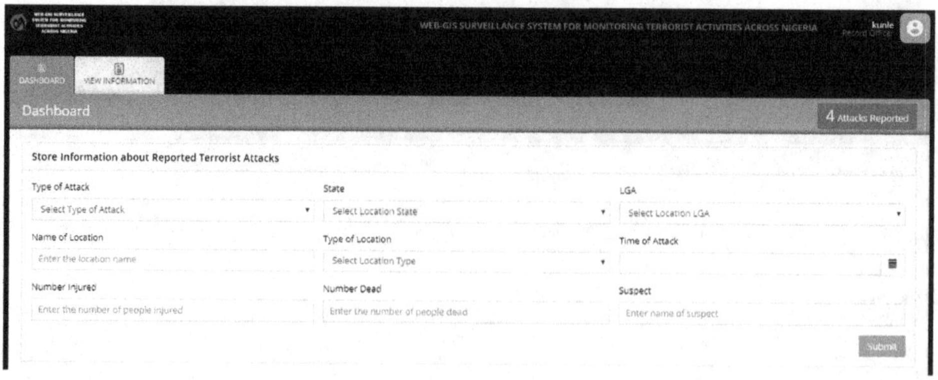

Figure 15. Screenshot of Sample Crime Event reported

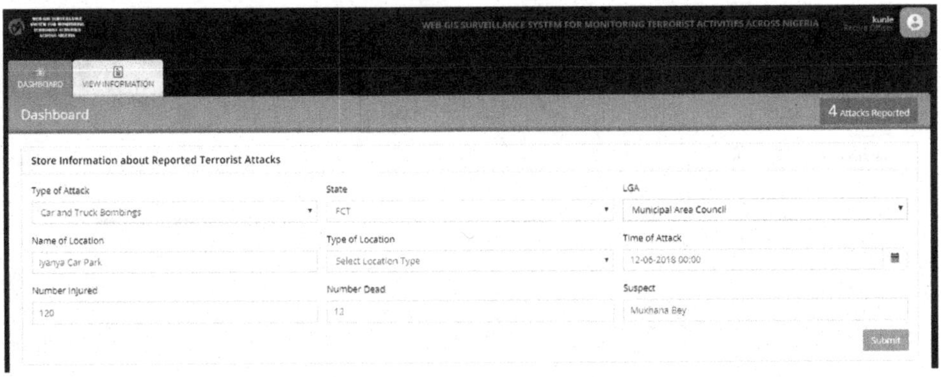

Figures 14 and 15 shows the results of the interface required by the data collator belonging to a security agency in order to add information about a newly reported crime event. The data collator is required to provide details about the reported crime events by providing information such as; the type of attack, state, LGA and ward where the attack took place, the name of the location affected, the type of location affected, time of attack, number of people injured and/or dead and the suspect. Figure 14 (b) shows the details that were provided regarding a particular crime event reported.

Figure 16 shows the results of the interface required by the data collator for viewing information about existing crimes events reported. Thus the interface shows details about reported crime events such as the day, month and year of the reported crime, type of attack, type of location attacked, number of injured and/or dead persons.

Figure 16. Data Collator Interface for viewing reported Crime

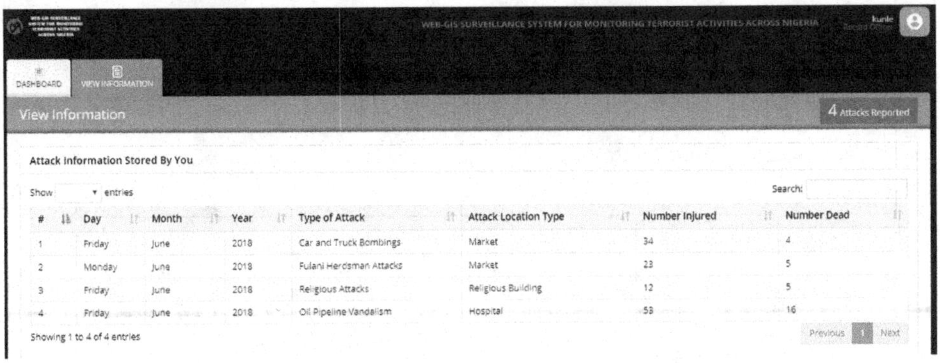

Figure 17. Investigator Interface for viewing reported Crimes

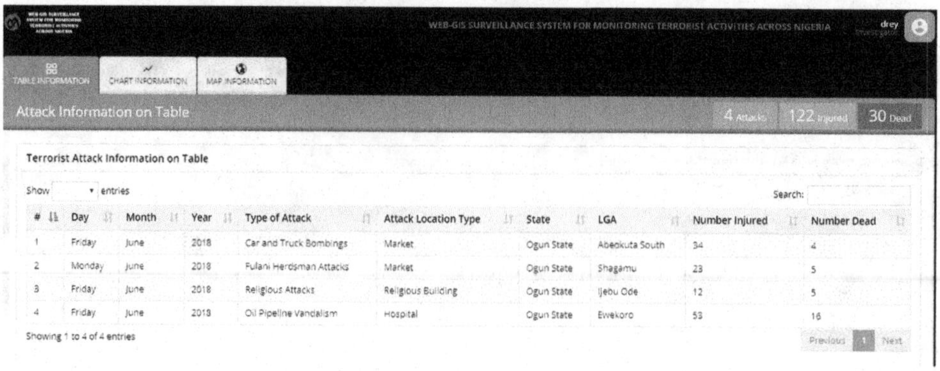

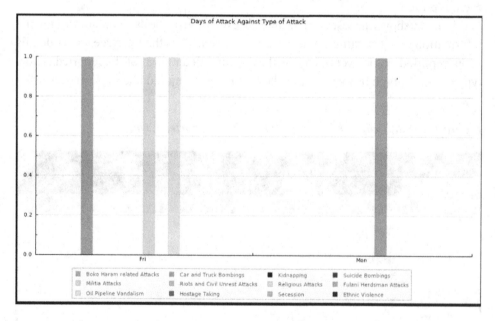

Figure 17 shows the results of the interface required by an investigator for viewing information about existing crimes events reported. Thus the interface shows details about reported crime events such as the day, month and year of the reported crime, type of attack, type of location attacked, number of injured and/or dead persons just as is observed by the data collator.

Figure 18. Chart Interface showing Type of Attack by Days

Figure 19. Chart Interface showing Type of Attack by Months

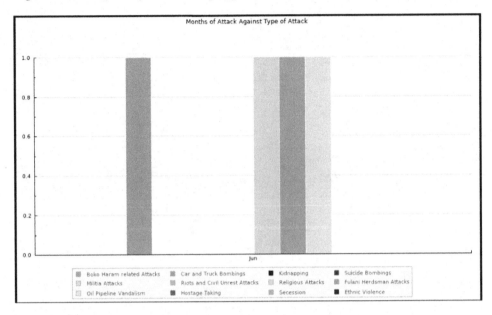

Figure 20. Chart Interface showing Type of Attack by Number of People Injured (blue) and Dead (red)

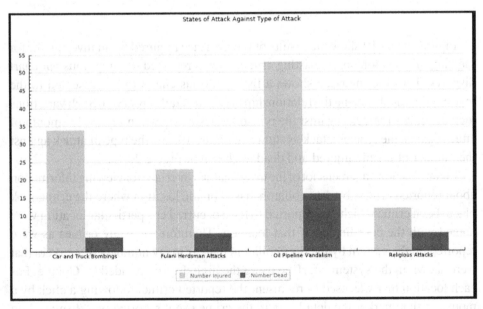

Figure 21. Interface showing Map View of Reported Crimes across Locations

Figure 18 and 19 show the results of the interface required by an investigator for viewing information about existing crimes events reported using various bar chart displays. Thus the interface shows a list of various charts to be presented to the investigator for observing the relationship between details observed. Such variations include: days of attacks against the type of attack as shown in Figure 18, month of attack against the type of attack as shown in Figure 19, and the type of attack against the number of people injured and dead as shown in Figure 20.

Figure 21 shows a screenshot of the investigator's interface for viewing information about reported crimes by data collators based on the location where the crime took place. Each crime which was reported to have occurred at a particular location were tagged with the coordinates of that location. Therefore, as many crimes as were reported on the system by the data collators then as many numbers of markers that were shown in the system interface using the digital map provided by Google. For each location that was used to represent the reported crime, following a click by a mouse of that marker the details about the crime event reported was displayed on a text pop-up as shown in the interfaces shown in Figure 21.

5. CONCLUSION

This study developed a web-based spatially enabled system which monitors the spatial distribution of reported criminal acts of terror in Nigeria. Interviews/Interactions were done with the prospective system users which are basically security agencies and the area of study was Ogun State. Numerous challenges were identified with the traditional mode of gathering and reporting crime related information hence the need for the web enabled system. The system was designed to improve the way and rate at which information about crimes gathered and reported for enhanced decision-making process. The system would also reduce the frequency of unreported crimes, increase transparency, and manage scarce resources in terms of man and machine. It is recommended for further studies that the designed system be integrated with crime mapping such that after the system might have collected crime data, it would analyze it and determine and (or) predict crime especially in hot spot areas for enhanced security. Spatial analysis would also be done in future studies so that crime patterns and relationships can be known or predicted for adequate and improved policing strategies. The system would also be improved on by using it to monitor a wider geographical area not just one state in a country.

REFERENCES

Adedeji, O. H., Adebayo, H. O., & Sotayo, E. I. (2014). Assessing Environmental Impacts of Inland Sand Mining in Parts of Ogun State, Nigeria. *Ethiopian Journal of Environmental Studies and Management, 7*(5), 478–487. doi:10.4314/ejesm.v7i5.2

Adelaja, A. O., Labo, A., & Penar, E. (2018). Public Opinion on the Root Causes of Terrorism and Objectives of Terrorists: A Boko Haram Case Study. *Perspectives on Terrorism, 12*(3), 35–49.

Adigun, A. A., Folorunso, S. O. & Uzoh, P. (2018). A Criminal Database System to Enhance National Security. *The Journal of Computer Science and its Applications, 25*(2), 176-183.

Africa Check. (2019). *Factsheet: South Africa's crime statistics for 2018/19.* Retrieved from https://africacheck.org/factsheets/factsheet-south-africas-crime-statistics-for-2018-19/

Ahishakiye, E., Danison, T., & Elisha, O. O. (2017). A Secure Web Based Records Management System for Prisons: A Case of Kisoro Prison in Uganda. *International Journal of Computer, 24*(1), 146–158.

Amin, M., Rahim, M., & Ayu, G. (2014). A trend analysis of violent crimes in Malaysia. *Health and the Environment Journal, 5*(2), 41–56.

Asmann, P., & O'Reilly, E. (2020). *InSight Crime's 2019 Homicide Round-Up.* Retrieved from https://www.insightcrime.org/news/analysis/insight-crime-2019-homicide-round-up/

Beynon-Davies, P, Carne, C, Mackay, H. & Tudhope, D. (1999). *Rapid Application Development (RAD): An empirical review.* Academic Press.

Bornman, E. (2012). The Mobile Phone in Africa: Has It Become a Highway to the Information Society or Not. *Contemporary Educational Technology, 3*(4), 278–292. doi:10.30935/cedtech/6084

British Broadcast Corporation (BBC) News. (2020). *How dangerous is Mexico?* Retrieved from https://www.bbc.com/news/world-latin-america-50315470

BusinessTech. (2019). *Crime levels in South Africa are far worse than what is reported.* Retrieved from https://businesstech.co.za/news/lifestyle/344284/crime-levels-in-south-africa-are-far-worse-than-what-is-reported/

Butler, D. (2006). Virtual Globes: The web-wide world. *Journal of Nature, 439*(7078), 776–778. doi:10.1038/439776a PMID:16482123

Chaudhuri, K., Chowdhury, P., & Kumbhakar, S. C. (2015). Crime in India: Specification and Estimation of violent crime index. *Journal of Productivity Analysis, 43*(1), 13–28. doi:10.100711123-014-0398-7

Chow, T. E. (2008). The Potential of Maps APIs for Internet GIS Applications. *Transactions in GIS Journal, 12*(2), 179–191. doi:10.1111/j.1467-9671.2008.01094.x

Crima and Safety Report. (2019). *Nigeria 2019 Crime & Safety Report: Lagos.* Retrieved from https://www.osac.gov/Country/Nigeria/Content/Detail/Report/4a5eaf52-3655-43e6-b540-1684bcb6f3de

Ejemeyovwi, D. O. (2015). Crime mapping using Time Series Analysis in Asaba, Delta State Nigeria: A Remote Sensing and GIS Approach. *European Journal of Basic and Applied Sciences, 2*(2), 52–71.

Falaye, A. A., Adama, N. V., & Agemerien, F. P. (2013). Design and Implementation of Crime Investigation System using Biometrics Approach (Nigeria Police Force). *Pacific Journal of Science and Technology, 14*(2), 242–253.

Idhoko, K. E., & Ojaiko, J. C. (2014). Integration of Geographical Information Systems (GIS) and Spatial Data Mining Techniques in Fight against Boko Haram Terrorist in Nigeria. *International Journal of Scientific Research*, 6(14), 1932–1934.

Mwiya, M., Phiri, J., & Lyoko, G. (2015). Public Crime Reporting and Monitoring System Model Using GSM and GIS Technologies: A Case of Zambia Police Service. *International Journal of Computer Science and Mobile Computing*, 4(11), 207–226.

Naz, R., & Khan, M. N. A. (2015). Rapid Applications Development Techniques: A Critical Review. *International Journal of Software Engineering and Its Applications*, 9(11), 163–176. doi:10.14257/ijseia.2015.9.11.15

Nwankwo, U. V., & James, O. (2016). Prevalence of Lethal and Non-lethal Crimes in Nigeria. *Journal of Advanced Research in Humanity and Social Science*, 3(1), 1–16.

Oguntade, P. E., Ojo, O.O., Okagbue, H. I., & Oguntade, O. A. (2015). Analysis of selected crime data in Nigeria between 1999 and 2013. *Data in Brief*. doi:10.1016/j.dib.2018.05.143i

Smiatek, G. (2005). SOAP Based web services in GIS/RDBMS Environment. *Journal of Environmental Modeling and Software*, 20(6), 775–782. doi:10.1016/j.envsoft.2004.04.008

Statista Research Department. (2019). *Total violent crime reported in the United States from 1990 to 2018*. Retrieved from https://www.statista.com/statistics/191129/reported-violent-crime-in-the-us-since-1990/

Statista Research Department. (2020). *Number of crimes in China 2018, by type*. Retrieved from https://www.statista.com/statistics/224776/number-of-crimes-in-china-by-type/

Wang, F. (2012). Why police and policing need GIS: An overview. *Annals of GIS*, 18(3), 159–171. doi:10.1080/19475683.2012.691900

World Population Review. (2020). *Crime Rate by Country 2020*. Retrieved from https://worldpopulationreview.com/countries/crime-rate-by-country/

Yasser, A. A., & Awatef, A. S. (2018). Fighting terrorism more effectively with the aid of GIS: The Kingdom of Saudi Arabia case study. *American Journal of Geographic Information System*, 7(91), 15–31.

Chapter 9
An IoT–Based Soil Properties Monitoring System for Crop Growth and Production

Harshit Bhatt
Shoolini University of Biotechnology and Management Sciences, India

Aaditya Sharma
Shoolini University of Biotechnology and Management Sciences, India

Brij Bhushan Sharma
(iD) https://orcid.org/0000-0002-8930-8102
Shoolini University of Biotechnology and Management Sciences, India

Ruchika Sharma
Shoolini University of Biotechnology and Management Sciences, India

Meenakshi Sharma
Shoolini University of Biotechnology and Management Sciences, India

ABSTRACT

Agriculture is very important for the economic growth of a country. Soil properties such as soil type, nutrients, pH level, temperature, and soil moisture play active role in the field of agriculture for the proper growth of any crop. The common primitive methods for soil testing involve collection of soil samples and testing these samples in the lab to provide real-time information of the soil. For continuous monitoring of these factors and to get accurate results, there is a need to modernize the traditional methods by using smart technologies such as IoT and WSN. With sensors, all the mentioned soil properties can be detected continuously, making it easier for any farmer to know the status of the soil and to further act upon accordingly. The highlighting feature of this chapter is the detection of pH level to monitor the system for better crop and yield as well as to minimize the use of water and fertilizers in IoT environment. Protecting the pH level is the biggest concern. In view of this, a note on securing the system with various suggestions is given in this chapter.

DOI: 10.4018/978-1-7998-7756-1.ch009

INTRODUCTION

The agriculture sector is an imperative part of the economic growth of any nation. If we talk about the role of agriculture in the development of an economy then we can say that it contributes to national income, is a source of food supply, improves the supply of raw material, employment, helps in the creation of infrastructure, is a source of foreign exchange for the nation and helps in tackling economic depression. In India, the agriculture sector contributes about 17% of the country's total GDP with a production of 284.95 million tonnes of major crops in 2018-19. In FY2019 agriculture exports were US$ 38.54 billion (Ibef, n.d.). Developmental activities towards better crop production meeting the requirements and standards at a global level are the need of the hour.

The growth and quality of any crop depend a lot on the quality of the soil. Soil is a blend of organic mineral particles and natural matter of differing size and arrangement. It is composed of five ingredients – minerals, soil organic matter, living organisms, gas and water. These ingredients play a huge role in the growth and quality of any crop. Out of the many factors affecting the growth and quality of the crop, one main factor discussed here is – pH (power of hydrogen) level of the soil and crop. Soil pH is a measure of the acidity or basicity (alkalinity) of soil. pH is defined as the negative logarithm of the activity of hydronium (H+ or H3O+aq.) in a solution. In soils, it is measured in a slurry of soil mixed with water. The pH of the soil (ranging between 0 and 14, where 0 to 6 is acidic, 7 is neutral and 8 to 14 is alkaline) affects the availability of nutrients. The effect of soil pH is great on the solubility of minerals or nutrients. Before a nutrient can be used by plants it must be dissolved properly in the soil solution. Most minerals and nutrients are more soluble or available in acid soils as compared to neutral or slightly alkaline soils. The soil may contain adequate nutrients, yet plant health may be limited by an unfavourable pH level and vice-versa. Although the best range for a crop to grow properly is 5.5 to 7 but some crops grow in more acidic soil and some in a more alkaline one. More acidic soil causes a reduction in the level of macronutrients and also increases aluminium, iron and manganese toxicity. While more alkaline soil leads to a decrease in the level of micronutrients in the soil. To monitor the status of properties associated with crop production, the significance of ICT seen worldwide. In this regard, IoT can play a very important role in agriculture (Sharma & Kumar, 2020; Jirapond et al., 2019). The quality of the crops can also be increased with the combination of wireless sensor networks and the internet of things (Kumar & Sharma, 2020). Meanwhile, there exists, several challenges in the field of smart technologies.

Figure 1. pH levels of soil

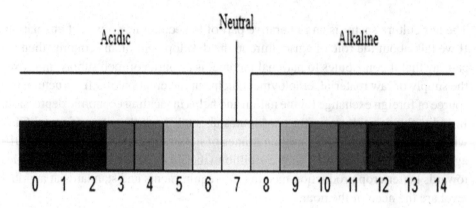

Table 1. List of pH detection methods

	1.	Indicator reagents
	2.	pH test strips
Common detection methods	3.	Metal electrode methods
	4.	Glass electrode methods
	1.	Optical-fibre-based pH sensors
	2.	Mass-sensitive pH sensor
	3.	Metal oxide pH sensors
New detection methods	4.	Conducting polymer pH sensors
	5.	Nano-constructedcantilever-basedpH
		sensors
	6.	ISFET-based pH sensors
	7.	EGFET-based pH sensors
	8.	CMOS FinFET-based pH sensors
	9.	pH-image sensor

The objective of this chapter is to come up with a device that can sense the pH level of the soil and water.

Further, to make the best possible use of available water and minimize the use of fertilizers. And also, highlights certain points on possible threats and challenges in the context of Smart Agriculture.

Advantages of Modern Techniques

The above-mentioned techniques to measure pH level prove to be much more beneficial as compared to the traditional techniques. The major advantages of modern techniques are:

(a) Reduce Human Efforts

Modern techniques require less manpower as compared to the traditional ones. Due to the huge production of any crop in traditional methods, farmers are required in abundance from the process of sowing till harvesting, but such is not the case with modern techniques as with less manpower all the processes can be taken care of.

(b) Reduce the Production Time

When using modern techniques, all the processes take place in time because the measured data is accurate enough to carry all the processes of agriculture very quickly.

(c) Helps in Proper Irrigation

Availability of fresh water for irrigation is a huge problem these days. In traditional techniques, the proper use of irrigation is not made thus causing wastage of water in large amount but when it comes to modern techniques, the use of water is done properly thus saving the water usage as well as using the minimum amount of water (Rani, Kumar, & Bhushan, 2019) & (Sharma, B. B., & Kumar, N. 2021).

(d) Improves Fertility of the Soil

The soil and any crop require fertilizers according to their needs. Modern techniques help in sensing the accurate amount of minerals present in the soil or the crop as well as fertilizers required by the soil or the crop.

(e) Increase the Price and Demand of the Products

Due to great and timely crop production, the price and the demand for any product manufactured from a crop automatically increases.

Study on IoT for Agriculture

In this chapter, a study of different research focused on the field of smart agriculture is discussed. The study has mainly focused on the works in India. Also, it starts with certain works done at a global level.

The significance of IoT in agriculture has been well discussed by Bo, Y., & Wang, H. (2011).

Xiangyu Hu et al. developed an IoT application involving IoT-Radio Frequency identification, GPS and sensors for transforming field-level data. The distributed mobile architecture developed by Richard K. Lomotey et al. (2014) focused on providing timely details for farmers. The system involved WiFi, Bluetooth, offline communications.

In this direction, this study provides the literature done for the work proposed in Table 2.

PROPOSED WORK

As discussed above, many techniques have been made available by researchers to measure the pH levels of soil and crop. Each researcher has tried to come up with a new technique that can measure the pH accurately at a low cost but meeting these conditions of accuracy and low cost is not that easy.

We have tried to meet both of the above-mentioned conditions and proposed a device that can help to sense the accurate pH level of soil and crop and further also help in choosing the suitable crop and make the optimum use of water. Knowledge of pH levels of soil, water and plant is very essential. The optimum pH range (5.5 to 7) is the range in which the bacteria change and release nitrogen from organic matter. This range may be suitable for some fertilizers and in turn, this may be suited for crop growth.

Soil samples were taken from the greenhouse to measure their pH levels. Along with this, the pH level of the available water in the greenhouse was also measured. The pH levels of 5 soil samples and water were observed to be almost neutral or in some cases on a slightly alkaline side too. The pH meter kit (digital pH meter Alpha – 01) used to measure the pH levels of soil and water consisted of a pH probe and a meter to display the final pH of a solution digitally. The pH probe has a glass electrode (sensor electrode) which has a chrome electrical wire suspended in a solution of potassium chloride, contained inside a thin bulb. This bulb (or membrane) is made from a special glass. The reference electrode, another electrode, is used to provide a stable zero-voltage connection to complete the whole circuit. The potential difference between these two electrodes is the main reason behind the

Table 2. Study on Smart Agriculture

Author	Paper description
Yuqing, Jianrong and Keming (2005)	Discussed in detail pH and its importance. Also, various methods for detecting pH have been dealt with.
Tiong and Qiao (1999)	Discussed the integration of the intelligent agriculture systems for solving problems of agriculture domains.
Staggenborg, S.A et al. 2007	Discussed pH values prediction methodologies.
Zhai et al. (2018)	Highlighted the use of intelligent techniques in agriculture.
(Ramane, Patil, & Shaligram, 2015)	An NPK sensor used in multimode and plastic optical fibres works on the colourimetric principle (absorption of light transmitted through the medium is directly proportional to the concentration of medium). The sensor gives output in terms of the deficient component in the soil and an LCDs the name of the deficient component and amount of it needed in the soil.
(Gaikwad & Galande S. G, 2015)	A wireless sensor node has been constructed to sense conditions like NPK (Nivo-press probe), temperature (LM35 sensor), moisture (sensed using two wires covered with soil), humidity (P-Hs-220), pH level (standard pH probe) and light intensity (light dependent resistor). The central control unit receives the data from the sensor node through RF transceivers which further compares data with the programmed data in PC and if these don't match then appropriate controlling action is taken.
(Patil, 2016)	The sensing of various parameters is done using Ubi-Sense mote which consists of different sensors like temperature, relative humidity, light intensity, buzzer etc. The sensed data (properties of soil, crops and environmental conditions) are gathered at the server and is further used for analysis. A web application or mobile application on an Android OS can be used by a user to receive and analyze the sensed data.
(Prathibha, Hongal & Jyothi, 2017)	The aim here is to monitor temperature and humidity in the agricultural field using sensors and in addition to this, a camera sensor has been used to capture images and send them to a farmer via MMS so that the condition of the crops can be known.
(Padalalu, Mahajan, Dabir, Mitkar, & Javale, 2017)	The system consists of sensors to sense the conditions of the crop soil and with the help of predefined values, it decides whether the pump used in the system should be in an on or off state. If there is a failure to water the crops, an alert is sent to the android application. In the case of natural conditions like the rainy season, the weather conditions are also taken into account because that is the time when there is less need for smart irrigation. The microcontroller used here is Arduino which helps in less consumption of power supply. The entire system can be controlled using a smartphone.
(Rahaman, 2017)	The proposed system senses pH level, humidity, temperature and moisture along with the NPK level of the soil. The property of electrical resistance is used to sense soil moisture, to sense temperature/humidity a DHT11 sensor has been used, pH has been measured using a pH analogue meter and the NPK ratio has been sensed using soil image processing. The sensed data is fed to the microcontroller for processing while the Blynk app has been used to display data. Grey-level co-event matrix (GLCM) and support vector machine (SVM) algorithm have been used to distinguish
(N & M, 2017)	A system has been proposed for the estimation of nutrient level and disease detection. The image processing unit depicts the pH level and NPK ratio in the soil sample. For disease detection, digital cameras have been used to keep track of plant body surface. The classification of data has been done using the SVM algorithm. The data is finally sent to the cloud for storage and to the farmer's smartphone to take any necessary action.
(Rao, R. Nageswara., 2018)	The sensed data (temperature and humidity) in the form of analogue values are firstly converted to digital values and then processed by raspberry-pi which is finally sent to the database after which starts the application of the irrigation system once the sensed data is properly analysed.
(Aswathy, Manimegalai, Fernando, & Vijay, 2018)	Most of the farmers still use the traditional methods for soil testing in the soil testing labs which may take days and hence real-time monitoring of soil parameters is also not possible. Hence, in this paper, a smart way of testing or sensing the soil parameters has been proposed with the help of sensors like pH, moisture and EC sensors. The link of the website containing these reports are sent to the farmer via SMS and further, fertilizers are also recommended to a farmer according to his choice of the crop.
(P. Sindhu, 2018)	A node MCU 1.0 (ESP8266 12E Wi-Fi module) has been used for data processing and transmission along with soil moisture, soil pH, humidity and temperature sensors. The sensed data is sent to the cloud for storage and can be accessed anytime. The proposed system helps in improving the production of vegetables.
(Anand, J, S, & Sweatha, 2019)	A system has been proposed to monitor soil parameters like pH level, soil moisture and various important soil nutrients like nitrogen, phosphorus and potassium. Further, ultrasonic and PIR sensors have been used to monitor animal and human intrusion. These reports can be viewed by a farmer on this smartphone using an android application. The proposed system helps to reduce the use of water and fertilizers. Hence, reducing the cost of the production of crops and further improving it as well.
(Bhatt, Bhushan, & Kumar, 2019)	The paper discusses the advantages of IoT and WSN in agriculture. The farmers still use traditional methods for cultivation and harvesting of the crops hence decreasing the yield of crops so, it becomes important to use new techniques to get rid of old ones. Further, various sensors and sensors nodes have been discussed which can be used in smart agriculture to detect climatic and soil conditions like temperature, humidity, light, soil moisture and pH level.
(Saranya, 2019)	An automated system is designed and implemented by the authors in this research article, for the treatment of household wastewater. pH meter is designed to make the wastewater usable for irrigation.
(Ramane et al., 2015)	The authors proposed an ultrasonic sensor-based system as a repellent for the pest in agriculture. A pH meter is used to maintain and check the quality of the water used in fields. Continuous usage of pesticides decreases the groundwater level. They proposed that different frequencies of the ultrasonic sensor can repel pests from the crops.

pH measurement of any aqueous solution. The digital pH meter gives the pH of the aqueous solution in a digital form.

The results (pH readings) obtained are given below:

As discussed above and also can be seen in the above-given figures, the pH levels of the 5 soil samples and available water are almost neutral or slightly on the alkaline side making the soil and water suitable enough for good crop growth and production. The main aim here is to develop a system which a common farmer or user can use to sense pH level easily and at a low cost. The system further aims to decrease human intervention and give the results as soon as possible so that a farmer or user doesn't need to wait for days for results to come.

The main goal is to develop a sensing module to sense the pH levels needed for plant growth. The proposed system consists of the following components:

1. Gravity pH sensor
2. Arduino Uno Microcontroller
3. Power supply
4. LCD (Output)
5. ESP8266

In the proposed model ESP8266 WiFi module is used. All sensed data from the pH sensor can be stored in a cloud platform for future purposes. Whereas, Internet and Cloud platforms are associated with this proposed model.

RESULTS AND DISCUSSIONS

The major outcome of this project is providing soil specific crop recommendation and good utilization of the irrigation system. It is very difficult to test all the soil samples in time by the laboratories. By the time test reports are generated, harvesting is on the verge of completion. Hence there is a need for a soil analysis to be made available to the farmer as early as possible. Before choosing a crop, which is to be grown by a farmer, he/ she needs to know the available soil well. We have been able to successfully sense the pH of the soil and water so that it becomes easy for the farmer to choose the crop and water them accordingly. As pH also affects the presence of nutrients in the soil, hence a farmer can get a rough idea of the nutrients present in the soil and make use of suitable fertilizers to keep the growth and production of the crop as good as possible. According to the pH value of sensed soil, we can recommend farmer grow specific crops like mentioned in table 3 according to the max pH value crop can survive. Moreover, this article also provides the various security concerns related to the Internet of Things while dealing in a real-time environment and this can contribute towards the literature to the mentioned field.

Figure 2. Soil Sample – 1

Figure 3. Soil Sample – 2

Figure 4. Soil Sample – 3

Figure 5. Soil Sample – 4

Figure 6. Soil Sample – 5

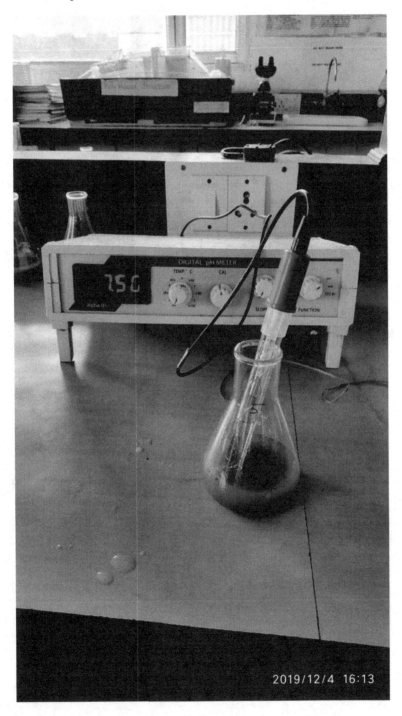

Figure 7. Water Sample

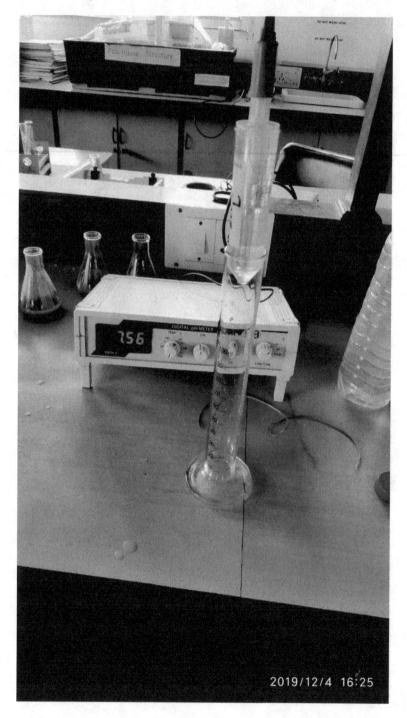

Figure 8. Block diagram of the proposed system

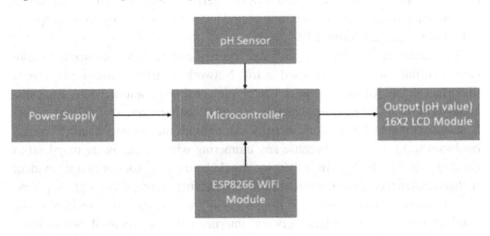

Table 3. Recommend Crops as per the pH value

Sr. No	pH value	Crops Recommended (according to max pH value)		
		Flowers	Vegetables	Trees and Shrubs
1.	8.13	Canna, Cosmos, Crocus, Shasta daisy, Daylily and Geranium	Asparagus, Garlic	Elder, box, Pecan, Plum, Walnut, black and Willow
2.	7.58	Alyssum, Beebalm, Chrysanthemum, Coneflower, Dahlia &Marigold	Cauliflower, Kale, Pumpkin, Spinach, Tomato	Ash, Beautybush, Lemon, Orange, Pear

Security Issues and Management

An eye should also be kept on security concerns. Malware has proven to be a big issue in IoT security. Even if the data is stored securely in the cloud, still the malware can lock down the entire functionality of an IoT device hence making it impossible for the IoT device to work in any manner. With a lack of IoT security, (improper passwords, personal data in internet cloud etc.) an intruder or spy can alter the sensitive data by taking control of the IoT device and can even send false signals which may lead to taking wrong decisions because of the presence of inaccurate data in the IoT device.

One of the biggest advantages of an IoT device is that it can be easily accessed from a remote location. But this proves to be a huge disadvantage as well. Usually, an IoT device functions successfully without any user intervention but any IoT device needs to be physically secured from external threats. An IoT device can be located in a remote location for a long period hence making it easy to be tampered with if not protected adequately.

To protect an IoT device from such security concerns, a user needs to take care of certain vital aspects related to IoT. Network security is discussed above is important in any IoT device which can be protected using antimalware, firewalls, and even intrusion detection/prevention system. Blocking unauthorized IP addresses is another solution for network security. Along with the network security comes hardware security as well because any tampering with the hardware may lead to damage to an IoT device. An IoT device should be tamper-proof or tamper-evident so that it can survive a harsh environment or even function properly for a long period even if not monitored regularly. Various security issues in the IoT are related to the wireless transmission medium, network, internet and access control. Some of the issues are listed and described below(Hanan Aldowah, Shafiq Ul Rehman, 2019).

Security Requirements of the Internet of Things

Security Concerns related to the Internet of things should be considered throughout the life span of the particular device. Some of the key requirements of security in the Internet of things are mentioned & described below(Jaiswal, 2017).

1. **Cryptography and Encryption:** The IoT devices are required to implement the encryption to the sensor modules. So that data can be protected, and these encryption standards should be decided according to the sensing units. Most of the IoT devices do not have any authentication keys or they have global keys, this makes the particular device vulnerable. As symmetric algorithms are light as compared to asymmetric, they may be implemented.
2. **Safe and Secure OS:** An IoT working framework ought to have restricted access rights and decrease the permeability of the framework which is heavily based on safe and secured O.S.
3. **Event Logging Protection:** The log files must be kept or generated at various levels of IoT scenarios must be analyzed at a periodic time- period to detect whether there is any fault in the data or not if there is a data fault then immediate action must be taken.
4. **Protection of devices:** At the time of manufacturing of any IoT device, so many peripherals are used in the manufacturing process. All these kinds of peripherals should be removed before any kind of deployment. Proper access to all the ports should be provided.

Figure 9. Security Issues related to IoT

5. **Application Safety:** Applications are developed for IoT devices when they are deployed in an open environment. These applications should be provided with proper safety precautions. As the data gathered by the sensors of the IoT devices are validated by these applications before any kind of processing of the data.

6. **Credentials:** All credentials like passwords, digital certificates, and other keys which are used for different purposes in the IoT need to be stronger and never to be shared with anyone.

Figure 10. Key Security Requirements of Internet of Things

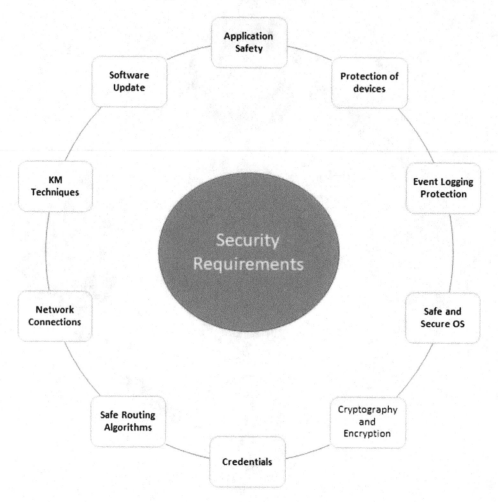

7.   **Safe Routing Algorithms:** As data can be transferred using wireless media or over the internet, and the traditionally available routing algorithms are not appropriate or cannot be applied to the IoT devices. So, a safe routing algorithm is required in IoT devices to protect the data transmission from the attacks such as selective forwarding, warm hole, and Dos etc.

8.   **Network Connections:** Network connections are used for the connection of the IoT devices with the external world. IoT device should have a single network port or minimum ports for connection purposes. Secured protocols like SFTP should be used and proper acknowledgement messages should be used by the receiver while transmission of the data takes place.

9. **KM Techniques:** These techniques are a very important feature in IoT devices. Secure communication is the Key requirement these techniques are used often in wireless sensor devices like shared key distribution, group, and broadcast. These are used to reduce power consumption.

10. **Software Update:** Proper software updates should be provided from time to time to keep the device updated up to date which will protect the device from various attacks.

FUTURE SCOPE

In this venture, we have just taken into account a single important factor (pH level) of agriculture for good crop growth and production. There are many other factors as well which need to be taken care of to further improve the sector of smart agriculture. The idea here was to take quick and accurate actions based on pH levels of crop and water keeping in mind the overall cost of the proposed system. To improve this further, the idea is to take into account the other soil properties like NPK, temperature, soil moisture etc. as well which also contribute a lot to crop growth and production. All this has to be done quickly, accurately and at a low cost like in the case of the proposed pH model. For a further enhancement to the work, the need and discussions on IoT related security aspects done.

REFERENCES

Anand, S., J, S. C., S, S. P., & Sweatha, A. (2019). Monitoring of Soil Nutrients Using IoT for Optimizing the Use of Fertilizers. *International Journal of Science Engineering And Technology Research*, 8(4), 105–107.

Aswathy, S., Manimegalai, S., Fernando, M. M. R., & Vijay, J. F. (2018). *Smart Soil Testing*. Academic Press.

Bhatt, H., Bhushan, B., & Kumar, N. (2019). IoT: The Current Scenario and Role of Sensors Involved in Smart Agriculture. *International Journal of Recent Technology and Engineering*, 8(4), 12011–12023. doi:10.35940/ijrte.D9285.118419

Bo, Y., & Wang, H. (2011). The Application of Cloud Computing and the Internet of Things in Agriculture and Forestry. *International Joint Conference on Service Sciences*, 168-172. 10.1109/IJCSS.2011.40

Gaikwad, S. V, & G, P. G. S. (2015). *Measurement of NPK, Temperature, Moisture, Humidity using*. Academic Press.

Gayatri, M. K., Jayasakthi, J., & Mala, G. S. A. (2015). Providing Smart Agricultural solutions to farmers for better yielding using IoT. *Proceedings - 2015 IEEE International Conference on Technological Innovations in ICT for Agriculture and Rural Development, TIAR 2015, 4*(22), 40–43. 10.1109/TIAR.2015.7358528

Hu, X. S. Q. (n.d.). IOT Application System with Crop Growth Models in Facility Agriculture. IEEE.

Ibef. (n.d.). *Agriculture in India: Information About Indian Agriculture & Its Importance*. Retrieved from https://www.ibef.org/industry/agriculture-india.aspx

Kumar, N., & Sharma, B. (2020). Opportunities and Challenges with WSN's in Smart Technologies: A Smart Agriculture Perspective. *Advances in Intelligent Systems and Computing, 1132*, 441–463. doi:10.1007/978-3-030-40305-8_22

Lomotey, R. D. (2014). Management of Mobile Data in a Crop Field. In *2014 IEEE International Conference on Mobile Services* (pp. 100-107). IEEE. 10.1109/MobServ.2014.23

Muangprathub, J., Boonnam, N., Kajornkasirat, S., Lekbangpong, N., Wanichsombat, A., & Nillaor, P. (2019). IoT and agriculture data analysis for smart farm. *Computers and Electronics in Agriculture, 156*, 467–474. doi:10.1016/j.compag.2018.12.011

N, M. S., & M, P. K. (2017). *Development of a System for Estimation of NPK and pH in Soil and Disease Detection in plants*. doi:10.9790/2834-1204055257

Padalalu, P., Mahajan, S., Dabir, K., Mitkar, S., & Javale, D. (2017). Smart water dripping system for agriculture/farming. *2017 2nd International Conference for Convergence in Technology, I2CT 2017*, (April), 659–662. 10.1109/I2CT.2017.8226212

Patil, P. K. A. (2016). *A Model for Smart Agriculture Using IoT*. Academic Press.

Prathibha, S. R., Hongal, A., & Jyothi, M. P. (2017). *IoT based monitoring system in smart agriculture*. Advance online publication. doi:10.1109/ICRAECT.2017.52

Rahaman, S. (2017). Detection of NPK Ratio Level Using SVM Algorithm And Smart Agro Sensor System. *International Journal of Latest Research in Engineering and Technology, 3*(7), 11–15. Www.Ijlret.Com

Ramane, D. V., Patil, S. S., & Shaligram, A. D. (2015). Detection of NPK nutrients of soil using Fiber Optic Sensor. *International Journal of Research in Advent Technology ACGT*, (April), 13–14.

Rani, D., Kumar, N., & Bhushan, B. (2019). Implementation of an Automated Irrigation System for Agriculture Monitoring using IoT Communication. *5th IEEE International Conference on Signal Processing, Computing and Control (ISPCC 2k19)*, 138–143. 10.1109/ISPCC48220.2019.8988390

Rao, R., & Nageswara, B. S. (2018). IoT based smart crop-field monitoring and automation irrigation system. *2018 2nd International Conference on Inventive Systems and Control (ICISC)*, 478–483.

Rasooli, M. W., Bhushan, B., & Kumar, N. (2020). Applicability of wireless sensor networks & IoT in saffron & wheat crops: A smart agriculture perspective. *International Journal of Scientific and Technology Research, 9*(2), 2456–2461.

Saranya, R. M. K. A. S. S. P. (2019). Design and Construction of Arduino Based pH Control System for Household Waste Water Reuse. *2019 3rd International Conference on Trends in Electronics and Informatics (ICOEI)*, 1037–1041.

Sharma, B. B., & Kumar, N. (2020). Internet of things-based hardware and software for smart agriculture: A review. *Lecture Notes in Electrical Engineering, 597*, 151–157. doi:10.1007/978-3-030-29407-6_13

Sharma, B. B., & Kumar, N. (2021). IoT-Based Intelligent Irrigation System for Paddy Crop Using an Internet-Controlled Water Pump. *International Journal of Agricultural and Environmental Information Systems, 12*(1), 21–36. doi:10.4018/IJAEIS.20210101.oa2

Sindhu, P., G. I. (2018). IoT Enabled Soil Testing. *Res Publica (Liverpool, England), 7*(1), 54–57.

Staggenborg, S. A., Carignano, M., & Haag, L. (2007). Predicting Soil pH and Buffer pH In Situ with a Real-Time Sensor. *Agronomy Journal, 99*(3), 854–861. doi:10.2134/agronj2006.0254

Xiong, F., & Qiao, K. (1999). Intelligent systems and its application in agriculture. *IFAC Proceedings Volumes, 32*(2), 5597–5602. 10.1016/S1474-6670(17)56954-2

Yuqing, M., Jianrong, C., & Keming, F. (2005). New technology for the detection of pH. *Journal of Biochemical and Biophysical Methods, 63*(1), 1–9. doi:10.1016/j.jbbm.2005.02.001 PMID:15892973

Zhai, Z., Martínez Ortega, J.-F., Lucas Martínez, N., & Rodríguez-Molina, J. (2018). A mission planning approach for precision farming systems based on multi-objective optimization. *Sensors (Basel), 18*(6), 1795. doi:10.339018061795 PMID:29865251

Chapter 10
An Improved Authentication Scheme for Wireless Sensor Network Using User Biometrics

Ambika N.

ⓘ https://orcid.org/0000-0003-4452-5514

Dept of Computer Applications, Sivananda Sarma Memorial RV College, Bangalore, India

ABSTRACT

Sensors are tiny devices deployed in an unsupervised environment. These devices monitor the readings, process them, and transmit them to the predefined destination. The internet has also availed the users to query the sensors and get the values directly. Users are to register themselves with the gateway node. After registration, they increase flexibility to query the sensors. The sensors are to authenticate the users for their legitimacy before dispatching the requested information. The proposal increases security by minimizing the replay attacks and enhance reliability in sensor-user communication. The proposed work hikes reliability as well as conserves energy substantially. Also, it minimizes replay attacks that are vulnerable in WSN.

1. INTRODUCTION

Due to the advances in mobile communication and information technology, Wireless Sensor Network (WSN) systems (Ambika N., 2020) have their fullest potential in varieties of modernday applications ranging from sending messages, making calls, accessing web sites, viewing video contents to mobile advertising, internet trading etc. (Lewis F.L., 2004; Yick et al, 2008; S.K.Noh et al., 2013).

DOI: 10.4018/978-1-7998-7756-1.ch010

Wireless sensor networks are composed of a finite set of sensor devices geographically distributed in a given environment, may be indoor or outdoor (Ambika & Raju, 2014) (Akyildiz, F., Su, Sankarasubramaniam, and Cayirci, 2002). These devices monitor or track any object of interest. Due to this feature, WSNs become suitable for high end applications such as military monitoring (Lee, Hyuk, Lee, Song, & Lee, 2009), home surveillance (Nasution, Hans & Emmanuel, 2007), habitat monitoring (Szewczyk, et al., 2004), elderly care (Abbate, et al., 2010), etc. The devices can self-configure, make a topology, and communicate with each other. The nodes gather sensed and processed data and then forward them to the predefined destination. (Figure 1). These devices are embedded with credentials to secure the transmitted data in the environment. Different methodologies have been explored and implemented to make the data secure in WSN environments.

Figure 1. Wireless Sensor Networks Connected to Internet
[Source:Kamgueu, P. O., Nataf, E., &Djotio, T. (2017).]

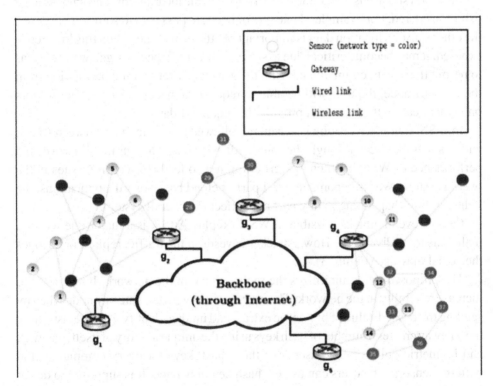

Gateway acts as the bridge between WSN and another network, usually the internet. Through the internet, users or the applications can see, control, transfer data to the WSN and also get data.The users may be connected to the sensor nodes available in various topologies (Figure 2).

Figure 2. Gateway connected to different sensor topologies
[Source:https://remotelab.fe.up.pt/nsensor/wsn-concepts.pdf]

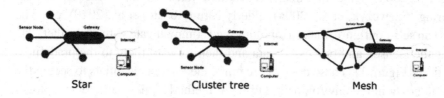

Star	Cluster tree	Mesh

In several situations, for collaboration purpose, the locations of sensor nodes need to be considered. For example, if one sensor needs to pass data to some other sensor, the other sensor's location data is important. At the same time, when this location is exposed, it may become critical due to security threats. Especially gateway node has to permit the user to communicate with the sensors. After gaining permission from the gateway node, the user will be able to request the necessary data. The sensors on authenticating the users can provide the requested data.

In WSN, multi-hop routing is in general followed to transfer data between source and destination nodes through the intermediate nodes. Though this improves the performance of WSN w.r.t. energy criterion, it also leads to security issues in the overall system. WSNs become integral part of cloud based or IoT applications, the vulnerabilities happening in any part may affect the overall system.

Out of several attacks possible in WSN, Replay Attack is a major one where a malicious node diverts the flow. Attacker eavesdrop the traffic, replays or changes the actual message (Figure 3).

The proposed work minimizes the replay attack in the network. It also aims to increase reliability in the network. The user registers with the gateway node when by sending the hashed value of biometric extract and unique identity. After registration, the gateway creates n number of hash keys using the unique identity of itself, gateway, and biometric pull-out. The user uses these hash keys for every communication with the sensors. The users can use the hash key only once. It is supposed to delete the same after use. The user creates the hash value of the credential and biometric extract. It is attached to the request and hashed timestamp. The transmitted message undergoes verification for the freshness and also its identity. The summary received by the nodes and the users undergoes evaluation by the gateway node.

Figure 3. Replay Attack

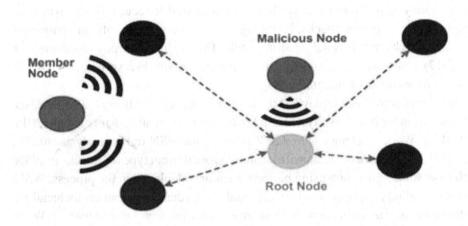

2. LITERATURE SURVEY

Security concerns over WSNs have been focused my many in terms of protocols, applications and products. In this line, this section highlights some of the major works for securing WSNs including schemes proposed against Replay attacks. There exist few proven mechanisms such as Lamports Password Authentication, Nance based, Timestamp based, and Sequence Number based for ensuring the authentication process (Sharma V and Hussain, 2016).

Hwang, Lee and Tang, (2002) proposed a basic remote client validation methodology utilizing smart cards. The card-based verification methodology contains three stages: enlistment, login, and confirmation. The proposition limits adjusting and replay assaults. The framework is additionally ensured by not uncovering the secret word to the server. The client has the opportunity to pick and change the undisclosed key discretionarily. Das et al. (2004) discussed a model with 2 stages namely enrollment and confirmation. The framework permits the client to get to the framework after a check of login credentials and works against replay attacks. Dua et al. (2013) proposed three password schemes with authentication server, verification server and ticket granting server to work against replay attacks.The framework by Smith et al., (2015)could recognize live individuals and parodying endeavors, for example, photos. The system deals with a way to counter replay assaults for face acknowledgment on brilliant customer gadgets utilizing a noninvasive test and reaction procedure. Works of Tseng et al., (2007), Goriparti et al., (2009), Ruj et al., (2012) and Chauhan et al. (2017) allaim at resolving the attacks expected in the transaction as well as access process.

Pirzada and McDonald (2004) utilized a variation of Kerberos for secure trade in impromptu systems. Work by Das A. K. (2013)discussed on securing systems against various known types of attacks, including strong replay attack, off-line password guessing attacks and parallel session attack. The RedDots corpus (Kinnunen, et al., 2017) deals with the assessment of automatic speaker verification (ASV) vulnerabilities to spoofing attack.

Securing control over replay attacks has been focused by Mo et al., (2009). User authentication for healthcaresystems in WSNs has been dealt by Kumar et al. (2011 and 2012). Work by Deng J et al.,(2006) deals with WSN traffic analysis attacks. Riaz et al. (2019) have come up with a solution for different types of attacks in WSN with hash value generation using biometric features deployed in the process. WSN design for military applications (Lee S.H. et. al.,2009) dealt with features for handling certain attacks. Authentication mechanism for securing smart phone users in WSN has been the focus of Lee et al., (2015). Das M.L. (2009) dealt with authentication scheme proposed in gateway nodes. For the current work, works of Liu and Ning (2004), Das M.L. (2009), Liu et al.,(2005), Han et al.,(2010) have been explored.

In the work proposed by Riaz et al. (2019), an authentication procedure is used that tackles different kinds of attacks. The procedure works in two phases. The user generates a hash value using the biometric features and transmits this value with identity to register him with the base station (trusted node). The node transmits a value using which the user can extract the required information. In the authentication phase, the user interacts with the sensor node communicates the hash value of biometrics, identity, time-stamp, and the requested information. The sensor continues the transmission after verifying the time-stamp (Nagaraj 2021). In this line, this chapter discusses the work proposed similar to Riaz et al. (2019) and highlights the outcome of the experiments.

3. PROPOSE STUDY

a. Objectives of the Study

The model handles replay attacks in WSN environment through similar experiments.

b. Notations Used in the Study

Table 1 provides the list of notations used in the study.

Table 1. Notations Used

Notations used	Description
G	Gateway node
U_i	i^{th} user of the network
N_i	i^{th} node of the network
Bio_u	Biometric extract of the user
id_u	Identity of the user
R_u	Request from the user
R_h	Request for the hash keys (sent from the user to the gateway node)
S_u	Summary of transmissions sent by the user to the gateway node
id_g	Unique identity of the gateway
T_u	Timestamp of the user
$h(..)$	Hashing algorithm

c. Assumptions Made in the Study

- The gateway node is the most reliable in the network. The gateway node provides credentials to the user. It is this node that has to authenticate the user before the actual transmission commences.
- The user device is capable of extracting the biometrics from the user. The device is capable of creating the hashed value of the biometric and identity of itself.
- The other nodes deployed in the network are assumed to be legitimate ones.
- The adversaries are capable of launching replay attacks in the network.

d. Methodology

The proposed work minimizes replay attacks in the network. It also aims to increase reliability in the network. The proposed work divides into two phases – The Registration phase and the Authentication phase. The user registers with the gateway node when the user registers by sending the hashed value of biometric extract and unique identity. After registration, the gateway creates n number of hash keys using the unique identity of itself, gateway, and biometric pullout. The user uses these hash keys for every communication with the sensors. The users can use the hash key only once, and it is supposed to delete the same. The keys will be deleted after they reach expiry time. The user creates the hash value of the hash key and biometric print. It attaches to the request and hashed timestamp. The transmitted message undergoes verification for the freshness and also its identity. The summary received by the nodes and the gateway node verifies the user. Figure 4 depicts the architecture of the system.

Figure 4. Architecture of the system

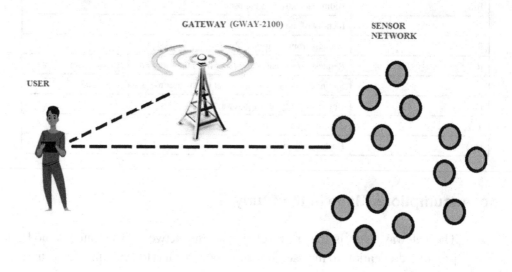

i. Registration Phase

The user sends the request to the gateway to join the group and send queries to the sensor. The user hashes his biometric and identity of the device and transmits the same to the gateway. In equation (1) the user U_i calculates the hash value. He uses the identity id_u and hash value of the biometric extract of the user bio_u. it transmits the same to the gateway G.

$$U_i \rightarrow G : h(id_u) \| h(bio_u) \tag{1}$$

The gateway uses the transmitted values to generate a series of hash keys. The gateway regenerates the identity and biometric values of the user. It generates a series of hash keys using three parameters. They are the biometric value of the user, identity of the user, and identity of the gateway. In equation (2) the gateway G is generating the hash keys using the identity U_i, biometric extract of the user bio_u, and identity of the gateway id_g. These key credentials are transmitted to the user. The hash keys $h_i, h_j, \ldots . . h_n$ are transmitted to the user U_i by the gateway G in equation (3).

$$G : h\left(id_u, bio_u, id_g\right) \rightarrow \left(h_i, h_j \ldots . . h_n\right) \tag{2}$$

$$G \rightarrow U_i\left(h_i, h_j \ldots . . h_n\right) \tag{3}$$

ii. Authentication Phase

The user generates the hash value by using the hash key and the biometric extract. Each key can be used only once and discarded. Whenever the user sends a request to the sensor, it authenticates by transmitting the petition with the hash value of the biometric extract and the hash key. This message suffixes with the hash value of the timestamp. In the equation (4), the user regenerates freshly generated biometric extract bio_u and the hash key h_i. It suffixes the same with the request R_i and the hash value of the timestamp T_u.

$$U_i \rightarrow N_i : R_u \left\| h\left(bio_u, h_i\right) \right\| h\left(T_u\right) \tag{4}$$

The node evaluates the timestamp and hashed biometric extract and hash credential values for the authentication.

After the hash keys are exhausted, the user has to provide a summary of the transmissions. Similarly, the nodes deployed also provide the overall outline of the communication with the user details. In equation (5), the user U_i is requesting the gateway G for the next set of hash keys. In equation R_h request for the hash keys, hashed summary S_u and hashed biometric extract bio_u.

$$U_i \rightarrow G : R_h \left\| h\left(bio_u\right) \right\| h(S_u) \tag{5}$$

This procedure aims to bring better reliability to the system. It minimizes the occurrence of replay attacks in the network compared to previous work.

4. SECURITY ANALYSIS

The work is experimented using NS2 simulator. Table 2 provides the details of the parameters used in the study.

Table 2. List of parameters used in study

Parameters	Description
Dimension of the network	200m*200m
Number of nodes deployed in the network	25 nodes
Number of users	4 users
Time duration	60ms
Length of hash message(timestamp)	8 bits
Length of hash extract (unique identity)	12 bits
Length of biometric extract (biometric)	10 bits
Length of request	6 bits
Length of summary Length of the user identification Length of the gateway identification	20 bits 24 bits 42 bits

Table 3. Generation of hash keys

Step 1: Input user identification (24 bits), gateway identification (42 bits), biometric extract (10 bits) *For i=0 to n key generation* *Step 2: Substitute the bits by its complement in (i+10) % 76 positions* *Step 3: Divide the outcome into 2 sets (38 bits each)* *Step 4: Right Shift the second set by i* *Step 5: Add both the sets (Resultant 39 bits)* *Step 6: Divide the resultant into 2 (even position bits belong to 1 set and odd position bits belong to 2 set i.e2,4,.........38 belong to set 1 and 1,3,............39 belong to set 2)* *Step 7: Reverse the 1 set and concatenate with the set 2 (hash key)*

a. Energy Consumption

Power is one of the priority resources in a kind of network. The users and the nodes of the network should be able to use minimum electricity. If the user's device consumes too much energy, it requires recharging. But the sensors are not rechargeable. Hence the energy consumption has to be minimum. If the adversary launches a replay attack, the energy consumption will hike.

The previous proposal (Riaz, Gillani, Rizvi, Shokat, & Kwon, 2019) tries to minimize the replay attack using a hashed timestamp. The summary on both sides reaches the gateway, and hence the gateway will be able to reduce different kinds of attacks. This methodology minimizes the energy consumption in the network. The suggestion decreases energy consumption by 8.79% compared to (Riaz, Gillani, Rizvi, Shokat, & Kwon, 2019). The same is represented in figure 5.

Figure 5. Energy consumption

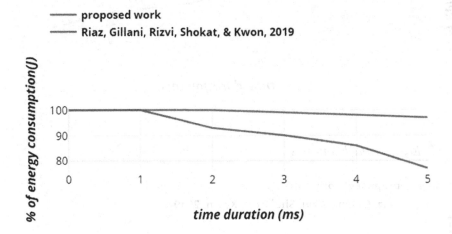

b. Reliability

The suggested work provides a summary of communicating parties to the gateway. It happens regularly. The gateway hence will be able to trace any irregularities in the system. The suggested work will increase reliability by 8.71% compared to (Riaz, Gillani, Rizvi, Shokat, & Kwon, 2019). The same is represented in figure 6.

Figure 6. Reliability of the proposed system

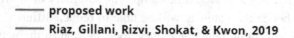

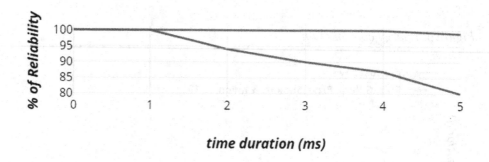

time duration (ms)

Figure 7. Replay Attack Analysis

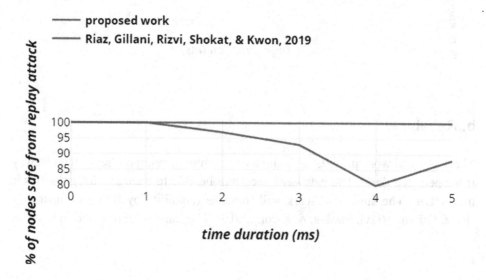

time duration (ms)

c. Replay Attack

The proposed work minimizes the replay attack by adding some measures. The gateway transmits the hash key. Its usage by the user device is the identity of the device for that session. The hash key get disposed after use. The user requests the hash key after exhausting it. The user and sensors transmit the outline. The summary of the transmission received from both ends matches to validate the reports. The suggestion minimizes the replay attack by 7.53% compared to the earlier approach. The same is represented in figure 7.

5. CONCLUSION

Sensors are tiny devices deployed in an unsupervised environment. These devices deploy to monitor and provide readings to pre-defined destinations. The user can register them with the gateway and query the sensors. The sensors on authentication provide the requested data. The proposed work minimizes the replay attack in the network. It also aims to increase reliability in the network. This work has done a study on a proposed mechanism w.r.t. handling replay attacks and ensuring reliability.

REFERENCES

Abbate, S., Avvenuti, M., Corsini, P., Light, J., & Vecchio, A. (2010). Monitoring of human movements for fall detection and activities recognition in elderly care using wireless sensor network: a survey. *Wireless Sensor Networks: Application-Centric Design.*

Akyildiz, F. I., Su, W., Sankarasubramaniam, Y., & Cayirci, E. (2002). A survey on sensor networks. *IEEE Communications Magazine*, *40*(8), 102–114. doi:10.1109/MCOM.2002.1024422

Ambalakat, P. (2005). Security of biometric authentication systems. *21st Computer Science Seminar*, 1.

Ambika, N. (2020). SYSLOC: Hybrid Key Generation in Sensor Network. In Handbook of Wireless Sensor Networks: Issues and Challenges in Current Scenario's (pp. 325-347). Springer.

Ambika, N., & Raju, G. T. (2014). ECAWSN: Eliminating compromised node with the help of auxiliary nodes in wireless sensor network. *International Journal of Security and Networks*, *9*(2), 78–84. doi:10.1504/IJSN.2014.060743

Chauhan, J., Hu, Y., Seneviratne, S., Misra, A., Seneviratne, A., & Lee, Y. (2017). BreathPrint: Breathing Acoustics-based User Authentication. *15th Annual International Conference on Mobile Systems, Applications, and Services* (pp. 278-291). Niagara Falls, NY: IEEE. 10.1145/3081333.3081355

Das, A. K. (2013). A secure and effective user authentication and privacy preserving protocol with smart cards for wireless communications. *Network Science*, *2*(1-2), 12–27. doi:10.100713119-012-0009-8

Das, M. L. (2009). Two-factor user authentication in wireless sensor networks. *IEEE Transactions on Wireless Communications*, *8*(3), 1086–1090. doi:10.1109/TWC.2008.080128

Das, M. L., Saxena, A., & Gulati, V. P. (2004). A Dynamic ID-based Remote User Authentication Scheme. *IEEE Transactions on Consumer Electronics*, *50*(2), 629–631. doi:10.1109/TCE.2004.1309441

Deng, J., Han, R., & Mishra, S. (2006). Decorrelating wireless sensor network traffic to inhibit traffic analysis attacks. *Pervasive and Mobile Computing*, *2*(2), 159–186. doi:10.1016/j.pmcj.2005.12.003

Dua, G., Gautam, N., Sharma, D., & Arora, A. (2013). Replay attack prevention in kerberos authentication protocol using triple password. *International Journal of Computer Networks & Communications*, *5*(2), 59–70. doi:10.5121/ijcnc.2013.5205

Goriparthi, T., Das, M. L., & Saxena, A. (2009). An improved bilinear pairing based remote user authentication scheme. *Computer Standards & Interfaces*, *31*(1), 181–185. doi:10.1016/j.csi.2007.11.016

Han, K., Shon, T., & Kim, K. (2010). Efficient mobile sensor authentication in smart home and WPAN. *IEEE Transactions on Consumer Electronics*, *56*(2), 591–596. doi:10.1109/TCE.2010.5505975

Hwang, M.-S., Lee, C.-C., & Tang, Y.-L. (2002). A Simple Remote User Authentication Scheme. *Mathematical and Computer Modelling*, *36*(1-2), 103–107. doi:10.1016/S0895-7177(02)00106-1

Kinnunen, T., Sahidullah, M., Falcone, M., Costantini, L., Hautamäki, R., Thomsen, D., ... Evans, N. (2017). Reddots replayed: A new replay spoofing attack corpus for text-dependent speaker verification research. In *IEEE International Conference on Acoustics, Speech and Signal Processing (ICASSP)* (pp. 5395-5399). New Orleans, LA: IEEE. 10.1109/ICASSP.2017.7953187

Kumar, P., Lee, S. G., & Lee, H. J. (2011). A user authentication for healthcare application using wireless medical sensor networks. In *International Conference on High Performance Computing and Communications* (pp. 647-652). Banff, Canada: IEEE. 10.1109/HPCC.2011.92

Kumar, P., Lee, S. G., & Lee, H. J. (2012). E-SAP: Efficient-strong authentication protocol for healthcare applications using wireless medical sensor networks. *Sensors (Basel)*, *12*(2), 1625–1647. doi:10.3390120201625 PMID:22438729

Lee, H. S., Lee, S., Song, H., & Lee, H. S. (2009). Wireless sensor network design for tactical military applications: Remote large-scale environments. In IEEE Military communications conference (MILCOM) (pp. 1-7). Boston, MA: IEEE.

Lee, W. H., & Lee, R. B. (2015). Multi-sensor authentication to improve smartphone security. In *International conference on information systems security and privacy (ICISSP)* (pp. 1-11). Angers, France: IEEE.

Liu, D., & Ning, P. (2004). Multilevel μTESLA: Broadcast authentication for distributed sensor networks. *ACM Transactions on Embedded Computing Systems*, *3*(4), 800–836. doi:10.1145/1027794.1027800

Liu, D., Ning, P., Zhu, S., & Jajodia, S. (2005). Practical broadcast authentication in sensor networks. In *Second Annual International Conference on Mobile and Ubiquitous Systems: Networking and Services* (pp. 118-129). San Diego, CA: IEEE.

Mo, Y., & Sinopoli, B. (2009). Secure control against replay attacks. In *47th annual Allerton conference on communication, control, and computing (Allerton)* (pp. 911-918). Monticello, IL: Academic Press.

Nagaraj, A. (2021). *Introduction to Sensors in IoT and Cloud Computing Applications*. Bentham Science Publishers.

Nasution, H. A., & Emmanuel, S. (2007). Intelligent video surveillance for monitoring elderly in home environments. In *9th Workshop on Multimedia Signal Processing* (pp. 203-206). IEEE. 10.1109/MMSP.2007.4412853

Pirzada, A. A., & McDonald, C. (2004). Kerberos Assisted Authentication in Mobile Ad-hoc Networks. In *27th Australasian Computer Science conference* (pp. 41-46). Dunedin, New Zealand: Australian Computer Society.

Riaz, R., Gillani, N.-A., Rizvi, S. S., Shokat, S., & Kwon, S. J. (2019). SUBBASE: An Authentication Scheme for Wireless Sensor Networks Based on User Biometrics. *Wireless Communications and Mobile Computing*, *2019*, 1–11. doi:10.1155/2019/6370742

Ruj, S., Stojmenovic, M., & Nayak, A. (2012). Privacy Preserving Access Control with Authentication for Securing Data in Clouds. In *12th IEEE/ACM International Symposium on Cluster, Cloud and Grid Computing* (pp. 556-563). Ottawa, Canada: IEEE. 10.1109/CCGrid.2012.92

Shelton, J., Roy, K., O'Connor, B., & Dozier, G. V. (2014). Mitigating Iris-Based Replay Attacks. *International Journal of Machine Learning and Computing, 4*(3), 204–209. doi:10.7763/IJMLC.2014.V4.413

Smith, D. F., Wiliem, A., & Lovell, B. C. (2015). Face Recognition on Consumer Devices: Reflections on Replay Attacks. *IEEE Transactions on Information Forensics and Security, 10*(4), 736–745. doi:10.1109/TIFS.2015.2398819

Szewczyk, R., Osterweil, E., Polastre, J., Hamilton, M., Mainwaring, A., & Estrin, D. (2004). Habitat monitoring with sensor networks. *Center for Embedded Network Sensing, 47*(6), 33–40.

Tseng, H. R., Jan, R. H., & Yang, W. (2007). An improved dynamic user authentication scheme for wireless sensor networks. In *IEEE Global Communications Conference (GLOBECOM'07)* (pp. 986-990). Washington, DC: IEEE. 10.1109/GLOCOM.2007.190

Compilation of References

A report on awareness of ATM Threats to Parents by CDAC. (n.d.). Available at https://www.infosecawareness.in/parents/atm-threats

A Report on —Updated Mobile Malware Targets Android‖, Bank Info Security. (2016). https://bankinfosecurity.com/

Abada, L., & Aouat, S. (2016). Facial shape-from-shading using features detection method. *International Journal of Advanced Intelligence Paradigms*, 8(1), 3–19. doi:10.1504/IJAIP.2016.074774

Abbas, R., Michael, K., & Michael, M. G. (2015). Location-Based Privacy, Protection, Safety, and Security. In S. Zeadally & M. Badra (Eds.), *Privacy in a Digital, Networked World. Computer Communications and Networks*. Springer. doi:10.1007/978-3-319-08470-1_16

Abbate, S., Avvenuti, M., Corsini, P., Light, J., & Vecchio, A. (2010). Monitoring of human movements for fall detection and activities recognition in elderly care using wireless sensor network: a survey. *Wireless Sensor Networks: Application-Centric Design*.

Abdul Shukor, S. A., Amiruddin, S., & Ilias, B. (2016). Analysis and Evaluation of Human Tracking Methods from Video. *The 6th IEEE International Conference on Control System, Computing and Engineering*, 310-315.

Abou-zeid, H., Hassanein, H. S., & Valentin, S. (2013). Optimal predictive resource allocation: exploiting mobility patterns and radio maps. In *IEEE global communications conference 2013* (pp. 4877–4882). GLOBECOM. doi:10.1109/GLOCOMW.2013.6855723

Adedeji, O. H., Adebayo, H. O., & Sotayo, E. I. (2014). Assessing Environmental Impacts of Inland Sand Mining in Parts of Ogun State, Nigeria. *Ethiopian Journal of Environmental Studies and Management*, 7(5), 478–487. doi:10.4314/ejesm.v7i5.2

Adelaja, A. O., Labo, A., & Penar, E. (2018). Public Opinion on the Root Causes of Terrorism and Objectives of Terrorists: A Boko Haram Case Study. *Perspectives on Terrorism*, 12(3), 35–49.

Adigun, A. A., Folorunso, S. O. & Uzoh, P. (2018). A Criminal Database System to Enhance National Security. *The Journal of Computer Science and its Applications, 25*(2), 176-183.

Adlakha, D., Adlakha, D., & Tanwar, R. (2016). Analytical Comparison between Sobel and Prewitt Edge Detection Techniques. *International Journal of Scientific and Engineering Research, 7*(1), 1482–1488.

Africa Check. (2019). *Factsheet: South Africa's crime statistics for 2018/19*. Retrieved from https://africacheck.org/factsheets/factsheet-south-africas-crime-statistics-for-2018-19/

Aggarwal, J. K., & Cai, Q. (1999). Human motion analysis: A review. *Computer Vision and Image Understanding, 73*(3), 428–440. doi:10.1006/cviu.1998.0744

Ahishakiye, E., Danison, T., & Elisha, O. O. (2017). A Secure Web Based Records Management System for Prisons: A Case of Kisoro Prison in Uganda. *International Journal of Computer, 24*(1), 146–158.

Ajitha, J. M, & Jaba, K., & M.phil, M. (. (2017). Video Image Filtering Technique - A Review. *International Journal of Engineering Trends and Technology, 46*(3), 159–161. doi:10.14445/22315381/IJETT-V46P227

Akon, M., Islam, M., Shen, X., & Singh, A. (2011). OUR: Optimal Update-based Replacement policy for cache in wireless data access networks with optimal effective hits and bandwidth requirements. *Wireless Communications and Mobile Computing, 13*. doi:10.1002/wcm.1182

Akyildiz, F. I., Su, W., Sankarasubramaniam, Y., & Cayirci, E. (2002). A survey on sensor networks. *IEEE Communications Magazine, 40*(8), 102–114. doi:10.1109/MCOM.2002.1024422

Alahuhta. (2010). *SWAMI- Dark scenarios in ambient intelligence: Highlighting risks and vulnerabilities.* Information Society Technologies, Sixth Frame Work Programme.

Al-Molegi, A., Alsmadi, I., & Martínez-Ballesté, A. (2018). Regions-of-interest discovering and predicting in smartphone environments. *Pervasive and Mobile Computing, 47*, 31–53. doi:10.1016/j.pmcj.2018.05.001

Al-Molegi, A., Jabreel, M., & Martínez-Ballesté, A. (2018). Move, Attend and Predict: An attention-based neural model for people's movement prediction. *Pattern Recognition Letters, 112*, 34–40. doi:10.1016/j.patrec.2018.05.015

Alrababah, Z. (2020). *Privacy and Security of Wearable Devices*. Academic Press.

Ambalakat, P. (2005). Security of biometric authentication systems. *21st Computer Science Seminar, 1*.

Ambika, N. (2020). SYSLOC: Hybrid Key Generation in Sensor Network. In Handbook of Wireless Sensor Networks: Issues and Challenges in Current Scenario's (pp. 325-347). Springer.

Ambika, N., & Raju, G. T. (2014). ECAWSN: Eliminating compromised node with the help of auxiliary nodes in wireless sensor network. *International Journal of Security and Networks, 9*(2), 78–84. doi:10.1504/IJSN.2014.060743

Amin, M., Rahim, M., & Ayu, G. (2014). A trend analysis of violent crimes in Malaysia. *Health and the Environment Journal, 5*(2), 41–56.

Anand, S., J, S. C., S, S. P., & Sweatha, A. (2019). Monitoring of Soil Nutrients Using IoT for Optimizing the Use of Fertilizers. *International Journal of Science Engineering And Technology Research, 8*(4), 105–107.

Arachchilage, N. A. G., Love, S., & Beznosov, K. (2016). Phishing threat avoidance behaviour: An empirical investigation. *Computers in Human Behavior, 60*, 185–197. doi:10.1016/j.chb.2016.02.065

Asmann, P., & O'Reilly, E. (2020). *InSight Crime's 2019 Homicide Round-Up*. Retrieved from https://www.insightcrime.org/news/analysis/insight-crime-2019-homicide-round-up/

Aswathy, S., Manimegalai, S., Fernando, M. M. R., & Vijay, J. F. (2018). *Smart Soil Testing*. Academic Press.

Atzori & Iera. (2010). The internet of things: A survey. *Elsevier Journal on Computer Networks, 54*, 2787–2805.

Babuška, R. (2012). *Fuzzy modeling for control* (Vol. 12). Springer Science & Business Media.

Balan, A., Sigal, L., & Black, M. (2005). A Quantitative Evaluation of Video-based 3D Person Tracking. *The IEEE International Workshop on Visual Surveillance and Performance Evaluation of Tracking and Surveillance, 5*, 349–356. 10.1109/VSPETS.2005.1570935

Barnich, O., & Van Droogenbroeck, M. (2011). The vibe: A universal Background subtraction algorithm for video sequences. *IEEE Transactions on Image Processing, 20*(6), 1709–1724. doi:10.1109/TIP.2010.2101613 PMID:21189241

Beiró, M. G., Panisson, A., Tizzoni, M., & Cattuto, C. (2016). Predicting human mobility through the assimilation of social media traces into mobility models. *EPJ Data Science, 5*(1), 1–15. doi:10.1140/epjds13688-016-0092-2

Belimpasakis & Stirbu. (2012). A survey of techniques for remote access to home networks and resources. *Journal on Multimedia Tools and Applications*.

Ben Sassi, I., Mellouli, S., & Ben Yahia, S. (2017). Context-aware recommender systems in mobile environment: On the road of future research. *Information Systems, 72*, 27–61. doi:10.1016/j.is.2017.09.001

Benezeth, Y., Laurent, H., Emile, B., & Rosenberger, C. (2011). Towards a sensor for detecting human presence and activity. *Energy and Buildings, Elsevier, 43*(2-3), 305–314. doi:10.1016/j.enbuild.2010.09.014

Bewley, A., Ge, Z., Ott, L., Ramos, F., & Upcroft, B. (2016). Simple online and real-time tracking. *The IEEE International Conference on Image Processing (ICIP)*, 3464-3468.

Beynon-Davies, P., Carne, C, Mackay, H. & Tudhope, D. (1999). *Rapid Application Development (RAD): An empirical review.* Academic Press.

Bhattasali, T. (2017). Study of Security Issues in Pervasive Environment of Next Generation Internet of Things. In *12th International Conference on Information Systems and Information Management (CISIM).* Springer.

Bhatt, H., Bhushan, B., & Kumar, N. (2019). IoT: The Current Scenario and Role of Sensors Involved in Smart Agriculture. *International Journal of Recent Technology and Engineering, 8*(4), 12011–12023. doi:10.35940/ijrte.D9285.118419

Biradar, A., & Patil, S. S. (2018). Secure Communication Between Sensors in IoT. *International Journal of Computing, 7*(4).

Blum, A. L., & Langley, P. (1997). Selection of relevant features and examples in machine learning. *Artificial Intelligence, 1-2*(1-2), 245–271. doi:10.1016/S0004-3702(97)00063-5

Bodor, R., Jackson, B., & Papanikolopoulos, N. (2003). Vision Based Human Tracking and Activity Recognition. *The 11th Mediterranean Conference on Control Automation*, 18–20.

Bornman, E. (2012). The Mobile Phone in Africa: Has It Become a Highway to the Information Society or Not. *Contemporary Educational Technology, 3*(4), 278–292. doi:10.30935/cedtech/6084

Bouwmans, T. (2014). Traditional and recent approaches in background modeling for foreground detection: An overview. *Computer Science Review, 11-12*, 31–66. doi:10.1016/j.cosrev.2014.04.001

Bowyer, K., Kranenburg, C., & Dougherty, S. (2001). Edge detector evaluation using empirical ROC curve. *Computer Vision and Image Understanding, 10*(1), 77–103. doi:10.1006/cviu.2001.0931

Bo, Y., & Wang, H. (2011). The Application of Cloud Computing and the Internet of Things in Agriculture and Forestry. *International Joint Conference on Service Sciences*, 168-172. 10.1109/IJCSS.2011.40

Boyat, A. K., & Joshi, B. K. (2015). A review paper: Noise modes in digital image processing. [SIPIJ]. *Signal and Image Processing: an International Journal, 6*(2), 63–75. doi:10.5121ipij.2015.6206

Braganza, D., & Tulasi, B. (2017). RFID security issues in IoT: A comparative study. *Oriental Journal of Computer Science and Technology, 10*(1), 127–134. doi:10.13005/ojcst/10.01.17

British Broadcast Corporation (BBC) News. (2020). *How dangerous is Mexico?* Retrieved from https://www.bbc.com/news/world-latin-america-50315470

BusinessTech. (2019). *Crime levels in South Africa are far worse than what is reported.* Retrieved from https://businesstech.co.za/news/lifestyle/344284/crime-levels-in-south-africa-are-far-worse-than-what-is-reported/

Butler, D. (2006). Virtual Globes: The web-wide world. *Journal of Nature, 439*(7078), 776–778. doi:10.1038/439776a PMID:16482123

Cao, G. (2003). A scalable low-latency cache invalidation strategy for mobile environments. *IEEE Transactions on Knowledge and Data Engineering, 15*(5), 1251–1265. doi:10.1109/TKDE.2003.1232276

Cekerevac, Z., Dvorak, Z., Prigoda, L., & Cekerevac, P. (2017). Internet of things and the man-in-the-middle attacks–security and economic risks. *MEST Journal, 5*(2), 15–25. doi:10.12709/mest.05.05.02.03

Chaudhuri, K., Chowdhury, P., & Kumbhakar, S. C. (2015). Crime in India: Specification and Estimation of violent crime index. *Journal of Productivity Analysis, 43*(1), 13–28. doi:10.100711123-014-0398-7

Chauhan, J., Hu, Y., Seneviratne, S., Misra, A., Seneviratne, A., & Lee, Y. (2017). BreathPrint: Breathing Acoustics-based User Authentication. *15th Annual International Conference on Mobile Systems, Applications, and Services* (pp. 278-291). Niagara Falls, NY: IEEE. 10.1145/3081333.3081355

Checker ATM Security Report. (2011). *Protect your automatic teller machines against logical fraud.* GMV Soluciones Globales Internet.

Chen & Luo. (2012). *S2A: Secure Smart Household Appliances.* CODASPY '12, San Antonio, TX.

Chen, X., Huang, Q., Hu, P., Li, M., Tian, Y., & Li, C. (2009). Rapid and Precise Object Detection based on Color Histograms and Adaptive Bandwidth Mean Shift. *International IEEE/RSJ Conference on Intelligent Robots and Systems*, 4281-4286. 10.1109/IROS.2009.5354739

CherylR. (2012). https://www.army.mil/article/75165/Geotagging_poses_security_risks

Chow, T. E. (2008). The Potential of Maps APIs for Internet GIS Applications. *Transactions in GIS Journal, 12*(2), 179–191. doi:10.1111/j.1467-9671.2008.01094.x

Christaline, J. A., Ramesh, R., & Vaishali, D. (2015). Critical review of image analysis techniques. *International Journal of Advanced Intelligence Paradigms, 7*(3/4), 368–381. doi:10.1504/IJAIP.2015.073715

Christensen, T. C., Barrett, L. F., Bliss-Moreau, E., Lebo, K., & Kaschub, C. (2003). A practical guide to experience-sampling procedures. *Journal of Happiness Studies, 4*(1), 53–78. doi:10.1023/A:1023609306024

Comaniciu, D., & Meer, P. (1999). Mean shift analysis and applications. *The IEEE International Conference on Computer Vision (ICCV), 2*, 1197–1203.

Conner, T. (2015, May). *Experience sampling and ecological momentary assessment with mobile phones.* Retrieved on February 28, 2021 from https://www.otago.ac.nz/psychology/otago047475.pdf

Cornwell, J., & ... User-Controllable Security and Privacy for Pervasive Computing. *Eighth IEEE Workshop on Mobile Computing Systems and Applications.* 10.1109/HotMobile.2007.9

Crima and Safety Report. (2019). *Nigeria 2019 Crime & Safety Report: Lagos*. Retrieved from https://www.osac.gov/Country/Nigeria/Content/Detail/Report/4a5eaf52-3655-43e6-b540-1684bcb6f3de

Cucchiara, R., Piccardi, M., & Prati, A. (2003). Detecting Moving Objects, Ghosts, and Shadows in Video Streams. *IEEE Transactions on Pattern Analysis and Machine Intelligence*, 25(10), 1337–1342. doi:10.1109/TPAMI.2003.1233909

Cuenca-Jara, J., Terroso-Saenz, F., Valdes-Vela, M., Gonzalez-Vidal, A., &Skarmeta, A. F. (2017, June). Human mobility analysis based on social media and fuzzy clustering. In *2017 Global Internet of Things Summit (GIoTS)* (pp. 1-6). IEEE.

Cuttone, A., Lehmann, S., & González, M. C. (2018). Understanding predictability and exploration in human mobility. *EPJ Data Science*, 7(1), 1–17. doi:10.1140/epjds13688-017-0129-1

Darwish, S. M., El-Zoghabi, A., & El-Shnawy, A. G. (2018). Proactive cache replacement technique for mobile networks based on genetic programming. *IET Networks*, 7(6), 376–383. doi:10.1049/iet-net.2017.0261

Das, A. K. (2013). A secure and effective user authentication and privacy preserving protocol with smart cards for wireless communications. *Network Science*, 2(1-2), 12–27. doi:10.100713119-012-0009-8

Das, M. L. (2009). Two-factor user authentication in wireless sensor networks. *IEEE Transactions on Wireless Communications*, 8(3), 1086–1090. doi:10.1109/TWC.2008.080128

Das, M. L., Saxena, A., & Gulati, V. P. (2004). A Dynamic ID-based Remote User Authentication Scheme. *IEEE Transactions on Consumer Electronics*, 50(2), 629–631. doi:10.1109/TCE.2004.1309441

De Mooij, M. (2003). Convergence and divergence in consumer behaviour: Implications for global advertising. *International Journal of Advertising*, 22(2), 183–202. doi:10.1080/02650487.2003.11072848

Deng, J., Han, R., & Mishra, S. (2006). Decorrelating wireless sensor network traffic to inhibit traffic analysis attacks. *Pervasive and Mobile Computing*, 2(2), 159–186. doi:10.1016/j.pmcj.2005.12.003

Dhankhar, P., & Sahu, N. (2013). A Review and Research of Edge Detection Techniques for Image Segmentation. *International Journal of Computer Science and Mobile Computing, IJCSMC*, 2(7), 86–92.

Di Lascio, R., Foggia, P., Percannella, G., Saggese, A., & Vento, M. (2013). A real-time algorithm for people tracking using contextual reasoning. *Computer Vision and Image Understanding*, 117(8), 892–908. doi:10.1016/j.cviu.2013.04.004

Diab, G. M., El-Shennawy, N., & Sarhan, A. (2019). Implementation of Human Tracking System under Different Video Degradations. *The International Japan-Africa Conference on Electronics, and Communications (JAC-ECC 2019)*.

Compilation of References

Dobson, J. E., & Fisher, P. F. (2003). Geoslavery. *IEEE Technology and Society Magazine, 22*(1), 47–52. doi:10.1109/MTAS.2003.1188276

Drakatos, S., Pissinou, N., Makki, K., & Douligeris, C. (2009). A future location-aware replacement policy for the cache management at the mobile terminal. *Wireless Communications and Mobile Computing, 9*(5), 607–629. doi:10.1002/wcm.606

Dua, G., Gautam, N., Sharma, D., & Arora, A. (2013). Replay attack prevention in kerberos authentication protocol using triple password. *International Journal of Computer Networks & Communications, 5*(2), 59–70. doi:10.5121/ijcnc.2013.5205

Dwyer, B. (n.d.). *Report on Dog's Sense of Smell by Dogwalkers.* http://dogwalkersmelbourne.com.au

Ejemeyovwi, D. O. (2015). Crime mapping using Time Series Analysis in Asaba, Delta State Nigeria: A Remote Sensing and GIS Approach. *European Journal of Basic and Applied Sciences, 2*(2), 52–71.

Elgammal, A., Harwood, D., & Davis, L. (2000). Non-parametric model for background subtraction. *The International Conference on Computer Vision (ECCV 2000)*, 751-767. 10.1007/3-540-45053-X_48

EraInnovator. (2020, September 1). EraInnovator. *Mobile Commerce.* Retrieved on February 27, 2021 from https://erainnovator.com/mobile-commerce/

Fairfield, J. A. T. (2012, Spring). Mixed reality: How the laws of virtual worlds govern everyday life. *Berkeley Technology Law Journal, 27*(1), 55–116.

Falaye, A. A., Adama, N. V., & Agemerien, F. P. (2013). Design and Implementation of Crime Investigation System using Biometrics Approach (Nigeria Police Force). *Pacific Journal of Science and Technology, 14*(2), 242–253.

Fan, C. M., & Namazi, N. M. (2000). Simultaneous Motion Estimation and Filtering of Image Sequences. *IEEE Transactions on Image Processing, 8*(12), 1788–1795. PMID:18267454

Fan, L., Wang, Z., Cail, B., Tao, C., Zhang, Z., Wang, Y., Li, S., Huang, F., Fu, S., & Zhang, F. (2016). A survey on multiple objects tracking algorithm. *The IEEE International Conference on Information and Automation (ICIA)*, 1855-1862. 10.1109/ICInfA.2016.7832121

Flannery, N. (n.d.). *Direct marketing and privacy: Striking that balance.* Retrieved on March 3, 2021 from http://uir.unisa.ac.za/bitstream/handle/10500/13073/10542-10553.pdf?sequence=10501

Friesland, K. (2018, June 2). 10 Worst internet privacy scandals to Date. *TechNadu.* Retrieved on June 23, 2019 from https://www.technadu.com/worst-internet-privacy-scandals/30236/

Gabrielli, L., Rinzivillo, S., Ronzano, F., & Villatoro, D. (2013, September). From tweets to semantic trajectories: mining anomalous urban mobility patterns. In *International Workshop on Citizen in Sensor Networks* (pp. 26-35). Springer.

Gaikwad, S. V, & G, P. G. S. (2015). *Measurement of NPK, Temperature, Moisture, Humidity using.* Academic Press.

Gal-Or, E., Gal-Or, R., & Penmetsa, N. (2018, September). The role of user privacy concerns in shaping competition among platforms. *Information Systems Research, 29*(3), 698–722. doi:10.1287/isre.2017.0730

Gao, H., & Liu, H. (2013). Data Analysis on Location-Based Social Networks. *Mobile Social Networking,* 165–194. . doi:10.1007/978-1-4614-8579-7_8

Gavrila, D. M. (1999). The visual analysis of human movement: A survey. *Computer Vision and Image Understanding, 73*(1), 82–98. doi:10.1006/cviu.1998.0716

Gayatri, M. K., Jayasakthi, J., & Mala, G. S. A. (2015). Providing Smart Agricultural solutions to farmers for better yielding using IoT. *Proceedings - 2015 IEEE International Conference on Technological Innovations in ICT for Agriculture and Rural Development, TIAR 2015, 4*(22), 40–43. 10.1109/TIAR.2015.7358528

Giaglis, G. M., Kourouthanassis, P., & Tsamakos, A. (2003). Towards a classification framework for mobile location-based services. In B. E. Mennecke & T. J. Strader (Eds.), *Mobile commerce: technology, theory and applications* (pp. 67–85). Idea Group Publishing. doi:10.4018/978-1-59140-044-8.ch004

Gonzalez, R. C., & Woods, R. E. (2002). *Digital Image Processing* (2nd ed.). Prentice Hall.

Goriparthi, T., Das, M. L., & Saxena, A. (2009). An improved bilinear pairing based remote user authentication scheme. *Computer Standards & Interfaces, 31*(1), 181–185. doi:10.1016/j.csi.2007.11.016

Grinstead, C., & Snell, J. L. (2021). Introduction to probability (2nd rev. ed). Academic Press.

Guizi, F., & Kurashima, C. S. (2016). Real-time people detection and tracking using 3d depth estimation. *The IEEE International Symposium on Consumer Electronics (ISCE),* 39–40. 10.1109/ISCE.2016.7797359

Guo, J. M., Hsia, C. H., Liu, Y. F., Shih, M. H., Chang, C. H., & Wu, J. Y. (2013). Fast background subtraction based on a multilayer codebook model for moving object detection. *IEEE Transactions on Circuits System Video Technology, 23*(10), 1809–1821. doi:10.1109/TCSVT.2013.2269011

Guo, J., Williams, B. M., & Huang, W. (2014). Adaptive Kalman filter approach for stochastic short-term traffic flow rate prediction and uncertainty quantification. *Transportation Research Part C, Emerging Technologies, 43*(1), 50–51. doi:10.1016/j.trc.2014.02.006

Gupta, A. K. (2020). Spam Mail Filtering Using Data Mining Approach: A comparative performance analysis. In Handling Priority Inversion in Time-Constrained Distributed Databases (pp. 253–282). Hershey, PA: IGI Global. doi:10.4018/978-1-7998-2491-6.ch015

Compilation of References

Gupta, A. K., & Shanker, U. (2018a). Location dependent information system's queries for mobile environment. Lecture Notes in Computer Science (Including Subseries Lecture Notes in Artificial Intelligence and Lecture Notes in Bioinformatics), 10829 LNCS. doi:10.1007/978-3-319-91455-8_19

Gupta, A. K., & Shanker, U. (2019). SPMC-PRRP: A Predicted Region Based Cache Replacement Policy. In Lecture Notes in Networks and Systems (Vol. 39). doi:10.1007/978-981-13-0277-0_26

Gupta, A. K., & Shanker, U. (2020b). MAD-RAPPEL: Mobility Aware Data Replacement &Prefetching Policy Enrooted LBS. *Journal of King Saud University - Computer and Information Sciences*.

Gupta, A. K., & Shanker, U. (2020d). *Study of fuzzy logic and particle swarm methods in map matching algorithm.* doi:10.100742452-020-2431-y

Gupta, A. K., & Shanker, U. (2020d). Study of fuzzy logic and particle swarm methods in map matching algorithm. doi:10.100742452-020-2431-y

Gupta, A. K., & Shanker, U. (2020e). Some Issues for Location Dependent Information System Query in Mobile Environment. *29th ACM International Conference on Information and Knowledge Management (CIKM '20)*, 4. doi:10.1145/3340531.3418504

Gupta, A. K., & Shanker, U. (2020f). MAD-RAPPEL: Mobility Aware Data Replacement &Prefetching Policy Enrooted LBS. Journal of King Saud University - Computer and Information Sciences.

Gupta, B. B., Joshi, R. C., & Misra, M. (2009). Defending against distributed denial of service attacks: issues and challenges. *Information Security Journal: A Global Perspective, 18*(5), 224-247.

Gupta, A. K., & Prakash, S. (2018). Secure Communication in Cluster-Based Ad Hoc Networks: A Review. In D. K. Lobiyal, V. Mansotra, & U. Singh (Eds.), *Advances in Intelligent Systems and Computing* (pp. 537–545). Springer Singapore.

Gupta, A. K., & Shanker, U. (2018). CELPB: A cache invalidation policy for location dependent data in mobile environment. *ACM International Conference Proceeding Series*. 10.1145/3216122.3216147

Gupta, A. K., & Shanker, U. (2018b). Modified predicted region based cache replacement policy for location-dependent data in mobile environment. *Procedia Computer Science, 125*, 917–924. Advance online publication. doi:10.1016/j.procs.2017.12.117

Gupta, A. K., & Shanker, U. (2020a). A Literature Review of Location-Aware Computing Policies: Taxonomy and Empirical Analysis in Mobile Environment. *International Journal of Mobile Human Computer Interaction, 12*(3), 21–45. doi:10.4018/IJMHCI.2020070102

Gupta, A. K., & Shanker, U. (2020b). CEMP-IR: A Novel Location Aware Cache Invalidation & Replacement Policy. *International Journal on Computer Science and Engineering, 2020*(1).

Gupta, A. K., & Shanker, U. (2020c). OMCPR: Optimal Mobility Aware Cache Data Pre-fetching and Replacement Policy Using Spatial K-Anonymity for LBS. *Wireless Personal Communications, 114*(2), 949–973. doi:10.100711277-020-07402-2

Gupta, B. B., Arachchilage, N. A., & Psannis, K. E. (2018). Defending against phishing attacks: Taxonomy of methods, current issues and future directions. *Telecommunication Systems, 67*(2), 247–267. doi:10.100711235-017-0334-z

Hambal, A. M., Pei, Z., & Ishabailu, F. L. (2017). Image Noise reduction and Filtering Techniques. *International Journal of Scientific Research, 6*(3), 2033–2038.

Han, K., Shon, T., & Kim, K. (2010). Efficient mobile sensor authentication in smart home and WPAN. *IEEE Transactions on Consumer Electronics, 56*(2), 591–596. doi:10.1109/TCE.2010.5505975

Haritaoglu, I., Harwood, D., & Davis, L. (2000). Real-time surveillance of people and their activities. *IEEE Transactions on Pattern Analysis and Machine Intelligence, 22*(8), 809–830. doi:10.1109/34.868683

Hektner, J. M., Schmidt, A., & Csikszentmihalyi, M. (2007). Experience sampling method: Measuring the quality of everyday life. Thousand Oaks, CA: Sage Publications.

Hess, A., Hummel, K.A., Gansterer, W.N., & Haring, G. (2015). Data-driven human mobility modeling: a survey and engineering guidance for mobile networking. *ACM Comput. Surv., 48*(3), 38:1–38:39.

Heyman, R., Wolf, R. D., & Pierson, J. (2014). Evaluating social media privacy settings for personal and advertising purposes. *Info, 16*(4), 18-32.

Hofstede, G. H. (2021, February 27). Country comparison. *Hofstede Insights*. Retrieved on February 27, 2021 from https://www.hofstede-insights.com/country-comparison/taiwan,the-usa/

Hofstede, G. H. (1991). *Cultures and organizations: Software of the mind*. McGraw-Hill.

Horak, R. (2012). *Telecommunications and Data Communications Handbook*. Wiley-Interscience.

Horwitz, L. (2014). Location-based marketing (LBM). *TechTarget*. Retrieved on February 28, 2021 from https://searchcustomerexperience.techtarget.com/definition/location-based-marketing-LBM

Hu, X. S. Q. (n.d.). IOT Application System with Crop Growth Models in Facility Agriculture. IEEE.

Hunter, G. L., & Taylor, S. A. (2019). The relationship between preference for privacy and social media usage. *Journal of Consumer Marketing, 37*(1), 43–54. doi:10.1108/JCM-11-2018-2927

Hu, W., Li, W., Zhang, X., & Maybank, S. (2015). Single and Multiple Object Tracking Using a Multi-Feature Joint Sparse Representation. *IEEE Transactions on Pattern Analysis and Machine Intelligence, 37*(4), 816–833. doi:10.1109/TPAMI.2014.2353628 PMID:26353296

Hwang, M.-S., Lee, C.-C., & Tang, Y.-L. (2002). A Simple Remote User Authentication Scheme. *Mathematical and Computer Modelling*, *36*(1-2), 103–107. doi:10.1016/S0895-7177(02)00106-1

Ibef. (n.d.). *Agriculture in India: Information About Indian Agriculture & Its Importance*. Retrieved from https://www.ibef.org/industry/agriculture-india.aspx

Idhoko, K. E., & Ojaiko, J. C. (2014). Integration of Geographical Information Systems (GIS) and Spatial Data Mining Techniques in Fight against Boko Haram Terrorist in Nigeria. *International Journal of Scientific Research*, *6*(14), 1932–1934.

Idler, C., Schweiger, R., Paulus, D., Mahlisch, M., & Ritter, W. (2006). Real-time vision based multi-target-tracking with particle filters in automotive applications. *The 13th IEEE Intelligent Vehicle Symposium*, 188–193.

Ikram, A. A. (2020). Privacy and Security Issues in Online Social Networks (OSN). *LGURJCSIT*, *4*(4), 43–54.

Ilayaraja, N., Mary Magdalene Jane, F., Safar, M., & Nadarajan, R. (2016). WARM Based Data Pre-fetching and Cache Replacement Strategies for Location Dependent Information System in Wireless Environment. *Wireless Personal Communications*, *90*(4), 1811–1842. doi:10.100711277-016-3425-3

Irion, K., & Helberger, N. (2017). Smart TV and the online media sector: User privacy in view of changing market realities. *Telecommunications Policy*, *41*(3), 170–184. doi:10.1016/j.telpol.2016.12.013

Islam. (2014). Systematic Literature Review: Security Challenges of Mobile Banking and Payments System. *International Journal of u- and e- Service, Science and Technology*, *7*(6), 107–116. doi:10.14257/ijunesst.2014.7.6.10

Jepson, A., Fleet, D., & Elmaraghi, T. (2003). Robust online appearance models for visual tracking. *IEEE Transactions on Pattern Analysis and Machine Intelligence*, *25*(10), 1296–1311. doi:10.1109/TPAMI.2003.1233903

Jing, W., & Wen-xing, B. (2009). A video supported moving object detection technique based on a different algorithm. *Computer Applications and Software*, *26*(12), 68–70.

Johnston, M. (2020, March 26). Smartphones are changing advertising & marketing. *Investopedia*. Retrieved on February 27, 2021 from https://www.investopedia.com/articles/personal-finance/062315/how-smartphones-are-changing-advertising-marketing.asp

Jordaan, Y. (2007). Information privacy issues: Implications for direct marketing. *International Journal of Retail and Marketing*, 42-53.

Joshua, O., Ibiyemi, T. S., & Adu, B. A. (2019). A Comprehensive Review on Various Types of Noise in Image Processing. *International Journal of Scientific and Engineering Research*, *10*(11), 388–393.

Jyotsna, P., & Sunita, J. (2013). A Comparative Study of Image Denoising Techniques. *International Journal of Innovative Research in Science, Engineering and Technology*, 2(3), 787–794.

Kang, Y. W., & Yang, K. C. C. (2020). Privacy concerns in the VR and AR applications in creative cultural industries: A text mining study. In Managerial Challenges and Social Impacts of Virtual and Augmented Reality (pp. 142-164). Hershey, PA: IGI-Global Publisher. doi:10.4018/978-1-7998-2874-7.ch009

Kang, Y. W., & Yang, K. C. C. (2021). Will social media and its consumption converge or diverge global consumer culture? In Analyzing global social media consumption (pp. 68-87). Hershey, PA: IGI-Global Publisher.

Kaur, S., & Singh, R. (2015). Image De-Noising Technique: A Review. *International Journal for Technological Research in Engineering*, 2(8), 2347–2352.

Khan, V. J., Markopoulos, I., & Jsselsteijn, W. A. (2007). Combining the Experience Sampling Method with the Day Reconstruction Method. *Proceedings 11th CHI Nederland Conference*.

Kim, Z. (2006). Real-time obstacle detection and tracking based on constrained Delaunay triangulation. *The IEEE Intelligent Transportation Systems Conference (ITSC)*, 548–553.

Kinnunen, T., Sahidullah, M., Falcone, M., Costantini, L., Hautamäki, R., Thomsen, D., ... Evans, N. (2017). Reddots replayed: A new replay spoofing attack corpus for text-dependent speaker verification research. In *IEEE International Conference on Acoustics, Speech and Signal Processing (ICASSP)* (pp. 5395-5399). New Orleans, LA: IEEE. 10.1109/ICASSP.2017.7953187

KMPG. (2016a). *Creepy or cool? Staying on the right side of the consumer privacy line.* Retrieved on March 22, 2020 from https://home.kpmg.com/sg/en/home/insights/2016/2011/crossing-the-line.html

KMPG. (2016b, November 7). *Companies that fail to see privacy as a business priority risk crossing the 'creepy line'.* KMPG, Retrieved on June 23, 2019 from https://home.kpmg/sg/en/home/media/press-releases/2016/2011/companies-that-fail-to-see-privacy-as-a-business-priority-risk-crossing-the-creepy-line.html

Ko, C. N., & Lee, C. M. (2012). Short-term load forecasting using SVR (support vector regression)-based radial basis function neural network with dual extended Kalman filter. *Energy, Elsevier*, 49, 413–416.

Konard, J. (2000). Handbook of Images and Video Processing. Academic Press.

Kong, H., Cinar, H., Sanjay, A., & Sanjay, S. (2013). A Generalized Laplacian of Gaussian Filter for Blob Detection and its Applications. *IEEE Transactions on Cybernetics*, 43(6), 1719–1733. doi:10.1109/TSMCB.2012.2228639 PMID:23757570

Koohang, A., Paliszkiewicz, J., & Goluchowski, J. (2018). Social media privacy concerns: Trusting beliefs and risk beliefs. *Industrial Management & Data Systems*, 118(6), 1209–1228. doi:10.1108/IMDS-12-2017-0558

Kouicem, D. E., Bouabdallah, A., & Lakhlef, H. (2018). Internet of things security: A top-down survey. *Computer Networks*, *141*, 199–221. doi:10.1016/j.comnet.2018.03.012

Krishna, M. K., Hexmoor, H., & Sogani, S., (2005). At-step ahead constrained optimal target detection algorithm for a multi-sensor surveillance system. *IEEE Intelligent Robots and Systems*, 357–362.

Kumar, A., Misra, M., & Sarje, A. K. (2008). A Predicted Region based Cache Replacement Policy for Location Dependent Data in Mobile Environment. *10th Inter-Research-Institute Student Seminar in Computer Science, IIIT Hyderabad, 7*(February), 1–8.

Kumar, A., Misra, M., & Sarje, A. K. (2006). A Predicted Region Based Cache Replacement Policy for Location Dependent Data in Mobile Environment. *2006 International Conference on Wireless Communications, Networking and Mobile Computing*, 1–4. 10.1109/WiCOM.2006.405

Kumar, N., & Sharma, B. (2020). Opportunities and Challenges with WSN's in Smart Technologies: A Smart Agriculture Perspective. *Advances in Intelligent Systems and Computing*, *1132*, 441–463. doi:10.1007/978-3-030-40305-8_22

Kumar, P., Lee, S. G., & Lee, H. J. (2011). A user authentication for healthcare application using wireless medical sensor networks. In *International Conference on High Performance Computing and Communications* (pp. 647-652). Banff, Canada: IEEE. 10.1109/HPCC.2011.92

Kumar, P., Lee, S. G., & Lee, H. J. (2012). E-SAP: Efficient-strong authentication protocol for healthcare applications using wireless medical sensor networks. *Sensors (Basel)*, *12*(2), 1625–1647. doi:10.3390120201625 PMID:22438729

Kumar, U., Navaneet, S., Kumar, N., & Pandey, S. C. (2020). Isolation of DDoS Attack in IoT: A New Perspective. *Wireless Personal Communications*, *114*(3), 2493–2510. doi:10.100711277-020-07486-w

Lai, K. Y., Tari, Z., & Bertok, P. (2004). Location-aware cache replacement for mobile environments. *Global Telecommunications Conference, GLOBECOM '04*, 3441-3447. 10.1109/GLOCOM.2004.1379006

Lakshmi, R. S., Ravichandran, K. S., Nathan, P. S., & Alagapan, A. N. (2016). Information retrieval by mining text and image. *International Journal of Advanced Intelligence Paradigms*, *8*(4), 451–459. doi:10.1504/IJAIP.2016.080199

Landman, M. (2010). Managing Smart Phone Security Risks. In *InfoSecCD '10, 2010* (p. 10). ACM.

Lazer, D., Pentland, A. S., Adamic, L., Aral, S., Barabasi, A. L., Brewer, D., & Van Alstyne, M. (2009). Life in the network: The coming age of computational social science. *Science*, *323*(5915), 721. doi:10.1126cience.1167742 PMID:19197046

Lee, B. Y., Liew, L. H., Cheah, W. S., & Wang, Y. C., (2012). Measuring the Effects of Occlusion on Kernel-Based Object Tracking Using Simulated Videos. *Procedia Engineering*, *41*, 764–770.

Lee, H. S., Lee, S., Song, H., & Lee, H. S. (2009). Wireless sensor network design for tactical military applications: Remote large-scale environments. In IEEE Military communications conference (MILCOM) (pp. 1-7). Boston, MA: IEEE.

Lee, S., Lim, J., Park, J., & Kim, K. (2016). *Next Place Prediction Based on Spatiotemporal Pattern Mining of Mobile Device Logs*. 1–19. doi:10.339016020145

Lee, W. H., & Lee, R. B. (2015). Multi-sensor authentication to improve smartphone security. In *International conference on information systems security and privacy (ICISSP)* (pp. 1-11). Angers, France: IEEE.

Lenormand, M., Tugores, A., Colet, P., & Ramasco, J. J. (2014). Tweets on the road. *PLoS One*, *9*(8), e105407. doi:10.1371/journal.pone.0105407 PMID:25141161

Levesque, R. J. R. (2017). *Adolescence, Privacy, and the Law: A Developmental Science Perspective*. Oxford University Press.

Li, C., Guo, L., & Hu, Y. (2010). A new method is combining HOG and Kalman filter for video-based human detection and tracking. *The 3rd International Conference on Image Signal Processing*, *1*, 290–293.

Liang, L., Zheng, K., Sheng, Q., & Huang, X. (2016, December). A denial of service attack method for an iot system. In *2016 8th international conference on Information Technology in Medicine and Education (ITME)* (pp. 360-364). IEEE. 10.1109/ITME.2016.0087

Liang, L., Zheng, K., Sheng, Q., Wang, W., Fu, R., & Huang, X. (2017, August). A denial of service attack method for iot system in photovoltaic energy system. In *International Conference on Network and System Security* (pp. 613-622). Springer. 10.1007/978-3-319-64701-2_48

Li, H., Liu, Y., Xiong, S., & Wang, L. (2014). Pedestrian detection algorithm based on video sequences and laser point cloud. *Frontiers of Computer Science*, *9*(3), 402–414. doi:10.100711704-014-3413-2

Li, M., Cai, Z., Wei, C., & Yuan, Y. (2015). A Survey of Video Object Tracking. *International Journal of Control and Automation*, *8*(9), 303–312. doi:10.14257/ijca.2015.8.9.29

Lima, A. (2016). *Digital traces of human mobility and interaction: models and applications*. University of Birmingham. Retrieved from https://etheses.bham.ac.uk/id/eprint/6833

Ling, S., Shuo, W., & Qing-Xia, L. (2009). A target detection method based on an adaptive threshold mixed difference. *Computer Applications and Software*, *26*(10), 94–97.

Liu, D., & Ning, P. (2004). Multilevel μTESLA: Broadcast authentication for distributed sensor networks. *ACM Transactions on Embedded Computing Systems*, *3*(4), 800–836. doi:10.1145/1027794.1027800

Liu, D., Ning, P., Zhu, S., & Jajodia, S. (2005). Practical broadcast authentication in sensor networks. In *Second Annual International Conference on Mobile and Ubiquitous Systems: Networking and Services* (pp. 118-129). San Diego, CA: IEEE.

Compilation of References

Lom, H. S., Thoo, A. C., Sulaiman, Z., & Adam, S. (2018, June). Moderating role of mobile users' information privacy concerns towards behavioural intention and use behaviour in mobile advertising. *Advanced Science Letters, 24*(6), 4259–4264. doi:10.1166/asl.2018.11584

Lomotey, R. D. (2014). Management of Mobile Data in a Crop Field. In *2014 IEEE International Conference on Mobile Services* (pp. 100-107). IEEE. 10.1109/MobServ.2014.23

Lowe, D. (2004). Distinctive image features from scale-invariant key points. *International Journal of Computer Vision, 60*(2), 91–110. doi:10.1023/B:VISI.0000029664.99615.94

Lubbe, C., Brodt, A., Cipriani, N., Großmann, M., & Mitschang, B. (2011). DiSCO: A Distributed Semantic Cache Overlay for Location-Based Services. *2011 IEEE 12th International Conference on Mobile Data Management, 1*, 17–26. 10.1109/MDM.2011.56

Mahmoud, R. O., Faheem, M. T., & Sarhan, A. (2008). Intelligent Denoising Technique for Spatial Video Denoising for real-time applications. *International Conference on Computers Engineering and Systems (ICCES08)*, 407-412. 10.1109/ICCES.2008.4773037

Marguta, R., & Parisi, A. (2015). Impact of human mobility on the periodicities and mechanisms underlying measles dynamics. *Journal of the Royal Society, Interface, 12*(104), 20141317. doi:10.1098/rsif.2014.1317 PMID:25673302

Mehta, M., Goyal, C., Srivastava, M., & Jain, R. (2010). Real-time object Detection and Tracking: Histogram Matching and Kalman Filter Approach. *The 2nd International Conference on Computer and Automation Engineering*, 796-801.

Merler, S., & Ajelli, M. (2010). The role of population heterogeneity and human mobility in the spread of pandemic influenza. *Proc R Soc Lond B, 277*(1681), 557-565.

Michael, S. D. (1996). Semantic Data Caching and Replacement. *Proceedings of the 22th International Conference on Very Large Data Bases, 22*(4), 333–341. 10.1.1.45.683

Miguel, N. (2012). *Next Place Prediction using Mobility Markov Chains.* Academic Press.

Mikolajczyk, K., & Schmid, C. (2002). An affine invariant interest point detector. *The European Conference on Computer Vision (ECCV), 1*, 128–142.

Mo, Y., & Sinopoli, B. (2009). Secure control against replay attacks. In *47th annual Allerton conference on communication, control, and computing (Allerton)* (pp. 911-918). Monticello, IL: Academic Press.

Moeslund, T., & Granum, E. (2001). A survey of computer vision-based human motion capture. *Computer Vision and Image Understanding, 81*(3), 231–268. doi:10.1006/cviu.2000.0897

Mohapatra, M. R., & Mohanty, J. R. (2021). Overview of IoT Privacy and Security Challenges for Smart Carpooling System. In *Proceedings of Second International Conference on Smart Energy and Communication* (pp. 727-733). Springer. 10.1007/978-981-15-6707-0_71

Monnet, A., Mittal, A., Paragios, N., & Ramesh, V. (2003). Background modeling and subtraction of dynamic scenes. *The IEEE International Conference on Computer Vision (ICCV)*, 1305–1312. 10.1109/ICCV.2003.1238641

Mosenia, A., & Jha, N. K. (2016). A comprehensive study of security of internet-of-things. *IEEE Transactions on Emerging Topics in Computing, 5*(4), 586–602. doi:10.1109/TETC.2016.2606384

Muangprathub, J., Boonnam, N., Kajornkasirat, S., Lekbangpong, N., Wanichsombat, A., & Nillaor, P. (2019). IoT and agriculture data analysis for smart farm. *Computers and Electronics in Agriculture, 156*, 467–474. doi:10.1016/j.compag.2018.12.011

Mwiya, M., Phiri, J., & Lyoko, G. (2015). Public Crime Reporting and Monitoring System Model Using GSM and GIS Technologies: A Case of Zambia Police Service. *International Journal of Computer Science and Mobile Computing, 4*(11), 207–226.

Myers, J., & Sar, S. (2015). The influence of consumer mood state as a contextual factor on imagery-inducing advertisements and brand attitude. *Journal of Marketing Communications, 21*(4), 284–299. doi:10.1080/13527266.2012.762421

N, M. S., & M, P. K. (2017). *Development of a System for Estimation of NPK and pH in Soil and Disease Detection in plants.* doi:10.9790/2834-1204055257

Nagaraj, A. (2021). *Introduction to Sensors in IoT and Cloud Computing Applications.* Bentham Science Publishers.

Nanni, L., Lumini, A., & Brahnam, S. (2014). Ensemble of shape descriptors for shape retrieval and classification. *International Journal of Advanced Intelligence Paradigms, 6*(2), 136–156. doi:10.1504/IJAIP.2014.062177

Nasution, H. A., & Emmanuel, S. (2007). Intelligent video surveillance for monitoring elderly in home environments. In *9th Workshop on Multimedia Signal Processing* (pp. 203-206). IEEE. 10.1109/MMSP.2007.4412853

Naz, R., & Khan, M. N. A. (2015). Rapid Applications Development Techniques: A Critical Review. *International Journal of Software Engineering and Its Applications, 9*(11), 163–176. doi:10.14257/ijseia.2015.9.11.15

Niu, B., Li, Q., Zhu, X., Cao, G., & Li, H. (2014). Achieving k-anonymity in privacy-aware location-based services. *IEEE INFOCOM 2014 - IEEE Conference on Computer Communications*, 754–762. 10.1109/INFOCOM.2014.6848002

Niu, B., Li, Q., Zhu, X., Cao, G., & Li, H. (2015). Enhancing privacy through caching in location-based services. *2015 IEEE Conference on Computer Communications (INFOCOM)*, 1017–1025. 10.1109/INFOCOM.2015.7218474

Nuevo, J., Parra, I., Sjoberg, J., & Bergasa, L. (2010). Estimating surrounding pedestrians' pose using computer vision. *The 13th IEEE Intelligent Transportation Systems Conference (ITSC)*, 1863–1868.

Nwankwo, U. V., & James, O. (2016). Prevalence of Lethal and Non-lethal Crimes in Nigeria. *Journal of Advanced Research in Humanity and Social Science, 3*(1), 1–16.

O'Rourke, J. (1994). *Computational geometry in C* (2nd ed.). Cambridge University Press.

Oguntade, P. E., Ojo, O.O., Okagbue, H. I., & Oguntade, O. A. (2015). Analysis of selected crime data in Nigeria between 1999 and 2013. *Data in Brief.* doi:10.1016/j.dib.2018.05.143i

Ohlhorst, F. (2021). Social Media Risks Increasing in 2021. *Security Boulevard.* Retrieved from https://securityboulevard.com/2021/03/social-media-risks-increasing-in-2021

Oliver, N., Rosario, B., & Pentland, A. (2000). A Bayesian computer vision system for modeling human interactions. *IEEE Transactions on Pattern Analysis and Machine Intelligence, 22*(8), 831–843. doi:10.1109/34.868684

Padalalu, P., Mahajan, S., Dabir, K., Mitkar, S., & Javale, D. (2017). Smart water dripping system for agriculture/farming. *2017 2nd International Conference for Convergence in Technology, I2CT 2017,* (April), 659–662. 10.1109/I2CT.2017.8226212

Palen, L., & Dourish, P. (2003, April). Unpacking" privacy" for a networked world. In *Proceedings of the SIGCHI conference on Human factors in computing systems* (pp. 129-136). 10.1145/642611.642635

Pallis, G., Vakali, A., & Pokorny, J. (2008). A clustering-based prefetching scheme on a Web cache environment. *Computers & Electrical Engineering, 34*(4), 309–323. doi:10.1016/j.compeleceng.2007.04.002

Papadopoulou, P. (2018). Exploring M-Commerce and social media: A comparative analysis of mobile phones and tablets. In Mobile Commerce: Concepts, Methodologies, Tools, and Applications (pp. 849-869). IGI Publishers.

Patil, P. K. A. (2016). *A Model for Smart Agriculture Using IoT.* Academic Press.

Patterson, R. H., Gibson, G. A., Ginting, E., Stodolsky, D., & Zelenka, J. (1995). Informed Prefetching and Caching. *Proceedings of the Fifteenth ACM Symposium on Operating Systems Principles,* 79–95. 10.1145/224056.224064

Pew Research Center. (2019, June 12). *Social Media Fact Sheet.* Washington, DC: Pew Research Center. Retrieved on July 31, 2019 from https://www.pewinternet.org/fact-sheet/social-media/

Pirretti, M., Zhu, S., Vijaykrishnan, N., McDaniel, P., Kandemir, M., & Brooks, R. (2006). The sleep deprivation attack in sensor networks: Analysis and methods of defense. *International Journal of Distributed Sensor Networks, 2*(3), 267–287. doi:10.1080/15501320600642718

Pirzada, A. A., & McDonald, C. (2004). Kerberos Assisted Authentication in Mobile Ad-hoc Networks. In *27th Australasian Computer Science conference* (pp. 41-46). Dunedin, New Zealand: Australian Computer Society.

Pitman, J., & Yor, M. (2018). *A guide to Brownian motion and related stochastic processes.* Academic Press.

Prathibha, S. R., Hongal, A., & Jyothi, M. P. (2017). *IoT based monitoring system in smart agriculture.* Advance online publication. doi:10.1109/ICRAECT.2017.52

Puri, N. V., & Devale, P. R. (2012). Development of Human Tracking in Video Surveillance System for Activity Analysis. *Journal of Computational Engineering, 4,* 26–30.

Quercia, D., Lathia, N., Calabrese, F., Di Lorenzo, G., & Crowcroft, J. (2010). Recommending social events from mobile phone location data. *International conference on data mining,* 971–976. 10.1109/ICDM.2010.152

Rahaman, S. (2017). Detection of NPK Ratio Level Using SVM Algorithm And Smart Agro Sensor System. *International Journal of Latest Research in Engineering and Technology, 3*(7), 11–15. Www.Ijlret.Com

Ramane, D. V., Patil, S. S., & Shaligram, A. D. (2015). Detection of NPK nutrients of soil using Fiber Optic Sensor. *International Journal of Research in Advent Technology ACGT,* (April), 13–14.

Rani, D., Kumar, N., & Bhushan, B. (2019). Implementation of an Automated Irrigation System for Agriculture Monitoring using IoT Communication. *5th IEEE International Conference on Signal Processing, Computing and Control (ISPCC 2k19),* 138–143. 10.1109/ISPCC48220.2019.8988390

Rao, R., & Nageswara, B. S. (2018). IoT based smart crop-field monitoring and automation irrigation system. *2018 2nd International Conference on Inventive Systems and Control (ICISC),* 478–483.

Rasooli, M. W., Bhushan, B., & Kumar, N. (2020). Applicability of wireless sensor networks & IoT in saffron & wheat crops: A smart agriculture perspective. *International Journal of Scientific and Technology Research, 9*(2), 2456–2461.

Ravenstein, E. G. (1885). The laws of migration. *Journal of the Statistical Society of London, 52*(2), 167–235. doi:10.2307/2979181

Ren, Q., & Dunham, M. H. (2000). Using Semantic Caching to Manage Location Dependent Data in Mobile Computing. 6th ACM/IEEE Mobile Computing and Networking (MobiCom), 3, 210–221.

Riaz, R., Gillani, N.-A., Rizvi, S. S., Shokat, S., & Kwon, S. J. (2019). SUBBASE: An Authentication Scheme for Wireless Sensor Networks Based on User Biometrics. *Wireless Communications and Mobile Computing, 2019,* 1–11. doi:10.1155/2019/6370742

Richter, F. (2021, March 1). Global 5G Adoption to Triple in 2021. *Statista.* Retrieved on March 2, 2021 from https://www.statista.com/chart/9604/2025g-subscription-forecast/?utm_source=Statista+Global&utm_campaign=2670c2873f2029e-All_InfographTicker_daily_COM_AM_KW2005_2021_Fr_COPY&utm_medium=email&utm_term=2020_afecd2219f2025-2670c2873f2029e-301917341

Ritter, A., Etzioni, O., & Clark, S. (2012, August). Open domain event extraction from twitter. In *Proceedings of the 18th ACM SIGKDD international conference on Knowledge discovery and data mining* (pp. 1104-1112). 10.1145/2339530.2339704

Roth, C., Kang, S. M., Batty, M., & Barthèlemy, M. (2011). Structure of urban movements: Polycentric activity and entangled hierarchical flows. *PLoS One*, *6*(1), e15923. doi:10.1371/journal.pone.0015923 PMID:21249210

Ruiz Espejo, M. (2002). Review of Statisticians of the Centuries. Computational Statistics & Data Analysis, 40, 209–210.

Ruj, S., Stojmenovic, M., & Nayak, A. (2012). Privacy Preserving Access Control with Authentication for Securing Data in Clouds. In *12th IEEE/ACM International Symposium on Cluster, Cloud and Grid Computing* (pp. 556-563). Ottawa, Canada: IEEE. 10.1109/CCGrid.2012.92

Sadri, A. A., Rahmani, A. M., Saberikamarposhti, M., & Hosseinzadeh, M. (2021). Fog data management: A vision, challenges, and future directions. *Journal of Network and Computer Applications*, *174*, 102882. Advance online publication. doi:10.1016/j.jnca.2020.102882

Salhi, A., & Jammoussi, A. Y. (2012). Object tracking system using Camshaft, Meanshift and Kalman filter. *World Academy of Science, Engineering and Technology*, *6*(4), 674–679.

Saranya, R. M. K. A. S. S. P. (2019). Design and Construction of Arduino Based pH Control System for Household Waste Water Reuse. *2019 3rd International Conference on Trends in Electronics and Informatics (ICOEI)*, 1037–1041.

Sather, T. (2014, November). Experience Sampling Method: An overview for researchers and clinicians. *CREd Library*. Retrieved on February 28, 2021 from https://academy.pubs.asha.org/2014/2011/experience-sampling-method/

Sengupta, J., Ruj, S., & Bit, S. D. (2020). A comprehensive survey on attacks, security issues and blockchain solutions for IoT and IIoT. *Journal of Network and Computer Applications*, *149*, 102481. doi:10.1016/j.jnca.2019.102481

Sharma, B. B., & Kumar, N. (2020). Internet of things-based hardware and software for smart agriculture: A review. *Lecture Notes in Electrical Engineering*, *597*, 151–157. doi:10.1007/978-3-030-29407-6_13

Sharma, B. B., & Kumar, N. (2021). IoT-Based Intelligent Irrigation System for Paddy Crop Using an Internet-Controlled Water Pump. *International Journal of Agricultural and Environmental Information Systems*, *12*(1), 21–36. doi:10.4018/IJAEIS.20210101.oa2

Sharma, P., Singh, G., & Kaur, A. (2013). Different Techniques of Edge Detection in Digital Image Processing. *International Journal of Engineering Research and Applications*, *3*(3), 458–461.

Sheikh, Y., & Shah, M. (2005). Bayesian Modeling of Dynamic Scenes for Object Detection. *IEEE Transactions on Pattern Analysis and Machine Intelligence*, *27*(11), 1778–1792. doi:10.1109/TPAMI.2005.213 PMID:16285376

Shelton, J., Roy, K., O'Connor, B., & Dozier, G. V. (2014). Mitigating Iris-Based Replay Attacks. *International Journal of Machine Learning and Computing, 4*(3), 204–209. doi:10.7763/IJMLC.2014.V4.413

Shi, J., & Malik, J. (2000). Normalized cuts and image segmentation. *IEEE Transactions on Pattern Analysis and Machine Intelligence, 22*(8), 888–905. doi:10.1109/34.868688

Shokri, R., Theodorakopoulos, G., Papadimitratos, P., Kazemi, E., & Hubaux, J. (2014). Hiding in the Mobile Crowd: LocationPrivacy through Collaboration. *IEEE Transactions on Dependable and Secure Computing, 11*(3), 266–279. doi:10.1109/TDSC.2013.57

Sidenbladh, H., & Black, M. J. (2003). Learning the statistics of people images and video. *International Journal of Computer Vision, 54*(1/2), 189–209. doi:10.1023/A:1023765619733

Silver, L., Smith, A., John, C., Jiang, J., Anderson, M., & Rainie, L. (2019, March 7). Majorities say mobile phones are good for society, even amid concerns about their impact on children. *Pew Research Center.* Retrieved on February 27, 2021 from https://www.pewresearch.org/internet/2019/2003/2007/majorities-say-mobile-phones-are-good-for-society-even-amid-concerns-about-their-impact-on-children/

Simini, F., González, M. C., Maritan, A., & Barabási, A.-L. (2012). A universal model for mobility and migration patterns. *Nature, 484*(7392), 96–100. doi:10.1038/nature10856 PMID:22367540

Sindhu, P., G. I. (2018). IoT Enabled Soil Testing. *Res Publica (Liverpool, England), 7*(1), 54–57.

Sivaraman, S., & Trivedi, M. (2013). Integrated lane and vehicle detection, localization, and tracking: A synergistic approach. *IEEE Transactions on Intelligent Transportation Systems, 14*(2), 907–917. doi:10.1109/TITS.2013.2246835

Smiatek, G. (2005). SOAP Based web services in GIS/RDBMS Environment. *Journal of Environmental Modeling and Software, 20*(6), 775–782. doi:10.1016/j.envsoft.2004.04.008

Smith, D. F., Wiliem, A., & Lovell, B. C. (2015). Face Recognition on Consumer Devices: Reflections on Replay Attacks. *IEEE Transactions on Information Forensics and Security, 10*(4), 736–745. doi:10.1109/TIFS.2015.2398819

Song, L., Kotz, D., Jain, R., & He, X. (2006). Evaluating next-cell predictors with extensive wi-fi mobility data. *IEEE Transactions on Mobile Computing, 5*(12), 1633–1649. doi:10.1109/TMC.2006.185

Staggenborg, S. A., Carignano, M., & Haag, L. (2007). Predicting Soil pH and Buffer pH In Situ with a Real-Time Sensor. *Agronomy Journal, 99*(3), 854–861. doi:10.2134/agronj2006.0254

Statista Research Department. (2019). *Total violent crime reported in the United States from 1990 to 2018.* Retrieved from https://www.statista.com/statistics/191129/reported-violent-crime-in-the-us-since-1990/

Statista Research Department. (2020). *Number of crimes in China 2018, by type.* Retrieved from https://www.statista.com/statistics/224776/number-of-crimes-in-china-by-type/

Statista. (2016, February 28). United States mobile phone penetration 2014-2020. *Statista*. Retrieved on February 27, 2021 from https://www.statista.com/statistics/222307/forecast-of-mobile-phone-penetration-in-the-us/

Statista. (2020, December 4). Household penetration of mobile phones in Taiwan 2007-2018. *Statista*. Retrieved on February 27, 2021 from https://www.statista.com/statistics/324757/taiwan-mobile-phone-household-penetration/

Stauffer, C., & Grimson, W. (2000). Learning patterns of activity using real-time tracking. *IEEE Transactions on Pattern Analysis and Machine Intelligence, 22*(8), 747–767. doi:10.1109/34.868677

Suganthi, G., & Korah, R. (2016). Computer-aided detection and identification of mine-like objects in infrared imagery using digital image processing. *International Journal of Advanced Intelligence Paradigms, 8*(4), 400–411. doi:10.1504/IJAIP.2016.080193

Sukaphat, S. (2011). An implementation of location-based service system with cell identifier for detecting lost mobile. *Procedia Computer Science, 3*, 949–953. doi:10.1016/j.procs.2010.12.155

Sun, Z., Di, L., Heo, G., Zhang, C., Fang, H., Yue, P., Jiang, L., Tan, X., Guo, L., & Lin, L. (2017). GeoFairy: Towards a one-stop and location based Service for Geospatial Information Retrieval. *Computers, Environment and Urban Systems, 62*, 156–167. doi:10.1016/j.compenvurbsys.2016.11.007

Suo, H., Wan, J., Zou, C., & Liu, J. (2012, March). Security in the internet of things: A review. In 2012 international conference on computer science and electronics engineering (Vol. 3, pp. 648-651). IEEE.

Sushama, C., Kumar, M. S., & Neelima, P. (2021). Privacy and security issues in the future: A social media. *Materials Today: Proceedings*. Advance online publication. doi:10.1016/j.matpr.2020.11.105

Swaroop, V., & Shanker, U. (2011). *Concept and Management Issues in Mobile Distributed Real Time Database*. Academic Press.

Swaroop, V., Gupta, G., & Shanker, U. (2011). Issues in mobile distributed real time databases: Performance and review. *International Journal of Engineering Science and Technology, 3*.

Szewczyk, R., Osterweil, E., Polastre, J., Hamilton, M., Mainwaring, A., & Estrin, D. (2004). Habitat monitoring with sensor networks. *Center for Embedded Network Sensing, 47*(6), 33–40.

Tedeschi, S., Emmanouilidis, C., Mehnen, J., & Roy, R. (2019). A design approach to IoT endpoint security for production machinery monitoring. *Sensors (Basel), 19*(10), 2355. doi:10.339019102355 PMID:31121892

The Economist. (2004, June 24). The harder hard sell. *The Economist*. Retrieved on February 27, 2021 from https://www.economist.com/special-report/2004/2006/2024/the-harder-hard-sell

Thilakarathna, K., Seneviratne, S., Gupta, K., Kaafar, M. A., & Seneviratne, A. (2017). A deep dive into location-based communities in social discovery networks. *Computer Communications, 100*, 78–90. doi:10.1016/j.comcom.2016.11.008

Tian, Y., Kaleemullah, M., Rodhaan, M., Song, B., Al-Dhelaan, A., & Ma, T. (2018). A privacy preserving location service for cloud-of-things system. *Journal of Parallel and Distributed Computing, 123*, 215–222. Advance online publication. doi:10.1016/j.jpdc.2018.09.005

Tournier, J., Lesueur, F., Le Mouël, F., Guyon, L., & Ben-Hassine, H. (2020). A survey of IoT protocols and their security issues through the lens of a generic IoT stack. *Internet of Things*, 100264.

Trivedi, K. (2016). *Discrete-Time Markov Chains*. doi:10.1002/9781119285441.ch7

Tseng, H. R., Jan, R. H., & Yang, W. (2007). An improved dynamic user authentication scheme for wireless sensor networks. In *IEEE Global Communications Conference (GLOBECOM'07)* (pp. 986-990). Washington, DC: IEEE. 10.1109/GLOCOM.2007.190

Udupa. (2011). *ATM Security Digest India, Skimming- the global threat*. Secure Systems Pvt. Ltd.

Uke, S. N., Mahajan, A. R., & Thool, R. C. (2013). UML modeling of physical and data link layer security attacks in WSN. *International Journal of Computers and Applications, 70*(11).

van der Sloot, B. (2017, August). Decisional privacy 2.0: the procedural requirements implicit in Article 8 ECHR and its potential impact on profiling. *International Data Privacy Law, 7*(3), 190-201, doi:https://doi.org/110.1093/idpl/ipx1011

Van Le, T., Burmester, M., & de Medeiros, B. (2007). Forward-secure RFID Authentication and Key Exchange. *IACR Cryptol. ePrint Arch., 2007*, 51.

Viola, P., & Jones, M. (2001). Rapid object detection using a boosted cascade of simple features. *The IEEE Computer Society Conference on Computer Vision and Pattern Recognition (CVPR)*, 511–518. 10.1109/CVPR.2001.990517

Viola, P., Jones, M., & Snow, D. (2003). Detecting pedestrians using patterns of motion and appearance. *The IEEE International Conference on Computer Vision (ICCV)*, 734–741. 10.1109/ICCV.2003.1238422

Walden, I., & Woods, L. (2011). Broadcasting privacy. *Journal of Medicine and Law, 3*(1), 117–141. https://dx.doi.org/110.5235/175776311796471323

Wang, F. (2012). Why police and policing need GIS: An overview. *Annals of GIS, 18*(3), 159–171. doi:10.1080/19475683.2012.691900

Wang, S., Zhang, X., Zhang, Y., Wang, L., Yang, J., & Wang, W. (2017). A Survey on Mobile Edge Networks: Convergence of Computing, Caching and Communications. *IEEE Access: Practical Innovations, Open Solutions, 5*, 6757–6779. doi:10.1109/ACCESS.2017.2685434

Wazid, Katal, Goudar, Singh, Tyagi, Sharma, & Bhakuni. (2013). A Framework for Detection and Prevention of Novel Keylogger Spyware Attacks. *7th International Conference on Intelligent Systems and Control (ISCO 2013)*.

Wen, J. T., Sar, S., & Anghelcev, G. (2017). The interaction effects of mood and ad appeals on type of elaboration and advertising effectiveness. *Journal of Current Issues and Research in Advertising*, *38*(1), 31–43.

Williams, M. (2009, July 10). Advertisers test alimented reality's durability. *Campaign, 9*.

World Population Review. (2020). *Crime Rate by Country 2020*. Retrieved from https://worldpopulationreview.com/countries/crime-rate-by-country/

Wurmser. (2020). *Location Intelligence 2020 - Privacy Concerns Start to Squeeze the Supply of Mobile Location Data*. Report. Retrieved from https://www.emarketer.com/content/location-intelligence-2020

Wu, Y., & Yu, T. (2006). A field model for human detection and tracking. *IEEE Transactions on Pattern Analysis and Machine Intelligence*, *28*(5), 753–765. doi:10.1109/TPAMI.2006.87 PMID:16640261

Xiong, F., & Qiao, K. (1999). Intelligent systems and its application in agriculture. *IFAC Proceedings Volumes*, *32*(2), 5597–5602. 10.1016/S1474-6670(17)56954-2

Xiong, W., & Lagerström, R. (2019). Threat modeling–A systematic literature review. *Computers & Security*, *84*, 53–69. doi:10.1016/j.cose.2019.03.010

Xue, L., Jiang, C., Chang, H., Yang, Y., Qin, W., & Yuan, W. (2012). A novel Kalman filter for combining outputs of MEMS gyroscope array. *Measurement, Elsevier*, *45*(4), 745–746. doi:10.1016/j.measurement.2011.12.016

Xu, H., Dinev, T., Smith, J., & Hart, P. (2011, December). Information privacy concerns: Linking individual perceptions with institutional privacy assurances. *Journal of the Association for Information Systems*, *12*(12), 798–824. doi:10.17705/1jais.00281

Xu, J., Hu, Q., Lee, W.-C., & Lee, D. L. (2004). Performance evaluation of an optimal cache replacement policy for wireless data dissemination. *IEEE Transactions on Knowledge and Data Engineering*, *16*(1), 125–139. doi:10.1109/TKDE.2004.1264827

Yang, K. C. C., & Kang, Y. W. (2020a). Framing national security concerns in mobile telecommunication infrastructure debates: A text mining study of Huawei. In Huawei goes global (volume II): Regional, geopolitical perspectives and crisis management (pp. 313-339). Palgrave-Macmillan.

Yang, K. C. C., & Kang, Y. W. (2020b). What Facebook users' responses to advertising: A computational and ESM analysis. In IoT, digital transformation, and the future of global marketing. Hershey, PA: IGI-Global Publisher. doi:10.4018/978-1-7998-1618-8.ch001

Yang, D., Zhang, D., Zheng, V. W., & Yu, Z. (2014). Modeling user activity preference by leveraging user spatial temporal characteristics in LBSNs. *IEEE Transactions on Systems, Man, and Cybernetics. Systems*, *45*(1), 129–142. doi:10.1109/TSMC.2014.2327053

Yasser, A. A., & Awatef, A. S. (2018). Fighting terrorism more effectively with the aid of GIS: The Kingdom of Saudi Arabia case study. *American Journal of Geographic Information System*, *7*(91), 15–31.

Yilmaz, A., Javed, O., & Shah, M. (2006). Object Tracking: A Survey. *ACM Computing Surveys*, *38*(4), 1–45. doi:10.1145/1177352.1177355

Yilmaz, A., Li, X., & Shah, M. (2004). Contour based object tracking with occlusion handling in video acquired using mobile cameras. *IEEE Transactions on Pattern Analysis and Machine Intelligence*, *26*(11), 1531–1536. doi:10.1109/TPAMI.2004.96 PMID:15521500

Yin, L., Cao, G., Das, C., & Ashraf, A. (2002). Power-aware prefetch in mobile environments. *Proceedings 22nd International Conference on Distributed Computing Systems*, 571–578. 10.1109/ICDCS.2002.1022307

Yuqing, M., Jianrong, C., & Keming, F. (2005). New technology for the detection of pH. *Journal of Biochemical and Biophysical Methods*, *63*(1), 1–9. doi:10.1016/j.jbbm.2005.02.001 PMID:15892973

Zhai, Z., Martínez Ortega, J.-F., Lucas Martínez, N., & Rodríguez-Molina, J. (2018). A mission planning approach for precision farming systems based on multi-objective optimization. *Sensors (Basel)*, *18*(6), 1795. doi:10.339018061795 PMID:29865251

Zhang, C., Sun, Z., Heo, G., Di, L., & Lin, L. (2016). A GeoPackage implementation of common map API on Google Maps and OpenLayers to manipulate agricultural data on mobile devices. *2016 Fifth International Conference on Agro-Geoinformatics (Agro-Geoinformatics)*, 1–4. 10.1109/Agro-Geoinformatics.2016.7577654

Zhang, K., Liang, X., Lu, R., & Shen, X. (2014). Sybil attacks and their defenses in the internet of things. *IEEE Internet of Things Journal*, *1*(5), 372–383. doi:10.1109/JIOT.2014.2344013

Zhang, S., Choo, K.-K. R., Liu, Q., & Wang, G. (2018). Enhancing privacy through uniform grid and caching in location-based services. *Future Generation Computer Systems*, *86*, 881–892. doi:10.1016/j.future.2017.06.022

Zhang, S., Li, X., Tan, Z., Peng, T., & Wang, G. (2019). A caching and spatial K-anonymity driven privacy enhancement scheme in continuous location-based services. *Future Generation Computer Systems*, *94*, 40–50. doi:10.1016/j.future.2018.10.053

Zhang, Z., Zhou, L., Zhao, X., Wang, G., Su, Y., Metzger, M., & Zhao, B. Y. (2013, November). On the validity of geosocial mobility traces. In *Proceedings of the Twelfth ACM Workshop on Hot Topics in Networks* (pp. 1-7). 10.1145/2535771.2535786

Zheng, B., Xu, J., Member, S., & Lee, D. L. (2002). *Cache Invalidation and Replacement Strategies for Location-Dependent Data in Mobile Environments*. Academic Press.

Zheng, Y., & Zhou, X. (Eds.). (2011). *Computing with spatial trajectories*. Springer Science & Business Media. doi:10.1007/978-1-4614-1629-6

Zhong, Q., Chen, Z., Zhang, X., & Hu, G. (2014). Feature-Based Object Location of IC Pins by Using Fast Run Length Encoding BLOB Analysis. *IEEE Transactions on Components, Packaging, and Manufacturing Technology*, *4*(11), 1887–1898. doi:10.1109/TCPMT.2014.2350015

Zhou, Y., Wang, L., Zhong, R., & Tan, Y. (2018). A Markov Chain Based Demand Prediction Model for Stations in Bike Sharing Systems. *Mathematical Problems in Engineering*, *2018*, 1–8. doi:10.1155/2018/8028714

Related References

To continue our tradition of advancing media and communications research, we have compiled a list of recommended IGI Global readings. These references will provide additional information and guidance to further enrich your knowledge and assist you with your own research and future publications.

Abashian, N., & Fisher, S. (2018). Intercultural Effectiveness in Libraries: Supporting Success Through Collaboration With Co-Curricular Programs. In B. Blummer, J. Kenton, & M. Wiatrowski (Eds.), *Promoting Ethnic Diversity and Multiculturalism in Higher Education* (pp. 219–236). Hershey, PA: IGI Global. doi:10.4018/978-1-5225-4097-7.ch012

Adebayo, O., Fagbohun, M. O., Esse, U. C., & Nwokeoma, N. M. (2018). Change Management in the Academic Library: Transition From Print to Digital Collections. In R. Bhardwaj (Ed.), *Digitizing the Modern Library and the Transition From Print to Electronic* (pp. 1–28). Hershey, PA: IGI Global. doi:10.4018/978-1-5225-2119-8.ch001

Adegbore, A. M., Quadri, M. O., & Oyewo, O. R. (2018). A Theoretical Approach to the Adoption of Electronic Resource Management Systems (ERMS) in Nigerian University Libraries. In A. Tella & T. Kwanya (Eds.), *Handbook of Research on Managing Intellectual Property in Digital Libraries* (pp. 292–311). Hershey, PA: IGI Global. doi:10.4018/978-1-5225-3093-0.ch015

Adesola, A. P., & Olla, G. O. (2018). Unlocking the Unlimited Potentials of Koha OSS/ILS for Library House-Keeping Functions: A Global View. In M. Khosrow-Pour (Ed.), *Optimizing Contemporary Application and Processes in Open Source Software* (pp. 124–163). Hershey, PA: IGI Global. doi:10.4018/978-1-5225-5314-4.ch006

Adigun, G. O., Sobalaje, A. J., & Salau, S. A. (2018). Social Media and Copyright in Digital Libraries. In A. Tella & T. Kwanya (Eds.), *Handbook of Research on Managing Intellectual Property in Digital Libraries* (pp. 19–36). Hershey, PA: IGI Global. doi:10.4018/978-1-5225-3093-0.ch002

Adomi, E. E., Eriki, J. A., Tiemo, P. A., & Akpojotor, L. O. (2016). Incidents of Cyberbullying Among Library and Information Science (LIS) Students at Delta State University, Abraka, Nigeria. *International Journal of Digital Literacy and Digital Competence*, 7(4), 52–63. doi:10.4018/IJDLDC.2016100104

Afolabi, O. A. (2018). Myths and Challenges of Building an Effective Digital Library in Developing Nations: An African Perspective. In A. Tella & T. Kwanya (Eds.), *Handbook of Research on Managing Intellectual Property in Digital Libraries* (pp. 51–79). Hershey, PA: IGI Global. doi:10.4018/978-1-5225-3093-0.ch004

Agrawal, P. R. (2016). Google Search: Digging into the Culture of Information Retrieval. In E. de Smet & S. Dhamdhere (Eds.), *E-Discovery Tools and Applications in Modern Libraries* (pp. 210–239). Hershey, PA: IGI Global. doi:10.4018/978-1-5225-0474-0.ch012

Ahuja, Y., & Kumar, P. (2017). Web 2.0 Tools and Application: Knowledge Management and Sharing in Libraries. In B. Gunjal (Ed.), *Managing Knowledge and Scholarly Assets in Academic Libraries* (pp. 218–234). Hershey, PA: IGI Global. doi:10.4018/978-1-5225-1741-2.ch010

Ajmi, A. (2018). Developing In-House Digital Tools: Case Studies From the UMKC School of Law Library. In L. Costello & M. Powers (Eds.), *Developing In-House Digital Tools in Library Spaces* (pp. 117–139). Hershey, PA: IGI Global. doi:10.4018/978-1-5225-2676-6.ch006

Akakandelwa, A. (2016). A Glimpse of the Information Seeking Behaviour Literature on the Web: A Bibliometric Approach. In A. Tella (Ed.), *Information Seeking Behavior and Challenges in Digital Libraries* (pp. 127–155). Hershey, PA: IGI Global. doi:10.4018/978-1-5225-0296-8.ch007

Akande, F. T., & Adewojo, A. A. (2016). Information Need and Seeking Behavior of Farmers in Laduba Community of Kwara State, Nigeria. In A. Tella (Ed.), *Information Seeking Behavior and Challenges in Digital Libraries* (pp. 238–271). Hershey, PA: IGI Global. doi:10.4018/978-1-5225-0296-8.ch012

Al-Kharousi, R., Al-Harrasi, N. H., Jabur, N. H., & Bouazza, A. (2018). Soft Systems Methodology (SSM) as an Interdisciplinary Approach: Reflection on the Use of SSM in Adoption of Web 2.0 Applications in Omani Academic Libraries. In M. Al-Suqri, A. Al-Kindi, S. AlKindi, & N. Saleem (Eds.), *Promoting Interdisciplinarity in Knowledge Generation and Problem Solving* (pp. 243–257). Hershey, PA: IGI Global. doi:10.4018/978-1-5225-3878-3.ch016

Alenzuela, R. (2017). Research, Leadership, and Resource-Sharing Initiatives: The Role of Local Library Consortia in Access to Medical Information. In S. Ram (Ed.), *Library and Information Services for Bioinformatics Education and Research* (pp. 199–211). Hershey, PA: IGI Global. doi:10.4018/978-1-5225-1871-6.ch012

Allison, D. (2017). When Sales Talk Meets Reality: Implementing a Self-Checkout Kiosk. In E. Iglesias (Ed.), *Library Technology Funding, Planning, and Deployment* (pp. 36–54). Hershey, PA: IGI Global. doi:10.4018/978-1-5225-1735-1.ch003

Anglim, C. T., & Rusk, F. (2018). Empowering DC's Future Through Information Access. In A. Burtin, J. Fleming, & P. Hampton-Garland (Eds.), *Changing Urban Landscapes Through Public Higher Education* (pp. 57–77). Hershey, PA: IGI Global. doi:10.4018/978-1-5225-3454-9.ch003

Asmi, N. A. (2017). Social Media and Library Services. *International Journal of Library and Information Services*, 6(2), 23–36. doi:10.4018/IJLIS.2017070103

Awoyemi, R. A. (2018). Adoption and Use of Innovative Mobile Technologies in Nigerian Academic Libraries. In J. Keengwe (Ed.), *Handbook of Research on Digital Content, Mobile Learning, and Technology Integration Models in Teacher Education* (pp. 354–389). Hershey, PA: IGI Global. doi:10.4018/978-1-5225-2953-8.ch019

Awoyemi, R. A. (2018). Adoption and Use of Innovative Mobile Technologies in Nigerian Academic Libraries. In J. Keengwe (Ed.), *Handbook of Research on Digital Content, Mobile Learning, and Technology Integration Models in Teacher Education* (pp. 354–389). Hershey, PA: IGI Global. doi:10.4018/978-1-5225-2953-8.ch019

Ayson, M. C. (2016). Maximizing Social Media Tools: Planning and Evaluating Social Media Strategies for Special Libraries. In J. Yap, M. Perez, M. Ayson, & G. Entico (Eds.), *Special Library Administration, Standardization and Technological Integration* (pp. 166–179). Hershey, PA: IGI Global. doi:10.4018/978-1-4666-9542-9.ch007

Babatope, I. S. (2018). Social Media Applications as Effective Service Delivery Tools for Librarians. In M. Khosrow-Pour, D.B.A. (Ed.), Encyclopedia of Information Science and Technology, Fourth Edition (pp. 5252-5261). Hershey, PA: IGI Global. doi:10.4018/978-1-5225-2255-3.ch456

Related References

Bakare, A. A. (2018). Digital Libraries and Copyright of Intellectual Property: An Ethical Practice Management. In A. Tella & T. Kwanya (Eds.), *Handbook of Research on Managing Intellectual Property in Digital Libraries* (pp. 377–395). Hershey, PA: IGI Global. doi:10.4018/978-1-5225-3093-0.ch019

Baker, W. (2016). Responding to High-Volume Water Disasters in the Research Library Context. In E. Decker & J. Townes (Eds.), *Handbook of Research on Disaster Management and Contingency Planning in Modern Libraries* (pp. 282–310). Hershey, PA: IGI Global. doi:10.4018/978-1-4666-8624-3.ch013

Baker-Gardner, R., & Smart, C. (2017). Ignorance or Intent?: A Case Study of Plagiarism in Higher Education among LIS Students in the Caribbean. In D. Velliaris (Ed.), *Handbook of Research on Academic Misconduct in Higher Education* (pp. 182–205). Hershey, PA: IGI Global. doi:10.4018/978-1-5225-1610-1.ch008

Baker-Gardner, R., & Stewart, P. (2018). Educating Caribbean Librarians to Provide Library Education in a Dynamic Information Environment. In S. Bhattacharyya & K. Patnaik (Eds.), *Changing the Scope of Library Instruction in the Digital Age* (pp. 187–226). Hershey, PA: IGI Global. doi:10.4018/978-1-5225-2802-9.ch008

Bassuener, L. (2016). Knowledge in the Shrinking Commons: Libraries and Open Access in a Market-Driven World. In E. Railean, G. Walker, A. Elçi, & L. Jackson (Eds.), *Handbook of Research on Applied Learning Theory and Design in Modern Education* (pp. 358–379). Hershey, PA: IGI Global. doi:10.4018/978-1-4666-9634-1.ch017

Baylen, D. M., & Cooper, O. P. (2016). Social Media and Special Collections: Exploring Presence, Prevalence, and Practices in Academic Libraries. In J. Yap, M. Perez, M. Ayson, & G. Entico (Eds.), *Special Library Administration, Standardization and Technological Integration* (pp. 180–201). Hershey, PA: IGI Global. doi:10.4018/978-1-4666-9542-9.ch008

Belden, D., Phillips, M. E., Carlisle, T., & Hartman, C. N. (2016). The Portal to Texas History: Building a Partnership Model for a Statewide Digital Library. In B. Doherty (Ed.), *Space and Organizational Considerations in Academic Library Partnerships and Collaborations* (pp. 182–204). Hershey, PA: IGI Global. doi:10.4018/978-1-5225-0326-2.ch009

Bengtson, J. (2017). Funding a Gamification Machine. In E. Iglesias (Ed.), *Library Technology Funding, Planning, and Deployment* (pp. 99–112). Hershey, PA: IGI Global. doi:10.4018/978-1-5225-1735-1.ch006

Bhebhe, S., & Ngwenya, S. (2016). Adoption and Use of Discovery Tools by Selected Academic Libraries in Zimbabwe. In E. de Smet & S. Dhamdhere (Eds.), *E-Discovery Tools and Applications in Modern Libraries* (pp. 168–180). Hershey, PA: IGI Global. doi:10.4018/978-1-5225-0474-0.ch009

Blummer, B., & Kenton, J. M. (2017). Access and Accessibility of Academic Libraries' Electronic Resources and Services: Identifying Themes in the Literature From 2000 to the Present. In H. Alphin Jr, J. Lavine, & R. Chan (Eds.), *Disability and Equity in Higher Education Accessibility* (pp. 242–267). Hershey, PA: IGI Global. doi:10.4018/978-1-5225-2665-0.ch011

Blummer, B., & Kenton, J. M. (2018). Academic and Research Libraries' Portals: A Literature Review From 2003 to the Present. In R. Bhardwaj (Ed.), *Digitizing the Modern Library and the Transition From Print to Electronic* (pp. 29–63). Hershey, PA: IGI Global. doi:10.4018/978-1-5225-2119-8.ch002

Blummer, B., & Kenton, J. M. (2018). International Students and Academic Libraries: Identifying Themes in the Literature From 2001 to the Present. In B. Blummer, J. Kenton, & M. Wiatrowski (Eds.), *Promoting Ethnic Diversity and Multiculturalism in Higher Education* (pp. 237–263). Hershey, PA: IGI Global. doi:10.4018/978-1-5225-4097-7.ch013

Bodolay, R., Frye, S., Kruse, C., & Luke, D. (2016). Moving from Co-Location to Cooperation to Collaboration: Redefining a Library's Role within the University. In B. Doherty (Ed.), *Space and Organizational Considerations in Academic Library Partnerships and Collaborations* (pp. 230–254). Hershey, PA: IGI Global. doi:10.4018/978-1-5225-0326-2.ch011

Boom, D. (2017). The Embedded Librarian: Do More With less. In B. Gunjal (Ed.), *Managing Knowledge and Scholarly Assets in Academic Libraries* (pp. 76–97). Hershey, PA: IGI Global. doi:10.4018/978-1-5225-1741-2.ch004

Bosire-Ogechi, E. (2018). Social Media, Social Networking, Copyright, and Digital Libraries. In A. Tella & T. Kwanya (Eds.), *Handbook of Research on Managing Intellectual Property in Digital Libraries* (pp. 37–50). Hershey, PA: IGI Global. doi:10.4018/978-1-5225-3093-0.ch003

Bradley-Sanders, C., & Rudshteyn, A. (2018). MyLibrary at Brooklyn College: Developing a Suite of Digital Tools. In L. Costello & M. Powers (Eds.), *Developing In-House Digital Tools in Library Spaces* (pp. 140–167). Hershey, PA: IGI Global. doi:10.4018/978-1-5225-2676-6.ch007

Brisk, A. T., Pittman, K., & Rosendahl, M. (2016). Collaborating Off Campus: Creating Communities of Practice with New Partners. In B. Doherty (Ed.), *Technology-Centered Academic Library Partnerships and Collaborations* (pp. 245–274). Hershey, PA: IGI Global. doi:10.4018/978-1-5225-0323-1.ch009

Brown, V. (2018). Technology Access Gap for Postsecondary Education: A Statewide Case Study. In M. Yildiz, S. Funk, & B. De Abreu (Eds.), *Promoting Global Competencies Through Media Literacy* (pp. 20–40). Hershey, PA: IGI Global. doi:10.4018/978-1-5225-3082-4.ch002

Carroll, V. (2016). Conservation Since 2000. In E. Decker & J. Townes (Eds.), *Handbook of Research on Disaster Management and Contingency Planning in Modern Libraries* (pp. 467–493). Hershey, PA: IGI Global. doi:10.4018/978-1-4666-8624-3.ch020

Chaiyasoonthorn, W., & Suksa-ngiam, W. (2018). Users' Acceptance of Online Literature Databases in a Thai University: A Test of UTAUT2. *International Journal of Information Systems in the Service Sector, 10*(1), 54–70. doi:10.4018/IJISSS.2018010104

Chandler, D. R. (2016). Prepared for Anything and Everything: Libraries, Archives, and Unexpected Small Scale Disasters. In E. Decker & J. Townes (Eds.), *Handbook of Research on Disaster Management and Contingency Planning in Modern Libraries* (pp. 240–256). Hershey, PA: IGI Global. doi:10.4018/978-1-4666-8624-3.ch011

Chaudron, G. (2016). After the Flood: Lessons Learned from Small-Scale Disasters. In E. Decker & J. Townes (Eds.), *Handbook of Research on Disaster Management and Contingency Planning in Modern Libraries* (pp. 389–411). Hershey, PA: IGI Global. doi:10.4018/978-1-4666-8624-3.ch017

Chaudron, G. (2016). Managing the Commonplace: Small Water Emergencies in Libraries. *International Journal of Risk and Contingency Management, 5*(1), 42–61. doi:10.4018/IJRCM.2016010104

Chaudron, G. (2018). Burst Pipes and Leaky Roofs: Small Emergencies Are a Challenge for Libraries. In K. Strang, M. Korstanje, & N. Vajjhala (Eds.), *Research, Practices, and Innovations in Global Risk and Contingency Management* (pp. 211–231). Hershey, PA: IGI Global. doi:10.4018/978-1-5225-4754-9.ch012

Chemulwo, M. J. (2018). Managing Intellectual Property in Digital Libraries and Copyright Challenges. In A. Tella & T. Kwanya (Eds.), *Handbook of Research on Managing Intellectual Property in Digital Libraries* (pp. 165–183). Hershey, PA: IGI Global. doi:10.4018/978-1-5225-3093-0.ch009

Chen, J., Lan, X., Huang, Q., Dong, J., & Chen, C. (2017). Scholarly Learning Commons. In L. Ruan, Q. Zhu, & Y. Ye (Eds.), *Academic Library Development and Administration in China* (pp. 90–109). Hershey, PA: IGI Global. doi:10.4018/978-1-5225-0550-1.ch006

Chigwada, J. P. (2018). Adoption of Open Source Software in Libraries in Developing Countries. *International Journal of Library and Information Services*, 7(1), 15–29. doi:10.4018/IJLIS.2018010102

Chisita, C. T., & Chinyemba, F. (2017). Utilising ICTs for Resource Sharing Initiatives in Academic Institutions in Zimbabwe: Towards a New Trajectory. In B. Gunjal (Ed.), *Managing Knowledge and Scholarly Assets in Academic Libraries* (pp. 174–187). Hershey, PA: IGI Global. doi:10.4018/978-1-5225-1741-2.ch008

Colmenero-Ruiz, M. (2016). Discussion on Digital Inclusion Good Practices at Europe's Libraries. In B. Passarelli, J. Straubhaar, & A. Cuevas-Cerveró (Eds.), *Handbook of Research on Comparative Approaches to the Digital Age Revolution in Europe and the Americas* (pp. 352–369). Hershey, PA: IGI Global. doi:10.4018/978-1-4666-8740-0.ch021

Costello, B. (2016). Academic Libraries in Partnership with the Government Publishing Office: A Changing Paradigm. In B. Doherty (Ed.), *Space and Organizational Considerations in Academic Library Partnerships and Collaborations* (pp. 87–110). Hershey, PA: IGI Global. doi:10.4018/978-1-5225-0326-2.ch005

Costello, L., & Fazal, S. (2018). Developing Unique Study Room Reservation Systems: Examples From Teachers College and Stony Brook University. In L. Costello & M. Powers (Eds.), *Developing In-House Digital Tools in Library Spaces* (pp. 168–176). Hershey, PA: IGI Global. doi:10.4018/978-1-5225-2676-6.ch008

Cowick, C., & Cowick, J. (2016). Planning for a Disaster: Effective Emergency Management in the 21st Century. In E. Decker & J. Townes (Eds.), *Handbook of Research on Disaster Management and Contingency Planning in Modern Libraries* (pp. 49–69). Hershey, PA: IGI Global. doi:10.4018/978-1-4666-8624-3.ch003

Cui, Y. (2017). Research Data Management: Models, Challenges, and Actions. In L. Ruan, Q. Zhu, & Y. Ye (Eds.), *Academic Library Development and Administration in China* (pp. 184–195). Hershey, PA: IGI Global. doi:10.4018/978-1-5225-0550-1.ch011

Das, T. (2016). Academic Library Collaborations to Strengthen Open Government Data and Expand Librarianship. In B. Doherty (Ed.), *Technology-Centered Academic Library Partnerships and Collaborations* (pp. 167–193). Hershey, PA: IGI Global. doi:10.4018/978-1-5225-0323-1.ch006 de Smet, E. (2016). E-Discovery with the ABCD Information Management System. In E. de Smet & S. Dhamdhere (Eds.), *E-Discovery Tools and Applications in Modern Libraries* (pp. 332–357). Hershey, PA: IGI Global. doi:10.4018/978-1-5225-0474-0.ch017

Decker, E. N., & Odom, R. Y. (2016). Publish or Perish: Librarians Collaborating to Support Junior Faculty to Publish within the Academic Environment. In B. Doherty (Ed.), *Space and Organizational Considerations in Academic Library Partnerships and Collaborations* (pp. 298–316). Hershey, PA: IGI Global. doi:10.4018/978-1-5225-0326-2.ch014

Desilets, M. R., DeJonghe, J., & Filkins, M. (2016). Better Together: The Successful Public/Academic Joint Use Library. In B. Doherty (Ed.), *Space and Organizational Considerations in Academic Library Partnerships and Collaborations* (pp. 1–21). Hershey, PA: IGI Global. doi:10.4018/978-1-5225-0326-2.ch001

Dhamdhere, S. N., De Smet, E., & Lihitkar, R. (2017). Web-Based Bibliographic Services Offered by Top World and Indian University Libraries: A Comparative Study. *International Journal of Library and Information Services*, *6*(1), 53–72. doi:10.4018/IJLIS.2017010104

Dhamdhere, S. N., & Lihitkar, R. (2016). Commercial and Open Access Integrated Information Search Tools in Indian Libraries. In E. de Smet & S. Dhamdhere (Eds.), *E-Discovery Tools and Applications in Modern Libraries* (pp. 41–55). Hershey, PA: IGI Global. doi:10.4018/978-1-5225-0474-0.ch002

Dixon, J., & Abashian, N. (2016). Beyond the Collection: Emergency Planning for Public and Staff Safety. In E. Decker & J. Townes (Eds.), *Handbook of Research on Disaster Management and Contingency Planning in Modern Libraries* (pp. 120–140). Hershey, PA: IGI Global. doi:10.4018/978-1-4666-8624-3.ch006

Doherty, B. (2016). Marriage after Divorce: The Challenges and Opportunities of a Shared Library after Institutions Separate. In B. Doherty (Ed.), *Space and Organizational Considerations in Academic Library Partnerships and Collaborations* (pp. 22–44). Hershey, PA: IGI Global. doi:10.4018/978-1-5225-0326-2.ch002

Dongardive, P. (2016). Digital Libraries as Information Superhighway. In A. Tella (Ed.), *Information Seeking Behavior and Challenges in Digital Libraries* (pp. 304–315). Hershey, PA: IGI Global. doi:10.4018/978-1-5225-0296-8.ch015

Dougan, K. (2016). Music Information Seeking Opportunities and Behavior Then and Now. In P. Kostagiolas, K. Martzoukou, & C. Lavranos (Eds.), *Trends in Music Information Seeking, Behavior, and Retrieval for Creativity* (pp. 42–57). Hershey, PA: IGI Global. doi:10.4018/978-1-5225-0270-8.ch003

Eiriemiokhale, K. A. (2018). Copyright Issues in a Digital Library Environment. In A. Tella & T. Kwanya (Eds.), *Handbook of Research on Managing Intellectual Property in Digital Libraries* (pp. 142–164). Hershey, PA: IGI Global. doi:10.4018/978-1-5225-3093-0.ch008

El Mimouni, H., Anderson, J., Tempelman-Kluit, N. F., & Dolan-Mescal, A. (2018). UX Work in Libraries: How (and Why) to Do It. In L. Costello & M. Powers (Eds.), *Developing In-House Digital Tools in Library Spaces* (pp. 1–36). Hershey, PA: IGI Global. doi:10.4018/978-1-5225-2676-6.ch001

Emiri, O. T. (2017). Digital Literacy Skills Among Librarians in University Libraries In the 21st Century in Edo And Delta States, Nigeria. *International Journal of Library and Information Services*, 6(1), 37–52. doi:10.4018/IJLIS.2017010103

Entico, G. J. (2016). Knowledge Management and the Medical Health Librarians: A Perception Study. In J. Yap, M. Perez, M. Ayson, & G. Entico (Eds.), *Special Library Administration, Standardization and Technological Integration* (pp. 52–77). Hershey, PA: IGI Global. doi:10.4018/978-1-4666-9542-9.ch003

Esposito, T. (2018). Exploring Opportunities in Health Science Information Instructional Outreach: A Case Study Highlighting One Academic Library's Experience. In S. Bhattacharyya & K. Patnaik (Eds.), *Changing the Scope of Library Instruction in the Digital Age* (pp. 118–135). Hershey, PA: IGI Global. doi:10.4018/978-1-5225-2802-9.ch005

Esse, U. C., & Ohaegbulam, H. (2016). Library and Information Services for Open and Distance Learning: Assessing the Role of Mobile Technologies and Distance Learning in Higher Education. In G. Eby, T. Yuzer, & S. Atay (Eds.), *Developing Successful Strategies for Global Policies and Cyber Transparency in E-Learning* (pp. 29–45). Hershey, PA: IGI Global. doi:10.4018/978-1-4666-8844-5.ch003

Fagbohun, M. O., Nwokocha, N. M., Itsekor, V., & Adebayo, O. (2016). Responsive Library Website Design and Adoption of Federated Search Tools for Library Services in Developing Countries. In E. de Smet & S. Dhamdhere (Eds.), *E-Discovery Tools and Applications in Modern Libraries* (pp. 76–108). Hershey, PA: IGI Global. doi:10.4018/978-1-5225-0474-0.ch005

Fagbola, O. O. (2016). Indexing and Abstracting as Tools for Information Retrieval in Digital Libraries: A Review of Literature. In A. Tella (Ed.), *Information Seeking Behavior and Challenges in Digital Libraries* (pp. 156–178). Hershey, PA: IGI Global. doi:10.4018/978-1-5225-0296-8.ch008

Fan, Y., Zhang, X., & Li, G. (2017). Research Initiatives and Projects in Academic Libraries. In L. Ruan, Q. Zhu, & Y. Ye (Eds.), *Academic Library Development and Administration in China* (pp. 230–252). Hershey, PA: IGI Global. doi:10.4018/978-1-5225-0550-1.ch014

Farmer, L. S. (2017). ICT Literacy Integration: Issues and Sample Efforts. In J. Keengwe & P. Bull (Eds.), *Handbook of Research on Transformative Digital Content and Learning Technologies* (pp. 59–80). Hershey, PA: IGI Global. doi:10.4018/978-1-5225-2000-9.ch004

Farmer, L. S. (2017). Data Analytics for Strategic Management: Getting the Right Data. In V. Wang (Ed.), *Encyclopedia of Strategic Leadership and Management* (pp. 810–822). Hershey, PA: IGI Global. doi:10.4018/978-1-5225-1049-9.ch056

Farmer, L. S. (2017). Managing Portable Technologies for Special Education. In V. Wang (Ed.), *Encyclopedia of Strategic Leadership and Management* (pp. 977–987). Hershey, PA: IGI Global. doi:10.4018/978-1-5225-1049-9.ch068

Fujishima, D., & Kamada, T. (2017). Collective Relocation for Associative Distributed Collections of Objects. *International Journal of Software Innovation*, *5*(2), 55–69. doi:10.4018/IJSI.2017040104

Gaetz, I. (2016). Processes, Opportunities, and Challenges Creating and Managing a Scholarly Open Access Journal: An Investigation of "Collaborative Librarianship". In B. Doherty (Ed.), *Space and Organizational Considerations in Academic Library Partnerships and Collaborations* (pp. 205–229). Hershey, PA: IGI Global. doi:10.4018/978-1-5225-0326-2.ch010

Galloup, A. (2016). One Plan, Four Libraries: A Case Study in Disaster Planning for a Four-Campus Academic Institution. In E. Decker & J. Townes (Eds.), *Handbook of Research on Disaster Management and Contingency Planning in Modern Libraries* (pp. 166–183). Hershey, PA: IGI Global. doi:10.4018/978-1-4666-8624-3.ch008

Gamtso, C. W., Vogt, R. B., Donahue, A., Donovan, K., & Jefferson, J. (2016). Librarian and Peer Research Mentor Partnerships that Promote Student Success. In B. Doherty (Ed.), *Space and Organizational Considerations in Academic Library Partnerships and Collaborations* (pp. 255–279). Hershey, PA: IGI Global. doi:10.4018/978-1-5225-0326-2.ch012

Ghani, S. R. (2017). Ontology: Advancing Flawless Library Services. In T. Ashraf & N. Kumar (Eds.), *Interdisciplinary Digital Preservation Tools and Technologies* (pp. 79–102). Hershey, PA: IGI Global. doi:10.4018/978-1-5225-1653-8.ch005

Gibbons, P. (2016). Disaster Management and Exhibition Loans: Contingency Planning for Items on Display. In E. Decker & J. Townes (Eds.), *Handbook of Research on Disaster Management and Contingency Planning in Modern Libraries* (pp. 141–165). Hershey, PA: IGI Global. doi:10.4018/978-1-4666-8624-3.ch007

Gibbons, P. (2016). Assessing Risk and Safeguarding Rare Library Materials During Exhibition Loans. *International Journal of Risk and Contingency Management*, 5(1), 15–25. doi:10.4018/IJRCM.2016010102

Gibson, R. (2016). Wearable Technologies in Academic Information Search. In J. Holland (Ed.), *Wearable Technology and Mobile Innovations for Next-Generation Education* (pp. 122–146). Hershey, PA: IGI Global. doi:10.4018/978-1-5225-0069-8.ch007

Goldman, B. (2016). Two Fires and a Flood: Lasting Impact on a Public Library, Its Staff, and Community. In E. Decker & J. Townes (Eds.), *Handbook of Research on Disaster Management and Contingency Planning in Modern Libraries* (pp. 560–581). Hershey, PA: IGI Global. doi:10.4018/978-1-4666-8624-3.ch024

Goovaerts, M., Nieuwenhuysen, P., & Dhamdhere, S. N. (2016). VLIR-UOS Workshop 'E-Info Discovery and Management for Institutes in the South': Presentations and Conclusions, Antwerp, 8-19 December, 2014. In E. de Smet, & S. Dhamdhere (Eds.), E-Discovery Tools and Applications in Modern Libraries (pp. 1-40). Hershey, PA: IGI Global. doi:10.4018/978-1-5225-0474-0.ch001

Gu, J. (2017). Library Buildings on New Campuses. In L. Ruan, Q. Zhu, & Y. Ye (Eds.), *Academic Library Development and Administration in China* (pp. 110–124). Hershey, PA: IGI Global. doi:10.4018/978-1-5225-0550-1.ch007

Guan, Z., & Wang, J. (2017). The China Academic Social Sciences and Humanities Library (CASHL). In L. Ruan, Q. Zhu, & Y. Ye (Eds.), *Academic Library Development and Administration in China* (pp. 31–54). Hershey, PA: IGI Global. doi:10.4018/978-1-5225-0550-1.ch003

Gul, S., & Shueb, S. (2018). Confronting/Managing the Crisis of Indian Libraries: E-Consortia Initiatives in India - A Way Forward. In R. Bhardwaj (Ed.), *Digitizing the Modern Library and the Transition From Print to Electronic* (pp. 129–163). Hershey, PA: IGI Global. doi:10.4018/978-1-5225-2119-8.ch006

Gunjal, B. (2017). Managing Knowledge and Scholarly Assets in Academic Libraries: Issues and Challenges. In B. Gunjal (Ed.), *Managing Knowledge and Scholarly Assets in Academic Libraries* (pp. 270–279). Hershey, PA: IGI Global. doi:10.4018/978-1-5225-1741-2.ch013

Guo, J., Zhang, H., & Zong, Y. (2017). Leadership Development and Career Planning. In L. Ruan, Q. Zhu, & Y. Ye (Eds.), *Academic Library Development and Administration in China* (pp. 264–279). Hershey, PA: IGI Global. doi:10.4018/978-1-5225-0550-1.ch016

Hallis, R. (2018). Leveraging Library Instruction in a Digital Age. In S. Bhattacharyya & K. Patnaik (Eds.), *Changing the Scope of Library Instruction in the Digital Age* (pp. 1–23). Hershey, PA: IGI Global. doi:10.4018/978-1-5225-2802-9.ch001

Hamilton, R., & Brown, D. (2016). Disaster Management and Continuity Planning in Libraries: Changes since the Year 2000. In E. Decker & J. Townes (Eds.), *Handbook of Research on Disaster Management and Contingency Planning in Modern Libraries* (pp. 1–24). Hershey, PA: IGI Global. doi:10.4018/978-1-4666-8624-3.ch001

Hamilton, R., & Brown, D. (2016). Disaster Management and Continuity Planning in Libraries: Literature Review. *International Journal of Risk and Contingency Management, 5*(1), 26–41. doi:10.4018/IJRCM.2016010103

Hartsock, R., & Alemneh, D. G. (2018). Electronic Theses and Dissertations (ETDs). In M. Khosrow-Pour, D.B.A. (Ed.), Encyclopedia of Information Science and Technology, Fourth Edition (pp. 6748-6755). Hershey, PA: IGI Global. doi:10.4018/978-1-5225-2255-3.ch584

Haugh, D. (2018). Mobile Applications for Libraries. In L. Costello & M. Powers (Eds.), *Developing In-House Digital Tools in Library Spaces* (pp. 76–90). Hershey, PA: IGI Global. doi:10.4018/978-1-5225-2676-6.ch004

Hill, V. (2017). Digital Citizens as Writers: New Literacies and New Responsibilities. In E. Monske & K. Blair (Eds.), *Handbook of Research on Writing and Composing in the Age of MOOCs* (pp. 56–74). Hershey, PA: IGI Global. doi:10.4018/978-1-5225-1718-4.ch004

Horne-Popp, L. M., Tessone, E. B., & Welker, J. (2018). If You Build It, They Will Come: Creating a Library Statistics Dashboard for Decision-Making. In L. Costello & M. Powers (Eds.), *Developing In-House Digital Tools in Library Spaces* (pp. 177–203). Hershey, PA: IGI Global. doi:10.4018/978-1-5225-2676-6.ch009

Huang, C., & Xue, H. F. (2017). The China Academic Digital Associative Library (CADAL). In L. Ruan, Q. Zhu, & Y. Ye (Eds.), *Academic Library Development and Administration in China* (pp. 20–30). Hershey, PA: IGI Global. doi:10.4018/978-1-5225-0550-1.ch002

Hunsaker, A. J., Majewski, N., & Rocke, L. E. (2018). Pulling Content out the Back Door: Creating an Interactive Digital Collections Experience. In L. Costello & M. Powers (Eds.), *Developing In-House Digital Tools in Library Spaces* (pp. 205–226). Hershey, PA: IGI Global. doi:10.4018/978-1-5225-2676-6.ch010

Ibrahim, H., Mustapa, R., Edzan, N., & Yahya, W. A. (2016). Profiling Prominent Malaysians in Bernama Library and Infolink Service. In J. Yap, M. Perez, M. Ayson, & G. Entico (Eds.), *Special Library Administration, Standardization and Technological Integration* (pp. 315–336). Hershey, PA: IGI Global. doi:10.4018/978-1-4666-9542-9.ch014

Idiegbeyan-Ose, J., Ifijeh, G., Iwu-James, J., & Ilogho, J. (2016). Management of Institutional Repositories (IR) in Developing Countries. In E. de Smet & S. Dhamdhere (Eds.), *E-Discovery Tools and Applications in Modern Libraries* (pp. 306–331). Hershey, PA: IGI Global. doi:10.4018/978-1-5225-0474-0.ch016

Idiegbeyan-ose, J., Nkiko, C., Idahosa, M., & Nwokocha, N. (2016). Digital Divide: Issues and Strategies for Intervention in Nigerian Libraries. *Journal of Cases on Information Technology*, *18*(3), 29–39. doi:10.4018/JCIT.2016070103

Ifijeh, G., Adebayo, O., Izuagbe, R., & Olawoyin, O. (2018). Institutional Repositories and Libraries in Nigeria: Interrogating the Nexus. *Journal of Cases on Information Technology*, *20*(2), 16–29. doi:10.4018/JCIT.2018040102

Ifijeh, G., Idiegbeyan-ose, J., Segun-Adeniran, C., & Ilogho, J. (2016). Disaster Management in Digital Libraries: Issues and Strategies in Developing Countries. *International Journal of Risk and Contingency Management*, *5*(1), 1–14. doi:10.4018/IJRCM.2016010101

Iglesias, E. (2017). Insourcing and Outsourcing of Library Technology. In E. Iglesias (Ed.), *Library Technology Funding, Planning, and Deployment* (pp. 113–123). Hershey, PA: IGI Global. doi:10.4018/978-1-5225-1735-1.ch007

Ikolo, V. E. (2018). Transformational Leadership for Academic Libraries in Nigeria. In M. Khosrow-Pour, D.B.A. (Ed.), Encyclopedia of Information Science and Technology, Fourth Edition (pp. 5726-5735). Hershey, PA: IGI Global. doi:10.4018/978-1-5225-2255-3.ch497

Jaafar, T. M. (2016). Law Library Consortium in Metro Manila: A Proposed Model and the Management of Law Libraries. In J. Yap, M. Perez, M. Ayson, & G. Entico (Eds.), *Special Library Administration, Standardization and Technological Integration* (pp. 134–164). Hershey, PA: IGI Global. doi:10.4018/978-1-4666-9542-9.ch006

Related References

Joe, J. A. (2018). Changing Expectations of Academic Libraries. In M. Khosrow-Pour, D.B.A. (Ed.), Encyclopedia of Information Science and Technology, Fourth Edition (pp. 5204-5212). Hershey, PA: IGI Global. doi:10.4018/978-1-5225-2255-3.ch452

Johnson, H., & Simms, S. (2016). Concept, Conversion, Cultivation, and Consequence: The Four Cs of Successful Collaboration. In B. Doherty (Ed.), *Space and Organizational Considerations in Academic Library Partnerships and Collaborations* (pp. 280–297). Hershey, PA: IGI Global. doi:10.4018/978-1-5225-0326-2.ch013

Jones, A. (2016). Shortcomings and Successes: A Small-Scale Disaster Case Study. In E. Decker & J. Townes (Eds.), *Handbook of Research on Disaster Management and Contingency Planning in Modern Libraries* (pp. 412–435). Hershey, PA: IGI Global. doi:10.4018/978-1-4666-8624-3.ch018

Juliana, I., Izuagbe, R., Itsekor, V., Fagbohun, M. O., Asaolu, A., & Nwokeoma, M. N. (2018). The Role of the School Library in Empowering Visually Impaired Children With Lifelong Information Literacy Skills. In P. Epler (Ed.), *Instructional Strategies in General Education and Putting the Individuals With Disabilities Act (IDEA) Into Practice* (pp. 245–271). Hershey, PA: IGI Global. doi:10.4018/978-1-5225-3111-1.ch009

Kalusopa, T. (2018). Preservation and Access to Digital Materials: Strategic Policy Options for Africa. In P. Ngulube (Ed.), *Handbook of Research on Heritage Management and Preservation* (pp. 150–174). Hershey, PA: IGI Global. doi:10.4018/978-1-5225-3137-1.ch008

Kamau, G. W. (2018). Copyright Challenges in Digital Libraries in Kenya From the Lens of a Librarian. In A. Tella & T. Kwanya (Eds.), *Handbook of Research on Managing Intellectual Property in Digital Libraries* (pp. 312–336). Hershey, PA: IGI Global. doi:10.4018/978-1-5225-3093-0.ch016

Karbach, L. (2016). Public Libraries: Analysis of Services for Immigrant Populations and Suggestions to Improve Outreach. In K. González & R. Frumkin (Eds.), *Handbook of Research on Effective Communication in Culturally Diverse Classrooms* (pp. 153–182). Hershey, PA: IGI Global. doi:10.4018/978-1-4666-9953-3.ch008

Karmakar, R. (2018). Development and Management of Digital Libraries in the Regime of IPR Paradigm. *International Journal of Library and Information Services*, 7(1), 44–57. doi:10.4018/IJLIS.2018010104

Kasemsap, K. (2016). Mastering Digital Libraries in the Digital Age. In E. de Smet & S. Dhamdhere (Eds.), *E-Discovery Tools and Applications in Modern Libraries* (pp. 275–305). Hershey, PA: IGI Global. doi:10.4018/978-1-5225-0474-0.ch015

Kasemsap, K. (2017). Mastering Knowledge Management in Academic Libraries. In B. Gunjal (Ed.), *Managing Knowledge and Scholarly Assets in Academic Libraries* (pp. 27–55). Hershey, PA: IGI Global. doi:10.4018/978-1-5225-1741-2.ch002

Kehinde, A. (2018). Digital Libraries and the Role of Digital Librarians. In A. Tella & T. Kwanya (Eds.), *Handbook of Research on Managing Intellectual Property in Digital Libraries* (pp. 98–119). Hershey, PA: IGI Global. doi:10.4018/978-1-5225-3093-0.ch006

Kenausis, V., & Herman, D. (2017). Don't Make Us Use the "Get Along Shirt": Communication and Consensus Building in an RFP Process. In E. Iglesias (Ed.), *Library Technology Funding, Planning, and Deployment* (pp. 1–22). Hershey, PA: IGI Global. doi:10.4018/978-1-5225-1735-1.ch001

Kohl, L. E., Lombardi, P., & Moroney, M. (2017). Moving from Local to Global via the Integrated Library System: Cost-Savings, ILS Management, Teams, and End-Users. In E. Iglesias (Ed.), *Library Technology Funding, Planning, and Deployment* (pp. 23–35). Hershey, PA: IGI Global. doi:10.4018/978-1-5225-1735-1.ch002

Kowalsky, M. (2016). Analysis of Initial Involvement of Librarians in the Online Virtual World of Second Life. In B. Baggio (Ed.), *Analyzing Digital Discourse and Human Behavior in Modern Virtual Environments* (pp. 126–148). Hershey, PA: IGI Global. doi:10.4018/978-1-4666-9899-4.ch007

Kumar, K. (2018). Library in Your Pocket Delivery of Instruction Service Through Library Mobile Apps: A World in Your Pocket. In S. Bhattacharyya & K. Patnaik (Eds.), *Changing the Scope of Library Instruction in the Digital Age* (pp. 228–249). Hershey, PA: IGI Global. doi:10.4018/978-1-5225-2802-9.ch009

Kwanya, T. (2016). Information Seeking Behaviour in Digital Library Contexts. In A. Tella (Ed.), *Information Seeking Behavior and Challenges in Digital Libraries* (pp. 1–25). Hershey, PA: IGI Global. doi:10.4018/978-1-5225-0296-8.ch001

Kwanya, T. (2018). Social Bookmarking in Digital Libraries: Intellectual Property Rights Implications. In A. Tella & T. Kwanya (Eds.), *Handbook of Research on Managing Intellectual Property in Digital Libraries* (pp. 1–18). Hershey, PA: IGI Global. doi:10.4018/978-1-5225-3093-0.ch001

LaMoreaux, N. E. (2016). Collaborating to Create a Fashionable Event: A Guide for Creating a Library-Sponsored Conference. In B. Doherty (Ed.), *Space and Organizational Considerations in Academic Library Partnerships and Collaborations* (pp. 317–334). Hershey, PA: IGI Global. doi:10.4018/978-1-5225-0326-2.ch015

Lewis, J. K. (2018). Change Leadership Styles and Behaviors in Academic Libraries. In M. Khosrow-Pour, D.B.A. (Ed.), Encyclopedia of Information Science and Technology, Fourth Edition (pp. 5194-5203). Hershey, PA: IGI Global. doi:10.4018/978-1-5225-2255-3.ch451

Lillard, L. L. (2018). Is Interdisciplinary Collaboration in Academia an Elusive Dream?: Can the Institutional Barriers Be Broken Down? A Review of the Literature and the Case of Library Science. In M. Al-Suqri, A. Al-Kindi, S. AlKindi, & N. Saleem (Eds.), *Promoting Interdisciplinarity in Knowledge Generation and Problem Solving* (pp. 139–147). Hershey, PA: IGI Global. doi:10.4018/978-1-5225-3878-3.ch010

Lock, M. B., Fansler, C., & Webb, M. (2016). (R)Evolutionary Emergency Planning: Adding Resilience through Continuous Review. *International Journal of Risk and Contingency Management, 5*(2), 47–65. doi:10.4018/IJRCM.2016040103

Long, X., & Yao, B. (2017). The Construction and Development of the Academic Digital Library of Chinese Ancient Collections. In L. Ruan, Q. Zhu, & Y. Ye (Eds.), *Academic Library Development and Administration in China* (pp. 126–135). Hershey, PA: IGI Global. doi:10.4018/978-1-5225-0550-1.ch008

Lowe, M., & Reno, L. M. (2018). Academic Librarianship and Burnout. In *Examining the Emotional Dimensions of Academic Librarianship: Emerging Research and Opportunities* (pp. 72–89). Hershey, PA: IGI Global. doi:10.4018/978-1-5225-3761-8.ch005

Lowe, M., & Reno, L. M. (2018). Emotional Dimensions of Academic Librarianship. In *Examining the Emotional Dimensions of Academic Librarianship: Emerging Research and Opportunities* (pp. 54–71). Hershey, PA: IGI Global. doi:10.4018/978-1-5225-3761-8.ch004

Lowe, M., & Reno, L. M. (2018). Why Isn't This Being Studied? In *Examining the Emotional Dimensions of Academic Librarianship: Emerging Research and Opportunities* (pp. 90–108). Hershey, PA: IGI Global. doi:10.4018/978-1-5225-3761-8.ch006

Lowe, M., & Reno, L. M. (2018). Research Agenda: Research Ideas and Recommendations. In *Examining the Emotional Dimensions of Academic Librarianship: Emerging Research and Opportunities* (pp. 109–125). Hershey, PA: IGI Global. doi:10.4018/978-1-5225-3761-8.ch007

Luyombya, D., Kiyingi, G. W., & Naluwooza, M. (2018). The Nature and Utilisation of Archival Records Deposited in Makerere University Library, Uganda. In P. Ngulube (Ed.), *Handbook of Research on Heritage Management and Preservation* (pp. 96–113). Hershey, PA: IGI Global. doi:10.4018/978-1-5225-3137-1.ch005

Mabe, M., & Ashley, E. A. (2017). The Natural Role of the Public Library. In *The Developing Role of Public Libraries in Emergency Management: Emerging Research and Opportunities* (pp. 25–43). Hershey, PA: IGI Global. doi:10.4018/978-1-5225-2196-9.ch003

Mabe, M., & Ashley, E. A. (2017). I'm Trained, Now What? In *The Developing Role of Public Libraries in Emergency Management: Emerging Research and Opportunities* (pp. 87–95). Hershey, PA: IGI Global. doi:10.4018/978-1-5225-2196-9.ch007

Mabe, M., & Ashley, E. A. (2017). Emergency Preparation for the Library and Librarian. In *The Developing Role of Public Libraries in Emergency Management: Emerging Research and Opportunities* (pp. 61–78). Hershey, PA: IGI Global. doi:10.4018/978-1-5225-2196-9.ch005

Mabe, M., & Ashley, E. A. (2017). The CCPL Model. In *The Developing Role of Public Libraries in Emergency Management: Emerging Research and Opportunities* (pp. 15–24). Hershey, PA: IGI Global. doi:10.4018/978-1-5225-2196-9.ch002

Mabe, M., & Ashley, E. A. (2017). The Local Command Structure and How the Library Fits. In *In The Developing Role of Public Libraries in Emergency Management: Emerging Research and Opportunities* (pp. 44–60). Hershey, PA: IGI Global. doi:10.4018/978-1-5225-2196-9.ch004

Mabe, M. R. (2016). Libraries to the Rescue. *International Journal of Risk and Contingency Management, 5*(1), 62–81. doi:10.4018/IJRCM.2016010105

Mabe, M. R. (2016). The Library as Lifeboat. In E. Decker & J. Townes (Eds.), *Handbook of Research on Disaster Management and Contingency Planning in Modern Libraries* (pp. 494–515). Hershey, PA: IGI Global. doi:10.4018/978-1-4666-8624-3.ch021

Manzoor, A. (2018). Social Media: A Librarian's Tool for Instant and Direct Interaction With Library Users. In R. Bhardwaj (Ed.), *Digitizing the Modern Library and the Transition From Print to Electronic* (pp. 112–128). Hershey, PA: IGI Global. doi:10.4018/978-1-5225-2119-8.ch005

Maringanti, H. (2018). A Decision Making Paradigm for Software Development in Libraries. In L. Costello & M. Powers (Eds.), *Developing In-House Digital Tools in Library Spaces* (pp. 59–75). Hershey, PA: IGI Global. doi:10.4018/978-1-5225-2676-6.ch003

Markman, K. M., Ferrarini, M., & Deschenes, A. H. (2018). User Testing and Iterative Design in the Academic Library: A Case Study. In R. Roscoe, S. Craig, & I. Douglas (Eds.), *End-User Considerations in Educational Technology Design* (pp. 160–183). Hershey, PA: IGI Global. doi:10.4018/978-1-5225-2639-1.ch008

Marks, A. B., & Owen, E. (2016). It Is Everywhere: Handling a Mold Outbreak in a Library's High-Density Storage Collection. In E. Decker & J. Townes (Eds.), *Handbook of Research on Disaster Management and Contingency Planning in Modern Libraries* (pp. 311–339). Hershey, PA: IGI Global. doi:10.4018/978-1-4666-8624-3.ch014

Mavodza, J. (2016). Relationship between Knowledge Management and Academic Integrity in a Middle Eastern University. In A. Goel & P. Singhal (Eds.), *Product Innovation through Knowledge Management and Social Media Strategies* (pp. 241–264). Hershey, PA: IGI Global. doi:10.4018/978-1-4666-9607-5.ch011

Maynor, A. (2016). Response to the Unthinkable: Collecting and Archiving Condolence and Temporary Memorial Materials following Public Tragedies. In E. Decker & J. Townes (Eds.), *Handbook of Research on Disaster Management and Contingency Planning in Modern Libraries* (pp. 582–624). Hershey, PA: IGI Global. doi:10.4018/978-1-4666-8624-3.ch025

McFall, L. M., Simons, J. T., Lord, G., MacDonald, P. J., Nieves, A. D., & Young, S. (2016). Collaborations in Liberal Arts Colleges in Support of Digital Humanities. In B. Doherty (Ed.), *Technology-Centered Academic Library Partnerships and Collaborations* (pp. 31–60). Hershey, PA: IGI Global. doi:10.4018/978-1-5225-0323-1.ch002

Na, L. (2017). Library and Information Science Education and Graduate Programs in Academic Libraries. In L. Ruan, Q. Zhu, & Y. Ye (Eds.), *Academic Library Development and Administration in China* (pp. 218–229). Hershey, PA: IGI Global. doi:10.4018/978-1-5225-0550-1.ch013

Nagarkar, S. P. (2017). Biomedical Librarianship in the Post-Genomic Era. In S. Ram (Ed.), *Library and Information Services for Bioinformatics Education and Research* (pp. 1–17). Hershey, PA: IGI Global. doi:10.4018/978-1-5225-1871-6.ch001

Natarajan, M. (2016). Exploring the E-Discovery Tools on the Use of Library Collections by Users. In E. de Smet & S. Dhamdhere (Eds.), *E-Discovery Tools and Applications in Modern Libraries* (pp. 122–137). Hershey, PA: IGI Global. doi:10.4018/978-1-5225-0474-0.ch007

Natarajan, M. (2017). Exploring Knowledge Sharing over Social Media. In R. Chugh (Ed.), *Harnessing Social Media as a Knowledge Management Tool* (pp. 55–73). Hershey, PA: IGI Global. doi:10.4018/978-1-5225-0495-5.ch003

Nazir, T. (2017). Preservation Initiatives in E-Environment to Protect Information Assets. In T. Ashraf & N. Kumar (Eds.), *Interdisciplinary Digital Preservation Tools and Technologies* (pp. 193–208). Hershey, PA: IGI Global. doi:10.4018/978-1-5225-1653-8.ch010

Ngulube, P. (2017). Embedding Indigenous Knowledge in Library and Information Science Education in Anglophone Eastern and Southern Africa. In P. Ngulube (Ed.), *Handbook of Research on Social, Cultural, and Educational Considerations of Indigenous Knowledge in Developing Countries* (pp. 92–115). Hershey, PA: IGI Global. doi:10.4018/978-1-5225-0838-0.ch006

Nicolajsen, H. W., Sørensen, F., & Scupola, A. (2016). The Potential of Workshops vs Blogs for User Involvement in Service Innovation. *International Journal of E-Services and Mobile Applications*, 8(4), 1–19. doi:10.4018/IJESMA.2016100101

Nicolajsen, H. W., Sorensen, F., & Scupola, A. (2018). User Involvement in Service Innovation Processes. In M. Khosrow-Pour (Ed.), *Optimizing Current Practices in E-Services and Mobile Applications* (pp. 42–61). Hershey, PA: IGI Global. doi:10.4018/978-1-5225-5026-6.ch003

Nixon, M. L. (2016). Safety Doesn't Happen by Accident: Disaster Planning at the University of Pittsburgh. In E. Decker & J. Townes (Eds.), *Handbook of Research on Disaster Management and Contingency Planning in Modern Libraries* (pp. 184–206). Hershey, PA: IGI Global. doi:10.4018/978-1-4666-8624-3.ch009

Nwabueze, A. U., & Ibeh, B. O. (2016). Extent of ICT Literacy Possessed by Librarians in Federal University Libraries in South East Nigeria. *International Journal of Digital Literacy and Digital Competence*, 7(3), 13–22. doi:10.4018/IJDLDC.2016070102

O'Grady, A. R. (2016). The Boston Library Consortium and RapidR: Partnering to Develop an Unmediated Book Sharing Module. In B. Doherty (Ed.), *Technology-Centered Academic Library Partnerships and Collaborations* (pp. 194–219). Hershey, PA: IGI Global. doi:10.4018/978-1-5225-0323-1.ch007

Ochonogor, W. C., & Okite-Amughoro, F. A. (2018). Building an Effective Digital Library in a University Teaching Hospital (UTH) in Nigeria. In A. Tella & T. Kwanya (Eds.), *Handbook of Research on Managing Intellectual Property in Digital Libraries* (pp. 184–204). Hershey, PA: IGI Global. doi:10.4018/978-1-5225-3093-0.ch010

Oladapo, Y. O. (2018). Open Access to Knowledge and Challenges in Digital Libraries. In A. Tella & T. Kwanya (Eds.), *Handbook of Research on Managing Intellectual Property in Digital Libraries* (pp. 260–291). Hershey, PA: IGI Global. doi:10.4018/978-1-5225-3093-0.ch014

Oladokun, O., & Zulu, S. F. (2017). Document Description and Coding as Key Elements in Knowledge, Records, and Information Management. In P. Jain & N. Mnjama (Eds.), *Managing Knowledge Resources and Records in Modern Organizations* (pp. 179–197). Hershey, PA: IGI Global. doi:10.4018/978-1-5225-1965-2.ch011

Olin, J. R. (2016). Libraries and Digital Media. In B. Guzzetti & M. Lesley (Eds.), *Handbook of Research on the Societal Impact of Digital Media* (pp. 163–177). Hershey, PA: IGI Global. doi:10.4018/978-1-4666-8310-5.ch007

Oluwaseun, A. A. (2016). Barriers to Information Seeking in the Digital Libraries. In A. Tella (Ed.), *Information Seeking Behavior and Challenges in Digital Libraries* (pp. 291–303). Hershey, PA: IGI Global. doi:10.4018/978-1-5225-0296-8.ch014

Omeluzor, S. U., Abayomi, I., & Gbemi-Ogunleye, P. (2018). Contemporary Media for Library Users' Instruction in Academic Libraries in South-West Nigeria: Contemporary Library Instruction in the Digital Age. In S. Bhattacharyya & K. Patnaik (Eds.), *Changing the Scope of Library Instruction in the Digital Age* (pp. 162–185). Hershey, PA: IGI Global. doi:10.4018/978-1-5225-2802-9.ch007

Ondari-Okemwa, E. (2016). Information-Seeking Behaviour of Users in the Digital Libraries' Environment in Sub-Saharan Africa. In A. Tella (Ed.), *Information Seeking Behavior and Challenges in Digital Libraries* (pp. 26–56). Hershey, PA: IGI Global. doi:10.4018/978-1-5225-0296-8.ch002

Oshilalu, A. H., & Ogochukwu, E. T. (2017). Modeling a Software for Library and Information Centers. *International Journal of Library and Information Services*, 6(2), 1–10. doi:10.4018/IJLIS.2017070101

Osterman, A. C., O'Gara, G., & Armstrong, A. M. (2016). The Evolution of Collaborative Collection Development within a Library Consortium: Data Analysis Applied in a Cultural Context. In B. Doherty (Ed.), *Space and Organizational Considerations in Academic Library Partnerships and Collaborations* (pp. 157–181). Hershey, PA: IGI Global. doi:10.4018/978-1-5225-0326-2.ch008

Oswal, S. K. (2017). Institutional, Legal, and Attitudinal Barriers to the Accessibility of University Digital Libraries: Implications for Retention of Disabled Students. In H. Alphin Jr, J. Lavine, & R. Chan (Eds.), *Disability and Equity in Higher Education Accessibility* (pp. 223–241). Hershey, PA: IGI Global. doi:10.4018/978-1-5225-2665-0.ch010

Otike, J. (2016). Legal Considerations of Providing Information in Support of Distance Learning by Digital Libraries in Universities in Kenya. In A. Tella (Ed.), *Information Seeking Behavior and Challenges in Digital Libraries* (pp. 57–69). Hershey, PA: IGI Global. doi:10.4018/978-1-5225-0296-8.ch003

Oukrich, J., & Bouikhalene, B. (2017). A Survey of Users' Satisfaction in the University Library by Using a Pareto Analysis and the Automatic Classification Methods. *International Journal of Library and Information Services*, 6(1), 17–36. doi:10.4018/IJLIS.2017010102

Özel, N. (2018). Developing Visual Literacy Skills Through Library Instructions. In V. Osinska & G. Osinski (Eds.), *Information Visualization Techniques in the Social Sciences and Humanities* (pp. 32–48). Hershey, PA: IGI Global. doi:10.4018/978-1-5225-4990-1.ch003

Patel, D., & Thakur, D. (2017). Managing Open Access (OA) Scholarly Information Resources in a University. In A. Munigal (Ed.), *Scholarly Communication and the Publish or Perish Pressures of Academia* (pp. 224–255). Hershey, PA: IGI Global. doi:10.4018/978-1-5225-1697-2.ch011

Patnaik, K. R. (2018). Crafting a Framework for Copyright Literacy and Licensed Content: A Case Study at an Advanced Management Education and Research Library. In S. Bhattacharyya & K. Patnaik (Eds.), *Changing the Scope of Library Instruction in the Digital Age* (pp. 136–160). Hershey, PA: IGI Global. doi:10.4018/978-1-5225-2802-9.ch006

Paynter, K. (2017). Elementary Library Media Specialists' Roles in the Implementation of the Common Core State Standards. In M. Grassetti & S. Brookby (Eds.), *Advancing Next-Generation Teacher Education through Digital Tools and Applications* (pp. 262–283). Hershey, PA: IGI Global. doi:10.4018/978-1-5225-0965-3.ch014

Perez, M. J. (2016). Local Studies Centers in the Philippines: An Introductory Text. In J. Yap, M. Perez, M. Ayson, & G. Entico (Eds.), *Special Library Administration, Standardization and Technological Integration* (pp. 249–266). Hershey, PA: IGI Global. doi:10.4018/978-1-4666-9542-9.ch011

Perry, S. C., & Waggoner, J. (2018). Processes for User-Centered Design and Development: The Omeka Curator Dashboard Project. In L. Costello & M. Powers (Eds.), *Developing In-House Digital Tools in Library Spaces* (pp. 37–58). Hershey, PA: IGI Global. doi:10.4018/978-1-5225-2676-6.ch002

Phuritsabam, B., & Devi, A. B. (2017). Information Seeking Behavior of Medical Scientists at Jawaharlal Nehru Institute of Medical Science: A Study. In S. Ram (Ed.), *Library and Information Services for Bioinformatics Education and Research* (pp. 177–187). Hershey, PA: IGI Global. doi:10.4018/978-1-5225-1871-6.ch010

Pina, P. (2016). Copyright Issues in the Context of the Digital Library. In A. Tella (Ed.), *Information Seeking Behavior and Challenges in Digital Libraries* (pp. 70–83). Hershey, PA: IGI Global. doi:10.4018/978-1-5225-0296-8.ch004

Pionke, J. (2016). Disaster is in the Eye of the Beholder. In E. Decker & J. Townes (Eds.), *Handbook of Research on Disaster Management and Contingency Planning in Modern Libraries* (pp. 516–533). Hershey, PA: IGI Global. doi:10.4018/978-1-4666-8624-3.ch022

Quadri, R. F., & Sodiq, O. A. (2018). Managing Intellectual Property in Digital Libraries: The Roles of Digital Librarians. In A. Tella & T. Kwanya (Eds.), *Handbook of Research on Managing Intellectual Property in Digital Libraries* (pp. 337–355). Hershey, PA: IGI Global. doi:10.4018/978-1-5225-3093-0.ch017

Ram, S. (2017). Library Services for Bioinformatics: Establishing Synergy Data Information and Knowledge. In S. Ram (Ed.), *Library and Information Services for Bioinformatics Education and Research* (pp. 18–33). Hershey, PA: IGI Global. doi:10.4018/978-1-5225-1871-6.ch002

Rao, M. (2017). Use of Institutional Repository for Information Dissemination and Knowledge Management. In B. Gunjal (Ed.), *Managing Knowledge and Scholarly Assets in Academic Libraries* (pp. 156–173). Hershey, PA: IGI Global. doi:10.4018/978-1-5225-1741-2.ch007

Rao, Y., & Zhang, Y. (2017). The Construction and Development of Academic Library Digital Special Subject Databases. In L. Ruan, Q. Zhu, & Y. Ye (Eds.), *Academic Library Development and Administration in China* (pp. 163–183). Hershey, PA: IGI Global. doi:10.4018/978-1-5225-0550-1.ch010

Razip, S. N., Kadir, S. F., Saim, S. N., Dolhan, F. N., Jarmil, N., Salleh, N. H., & Rajin, G. (2017). Predicting Users' Intention towards Using Library Self-Issue and Return Systems. In N. Suki (Ed.), *Handbook of Research on Leveraging Consumer Psychology for Effective Customer Engagement* (pp. 102–115). Hershey, PA: IGI Global. doi:10.4018/978-1-5225-0746-8.ch007

Ress, A. D., McLaughlin, J. A., & Bertuca, C. (2016). Online Video Tutorials and Interlibrary Resource Sharing: A Model for Understanding the Role of Internet Video in Library Science and Education. In B. Doherty (Ed.), *Technology-Centered Academic Library Partnerships and Collaborations* (pp. 61–88). Hershey, PA: IGI Global. doi:10.4018/978-1-5225-0323-1.ch003

Rothwell, S. L. (2018). Librarians and Instructional Design Challenges: Concepts, Examples, and a Flexible Design Framework. In S. Bhattacharyya & K. Patnaik (Eds.), *Changing the Scope of Library Instruction in the Digital Age* (pp. 24–59). Hershey, PA: IGI Global. doi:10.4018/978-1-5225-2802-9.ch002

Roy, L., & Frydman, A. (2018). Community Outreach. In M. Khosrow-Pour, D.B.A. (Ed.), Encyclopedia of Information Science and Technology, Fourth Edition (pp. 6685-6694). Hershey, PA: IGI Global. doi:10.4018/978-1-5225-2255-3.ch579

Rutto, D., & Yudah, O. (2018). E-Books in University Libraries in Kenya: Trends, Usage, and Intellectual Property Issues. In A. Tella & T. Kwanya (Eds.), *Handbook of Research on Managing Intellectual Property in Digital Libraries* (pp. 120–141). Hershey, PA: IGI Global. doi:10.4018/978-1-5225-3093-0.ch007

Ryan, S. M., & Grubbs, W. T. (2016). Curricular Collaborations: Using Emerging Technologies to Foster Innovative Partnerships. In B. Doherty (Ed.), *Technology-Centered Academic Library Partnerships and Collaborations* (pp. 89–125). Hershey, PA: IGI Global. doi:10.4018/978-1-5225-0323-1.ch004

Sabharwal, A. (2017). The Transformative Role of Institutional Repositories in Academic Knowledge Management. In B. Gunjal (Ed.), *Managing Knowledge and Scholarly Assets in Academic Libraries* (pp. 127–155). Hershey, PA: IGI Global. doi:10.4018/978-1-5225-1741-2.ch006

Sadiku, S. A., Kpakiko, M. M., & Tsafe, A. G. (2018). Institutional Digital Repository and the Challenges of Global Visibility in Nigeria. In A. Tella & T. Kwanya (Eds.), *Handbook of Research on Managing Intellectual Property in Digital Libraries* (pp. 356–376). Hershey, PA: IGI Global. doi:10.4018/978-1-5225-3093-0.ch018

Sahu, M. K. (2018). Web-Scale Discovery Service in Academic Library Environment: A Birds Eye View. *International Journal of Library and Information Services*, 7(1), 1–14. doi:10.4018/IJLIS.2018010101

Salim, F., Saigar, B., Armoham, P. K., Gobalakrishnan, S., Jap, M. Y., & Lim, N. A. (2017). Students' Information-Seeking Intention in Academic Digital Libraries. In N. Suki (Ed.), *Handbook of Research on Leveraging Consumer Psychology for Effective Customer Engagement* (pp. 259–273). Hershey, PA: IGI Global. doi:10.4018/978-1-5225-0746-8.ch017

Related References

San Kong, E. W., Chiu, D. K., & Ho, K. K. (2016). Applications of Social Media in Academic Library Services: A Case of the Hong Kong Polytechnic University Library. *International Journal of Systems and Service-Oriented Engineering*, 6(2), 53–65. doi:10.4018/IJSSOE.2016040103

Saroja, G. (2017). Changing Face of Scholarly Communication and Its Impact on Library and Information Centres. In A. Munigal (Ed.), *Scholarly Communication and the Publish or Perish Pressures of Academia* (pp. 100–117). Hershey, PA: IGI Global. doi:10.4018/978-1-5225-1697-2.ch006

Sawant, S. (2016). Collaborative Online Learning Tools and Types: Few Perspectives of Its Use in Academic Library. In H. Rahman (Ed.), *Human Development and Interaction in the Age of Ubiquitous Technology* (pp. 94–119). Hershey, PA: IGI Global. doi:10.4018/978-1-5225-0556-3.ch005

Sawsaa, A. F., & Lu, J. (2017). Research Background on Ontology. In J. Lu & Q. Xu (Eds.), *Ontologies and Big Data Considerations for Effective Intelligence* (pp. 443–509). Hershey, PA: IGI Global. doi:10.4018/978-1-5225-2058-0.ch011

Schuster, D. W. (2017). Selection Process for Free Open Source Software. In E. Iglesias (Ed.), *Library Technology Funding, Planning, and Deployment* (pp. 55–71). Hershey, PA: IGI Global. doi:10.4018/978-1-5225-1735-1.ch004

Segaetsho, T. (2018). Environmental Consideration in the Preservation of Paper Materials in Heritage Institutions in the East and Southern African Region. In P. Ngulube (Ed.), *Handbook of Research on Heritage Management and Preservation* (pp. 183–212). Hershey, PA: IGI Global. doi:10.4018/978-1-5225-3137-1.ch010

Shakhsi, L. (2017). Cataloging Images in Library, Archive, and Museum. In T. Ashraf & N. Kumar (Eds.), *Interdisciplinary Digital Preservation Tools and Technologies* (pp. 119–141). Hershey, PA: IGI Global. doi:10.4018/978-1-5225-1653-8.ch007

Sharma, C. (2017). Digital Initiatives of the Indian Council of World Affairs' Library. In T. Ashraf & N. Kumar (Eds.), *Interdisciplinary Digital Preservation Tools and Technologies* (pp. 231–241). Hershey, PA: IGI Global. doi:10.4018/978-1-5225-1653-8.ch012

Shaw, M. D. (2016). Navigating Campus Disasters from Within the Library: Lessons and Implications from Gulf Coast Institutions. In E. Decker & J. Townes (Eds.), *Handbook of Research on Disaster Management and Contingency Planning in Modern Libraries* (pp. 340–365). Hershey, PA: IGI Global. doi:10.4018/978-1-4666-8624-3.ch015

Shawish, A., & Salama, M. (2016). Cloud-Based Digital Library Era. In J. Yap, M. Perez, M. Ayson, & G. Entico (Eds.), *Special Library Administration, Standardization and Technological Integration* (pp. 226–247). Hershey, PA: IGI Global. doi:10.4018/978-1-4666-9542-9.ch010

Siddaiah, D. K. (2018). Commonwealth Professional Fellowship: A Gateway for the Strategic Development of Libraries in India. In R. Bhardwaj (Ed.), *Digitizing the Modern Library and the Transition From Print to Electronic* (pp. 270–286). Hershey, PA: IGI Global. doi:10.4018/978-1-5225-2119-8.ch012

Silvana de Rosa, A. (2018). Mission, Tools, and Ongoing Developments in the So.Re.Com. "A.S. de Rosa" @-library. In M. Khosrow-Pour, D.B.A. (Ed.), Encyclopedia of Information Science and Technology, Fourth Edition (pp. 5237-5251). Hershey, PA: IGI Global. doi:10.4018/978-1-5225-2255-3.ch455

Silverman, R., Nakashima, T., Hunt, J. M., & Tuia, J. (2016). A Stitch in Time: Disaster Mitigation Strategies for Cultural Heritage Collections. In E. Decker & J. Townes (Eds.), *Handbook of Research on Disaster Management and Contingency Planning in Modern Libraries* (pp. 208–239). Hershey, PA: IGI Global. doi:10.4018/978-1-4666-8624-3.ch010

Smart, C. (2016). The Public Library's Role in Enabling E-Government: A View of Two Countries in the English-Speaking Caribbean. *International Journal of Public Administration in the Digital Age, 3*(3), 18–32. doi:10.4018/IJPADA.2016070102

Smolenski, N., Kostic, M., & Sofronijevic, A. M. (2018). Intrapreneurship and Enterprise 2.0 as Grounds for Developing In-House Digital Tools for Handling METS/ALTO Files at the University Library Belgrade. In L. Costello & M. Powers (Eds.), *Developing In-House Digital Tools in Library Spaces* (pp. 92–116). Hershey, PA: IGI Global. doi:10.4018/978-1-5225-2676-6.ch005

Sochay, L., & Junus, R. (2017). From Summon to SearchPlus: The RFP Process for a Discovery Tool at the MSU Libraries. In E. Iglesias (Ed.), *Library Technology Funding, Planning, and Deployment* (pp. 72–98). Hershey, PA: IGI Global. doi:10.4018/978-1-5225-1735-1.ch005

Sonawane, C. S. (2018). Library Catalogue in the Internet Age. In R. Bhardwaj (Ed.), *Digitizing the Modern Library and the Transition From Print to Electronic* (pp. 204–223). Hershey, PA: IGI Global. doi:10.4018/978-1-5225-2119-8.ch009

Sonawane, M. (2016). Creating an Agile Library. In E. de Smet & S. Dhamdhere (Eds.), *E-Discovery Tools and Applications in Modern Libraries* (pp. 109–121). Hershey, PA: IGI Global. doi:10.4018/978-1-5225-0474-0.ch006

Staley, C., Kenyon, R. S., & Marcovitz, D. M. (2018). Embedded Services: Going Beyond the Field of Dreams Model for Online Programs. In D. Polly, M. Putman, T. Petty, & A. Good (Eds.), *Innovative Practices in Teacher Preparation and Graduate-Level Teacher Education Programs* (pp. 368–381). Hershey, PA: IGI Global. doi:10.4018/978-1-5225-3068-8.ch020

Stavridi, S. V., & Hamada, D. R. (2016). Children and Youth Librarians: Competencies Required in Technology-Based Environment. In J. Yap, M. Perez, M. Ayson, & G. Entico (Eds.), *Special Library Administration, Standardization and Technological Integration* (pp. 25–50). Hershey, PA: IGI Global. doi:10.4018/978-1-4666-9542-9.ch002

Stewart, M. C., Atilano, M., & Arnold, C. L. (2017). Improving Customer Relations with Social Listening: A Case Study of an American Academic Library. *International Journal of Customer Relationship Marketing and Management*, 8(1), 49–63. doi:10.4018/IJCRMM.2017010104

Sukula, S. K., & Bhardwaj, R. K. (2018). An Extensive Discussion on Transition of Libraries: The Panoramic View of Library Resources, Services, and Evolved Librarianship. In R. Bhardwaj (Ed.), *Digitizing the Modern Library and the Transition From Print to Electronic* (pp. 255–269). Hershey, PA: IGI Global. doi:10.4018/978-1-5225-2119-8.ch011

Taylor, L. N., Alteri, S. A., Minson, V. I., Walker, B., Hawley, E. H., Dinsmore, C. S., & Jefferson, R. J. (2016). Library Collaborative Networks Forging Scholarly Cyberinfrastructure and Radical Collaboration. In B. Doherty (Ed.), *Technology-Centered Academic Library Partnerships and Collaborations* (pp. 1–30). Hershey, PA: IGI Global. doi:10.4018/978-1-5225-0323-1.ch001

Tella, A., & Babatunde, B. J. (2017). Determinants of Continuance Intention of Facebook Usage Among Library and Information Science Female Undergraduates in Selected Nigerian Universities. *International Journal of E-Adoption*, 9(2), 59–76. doi:10.4018/IJEA.2017070104

Tella, A., Okojie, V., & Olaniyi, O. T. (2018). Social Bookmarking Tools and Digital Libraries. In A. Tella & T. Kwanya (Eds.), *Handbook of Research on Managing Intellectual Property in Digital Libraries* (pp. 396–409). Hershey, PA: IGI Global. doi:10.4018/978-1-5225-3093-0.ch020

Tella, A., Oyeniran, S., & Ojo, O. J. (2016). Digital Libraries and Copyright Issues. In A. Tella (Ed.), *Information Seeking Behavior and Challenges in Digital Libraries* (pp. 108–126). Hershey, PA: IGI Global. doi:10.4018/978-1-5225-0296-8.ch006

Thull, J. J. (2018). Librarians and the Evolving Research Needs of Distance Students. In I. Oncioiu (Ed.), *Ethics and Decision-Making for Sustainable Business Practices* (pp. 203–216). Hershey, PA: IGI Global. doi:10.4018/978-1-5225-3773-1.ch012

Titilope, A. O. (2017). Ethical Issues in Library and Information Science Profession in Nigeria: An Appraisal. *International Journal of Library and Information Services*, *6*(2), 11–22. doi:10.4018/IJLIS.2017070102

Tutu, J. M. (2018). Intellectual Property Challenges in Digital Library Environments. In A. Tella & T. Kwanya (Eds.), *Handbook of Research on Managing Intellectual Property in Digital Libraries* (pp. 225–240). Hershey, PA: IGI Global. doi:10.4018/978-1-5225-3093-0.ch012

Upev, M. T., Beetseh, K., & Idachaba, J. A. (2016). Usability of Digital Resources: A Study of Francis Sulemanu Idachaba Library University of Agriculture Makurdi. In A. Tella (Ed.), *Information Seeking Behavior and Challenges in Digital Libraries* (pp. 224–237). Hershey, PA: IGI Global. doi:10.4018/978-1-5225-0296-8.ch011

Verplaetse, A., Mascareñas, P., & O'Neill, K. (2016). Zen and the Art of Disaster Planning: Collaboration Challenges in Library Disaster Plan Design and Execution. In E. Decker & J. Townes (Eds.), *Handbook of Research on Disaster Management and Contingency Planning in Modern Libraries* (pp. 96–119). Hershey, PA: IGI Global. doi:10.4018/978-1-4666-8624-3.ch005

Walker, B., & Pursley, T. (2016). A Statewide Collaborative Storage and Print Repository Model: The Florida Academic Repository (FLARE). In B. Doherty (Ed.), *Space and Organizational Considerations in Academic Library Partnerships and Collaborations* (pp. 111–129). Hershey, PA: IGI Global. doi:10.4018/978-1-5225-0326-2.ch006

Wallace, D., & Hemment, M. (2018). Enabling Scholarship in the Digital Age: A Case for Libraries Creating Value at HBS. In S. Bhattacharyya & K. Patnaik (Eds.), *Changing the Scope of Library Instruction in the Digital Age* (pp. 86–117). Hershey, PA: IGI Global. doi:10.4018/978-1-5225-2802-9.ch004

Wani, Z. A., Zainab, T., & Hussain, S. (2018). Web 2.0 From Evolution to Revolutionary Impact in Library and Information Centers. In M. Khosrow-Pour, D.B.A. (Ed.), Encyclopedia of Information Science and Technology, Fourth Edition (pp. 5262-5271). Hershey, PA: IGI Global. doi:10.4018/978-1-5225-2255-3.ch457

Waring, S. M. (2016). Teaching with Primary Sources: Moving from Professional Development to a Model of Professional Learning. In T. Petty, A. Good, & S. Putman (Eds.), *Handbook of Research on Professional Development for Quality Teaching and Learning* (pp. 295–306). Hershey, PA: IGI Global. doi:10.4018/978-1-5225-0204-3.ch014

Weiss, A. P. (2018). Massive Digital Libraries (MDLs). In M. Khosrow-Pour, D.B.A. (Ed.), Encyclopedia of Information Science and Technology, Fourth Edition (pp. 5226-5236). Hershey, PA: IGI Global. doi:10.4018/978-1-5225-2255-3.ch454

Wentao, C., Jinyu, Z., & Zhonggen, Y. (2016). Learning Outcomes and Affective Factors of Blended Learning of English for Library Science. *International Journal of Information and Communication Technology Education, 12*(3), 13–25. doi:10.4018/IJICTE.2016070102

White, G. W. (2016). The Library as a Center for Innovation: A Collaboration at the University of Maryland. In B. Doherty (Ed.), *Space and Organizational Considerations in Academic Library Partnerships and Collaborations* (pp. 68–86). Hershey, PA: IGI Global. doi:10.4018/978-1-5225-0326-2.ch004

Wu, S. K., Bess, M., & Price, B. R. (2018). Digitizing Library Outreach: Leveraging Bluetooth Beacons and Mobile Applications to Expand Library Outreach. In R. Bhardwaj (Ed.), *Digitizing the Modern Library and the Transition From Print to Electronic* (pp. 193–203). Hershey, PA: IGI Global. doi:10.4018/978-1-5225-2119-8.ch008

Wulff, E. (2018). Evaluation of Digital Collections and Political Visibility of the Library. In R. Bhardwaj (Ed.), *Digitizing the Modern Library and the Transition From Print to Electronic* (pp. 64–89). Hershey, PA: IGI Global. doi:10.4018/978-1-5225-2119-8.ch003

Xiao, L., & Liu, Y. (2017). Development of Innovative User Services. In L. Ruan, Q. Zhu, & Y. Ye (Eds.), *Academic Library Development and Administration in China* (pp. 56–73). Hershey, PA: IGI Global. doi:10.4018/978-1-5225-0550-1.ch004

Xin, X., & Wu, X. (2017). The Practice of Outreach Services in Chinese Special Libraries. In L. Ruan, Q. Zhu, & Y. Ye (Eds.), *Academic Library Development and Administration in China* (pp. 74–89). Hershey, PA: IGI Global. doi:10.4018/978-1-5225-0550-1.ch005

Yao, X., Zhu, Q., & Liu, J. (2017). The China Academic Library and Information System (CALIS). In L. Ruan, Q. Zhu, & Y. Ye (Eds.), *Academic Library Development and Administration in China* (pp. 1–19). Hershey, PA: IGI Global. doi:10.4018/978-1-5225-0550-1.ch001

Yap, J. M. (2016). Social Media Literacy of Agricultural Librarians in the Philippines. In J. Yap, M. Perez, M. Ayson, & G. Entico (Eds.), *Special Library Administration, Standardization and Technological Integration* (pp. 202–224). Hershey, PA: IGI Global. doi:10.4018/978-1-4666-9542-9.ch009

Yasue, A. (2016). Preservation Management in Company Libraries. In J. Yap, M. Perez, M. Ayson, & G. Entico (Eds.), *Special Library Administration, Standardization and Technological Integration* (pp. 305–314). Hershey, PA: IGI Global. doi:10.4018/978-1-4666-9542-9.ch013

Yin, Q., Yingying, W., Yan, Z., & Xiaojia, M. (2017). Resource Sharing and Mutually Beneficial Cooperation: A Look at the New United Model in Public and College Libraries. In L. Ruan, Q. Zhu, & Y. Ye (Eds.), *Academic Library Development and Administration in China* (pp. 334–352). Hershey, PA: IGI Global. doi:10.4018/978-1-5225-0550-1.ch019

Yuhua, F. (2018). Computer Information Library Clusters. In M. Khosrow-Pour, D.B.A. (Ed.), Encyclopedia of Information Science and Technology, Fourth Edition (pp. 4399-4403). Hershey, PA: IGI Global. doi:10.4018/978-1-5225-2255-3.ch382

Yusuf, F., Owolabi, S., Aregbesola, A., Oguntayo, S., Okocha, F., & Eyiolorunse, T. (2016). Demographics, Socio-Economic and Cognitive Skills as Barriers to Information Seeking in a Digital Library Environment. In A. Tella (Ed.), *Information Seeking Behavior and Challenges in Digital Libraries* (pp. 179–202). Hershey, PA: IGI Global. doi:10.4018/978-1-5225-0296-8.ch009

Yusuf, F., & Owolabi, S. E. (2018). Open Access to Knowledge and Challenges in Digital Libraries: Nigeria's Peculiarity. In A. Tella & T. Kwanya (Eds.), *Handbook of Research on Managing Intellectual Property in Digital Libraries* (pp. 241–259). Hershey, PA: IGI Global. doi:10.4018/978-1-5225-3093-0.ch013

Yuvaraj, M. (2016). Impact of Discovery Layers on Accessing E-Resources in Academic Libraries: A Case Study of Central University of Bihar. In E. de Smet & S. Dhamdhere (Eds.), *E-Discovery Tools and Applications in Modern Libraries* (pp. 181–200). Hershey, PA: IGI Global. doi:10.4018/978-1-5225-0474-0.ch010

Zaremohzzabieh, Z., Ahrari, S., Abu Samah, B., & Bolong, J. (2016). Researching Information Seeking in Digital Libraries through Information-Seeking Models. In A. Tella (Ed.), *Information Seeking Behavior and Challenges in Digital Libraries* (pp. 84–107). Hershey, PA: IGI Global. doi:10.4018/978-1-5225-0296-8.ch005

Related References

Zhu, S., & Shi, W. (2017). A Bibliometric Analysis of Research and Services in Chinese Academic Libraries. In L. Ruan, Q. Zhu, & Y. Ye (Eds.), *Academic Library Development and Administration in China* (pp. 253–262). Hershey, PA: IGI Global. doi:10.4018/978-1-5225-0550-1.ch015

Zimeras, S., Kostagiolas, P., & Lavranos, C. (2016). Dealing with the Uncertainty of Satisfaction Surveys in Organizations That Employ Interactive Multimedia: An Analysis of False Answers Statistical Models through a Digital Music Library Case Study. In I. Deliyannis, P. Kostagiolas, & C. Banou (Eds.), *Experimental Multimedia Systems for Interactivity and Strategic Innovation* (pp. 160–175). Hershey, PA: IGI Global. doi:10.4018/978-1-4666-8659-5.ch008

About the Contributors

P. Shanthi Saravanan received B.E degree in Computer Science and Engineering from Bharathidasan University, Trichy, India, M.E degree in Computer Science and Engineering from Anna University, Trichy, India, and completed Ph.D. in Privacy preservation in Location based services at National Institute of Technology, Trichy, India. Her research interests include location privacy, information security and mobile/ubiquitous computing. She has authored over 10 technical papers in international journals and conference proceedings. Currently working at J.J. College of Engineering and Technology, Trichy, India as an Assistant Professor. Subjects of interests are Computer Networks, Computer Programming, Computer Architecture, Web Technologies, Object Oriented Analysis and Design, Mobile Computing and Graph Theory. She is a life member of the CSI and the ISTE.

S. R. Balasundaram has been working since 1987 at National Institute of Technology (formerly known as Regional Engineering College) Tiruchirappalli, After completing M.C.A. from PSG College of Technology, Coimbatore, he joined REC Trichy during 1987 as Computer Programmer. He completed M.E. in Computer Science & Engineering during 1992. Currently he is working as Professor in the Department of Computer Applications. He earned his doctorate in "E-Learning and Assessment" from NIT, Trichy. Has more than 40 papers in reputed Journals and Proceedings of International conferences. His areas of interests are Web & Mobile Technologies, Cognitive Sciences and e-Learning Technologies.

* * *

Bodunde Akinyemi obtained a B.Tech in Computer Science from Ladoke Akintola University of Technology, Ogbomoso, Nigeria in 2005. She joined the services of Obafemi Awolowo University, Ile –Ife in 2007 as a Graduate Assistant in the Department of Computer Science and Engineering. She obtained M.Sc. and Ph.D. in Computer Science from Obafemi Awolowo University, Ile-Ife, Nigeria in 2011 and 2014 respectively. She is currently a Senior Lecturer and a researcher. Her research interests centered mainly on Data Communication and Network Security and Performance Management (NSPM). She has supervised 7 MSc and 1 PhD projects students. She has over 13years of experience in teaching and research and has published over 20 journals articles both locally and internationally. She is one of the team members that won the Africa Knowledge Transfer Partnership grant, World Bank/STEP-B Institutional Grant to Setup the OAU ICT Centre of Excellence in Software Engineering and the World Bank Grant to setup Africa Centre of Excellence (ACE) in OAU ICT Driven Knowledge Park. Currently, she won a TETFUND- NRF research grant as the Principal Investigator. She has actively participated in organizing a number of learned conferences. She is an active member of the Local Organizing Committee (LOC) of the Application of Information Communication Technologies to Teaching, Research and Administration (AICTTRA) international conference and the Faculty of Technology international conference, Obafemi Awolowo University, Ile Ife. She is also a reviewer of many reputable journals both locally and internationally. She is an active member of the Nigeria Computer Society (NCS) and Computer Professional Registration Council of Nigeria (CPN), International Association of Engineers (IAENG), Institute of Electrical and Electronics Engineers (IEEE), Organization for Women in Science for the Developing World (OWSD) and Nigeria Women in Information Technology (NIWIIT).

Ibidapo Akinyemi has B.Sc degree in Mathematical Sciences (option in Computer Science), M.Sc. in Computer Science and Ph.D degree in Computer Science. His research interest includes Artificial Intelligence, Soft Computing and Software Engineering.

Jeremiah Balogun is an Assistant Lecturer in the Department of Computer Science and Mathematics at Mountain Top University (MTU), MFM Prayer City, Ibafo, Ogun State. He has B.Sc. (Computer Science with Mathematics) and M.Sc. (Computer Science) both from Obafemi Awolowo University (OAU), Ile-Ife, Osun State in Nigeria. He is presently running his Ph.D. (Computer Science) at the same institution (OAU). He has published over twenty (20) scientific articles, contributed to book chapters. His interests include: Preventive Medicine, Classification Modeling, Database Design and Modeling, Data Mining and Machine Learning.

Harshit Bhatt is an M.Tech major research areas are IoT and Wireless Sensor networks.

Sabin Deorai, completed his M.Tech Data Analytics at NIT Tiruchirappalli, India. His areas of interests are AI, Big Data, Machine Learning, NLP and Location Aware Systems. He is a researcher living at Sivasagar, Assam.

Ghadeer M. Diab, graduaded from Faculty of Engineering, Computer and Automatic Control, Tanta University, Egypt.

Nada M. Elshennawy is an assistant professor in Computers and Control Engineering Department, Faculty of Engineering, Tanta University, Egypt. She was born in 1978, Egypt. Her B.Sc., M.Sc., and Ph.D. degrees taken from Computers and Control Engineering Department, Faculty of Engineering, Tanta University in 2001, 2007, and 2014, respectively. Nada works as a manager at Information Technology (IT) Unit, Faculty of Engineering Tanta University, Egypt from 2016 until 2018. Her research interests are in machine learning, computer vision and human behavior recognition, wireless networks, wireless sensor networks, and neural networks.

Ajay Kr. Gupta is credited with PhD from the Department of Computer Sc. & Engineering of M. M. M. University of Technology, Gorakhpur 273010. He is authors of 15 research papers, which have been published in various National & International Journals/Conferences. His current research areas are Spatio-Temporal Database, Location Dependent Database, and Mobile Distributed Database.

Peter Adebayo Idowu is an Associate Professor in the Department of Computer Science and Engineering, Obafemi Awolowo University, Nigeria. He received MPhil (Computer Science) and PhD (Computer Science) from Aston University, Birmingham, United Kingdom and Obafemi Awolowo University, Ile-Ife, Nigeria. His research focuses on Applied Computing, that is, application of computing to address and solve health related problems in Africa. He developed the first Health Data Model for Nigeria. He is currently researching into HIV/AIDS, Sickle Cell Anaemia, Sex Classification Model, disease modelling and cloud computing in health care delivery. He is a Member of British Computer Society, Internet Society Nigeria Chapter, Nigerian Computer Society, Computer Professional Registration Council of Nigeria, Nigerian Young Academy, International Geospatial Society, International Association of Engineers and International Federation of Information Processing WG 9.4. His research interests include Health Informatics, Data Mining, Software Engineering, Geographical Information System, and Informatics. Within the last seven years, Dr Idowu has successfully trained over 30 graduate students (including PhDs). He has published over 90 scientific research articles in reputable journals and referred conference proceedings in which a large number of them are Scopus indexed. He is blessed with three Research Associates; Praise, Vicky and Peter. He enjoys reading and driving.

Madhusudanan J., Associate Professor, Department of Computer Science and Engineering in Sri Manakula Vinayagar Engineering College. He holds M.E in

Computer Science and Engineering. He has completed his Ph.D., in Banking Technology from Pondicherry University, India. His areas of Interest are Context Aware Computing, Pervasive Middleware, Ubiquitous Computing and Smart Banking. He has many International and National Journal Publications

Yowei Kang (Ph.D.) is Assistant Professor at Bachelor Degree Program in Oceanic Cultural Creative Design Industries, National Taiwan Ocean University, TAIWAN. His research interests focus on new media design, digital game research, visual communication, and experiential rhetoric. Some of his works have been published in International Journal of Strategic Communication, and Journal of Intercultural Communication Studies. He has received government funding to support his research in location-based advertising and consumer privacy management strategies.

Funmilayo Kasali is a Lecturer in the Department of Computer Science and Mathematics, College of Basic and Applied Sciences in Mountain Top University. She has a BSc. degree in Computer Mathematics from Olabisi Onabanjo University Ago-Iwoye, Ogun State in 2008, Post graduate Diploma in Education from Federal College of Technology Akoka, Lagos State to understand the basic rudiments of being a great teacher. She also obtained her PGD, M.Sc and PhD in Computer Science from Babcock University, Ilishan-Remo, Ogun State, Nigeria in 2012, 2015 and 2018 respectively. She joined the service of Mountain Top University, Ibafo, Ogun State in September, 2018. She is currently a lecturer in the Department of Computer Science and Mathematics. Her areas of research interest are on Software Usability Engineering, Data Science, Big Data Analytics, Health Informatics, User Centered Systems Design, Management Information Systems and Business Intelligence. In addition, she is passionate about women and child health care and how recent technological innovations can be used positively in these areas for better health care in Nigeria. She is a member of Nigeria Computer Science. She also holds a Certificate in Block chain Mastery Award by IBM.

Sujaritha M. was born in Thiyagaduram, Villupuram District, TamilNadu, India, in 1973. She received A.M.I.E degree in Computer Science and Engineering in the year 2000 from Institution of Engineers (India). She was awarded Suman Sharma prize award for securing second highest mark in AMIE amongst women students in the year 1994. She received M.E. degree from Bharathiar University at Government College of Technology Coimbatore during 2003. She has secured GATE scholarship during her P.G. course. She completed her Ph.D degree in Anna University, Chennai, under the guidance of Dr.S.Annadurai in the year 2011. She has fifteen years of teaching experience and ten years of research experience in the field of Computer Vision, Image Processing and Soft Computing. Currently she is serving as Professor at Sri Krishna College of Engineering and Technology, Coimbatore. She has visited Malaysia to present her research papers and Chair a session in an International Conference. She has completed two research projects funded by Government of India. She is currently involved in Women Entrepreneurship Development project sponsored by Department of Science and Technology, Government of India. She has published fifteen research papers in International Journals, more than thirty research papers in National and International Conferences. She is guiding three research scholars in the field of internet of things in agriculture.

Ambika. N has completed her MCA in the year 2001 and M.Phil in the year 2008. She completed her Ph.D. from Bharathiar University, Coimbatore in the year 2015. She has 13 years of experience. She has published papers in International conferences, books and Journals. She has guided significant number of students in their projects which include under-graduate and graduate students. Her areas of interest include Wireless sensor network, Internet-of-things (IoT), and Cyber Security. She is working as faculty in the Department of Computer Applications, SSMRV College, Bangalore.

Shunmuga Priya S. was born in Palayamkottai, Tirunelveil, TamilNadu, India in 1991. She pursued her Bachelor degree in Anna University, Tiruchirapalli. She has cleared various competitive exams like GATE, Talent Search exams. She pursued her Master degree in Thiagarajar College of Engg., Madurai. She was the department topper. She has published various articles in reputed international journals and international conferences and has filed a patent. She is the Editorial Board member for the website "eezytutorials.com" and content developer for the youtube channel "eezytutorials". Currently she is working as an Asst. Professor in Dept. of Computer Science and Engineering, Sri Krishna College of Engineering and Technology, Coimbatore. She is also pursuing her Ph.D in Anna University, Chennai under the guidance of Dr. M. Sujaritha. Her research interest includes Network Security, Wireless adhoc networks, Cryptography, Programming and Internet of Things.

Amany Sarhan received the B.Sc degree in Electronics Engineering, and M.Sc. in Computer Engineering from the Faculty of Engineering, Mansoura University, in 1990, and 1997, respectively. She awarded the Ph.D. degree as a joint research between Tanta Univ., Egypt and Univ. of Connecticut, USA. She is working now as a Full Prof. and head Computers and Control Dept., Tanta Univ., Egypt. Her interests are in the area of: Distributed Systems, Software Restructuring, Object-oriented Databases, and Image and video processing, GPU and Distributed Computations.

Udai Shanker is presently Professor in the Department of Computer Sc. & Engineering of M. M. M. University of Technology, Gorakhpur-273010. He is credited with PhD from Indian Institute of Technology Roorkee and is recipient of awards from Institution of Engineers (India), Calcutta twice for his technical papers. He is authors of 95 research papers, which have been published in various National & International Journals/Conferences. He is reviewer of many International Conferences/Journals and also Editorial Board Member of 30 International Journals.

Aaditya Sharma is Pursuing B.Tech in Electrical Engineering from Shoolini University.

Brij Sharma is working as Assistant Professor, M. Tech (ECE), Pursuing PhD, Yogananda School of AI, Computer & Data Sciences Shoolini University. Research Area: Wireless Sensor Networks, Internet of Things and Embedded Electronics.

Meenakshi Sharma is currently serving as an Executive Assistant at Shoolini University, Solan (HP) India. She holds more than twelve years of experience in administration. She has done MA (English) from Himachal Pradesh University with three years Diploma in Computer Science and Engineering.

Ruchika Sharma is a PhD scholar at Yogananda School Of AI, Computer and Data Sciences Shoolini university of Biotechnology and Management Sciences. MCA in 2016 from HPTU. Research interests/area Artificial Intelligence, IOT, Big Data.

Prasanna Venkatesan Venkatasamy, Associate Professor, Dept. of Banking Technology, Pondicherry University, Puducherry, India. He has more than 20 years teaching and research experience in the field of Computer Science and Engineering. His research interest includes software engineering, Business intelligence, Software Architecture and banking technology. He has designed Multilingual Compiler. He has many international Journal publications. He is co– author of the book titled as Service Composition and Orchestration: Concepts and Approaches published by Vdm Verlag Dr. Müller e.K.

Kenneth C. C. Yang (Ph.D.) is Professor in the Department of Communication at the University of Texas at El Paso, USA. His research focuses on new media advertising, consumer behavior, and international advertising. Some of his many works have been published in Cyberpsychology, Journal of Strategic Communication, International Journal of Consumer Marketing, Journal of Intercultural Communication Studies, Journal of Marketing Communication, and Telematics and Informatics. He has edited or co-edited three books, Asia.com: Asia encounters the Internet (Routledge, 2003), Multi-Platform Advertising Strategies in the Global Marketplace (IGI Global, 2018), and Cases on Immersive Virtual Reality Techniques (IGI Global, 2019).

Index

A

acts of terrorism 177
agriculture 149, 200-205, 217-219
applications and services 2
attacks 66, 126-128, 131, 145, 147-149, 151-153, 155-157, 160, 162-165, 168-169, 173-177, 182, 189, 196, 216-217, 220, 222-225, 227, 229, 231-234

B

Bio-Inspired Computing 126
bot 161-162, 168

C

challenging weather conditions 72, 86, 100
consumer behavior 24
content caching 30, 110, 121
Context-aware mobility 109
Context-awareness 126-127, 129, 146
Cross-National Study 1

D

direct marketing 3-4, 6-7, 18-20, 24

E

Experience Sampling Method (ESM) 1, 9

G

Geographical Information Systems 177, 199
geo-tagged data 52, 54
GPS 24, 27, 32-33, 53-56, 151, 153, 157, 204

H

hashing 31
human detection and tracking 72, 74-75, 77-78, 80-81, 86, 100, 105, 107
human mobility 32, 52-53, 55, 67-69

I

information privacy 18, 20-24
Internet of Thing 200
IoT 22, 69, 148-159, 167, 173-176, 200-201, 204, 213-219, 222, 233

K

Kalman filter 75, 80-81, 86, 88, 93, 96, 100, 103-107

L

LBS 26-31, 33, 36, 43, 46-49, 112-113, 122-124
Location Based Services 26, 66, 169
location based social networking 52
location tracking 27, 52
Location-Awareness 24

M

malware 147, 165-168, 173, 213
Mixed Research Method 24
mobile advertising 3, 6, 21, 24, 220
Mobile Commerce 4, 6-7, 19, 21, 24, 69
mobile communications 2-3, 16, 25
Mobile Environment 48-49, 109, 122-124
Mobile Social Media 25

N

Nigeria 177-179, 182, 197-199

P

pH 200-204, 206, 213, 217-219
prefetching 26-27, 29-31, 46-47, 49, 109-110, 113-114, 117-118, 121-124
privacy 1, 3-7, 9, 16, 18-29, 31, 36, 43, 46-47, 49-52, 54, 66-70, 127, 147-149, 151-152, 171, 232-233
Privacy Preserving Models 26
Proactive caching 109-110, 117, 121

R

reliability 179, 220, 222, 225, 227, 229-231
replay attack 158-159, 222-224, 228-232

S

security 22, 28-29, 43, 46, 52, 54, 66-70, 72-73, 122, 126-132, 134, 138, 140-141, 143-149, 151-153, 157, 165, 167, 169, 171-186, 189, 191, 193, 197, 206, 213-217, 220, 222-223, 228, 231, 233-234
security issues 69-70, 127-129, 147, 171, 174-176, 213-215, 222
sensors 132, 149-150, 153, 155, 175-176, 200, 204, 215, 217, 219-220, 222, 225, 228, 230-231, 233
Smart ATM 126-127, 131-133, 135-137, 143-144
smart phone 13, 147, 224
smart technologies 126, 200-201, 218
smartphone 2-4, 6, 8, 10-11, 14, 16, 25, 27, 30-31, 43, 46-47, 66, 110, 233
social media 4, 7, 19-21, 23-25, 59, 66, 68, 70
soil 200-204, 206-211, 217-219
surveillance videos 72, 77
survey 2, 6, 9, 15, 23, 28, 50, 66, 69, 103, 105-107, 147, 175-176, 181, 223, 231

U

user authentication 220, 224, 231-232, 234

V

vulnerability 122, 171

W

Watch Dog Mechanism 126
Wireless Sensor Networks 200-201, 219, 221, 231-234

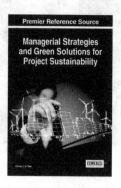

IGI Global's Transformative Open Access (OA) Model:
How to Turn Your University Library's Database Acquisitions Into a Source of OA Funding

Well in advance of Plan S, IGI Global unveiled their OA Fee Waiver (Read & Publish) Initiative. Under this initiative, librarians who invest in IGI Global's InfoSci-Books and/or InfoSci-Journals databases will be able to subsidize their patrons' OA article processing charges (APCs) when their work is submitted and accepted (after the peer review process) into an IGI Global journal.

How Does it Work?

Step 1: **Library Invests in the InfoSci-Databases:** A library perpetually purchases or subscribes to the InfoSci-Books, InfoSci-Journals, or discipline/subject databases.

Step 2: **IGI Global Matches the Library Investment with OA Subsidies Fund:** IGI Global provides a fund to go towards subsidizing the OA APCs for the library's patrons.

Step 3: **Patron of the Library is Accepted into IGI Global Journal (After Peer Review):** When a patron's paper is accepted into an IGI Global journal, they option to have their paper published under a traditional publishing model or as OA.

Step 4: **IGI Global Will Deduct APC Cost from OA Subsidies Fund:** If the author decides to publish under OA, the OA APC fee will be deducted from the OA subsidies fund.

Step 5: **Author's Work Becomes Freely Available:** The patron's work will be freely available under CC BY copyright license, enabling them to share it freely with the academic community.

Note: This fund will be offered on an annual basis and will renew as the subscription is renewed for each year thereafter. IGI Global will manage the fund and award the APC waivers unless the librarian has a preference as to how the funds should be managed.

Hear From the Experts on This Initiative:

"I'm very happy to have been able to make one of my recent research contributions *freely available* along with having access to the *valuable resources* found within IGI Global's InfoSci-Journals database."

– **Prof. Stuart Palmer**, Deakin University, Australia

"Receiving the support from IGI Global's OA Fee Waiver Initiative *encourages me to continue my research work without any hesitation.*"

– **Prof. Wenlong Liu**, College of Economics and Management at Nanjing University of Aeronautics & Astronautics, China

Printed in the United States
by Baker & Taylor Publisher Services